T5-CVF-858

PRAGMATIC UTOPIAS
Ideals and Communities, 1200–1630

This collection of essays is presented to Barrie Dobson in celebration of his seventieth birthday, and will be welcomed by all scholars of pre-modern religion and society. Spanning the artificial divide between medieval and early modern, the contributors – all acknowledged experts in their field – pursue the ways in which men and women tried to put their ideals into practice, sometimes alone, but more commonly in the shared environment of cloister, college or city.

The range of topics is testimony to the breadth of Barrie Dobson's own interests, but even more striking are the continuities and shared assumptions across time, and between the dissident and the impeccably orthodox. Taking the reader from a rural anchorhold to the London of Thomas More, and from the greenwood of Robin Hood to the central law courts, this collection builds into a richly satisfying exploration of the search for perfection in an imperfect world.

ROSEMARY HORROX is Fellow and Director of Studies in History, Fitzwilliam College, Cambridge

SARAH REES JONES is Lecturer in History, University of York

PRAGMATIC UTOPIAS

Ideals and Communities, 1200–1630

EDITED BY

ROSEMARY HORROX

AND

SARAH REES JONES

CAMBRIDGE
UNIVERSITY PRESS

PUBLISHED BY THE PRESS SYNDICATE OF THE UNIVERSITY OF CAMBRIDGE
The Pitt Building, Trumpington Street, Cambridge, United Kingdom

CAMBRIDGE UNIVERSITY PRESS
The Edinburgh Building, Cambridge CB2 2RU, UK
40 West 20th Street, New York, NY 10011-4211, USA
10 Stamford Road, Oakleigh, VIC 3166, Australia
Ruiz de Alarcón 13, 28014 Madrid, Spain
Dock House, The Waterfront, Cape Town 8001, South Africa

http://www.cambridge.org

© Cambridge University Press 2001

This book is in copyright. Subject to statutory exception
and to the provisions of relevant collective licensing agreements,
no reproduction of any part may take place without
the written permission of Cambridge University Press.

First published 2001

Printed in the United Kingdom at the University Press, Cambridge

Typeface Baskerville Monotype 11/12.5 pt.   *System* LaTeX 2ε   [TB]

A catalogue record for this book is available from the British Library

Library of Congress Cataloguing in Publication data

Pragmatic utopias: ideals and communities, 1200–1630/edited by Rosemary Horrox
and Sarah Rees Jones.
p.   cm.
Includes bibliographical references and index.
ISBN 0 521 65060 7
1. Sociology, Christian – England – History.   2. England – Church history.
I. Horrox, Rosemary.   II. Rees Jones, Sarah.
BR744 .P73 2001 942.03 – dc21   2001025828

ISBN 0 521 65060 7 hardback

Contents

Preface   *page* vii
    Rosemary Horrox
List of abbreviations   ix

   Richard Barrie Dobson: an appreciation   1
   John Taylor

1 'If heaven be on this earth, it is in cloister or in school':
   the monastic ideal in later medieval English literature   11
   Derek Pearsall

2 The 'Chariot of Aminadab' and the Yorkshire priory
   of Swine   26
   Janet Burton

3 Godliness and good learning: ideals and imagination
   in medieval university and college foundations   43
   R. N. Swanson

4 Hugh of Balsham, bishop of Ely 1256/7–1286   60
   Roger Lovatt

5 A cruel necessity? Christ's and St John's, two Cambridge
   refoundations   84
   Malcolm G. Underwood

6 Coventry's 'Lollard' programme of 1492 and the making
   of Utopia   97
   P. J. P. Goldberg

7 Thomas More's *Utopia* and medieval London   117
   Sarah Rees Jones

8 Social exclusivity or justice for all? Access to justice
   in fourteenth-century England   136
   Anthony Musson

9 Idealising criminality: Robin Hood in the fifteenth century   156
   A. J. Pollard

10 Fat Christian and Old Peter: ideals and compromises
    among the medieval Waldensians   174
    Peter Biller

11 Imageless devotion: what kind of an ideal?   188
    Margaret Aston

12 An English anchorite: the making, unmaking
    and remaking of Christine Carpenter   204
    Miri Rubin

13 Victorian values in fifteenth-century England: the
    Ewelme almshouse statutes   224
    Colin Richmond

14 Puritanism and the poor   242
    Patrick Collinson

15 Realising a utopian dream: the transformation of the clergy
    in the diocese of York, 1500–1630   259
    Claire Cross

Bibliography of Barrie Dobson's published works   277
Index   281

Preface

When the editors were considering a suitable topic for this *festschrift* they found themselves, as one might expect with an honorand of Barrie Dobson's range of interests, spoilt for choice. It was Sarah Rees Jones who came up with the theme of Utopias and Idealists, which pays tribute both to Barrie's strong interest in social justice, reflected in his work on the Peasants' Revolt and Robin Hood, and also to his long-standing engagement with the aspirations and achievements of medieval communities and their administrators, both ecclesiastical and secular. This wide range of interests, to which John Taylor pays proper tribute below, has equipped Barrie with a special understanding of the relationship between idealism and pragmatism that has informed his equally long-standing interest in the life and work of Thomas More.

The initial hope was that this would be a subject that would draw together contributions from modernists as well as medievalists. That, sadly, foundered. Collections of papers ranging from the early Middle Ages to the twentieth century are not thought viable publishing ventures these days. Several of Barrie's friends and colleagues who had hoped to contribute were accordingly unable to do so, and the choice of topic (and the need to keep the collection within reasonable length) excluded others. Those friends and colleagues of Barrie whose papers are included here are conscious that they stand for a great many others who wished to be involved, and whose good wishes go with them. It demonstrates the great affection in which Barrie is held by very many people, as well as his enormous influence on medieval studies, that two other volumes honouring him have also been produced. It was a comfort to the editors of this one that as far more offers of papers flooded in than could ever be included, some at least of the potential contributors could be diverted to other volumes. How many historians have been the recipient of three more or less simultaneous *festschriften*? Everyone who knows Barrie will understand how he comes to be in that, perhaps unique, position.

The original working title for the collection was *Utopias and Idealists*. When initial offers of papers were received it was striking that all the modernists who wished to be involved offered Utopian themes. Medievalists opted on the whole for Idealists. As it happens, the collection includes no treatments of what is perhaps the closest contemporaries came to envisaging the no place/good place model: the Millennium itself or the Land of Cockayne. Most of the papers are studies of pragmatic idealists, looking to achieve salvation or improvement within the structures of this world rather than the sort of visionaries or radicals who imagined a transformed society. There are dissidents – heretics and outlaws – but they are operating within recognised models of community and mutuality. Even anchoresses are shown here to be a facet of community rather than a simple denial of it. Indeed the theme that emerges strongly from the volume is what constitutes the best sort of attainable community and how it is to be achieved – which in most cases means imposed. Barrie's inaugural lecture at Cambridge in 1990 took as its theme contrasting communities. The communities in this volume are contrasting too, but there are powerful shared assumptions at work within all of them.

Fitzwilliam College   ROSEMARY HORROX
Cambridge

Abbreviations

CUL	Cambridge University Library
EETS e.s.	Early English Text Society, extra series
EETS o.s.	Early English Text Society, original series
DNB	*Dictionary of National Biography*
HMC	Historical Manuscripts Commission
PL	*Patrologia Latina*
PRO	Public Record Office
RS	Rolls Series
VCH	*Victoria County History*

Richard Barrie Dobson: an appreciation

John Taylor

One of the chief characteristics of Barrie must surely be his attachment to the north of England. Born at Stockton-on-Tees in 1931, he spent his earliest years in South America, where his father worked for the Great Western Railway of Brazil. After Barrie returned to England before the outbreak of the Second World War, he went to school at Barnard Castle, at which time he came to know those parts of the north which have later claimed so much of his attention as a medieval scholar. Although he has lived for some time in the south, his recent return to the north underlines his strong commitment to that area. For this determined and intrepid hill walker the Lake District has always held a special attraction. Walks where 'Cambridge waters hurry by' do not, one suspects, hold quite the same appeal as some well-remembered climbs on Helvellyn or Fairfield. *Beati omnes qui ambulant*. Happiest of all, Barrie would certainly say, are those who go where the contour lines on the map lie closest together.

Like those of other distinguished northern scholars, Barrie's career led him eventually to the University of Cambridge, where in 1988 he was appointed Professor of Medieval History and elected a Fellow of Christ's College. In retrospect his life appears to have been an almost inevitable progression to that point. After Barnard Castle School a period in the army followed, including service in Malaya during the Emergency. At the end of his military service in 1951 Barrie went up to Wadham College, where his tutors were A. F. Thompson and Lawrence Stone. The medieval tutor was Reggie Lennard, an authority on early agrarian systems, and one of the founder members of the Friends of the Lake District. It was on one of Reggie Lennard's reading parties in a highly appropriate setting outside the Fish Inn in Buttermere, and against the background of Red Pike, that the writer of these words first met Barrie in the summer of 1951. At the end of a highly enjoyable and successful time as an undergraduate Barrie obtained a first in History. In 1956 he was elected a Senior Demy at Magdalen, and became a Junior Lecturer in the college. At Magdalen in those post-war years K. B. (Bruce) McFarlane was the senior medievalist. A formidable scholar, and a no less formidable personality, McFarlane exercised a powerful influence over a generation of Oxford postgraduates. His prosopographical approach to the history of late medieval England offered a new and exciting advance in historical interpretation. The exploration of the relationships which bound together the governing classes of late medieval England is not perhaps an approach immediately associated with Barrie. Nonetheless something of that approach can be seen in his work on Durham monks and York canons. As he himself has written, 'it is not often appreciated that the major religious houses of medieval Christendom often provide much the best hunting ground for the medieval prosopographer'.[1] During the years at Magdalen Barrie worked on his D.Phil. thesis, 'The Priory of Durham in the time of Prior John Wessington, 1416–46'. In this project he was fortunate in his supervisor. 'Billy' Pantin was a scholar who could inspire his pupils, who knew the Durham archives well, and whose advice was invaluable. No less a source of inspiration was Dom David Knowles, who was to be one of his examiners later. The days working as a postgraduate in the Durham archives were a formative period, and a time to which Barrie has always looked back with particular affection. In the course of this work he made many friends. One scholar with whom he established a special rapport was J. Conway Davies, whose knowledge of the Durham archives was exceptional. The thesis on Durham, successfully completed in 1963 and considerably expanded later, resulted eventually in the publication of *Durham Priory, 1400–1450* (1973). Although it was not published until after Barrie moved to York, this distinguished study reveals one feature which was to characterise much of his subsequent work, namely an archive-based interest in monasticism and the northern Church. *Durham Priory, 1400–1450* itself, with its rigorous analysis of the recruitment, economy and intellectual interests of a monastic community, was very much more than 'an account of life in a medieval abbey'. A work worthy to be set alongside Barbara Harvey's studies on Westminster, it is, as one reviewer said, 'a massive contribution to the religious and social history of medieval England'. As regards his time at Oxford, however, one should not dwell exclusively upon Barrie's academic accomplishments. Not the least of his achievements was to meet in February 1958, at one Oxford party given by Beryl Smalley, Narda Leon, a young graduate of St Hilda's to whom he was introduced by Menna Prestwich. Narda was in the process of completing a B.Litt. thesis at the Institute of

Colonial Studies and was about to take up a post in Paris. This fortunate meeting, which occurred during Barrie's last year at Oxford, was to lead to their marriage in the following year.

In 1958 Barrie moved to a lectureship in Medieval History at St Andrews. Medieval history there consisted of a small department of four members which under the inspired leadership of Lionel Butler was to grow both in numbers and prestige in the decade which followed. The years at St Andrews were a good period. In the words of one of his friends, 'as a man from Barnard Castle with all the attractive prejudices of a northern Englishman, Barrie fitted happily into a Scottish environment'.[2] As the youngest member of a small but separate department which at that time was turning from the traditional Scottish dependence on lectures to a system which provided more tutorial experience, Barrie did his full share of teaching, lecturing on long historical periods, and taking seminars. His personal life also flourished. At the end of his first year at St Andrews Narda and Barrie were married. At St Andrews their children, Mark and Michelle, were born. The young couple entered fully into the social life of the university. As Donald Watt has said of these years, 'this was a good time to be alive'.

In 1964 Barrie moved to the north of England when he was appointed to a lectureship in the newly founded University of York. York in the 1960s was an exciting place to be. If the university was not exactly drawing new maps of learning, it was certainly encouraging new approaches to knowledge, and was encouraging university teachers to evaluate new ideas. Under the notable leadership of Gerald Aylmer these approaches were fully reflected in the Department of History. History at York had an organisation which involved all its members more fully than did most of the older, more traditional universities. It was also a department which experimented with new kinds of courses, and different types of examination. The sense of being part of a great enterprise released all Barrie's considerable energies. His time at York saw not only a long list of important publications, but also a considerable input into the teaching and administration of both the department and the university.[3]

An excellent tutor and lecturer at both undergraduate and graduate level, Barrie came into his own in a York setting. He had arrived at York in the second year of teaching, when the history staff had increased from five to ten. He soon began to teach a Special Subject on York and London, a topic which saw the beginning of his lasting interest in the medieval city of York. In a jointly taught first-year course in which students re-examined the traditional division between 'medieval' and 'modern' history Barrie led a series of seminars on a topic close to his heart, Sir Thomas More and his Utopia, 'a paean to an orderly and educated society, despising luxury and display'.⁴ Not surprisingly, medieval English monasticism featured in his teaching. When the Medieval Centre in York came into existence in the 1960s with Elizabeth Salter as its leading figure, Barrie played a major part in the contribution which History was to make. As Gerald Aylmer says, 'the B.Phil. in Medieval Studies would never have established itself as a genuinely inter-disciplinary degree course without his patience and firmness'. His sterling work in the Centre of which he became Co-Director (1977–88) emphasises the significant role he has always played in postgraduate studies, first at York and later at Cambridge. At York several of his postgraduate students, including Sarah Rees Jones and Heather Swanson, went on to make important contributions to the history of the city.

As regards his own writings, *Durham Priory, 1400–1450* duly appeared in 1973 in the Cambridge Studies in Medieval Life and Thought series. Apart from this publication Barrie's best-known work written during his time at York was undoubtedly *The Peasants' Revolt of 1381*: continuously in print (1970, rpr. 1983), useful to both student and specialist alike, and in constant demand. In this publication, which owed something to Gwyn Williams's original inspiration, Barrie brought together a wealth of documentation to illustrate both the course of the revolt and its subsequent interpretations. Written with his customary elegance, searching in its analysis, the book brings to life the documents upon which it is based. If the student of history 'should read the documents until he hears their authors speaking', here indeed was the opportunity to listen to some of the voices of fourteenth-century England. A somewhat similar approach was attempted in *Rymes of Robyn Hood* (1976, rpr. 1989, 1997), produced in collaboration with the present writer. Following the debate concerning the origins and audience of the Robin Hood ballads inaugurated by Rodney Hilton and Sir James Holt in the pages of *Past and Present* almost twenty years earlier, the authors sought to illustrate the development of the legend through a selection of ballad texts and other sources, and at the same time explore certain of the problems concerning its origins. The major partner in this enterprise, Barrie brought all his formidable knowledge to bear on the quest for the forest outlaw. Although he approached the topic with impeccable scholarship, it may be that – as with the Peasants' Revolt and the seminars on Sir Thomas More – he found in this subject one manifestation of an early search for 'the just society'.

No subject, however, was more central to Barrie's research interests at York than the northern Church. Here, after various articles had appeared on Durham, his interest centred principally on the diocese of York. Work on the perpetual chantries at York and Selby Abbey[5] was followed by a magisterial chapter on the 'Minster in the Later Middle Ages', written for the *History of York Minster* (1977), edited by Gerald Aylmer and Reginald Cant. In his treatment of the canons of the Minster, whose wealth 'sustained active careers in the service of the chapter and archbishop, endowed chantries, maintained great households, and helped to rebuild the Minster itself', we see an example of the prosopographical approach. Equally, if not more, revealing of this approach was his treatment of the residentiary canons of York in the fifteenth century, in which (and perhaps prophetically in his own case) he noted the connection between northern clerks of exceptional ability and the University of Cambridge.[6] As he was to remark later, northern clerks, none of whom was more significant than the Yorkshireman John Fisher, were to play a major part in the great days of Renaissance Cambridge.[7] A further paper on 'Mendicant Ideal and Practice in late Medieval York' (1984) arose from his involvement with the York Archaeological Trust, of which he had been a member from the beginning, and to which he gave unstinting support during the difficult days of the early 1990s.[8] His involvement with the Trust and its work on medieval urban archaeology underlined his continuing concern with urban history. His interest in these 'electric transformers' of medieval society found expression in articles on the city of York and other northern towns[9] as well as in his edition of the *York City Chamberlains' Account Rolls 1396–1500* (1980). York was again the scene for Barrie's monograph on *The Jews of York and the Massacre of March 1190* (1974), one of the weightiest of the Borthwick Institute Papers. Yet another publication, which he edited, *The Church, Politics and Patronage in the Fifteenth Century* (1984), arose from his highly successful organisation of a colloquium of late medieval historians at York in 1982.

Through his teaching and his publications Barrie had by the middle years of the 1970s reached, according to Gerald Aylmer, 'a position of leadership, almost of dominance' among the medievalists at York. In 1977 he became Professor of Medieval History. To his effectiveness as a lecturer, and his achievements in research and publication, he also added for good measure a flair for academic organisation and management. At York, in addition to being a co-director of the Centre of Medieval Studies, he acted for (the customary) two years as Chairman of the History Board of Studies. Influential outside the department as well as within it, he served as Deputy Vice-Chancellor of the University from 1984 to 1987. He had just become Head of the History Department, in succession to Professor Norman Hampson, when in 1988 he was offered the chair of Medieval History at Cambridge. His ability to get on well with others ensured success in administrative matters. He enjoyed challenges. Just as he is reported to have said on one occasion that he enjoyed driving through heavy traffic because it was a challenge, so the sorting out of academic difficulties he saw perhaps as a similar sort of challenge. Barrie's administrative ability has led to his being much in demand. On the national level he has been a Vice-President of the Royal Historical Society (1985–9), President of the Jewish Historical Society of England (1990–1), President of the Ecclesiastical History Society (1991–2), Chairman of the Friends of the Public Record Office, member of the Victoria County History Advisory Committee (1982–), and of the Advisory Committee for the Public Records. In the north he has been Chairman of the Council of the York Archaeological Trust (1990–6), a position which involved frequent journeys from Cambridge. He is Chairman of the British Academy Episcopal Acta Committee (1995–), a project based on the Borthwick Institute, and was, with Claire Cross, General Editor of the Yorkshire Archaeological Society Record Series (1981–6). Since 1987 he has been President of the Surtees Society. As President of the Surtees Society he is, in the words of Gordon Forster, 'a fair-minded and patient chairman, with a relaxed manner, undogmatic and flexible in style . . . a striver for consensus with a disarming ability to see good in quite a range of arguments'.[10] Nonetheless, despite his very real administrative talents, Barrie has never allowed the administrative side to take precedence over his other contributions to academic life.

In 1988 Barrie moved to the Chair of Medieval History at Cambridge. There he followed in the footsteps of such distinguished scholars as Charles Previté-Orton, Zachary Brooke, and more recently Sir James Holt. He also followed, as he observed, a longer line of northern scholars, 'St Cuthbert's folk and the men from Eboracum', who had from late medieval times contributed much to the University of Cambridge. After such a lengthy period in the north the move to Cambridge was not without its problems. Housing was one such problem until Narda and Barrie found a suitable flat in Bateman Street where from his study (if he leaned perilously out of the window) he could just see the pinnacles of King's College Chapel. In the move to Cambridge Barrie was greatly helped by the fact that in Christopher Brooke, who held the Dixie Chair of Ecclesiastical History, he had an old friend from his time at York, when Christopher had taken groups of students to visit Yorkshire abbeys.[11] In Cambridge Barrie's formidable energies never let him down. As one colleague recalls, 'with a heavy load of teaching, and supervision of post-graduates, no call on his time was ignored'. In particular he attempted to ensure that in Part I of the History Tripos the history of the Church was given due recognition. He ran a Special Subject on late medieval towns. He presided over the new M.Phil. in Medieval History (an inheritance from Sir James Holt), and for much of the time presided over the Medieval Subject Group. Together with Rosamond McKitterick he conducted the affairs of the Medieval Research Seminar. No mere list of Barrie's teaching, however, does justice to the spirit which he brought to that task. As at St Andrews and York his great generosity of spirit was evident in all that he did, freely giving undergraduates and graduates alike time which on occasion he could ill afford. Christopher Brooke has remarked that Barrie is 'wonderfully supportive of colleagues', a feature which 'has had a deep influence in preserving the morale of medievalists in difficult times'. Barrie's wider sympathies have also been evident in his dealings with college fellows who did not have university appointments: he 'took special pains to get to know the wider constituency, to draw them into teaching, to make them feel full members of the university teaching staff'.

Despite a heavy teaching load Barrie was still able to make a significant contribution to Cambridge history. Throughout his time at Cambridge the publications continued to flow. In his Inaugural Lecture he dealt with those topics which had concerned him most over the years: medieval monasticism, medieval towns, and the medieval university – all examples of the richness of medieval group life.[12] These topics he continued to develop. Two substantial pieces to appear, highly impressive in their scholarship, were his chapter on 'The Religious Orders 1370–1540' in the *History of the University of Oxford*, and his contribution on 'The Monks of Canterbury in the Later Middle Ages' in the *History of Canterbury Cathedral*.[13] Articles on York chantries and the connection between York and the Universities of Oxford and Cambridge developed earlier themes.[14] The ties with Durham were not forgotten.[15] The extensive range of Barrie's writings on the north, and his deep affection for, and understanding of, his native region, all of which have made him the foremost historian of the northern Church, are clearly seen in his recent collection of papers, *Church and State in the Medieval North of England* (1996).[16] There is still to come his survey of English towns in the later

Middle Ages in the forthcoming Volume I of the *Cambridge Urban History*, edited by David Palliser.

With a scholar as exceptional as Barrie there are inevitably aspects of his work that have not been mentioned. It is not possible here to deal fully with all his publications and academically related interests.[17] Outside Cambridge his activities have been multifarious. He has been an indefatigable lecturer and examiner. As a reviewer he is in constant demand. He has been meticulous in his work for *Northern History*. He has been a frequent visitor to the United States and Canada, where he was British Academy Fellow in the Folger Library, Washington (1974), Visiting Professor at Swarthmore College (1987), and Visiting Fellow at Trinity College, Toronto (1994). A number of honours have come his way, most notably his election to the British Academy in 1988. One suspects that he values highly his Life Membership of the Merchant Taylors Company of York, of which he was Honorary Archivist. In 1999 he was appointed Honorary Professor at York University. At the same time there has been a life outside the university. He has a profound interest in the cinema, and at York was responsible for setting up a branch of the National Film Theatre in York (1968) which still flourishes. Above all there has been his family, Narda, and his children, Mark and Michelle. After his retirement from Cambridge in 1999 Barrie's return to the city of York has enabled him to see more of Michelle and Conrad, and of his grandson, Theo. It has taken him back to places he knows well.

In Barrie we have a very human person. His colleagues' judgements on him are unanimous, speaking of 'the generosity of his help, encourage-ment and friendship', his 'obvious integrity and likeability', his 'intense professional commitment', his 'strong sense of duty', his 'unswerving loyalty'. His warmth and the strength of his personality are apparent to all. It was once said by an eminent medieval scholar that intellec-tual friendships were the most valuable thing a university could offer. Those who have had the privilege of knowing Barrie and of sharing his friendship over the years will certainly have no difficulty in endorsing that judgement.

NOTES

1. See R. B. Dobson, 'Recent Prosopographical Research in Late Medieval English History: University Graduates, Durham Monks, and York Canons', in N. Bulst and J.-Ph. Genet (eds.) *Medieval Lives and the Historian: Studies in Medieval Prosopography* (Kalamazoo, Mich., 1986), pp. 181–200.

2. Professor Donald Watt, to whom I am indebted for these comments about St Andrews.

3. Information concerning York and other matters was generously provided by Dr Gerald Aylmer and Professor Claire Cross. For the York background see Gordon Leff, 'Gerald Aylmer in Manchester and York', in John Morrill, Paul Slack and Daniel Woolf (eds.), *Public Duty and Private Conscience in Seventeenth-Century England, Essays Presented to G. E. Aylmer* (Oxford, 1993), pp. 9–17.

4. C. S. L. Davies, *Peace, Print and Protestantism 1450–1558* (St Albans, 1977), p. 151. For a different view, see C. S. Lewis, *English Literature in the Sixteenth Century, Excluding Drama* (Oxford, 1954), p. 169.

5. 'The Foundation of Perpetual Chantries by the Citizens of Medieval York', *Studies in Church History* 4 (London, 1967), 22–38; 'The First Norman Abbey in Northern England', *The Ampleforth Journal* 74/2 (Summer 1969), 161–76. See also 'The Election of John Ousthorp as Abbot of Selby in 1436', *Yorkshire Archaeological Journal* 42 (1968), 38–40.

6. 'The Residentiary Canons of York in the Fifteenth Century', *Journal of Ecclesiastical History* 30 (1979), 145–74.

7. *'Preserving the Perishable': Contrasting Communities in Medieval England*, inaugural lecture, 22 February 1990 (Cambridge, 1991).

8. 'Mendicant Ideal and Practice in Late Medieval York', in P. V. Addyman and V. E. Black (eds.), *Archaeological Papers from York Presented to M. W. Barley* (York, 1984), pp. 109–22. For additional information on York I am indebted to Professor David Palliser and Professor David Smith.

9. See, for example, 'Admissions to the Freedom of the City of York in the Later Middle Ages', *Economic History Review*, Second Series 26 (1973), 1–22; 'Yorkshire Towns in the Late Fourteenth Century', *Publications of the Thoresby Society* 59 (1985), 1–21.

10. I am indebted to Mr Gordon Forster for a number of helpful comments.

11. The comments on Cambridge are considerably indebted to Professor Christopher Brooke. I am also grateful to Professor Patrick Collinson for information.

12. *'Preserving the Perishable'.*

13. 'The Religious Orders 1370–1540', in J. I. Catto and Ralph Evans (eds.), *The History of the University of Oxford*, vol. II, *Late Medieval Oxford* (Oxford, 1992), pp. 539–79; 'The Monks of Canterbury in the Later Middle Ages, 1220–1540', in Patrick Collinson, Nigel Ramsey and Margaret Sparks (eds.), *History of Canterbury Cathedral* (Oxford, 1995), pp. 69–153.

14. 'Citizens and Chantries in late medieval York', in D. Abulafia, M. Franklin and M. Rubin (eds.), *Church and City 1000–1500, Essays in Honour of Christopher Brooke* (Cambridge, 1992), pp. 311–32; 'The Educational Patronage of Archbishop Thomas Rotherham of York', *Northern History* 31 (1995), 65–85. See also 'Beverley in Conflict, Archbishop Neville and the Minster Clergy, 1381–8', in C. Wilson (ed.), *Medieval Art and Architecture in the East Riding of Yorkshire* (British Archaeological Association, 1989), pp. 149–64.

15. 'Contrasting Chronicles: Historical Writing in York and Durham in the Later Middle Ages', in I. Wood and G. Loud (eds.), *Church and Chronicle in the Middle Ages: Essays Presented to John Taylor* (London, 1991), pp. 201–18; 'The Church of Durham and the Scottish Borders, 1378–88', in A. Goodman and A. Tuck (eds.), *War and Border Societies in the Middle Ages* (London, 1992), pp. 124–54.

16. The recent publication, *The Church in Medieval York: Records Edited in Honour of Professor Barrie Dobson*, General Editor David M. Smith, Borthwick Texts and Calendars (York, 1999), is a fitting tribute to Barrie's own impressive contribution to the history of the Church in medieval York.

17. See, for example, his recent article, 'Robin Hood: The Genesis of a Popular Hero', in T. Hahn (ed.), *Robin Hood in Popular Culture: Violence, Transgression and Justice* (Cambridge, 2000), pp. 61–77.

CHAPTER I

'If heaven be on this earth, it is in cloister or in school': the monastic ideal in later medieval English literature

Derek Pearsall

Langland's glowing recommendation of the life of the cloister – 'For yf hevene be on this erthe, or eny ese to the soule, / Hit is in cloystre or in scole, by many skilles I fynde' (*Piers Plowman*, C.V.152–3)[1] – has often been taken to be in need of explanation. After all, monks, as we know from Chaucer, are fat and worldly and much more devoted to venery than the *opus Dei*. It has often been thought to be an indication that Langland himself had a monastic education. But it seems more likely that the views of both Langland and Chaucer are examples of cultural image-making. Monks are not portrayed as they 'really' are but in ways that serve particular cultural purposes. These images are powerful and vivid fictions, and they soon displace the shifting realities that must be laboriously, and inevitably imperfectly, reconstructed from other sources. In this paper I shall try to trace some of these various strains of thinking, including Langland's Utopian vision of the monastic life, in the secular English literature of the later medieval period.[2] Something will be said about the benefits that accrued to the monks from not being friars, but the main argument will concern the superseding of the stereotypes *ad bonum* and *ad malum* of Langland by a more pragmatic acknowledgement of the monk as a bureaucratic functionary, mischievously anticipated in Chaucer and embodied in person in the poet John Lydgate.

The image of the monk in later medieval English literature was based on very fragmentary information, heavily supplemented by literary stereotype. Traditionally, monks did not conduct their lives under the public gaze, and what went on in monasteries and nunneries was largely a matter for speculation. Episcopal visitors, infrequent and unwelcome as they were, would see something, and their reports, with all the biases of mutual hostility, are often hair-raising; but many monasteries, including many of the largest and most powerful, were exempt from visitation except from abbots of the same order. Royal and aristocratic guests saw the four-star quarters assigned to them, but little of the normal life of the monastery. Such concealment could encourage suspicion in the popular imagining, and worked to the disadvantage of monks during the monastic expansions of the twelfth century and then again by contrast with the friars during their first evangelical fervour in the thirteenth century.

But the comparative hiddenness of their lives turned to the monks' advantage as disillusion with the friars became more widespread and the corruption of the mendicant orders became more ostentatious. For whatever the friars did, good or bad, they did in public: they were ubiquitously visible. The Wife of Bath, speaking at the beginning of her Tale of the days of King Arthur, and how the land then was 'fulfild of fayerye', remarks that this is now all changed, and it is the friars who are everywhere:

> For ther as wont to walken was an elf
> Ther walketh now the lymytour hymself
> In undermeles and in morwenynges,
> And seyth his matyns and his hooly thynges
> As he gooth in his lymytacioun.[3]

Women used to be afraid of being in the elf-filled woods, and especially of the attentions of incubi; now there are just the friars.

The high public profile of friars, as preachers and confessors particularly, quite apart from the abuses they practised in those professions, meant that they were especially vulnerable to criticism. Meanwhile, the greed and self-indulgence of monks, though it went by no means uncriticised, met with less vehement denunciation – and one reason was that it was less visible to the outside world.

The difference in attitudes towards the two groups of orders is well illustrated in Langland. The fierceness of his condemnation of the friars, particularly for their perversion of their spiritual office – and even more for betraying the high hopes that they had inspired – is everywhere apparent, and provides one of the dominant themes of *Piers Plowman*. Near the beginning of the poem, it is the friars who are spoken of as the greatest threat to the true Church (Prologue 56–65), and it is the friars who bring the Church to the brink of destruction in the poem's final vision (XXII.230–379). In contrast, Langland's view of the monastic orders is remarkably benign, and his tolerance can hardly be attributed solely or at all to the possibility that he himself was educated in a Benedictine school.[4] (Indeed, whether such an education would or would not contribute to an exceptionally favourable opinion is a matter of debate.) One example of his good opinion of monks is that they make virtually no appearance in the confessions of the Seven Deadly Sins. The one appearance that they do make is in the confession of Wrath, who elaborates on the anger and irritability and spitefulness that he easily induces among nuns, but makes a special point of remarking on his lack of success among monks:

> Amonges monkes I myhte be, ac mony tyme I spare,
> For there aren many felle freke myne aferes to aspye,
> That is, priour and suppriour and oure *pater abbas*.
> And yf I telle eny tales they taken hem togyderes
> And doen me faste Fridayes to bred and to water.
> Yut am I chalenged in oure chapitre-hous as I a childe were
> And balayshed on the bare ers and no brech bytwene.
> I have no luste, lef me, to longe amonges monkes . . .
>
> (VI.151–8)

It does seem extraordinarily good-natured on Langland's part to view monks so benignly, especially given the traditional association of monks with envy and quarrelsomeness, though it is worth remarking that Chaucer too omits this unattractive vice from his portrait of the Monk.[5]

Elsewhere there is the famous passage in which Langland warns the religious of the fate that awaits them if they do not keep their rule – a passage which was interpreted by sixteenth-century readers as a notable prophecy of the Reformation and the dissolution of the monasteries. The tone is one of warning and reproof, but Langland clearly expresses the highest opinion of the monastic life, and makes a sharp contrast between the idealised life of the cloister and the corrupted life of monks in the world:

> For yf hevene be on this erthe, or eny ese to the soule
> Hit is in cloystre or in scole, by many skilles I fynde.
> For in cloystre cometh no man to chyde ne to fyhte;
> In scole is love and louhnesse and lykyng to lerne.
> Ac mony day, men telleth, bothe monkes and chanons
> Haen ryde out of aray, here reule evele yholde,
> Ledares of lawedays and londes ypurchaced
> And pryked aboute on palfrayes fram places to maneres,
> An hepe of houndes at here ers as he a lord were . . .
>
> (V.152–60)

In the preceding lines, Langland quoted the description by 'Gregory' of a monk out of his cloister as being like a fish out of water, alluding to a very familiar topos of anti-monastic criticism, also used by Chaucer, best known in the proverbial formulation of Gratian's *Decretum*: 'Sicut piscis sine aqua caret vita, ita sine monasterio monachus'.[6] How vividly, in these lines (v.148–51), Langland materialises the implication of the comparison, with his image of a monk out of his cloister rotting and dying like a stinking dead fish.[7] How vividly too he brings before us the equally familiar topos of the hunting monk who behaves like a secular lord.

By contrast, how unrealised, how gently remote, is his picture of the life of the cloister in terms of the traditional imagery of the claustral paradise, a medieval commonplace derived from Jerome through Peter of Blois.[8] The four lines describing what actually goes on in cloister or 'in scole' could hardly be more vague. The last line (155) is actually a reworking of the line in the B version:

> But al is buxomnesse there and bokes, to rede and to lerne.
>
> (B.V.302)

Langland refers here to the monastic activity in which he can be presumed to have taken the keenest personal interest.[9]

But the sense of the personal and the specific is momentary and it is not to the main point, which is why it is removed in the C version. The contrast between the ideal and the real must be expressed in terms of the abstract place, and not the real men who inhabit it or any too precise indication of what they do there (note too how all reference to learning is transferred in C from cloister to 'scole'). It is a difference in poetic vitality between what is *known about* and what is *known* (a distinction Langland makes frequently, referring to the latter as *kynde knowyng*, e.g. C.I.136, X.56). It is also a difference between what can be idealisingly admired from a distance and what reveals ugly or merely irrelevant features when seen close to.

Langland's monk here is an 'outrider', one who has licence to ride from one monastic manor to another on the monastery's business and behaves as a result like a manorial lord. It was these 'outriders' whom we can presume to have been most prominent to the lay observer, and to have provided therefore the material for the severest criticism. They appear again in *Piers Plowman* in the list of *impossibilia* that are proposed by the king's advisor Reason as the conditions for looking favourably on the lady Meed: he will not relent, he says, until all 'religious outryderes be reclused in here cloistres' (C.IV.116).

And of course it is as an 'outridere', and as the 'kepere' of an outlying cell, that Chaucer's Monk appears on pilgrimage (perhaps he had to be one in order to be on pilgrimage, if Chaucer cared about this kind of thing). It is the first specific detail that we have of him (General Prologue[GP] 166), and it sets the context for the description of the worldly monk, or monk in the world, that follows. Chaucer calls here upon a long tradition of anti-monastic commentary in estates satire, and what he says can be compared, detail by detail, with satirical writing in Latin and French and Anglo-Norman as well as with Gower and Langland. He gives us what Jill Mann has described as a reworking of a rich literary tradition more than the result of a direct observation of real life.[10] Chaucer's gift, of course, is that he convinces us otherwise – that he has just been having a chat with the Monk and jotting down details of his conversation and appearance which he now relays to us straight from his notebook: his success in creating that kind of illusion, whilst working with familiar materials, is characteristically Chaucerian. He speaks of the Monk's love of food, his fine clothes, his fine horses, his fondness for hunting, his dislike of claustration (GP 172–89) – all of them topics of anti-monastic satire – and in the process one can see how Chaucer gives vitality to these venerable commonplaces. The poetry seems actually to resonate with the Monk's own tone of voice, as if Chaucer were remembering what the Monk had just told him.

The implications of Chaucer's portrait are, as always, by no means unambiguous. A traditional view would argue that the many hints of irony in the portrait, the several occasions on which the Monk is praised for qualities that are not usually considered relevant to his profession (e.g. 'A manly man, to been an abbot able', GP 33), constitute a series of signals that direct us to an orthodox moral evaluation of the Monk as a bad representative of his profession. This is certainly the way such ironies would be read in traditional estates satire. But Chaucer is different, and there are two possible ways in which the subtleties of his portrait can be drawn out, or explained.

One is to see his Monk as a portrait of a 'new monk', and use here can be made of the careful case presented by Paul Beichner, CSC.[11] Modern exegetes, argues Beichner, are more familiar with claustration as it is defined in the sixth-century Rule of St Benedict than with the realities of monastic administration in the late fourteenth century and with the provisions made for administrators by the chapters of the Benedictine order. Chaucer's is a sympathetic portrait of a monastic administrator, an 'organisation man' who puts his own particular abilities, not themselves notably spiritual, to the service of the larger spiritual good. If monasteries are to be effective they have to be properly run, the estates efficiently managed, public relations assiduously cultivated – something like, in fact, the case put forward by the Monk himself through his admiring press agent, cub-reporter Geoffrey Chaucer. So the Monk's hunting activities are not a form of self-indulgence, but a carefully planned way of getting on to good business terms with the local landowners. No deal can be better discussed than in the atmosphere of personal bonhomie that follows on a good day's hunting, at the medieval equivalent of the nineteenth hole. Henry Knighton says of William de Cloune, the famous hunting abbot of the Augustinian house at Leicester, that he would frequently assert in private that he did not delight in such frivolous hunting but took part in it only to show deference to the lords of the realm, and to capture their kindness and gain their favour in his business.[12] And as for the Monk's fine horse, it is no more, says Beichner, than the monastery Cadillac, designed to impress the local landowners and make them realise they are dealing with a successful business enterprise and not just a community of souls dedicated to God. Beichner finds a modern parallel with 'the business officer of a college or university, church-related or not, or the official in charge of fund raising or public relations', and concludes that 'one can find his reincarnation, *mutatis mutandis*, on many a pleasant American campus'.[13] People in English universities can no longer afford to laugh at this.

Chaucer may be recognising, or anticipating, certain developments in the role of monks as bureaucratic functionaries, but the function of his portrait in neutralising moral outrage (and also making it impossible to idealise the monastic life) has to be set in the larger context of the Prologue, and the fairly systematic way in which Chaucer detaches the portraits from their traditional moral moorings. Jill Mann argues that Chaucer's obliqueness of approach in the General Prologue is not a way of hiding moral comment so that we shall enjoy finding it for ourselves, but rather that various ways of looking at people are being played out before us. It is our perceptions, the way we commonly come to make judgements on people, that are being exposed to us, so that we can take no quick or habitual route to moral evaluation. Chaucer constantly stresses the attractiveness of features we are used to associating with moral weakness (the Monk's corpulence, his love of hunting) and thus, though reminding us of traditional moral satire, constantly discourages or circumvents the traditional moral judgement.[14] The difference between Chaucer and Langland, for whom the moral judgement is paramount, is profound.

Chaucer enlarges on his portrait of the 'new monk' in the Shipman's Tale, set in Paris and Saint-Denis, where the role of the *fabliau* intruder upon the marriage of the bourgeois merchant and his wife is taken by a monk. One might have expected here a conventional portrait of a lascivious monk, sexually hungry with the special kind of pent-up appetite that was associated with the cloister in the popular imagination, as in the Host's remarks to the Monk preceding his Tale (*Canterbury Tales*, VII.1943–62). Instead we get an easy-going philanderer, always ready to oblige a lady, or to give a friend the pleasure of showing him hospitality, or to tip the servants handsomely. It is not he who pushes the lady into a liaison, but she who pushes him, and then not for any sexual reasons but for respectable reasons of monetary exchange. The monk behaves with perfect amiableness throughout. It would be too much even to call him a cad: it is just unfortunate that to oblige the lady he has to disoblige his friend, her husband.

Most striking, in the context of present discussion, however, is the apparently cool acceptance of a completely worldly role for the monk. The monk is again an outrider, one who has licence from his abbot 'out for to ryde, / To seen hir graunges and hire bernes wyde' (Shipman's Tale, *Canterbury Tales*, VII.65–6), and he is a regular visitor to the house of the merchant, his friend. His pretext in asking for the loan of a hundred francs (which he is going to give to the wife in return for her sexual favours) is that he needs to buy 'certain beestes'

> To stoore with a place that is oures.
> (Shipman's Tale, VII.272–3)

The abbey to which we are told he returns periodically is a kind of business headquarters, and there is not the least suggestion that he is any kind of fish out of water when he is not there. The only thing that distinguishes him from his friend the merchant, it appears, is his celibacy, and that, as we have seen, is more of an opportunity than a restriction.

Chaucer has, however, a surprise in store for us. The pilgrim-Monk later suffers under a concentrated burst of the Host's most complacent raillery, taking in patience all the Host's lewd allusions to his prematurely bottled-up virility, the finest stud stock going to (lack of) seed in the cloister. The Monk does not respond to the Host's provocations but stands on his dignity and proposes instead a programme of tale-telling so vast – a selection of 'tragedies' from his repertoire of a hundred or so, with perhaps a life of St Edward to follow (*Canterbury Tales*, VII.1968–71) – that the Host is completely deflated. The Monk knows what a monk is supposed to do – pore over books and be a guardian of learning – even if he doesn't himself do it.

Chaucer had an uncanny premonition, in his Monk's Tale, of the voluminous monkish bookishness of Lydgate, and it is to Lydgate that we now turn to seek in him and his writing evidences of the paradise of claustrality or of other developments in attitudes to monastic life. The difference here is that Lydgate was himself a monk, and therefore knew from the inside what the monastic life was like, though whether this would make him more or less prone to take up conventional attitudes is not as clear as might be thought.

It is the poem of the *Dance Macabre* that comes closest to presenting an idealised view of the monk's existence. Written in Paris in 1426, it is in large part a translation of the French verses inscribed on the walls of the charnel-houses around the cemetery of the church of the Holy Innocents in Paris. It consists of a series of paired stanzas in which Death, personified as a skeleton, summons his victims to death, and the victim, always a representative of one of the estates, replies with some kind of confession of mis-spent life. It is, in relation to Chaucer's General Prologue, a kind of General Epilogue.

The portraits of the fat and luxury-loving Abbot and the richly dressed Abbess are in this context entirely predictable,[15] but interestingly enough Death's summons to the ordinary monk (in his 'blake abite') accuses him of nothing and merely reminds him that life is transitory and that he must now make his reckoning. Lydgate follows the French closely here and in the monk's reply, which is sober enough:

> I had levere in the cloystre be
> Atte my boke and studie my service.
>
> (385–6)

He confesses that he has mis-spent his life 'in many vise / Liche as a fole dissolute and nyce' (388–9), but there are no specificities from the tradition of estates satire, any more than there are in Lydgate's perfunctory apology for his life in the epilogue to the *Troy-Book* ('usynge an habite of perfeccioun, / Al-be my lyfe acorde nat ther-to'),[16] or in Lydgate's personal confession, conventionalised as it is, in his *Testament*. The exemption of monks from the usual severities of anti-clerical satire is remarkable here, in both the French and the English, and the claustral ideal itself comes close to being presented in the *Dance Macabre* by the Carthusian monk. The Carthusians took the spiritual initiative from the other orders, as well as the lion's share of endowments, in the fifteenth century, and the Carthusian monk here answers the summons of Death with severe correctness by pointing out that the coming of death is a mere physical confirmation of a spiritual choice he had already made:

> Unto the worlde I was dede longe agon
> Be my ordre and my professioun.
>
> (353–4)

This of course is the explicit statement of the basic implication of the 'heaven on earth' topos: the life of the monk, since he is dead to the world, is an adumbration of the life in heaven hereafter. So much for the so-called late medieval love of the 'macabre'.

Elsewhere we find Lydgate representing himself, on solitary pilgrimage to Canterbury, meeting with Chaucer's pilgrims at their inn in Canterbury, and falling into their company for the return journey. He agrees to tell a story – a Canterbury tale with a Lydgatian difference, the 4716-line *Siege of Thebes*. It may be that Lydgate is simply falling in with Chaucer's fiction, and that his presence on the road to Canterbury in association with a group of secular pilgrims is no more a representation of reality than some of the elements of Chaucer's illusion of the roadside drama. But something of his own and his reader's pleasure in the imitation of Chaucer would be lost if there were not some obliquely mimetic purpose. He portrays himself as riding to Canterbury to fulfil a vow made in a recent sickness:

> In a cope of blak and not of grene,
> On a palfrey slender, long and lene,
> With rusty brydel mad nat for sale,
> My man to-forn with a voide male.[17]

Point by point, this is a refutation of the traditional image of the monk in estates satire, as if Lydgate were earnest to redeem the profession from traditional obloquy and also perhaps to say something reassuring to Henry V, his long-time patron, amidst the king's vigorous continuing efforts to effect a reform in the Benedictine order. Black monks, he might be saying, are not all fat and greedy and lazy.

There is one other Lydgate poem that touches on the theme of claustration and that is the love-vision of *The Temple of Glass*. A central feature of the poem is the lament of the lovers in the Temple of Venus, and amongst them appears, rather touchingly, not a group of monks (since that might have appeared too personal) but a group of nuns. They follow groups of ladies who make their complaint, with a specificity and bitterness which is rare in the genre, of having been forced into loveless marriages for wealth or as children. In the case of the nuns, their complaint is of having been dedicated to the cloister before they had reached years of discretion, that is, in pre-puberty, or when too young to have experienced the delights of love:

> Y-rendred were into religioun
> Or thei hade yeris of discresioun.[18]

It is rather difficult to know what the nuns are doing in the Temple of Venus in the first place, and there is a suspicion that Lydgate's desire to be encyclopaedically comprehensive has led him into indecorum – he just had to include every kind of woman's sexual frustration he could think of. But the lines may be taken more personally, as some kind of indirect expression on Lydgate's part of the longings for the what-might-have-been that must have been a frequent irritation in the cloister.[19]

Certainly, John Shirley recognised some novelty in Lydgate's role as a secular poet-monk, and he has a good deal of heavily ironic amusement at Lydgate's expense when the poet speaks of love. Shirley seems to have acted as a kind of gossipy 'literary agent' for Lydgate and he provides chatty headings for many of Lydgate's poems, describing, embroidering and often probably inventing occasions when they were or might have been composed. Shirley also provides running commentary on some of Lydgate's remarks about women and love, drawing attention to the amusing contrast between literary propriety and personal impropriety. When Lydgate writes of women's doubleness, Shirley adds in the margin 'Be stille, daun Johan, suche is youre fortune', and when Lydgate follows Boccaccio in a long tirade against women in *The Fall of Princes* (copied as extracts in MS Harley 2251), Shirley has a whole string of cries of mock-outrage – 'Holdith your pees . . . Ye have no cause to sey so . . . Ye wil be shent . . . Be pees or I wil rende this leef out of your booke'. In another poem, where Lydgate praises women's truth and fidelity, Shirley asks laconically, 'A, daun John, est yvray?'[20] Shirley's consciousness of Lydgate's monkish profession is clear when Lydgate writes on such matters, and when he and other writers refer to Lydgate it is most often as the 'Monk of Bury', as if this were ever present in their minds as a significant aspect of his literary presence. Yet he and his contemporaries have no hesitation in integrating Lydgate into the normal networks of cultural production and manuscript transmission: it seems to them a matter of remark that he is a monk, but not a matter of surprise or scandal.

Lydgate's own life is the most striking witness to the changes that were taking place in monastic life and attitudes towards it in the fifteenth century. He was admitted into the abbey of Bury St Edmund's as a boy of fifteen, about 1386, and eventually ordained priest in 1397; he studied at Gloucester College, the Benedictine house at Oxford, from about 1406 to 1408, or longer, and from 1423 to 1434 he was prior of the Bury cell at Hatfield Broadoak in Essex. The priorate was probably a kind of sinecure, since during this period he spent much time out of the cloister. He was in attendance upon the duke of Bedford and the earl of Warwick in Paris in

1426, was frequently in the royal retinue, and was in the royal household at Christmas and other festival-times. He wrote mummings for royal and civic occasions, and poems both secular and religious for all kinds of patron – kings and queens, dukes and earls, duchesses and countesses, London guilds and citizens, abbots, local gentry and ladies. He received payment for poems that he wrote on commission, for instance from Humphrey, duke of Gloucester, and the abbot of St Alban's, and was integrated into the financial world of secular patronage to a degree that seems unusual in terms of conventional expectations of the monastic life and its obligations. He received an annuity from the crown in his later years, which was strictly against the monastic rule, and he went to some lengths to secure payment of it so that he might benefit personally.[21]

Lydgate's time at Oxford was not that of a 'normal student'. He was a middle-aged man, and Gloucester College was a religious house, its intention to preserve the monastic atmosphere as much as possible. But the life of the monk-student was inevitably somewhat more relaxed than life in the cloister: certain modest tastes – having one's own room and books, and greater freedom to dispose one's own time and to meet and make friends – would have been implanted that make Lydgate's subsequent career easier to understand.[22] It is not easy to say with any conviction what Lydgate was 'really' like: his poetry is too conventional to allow even room for reasonable speculation. But one thing is certain about his character: he enjoyed the comforts and privileges that fame and money procured, and he put himself to considerable effort to make sure that he had them. In his own way, he was a representative of the 'new monk'.

Henry V, who as prince of Wales had been Lydgate's patron at Oxford, presented articles to the great chapter of the English Benedictines in 1421 in which he recommended a tightening of the rule, including strict injunctions against the receipt of money-allowances by individual monks, restrictions upon movement outside the cloister, and upon private property.[23] But discussion was deferred, the king died, and nothing happened. The general development of Benedictine monasticism during the fifteenth century continued to be towards a relaxation of the bonds of community life, an increase in the availability of private space, servants, books and income, and an increase in patronal relationships between secular families and individual monks.[24]

There had always been a strongly practical side to Benedictine monasticism, justified by the need for efficient administration of the vast estates of the black abbeys, and as long ago as the twelfth century Abbot Samson

of Bury is reported by Jocelin of Brakelond to have preferred the active
to the contemplative life in that he 'praised good obedientiaries more
highly than good cloistered monks'.[25] But the shift of emphasis in the
fifteenth century was still marked. There were now many more obedientiaries, perhaps half the total number of members of the house appointed
to some form of office and therefore with a lawful reason for not being in
the cloister. Neglect of enclosure was a common complaint of visitation
records, and an important article in Henry V's programme for reforming
the order in 1421 was a call for a curtailment of visits in society.[26]

We can return to literary texts (and to yet another field of study where
Barrie Dobson has put us all in his debt) to see how these developments
were picked up in the lay imagining. The hostility towards monks in
the Robin Hood ballads has some traditional features – they are still
fat, greedy and greasy – but it also now seems little different from the
hostility towards other bureaucratic functionaries such as sheriffs and
tax-collectors. There is no particular sense that their involvement in the
world of business and finance is specially offensive as a violation of their
rule. Their meanness and greed as agents of a mean and greedy system
is taken for granted. In the mid-fifteenth-century ballad of *Robin Hood
and the Monk*[27] it is the monk, who has been robbed of £100 in the past
by Robin Hood, who recognises the outlaw in the church at Nottingham
and calls out the sheriff's men to seize him. He acts in effect almost as
the sheriff's agent and messenger, and spends all his time on the road
and in the town's streets. In *A Gest of Robyn Hode* (*c.*1500),[28] the black
monk who is intercepted on his way south through Barnsdale by Robin
Hood's men is the cellarer of St Mary's abbey in York (stanza 233). He
claims to be going to an outlying manor to check on the reeves who have
been cheating (st. 254). Like the other monks we have been meeting he
is an 'outrider', but it is hard now to have any strong sense of what he is
riding out *from*. He seems to be part of ordinary society, and indeed in
the fifteenth century many of these monk-wardens, in charge of outlying
granges, were being replaced by lay functionaries.[29]

Such developments as these, of which Lydgate acted as a harbinger,
made the ideal of paradisal claustration obsolete. They removed the
opportunity or need for either idealisation or vituperation. Utopias are
built on denial (they are 'no-places' not 'nice places'), and the Utopian
vision of monastic perfection was built to some extent upon the satirical
condemnation of monastic abuse. When both became superfluous, the
monasteries had no special reason for remaining in existence. When the

royal visitor, Dr John London, arrived to close the Carthusian house at Beauvale, he found the prior of the Charterhouse 'in hys shortt gowen and velvytt cappe, redy before our commyng', and he noted that in all houses, 'as well of men as of wemen, they be in maner all gon that night I have taken ther surendre and streightway in new apparell'.[30] The entry into secular life had long been prepared for.

NOTES

1. All citations from *Piers Plowman* are from the C version, unless otherwise specified: *Piers Plowman, by William Langland: An Edition of the C-Text*, by Derek Pearsall (London, 1978). B and C are cited from A. V. C. Schmidt (ed.), *William Langland, Piers Plowman: A Parallel-Text Edition of the A, B, C and Ƶ Versions*, vol. I, *Text* (London, 1995), with some modification of spelling.

2. For a survey of attitudes to claustration in the French, Italian and German literature of the thirteenth century, see Joan M. Ferrante, 'Images of the Cloister – Haven or Prison', *Mediaevalia: A Journal of Medieval Studies* 12 (1989, for 1986), 57–66. She shows that many writers, including Dante (who calls the eighth circle of Hell a 'cloister' filled with 'lay brothers', *Inferno*, XXIX. 40–1), are inclined to regard the enclosed monastic life as a refuge from the real spiritual responsibilities of being in the world.

3. *Canterbury Tales*, III. 873–7. All citations from Chaucer are from Larry D. Benson (ed.), *The Riverside Chaucer* (Boston, 1987). The Summoner's image, in his Prologue, of friars swarming around the devil's arse in hell is a coarser expression of the same sense of the friars' oppressively numerous presence (*Canterbury Tales*, III.1692–8); *cf. Piers Plowman*, C.XXII.264–72.

4. A suggestion made by Morton W. Bloomfield, 'Was William Langland a Benedictine Monk?' *Modern Language Quarterly* 4 (1943), 57–61. Bloomfield generally associated Langland's poem very closely with the monastic tradition of perfection, the idea of the ascetic life of the monk as the anticipation in this world of the Kingdom of God: see *Piers Plowman as a Fourteenth-Century Apocalypse* (New Brunswick, NJ, 1961), especially pp. 68–97.

5. See Jill Mann, *Chaucer and Medieval Estates Satire: The Literature of Social Classes and the General Prologue to the Canterbury Tales* (Cambridge, 1973), p. 225. Mann makes a distinction between 'attractive' sins (e.g. worldliness among clerics) and 'unattractive' sins (e.g. avarice).

6. Cited by W. W. Skeat in his note to General Prologue 179 in *The Complete Works of Geoffrey Chaucer*, vol. V (Oxford, 1900), p. 22. John V. Fleming, in 'Daun Piers and Dom Pier: Waterless Fish and Unholy Hunters', *Chaucer Review* 15 (1980–1), 287–94, cites from Walther the proverb 'Monachus extra claustrum est sicut piscis extra aquam' (p. 294).

7. A point made by Mann, *Chaucer and Medieval Estates Satire*, p. 31, who cites also Gower's *Vox Clamantis* and *Mirour de l'Omme*.

8. See Bloomfield, *Piers Plowman as a Fourteenth-Century Apocalypse*, p. 72; G. G. Coulton, *Five Centuries of Religion*, 4 vols. (Cambridge, 1923–50), II, p. 56. R. E. Kaske, in 'Langland and the *Paradisus Claustralis*', *Modern Language Notes* 72 (1957), 481–3, suggests that Langland's praise of the life of the cloister as 'heaven on earth' is derived from Benvenuto da Imola's commentary on Dante. This seems highly unlikely; but Kaske emphasises too that it was a common topos, and not evidence of personal experience. Less unlikely is the suggestion by Elisabeth M. Orsten, in '"Heaven on Earth" – Langland's Vision of Life within the Cloister', *American Benedictine Review* 21 (1970), 526–34, that Langland drew the paradisal topos from a popular saying alluded to by Bishop Brinton in one of his sermons.

9. By contrast, books are one of the aversions of Chaucer's Monk: why should he be expected always to be poring over books? says the forward-looking 'new monk'.

10. Mann, *Chaucer and Medieval Estates Satire*, p. 17.

11. Paul E. Beichner, 'Daun Piers, Monk – Business Administrator', *Speculum* 34 (1959), 611–19.

12. Ibid., 618.

13. Ibid., 612, 619.

14. Mann, *Chaucer and Medieval Estates Satire*, pp. 193–202.

15. See Florence Warren and Beatrice White (eds.), *The Dance of Death*, EETS o.s. 181 (1931), lines 233–64 (Ellesmere MS).

16. H. Bergen (ed.), *Troy-Book*, EETS e.s. 97, 103, 106, 126 (1906–35), V.3470–1.

17. A. Erdmann (ed.), *Siege of Thebes*, EETS e.s. 108 (1911), lines 73–4.

18. *The Temple of Glass*, in John Lydgate, *Poems*, ed. John Norton-Smith (Oxford, 1966), p. 72. In his edition of the poem in EETS e.s. 60 (1891), J. Schick gives parallels for this scene in *The Kingis Quair* and *The Court of Love*, no doubt introduced in imitation of Lydgate.

19. The episode is the more striking in that the tradition, as Ferrante points out in the essay cited in note 2 above, is for women to regard the nunnery as a haven, not a prison.

20. See Aage Brusendorff, *The Chaucer Tradition* (Oxford, 1925), pp. 461–5.

21. See Derek Pearsall, *John Lydgate (1371–1449): A Bio-bibliography*, English Literary Studies 71 (University of Victoria, 1997), pp. 36–9.

22. Ibid., pp. 15–17.

23. See W. A. Pantin (ed.), *Documents Illustrating the Activities of the General and Provincial Chapters of the English Black Monks 1215–1540*, 3 vols., Camden Society, third series 45, 47, 54 (1931–37), II, pp. 113–14.

24. See David Knowles, *The Religious Orders in England*, II: *The End of the Middle Ages* (Cambridge, 1955), p. 274.

25. Jocelin of Brakelond, *Chronicle of the Abbey of Bury St Edmunds*, trans. Diana Greenway and Jane Sayers (Oxford, 1989), p. 37: cited in the essay on 'Monastic productions' by Christopher Cannon in David Wallace (ed.), *The Cambridge History of Medieval English Literature* (Cambridge, 1999), pp. 316–48 (p. 317).

26. See Knowles, *Religious Orders*, p. 184.
27. Printed in R. B. Dobson and J. Taylor, *Rymes of Robyn Hood: An Introduction to the English Outlaw* (London, 1976), pp. 113–22.
28. Ibid., pp. 71–112.
29. Knowles, *Religious Orders*, p. 312.
30. Ibid., p. 357 (cited in Cannon, 'Monastic Productions', p. 348).

The 'Chariot of Aminadab' and the Yorkshire priory of Swine

Janet Burton

The Gilbertine Order has the distinction of being the only medieval monastic congregation to have its origins in Britain. Moreover, of the many new orders of the twelfth century it was one of the few which brought to the foreground the vocation and needs of women, constructing and evolving over a period of several decades a constitution of which the *raison d'être* was the provision of a way of life for nuns. The mature Gilbertine arrangement was reached around 1150. To the anchoritic women who were now professed nuns according to the Rule of St Benedict, the lay sisters who were added on the advice of Abbot William of Rievaulx (1132–45) to serve the nuns, and the lay brothers who took charge of external affairs of the house, were now attached Augustinian canons, literate men to minister to the women.[1] Although the details concerned with the organisation of daily life and government were augmented and adapted over the years which followed, the basis of the Gilbertine houses remained this fourfold arrangement, which the author of the life of St Gilbert likened to the biblical 'Chariot of Aminadab':

This is the chariot of Aminadab, in other words of a willing people who of their own accord have become poor for Christ. It has two sides, one of men, the other of women; and four wheels, two of men, clerks and laymen, and two of women, educated and unlettered.[2]

The four wheels were to work together, in balance and harmony, to produce as near to an ideal monastic community as human fragility allowed.

The Gilbertine double houses comprising these four elements contain perhaps the easiest group of religious women to define, at least from a twentieth-century perspective, because the Gilbertines had a written constitution.[3] In the twelfth century such definition was not always easy – witness Gervase of Canterbury's efforts in the *Mappa Mundi*, which confused the 'white nuns' of the Gilbertines and Cistercians.[4] Increasingly, research into women's monastic history has revealed a much less clear-cut picture than the traditional labels Benedictine, Cistercian, Gilbertine, Cluniac and Augustinian, as detailed in the pages of Knowles and Hadcock, suggest.[5] Exigencies of female religious life, the demands of seclusion, perceived gender roles, and the place of men in female communities, all led to a diversity of practices, and a cross-fertilisation of influences. This process is exemplified at the female priory of Swine (East Yorkshire), founded some time before 1153 in a small area which also saw foundations, at roughly the same time, at Watton (Gilbertine double house), Meaux (Cistercian men) and Nunkeeling (women). Swine was – at least for part of its existence – a double house, incorporating all four wheels of the Chariot of Aminadab, possibly Gilbertine-influenced, yet not Gilbertine, calling itself Cistercian, yet not officially recognised as such. This paper argues that the arrangement at Swine was a product of intense cross-influence of monastic ideals in a small area which, in microcosm, reflects patterns of monastic change in Europe. It looks at the origins and development of the community, the relationship of its parts and the harmony – or a lack of harmony – that the arrangement allowed. It uses charters, visitation returns, wills and chronicle evidence to produce the first modern study of this religious community. Finally it draws some comparisons between Swine and the nearby Gilbertine nunnery of Watton, and argues that where the Gilbertine women were constrained by the Chariot of Aminadab, the nuns of Swine were liberated by it.

Swine Priory owed its foundation to Brother Robert de Verli, priest of Swine, who sought confirmation for his new house from Hugh du Puiset, archdeacon of the East Riding, some time before Hugh's promotion to the bishopric of Durham in January 1153.[6] Hugh confirmed the grant of the church of St Mary of Swine, made by Robert 'cujus ipsa ecclesia esse dinoscitur' (whose church this is known to be), to nuns serving God 'secundum institutionem sancti Benedicti' (according to the institution of St Benedict). In 1177 there is evidence of Cistercian influence: the nuns of Swine received a bull from Pope Alexander III, in which he described them, and the nuns of Nun Cotham in Lincolnshire, as enjoying the privilege of Cistercian monks, that is, of freedom from the payment of tithes on lands which they cultivated themselves.[7] Thus, Swine is one of the earliest of English nunneries to claim a Cistercian identity. What precisely such claims meant is problematic, as is the impetus which drew nunneries – officially not a part of the Cistercian Order until the thirteenth century – to emulate the White Monks. However, it is worthy of note that at roughly the same time as Robert de Verli was converting his parish church to accommodate religious women, the Cistercians, under the patronage of William of Aumale, earl of Yorkshire, settled at Meaux, some four miles to the north-west of Swine. The founding colony came from Fountains Abbey, whose abbot, Henry Murdac, was also archbishop of York. Until his reconciliation to the citizens of York in 1151, Murdac had divided his time between Ripon and Beverley – the latter only about four miles from Meaux and seven or eight from Swine.[8] The foundation of Swine was also roughly contemporary with the establishment, by Eustace Fitz John, of a Gilbertine house at Watton, which lies about twelve miles to the north-west of Swine;[9] and one of the early benefactors of Watton was Archbishop Henry Murdac.[10] The proto-Gilbertine house at Sempringham had many features in common with Swine – not least its foundation by the parish priest and its location in the parish church. The vibrancy of monastic growth in this small area of east Yorkshire thus mirrors many features of the wider European scene.

It is fairly early in its history that we begin to see evidence that Swine was a double house. When Ernegata de Burton, apparently between 1155 and 1170, issued a charter for Swine, she referred to the community as brothers and sisters serving God there.[11] In 1181, when King Henry II issued a confirmation charter, he took under his protection 'his house' of Swine and its master, canons, brothers and nuns – and the sequence in which the residents were listed may say something about their perceived significance within the community at that time.[12] It will be useful to consider these residents in turn, beginning with the master. Records of masters occur at fifteen of the twenty-seven English nunneries which appear to have been Cistercian at some time in their history.[13] At Swine it is likely that the individual named Robert, who occurs between 1170 and 1195 as master or as prior of Swine, was its founder, Robert de Verli – and this provides another parallel with the order of Sempringham, whose founder, Gilbert, became master. By the late 1180s there was another master of Swine named Philip.[14] Thereafter there is sporadic evidence for the holder of the post.[15] At some point between 1235 and 1249 it was held by Hamo, canon of the Augustinian house of Healaugh Park, which lies about seven miles south-west of York.[16] In April 1287 Archbishop Le Romeyn appointed Robert de Spalding, canon of the Premonstratensian house of Croxton, as master, and ordered the prioress and nuns, canons and brethren, to profess obedience to him. The significance of the appointment is perhaps underlined by the request of the archbishop to the Premonstratensian general chapter that Robert, who in the three months since his appointment had brought the 'domus pauperum monialium de Swyna' (the house of poor nuns at Swine) back from ruin, should be allowed to continue in his good work.[17] This request was repeated in January 1290, although by April the post had passed to John Bustard, brother of the Trinitarian friary of St Robert of Knaresborough, who was not a great success.[18] The post was not always held by a member of the religious orders: in 1298 William Darrains, vicar of Londesborough, near Pocklington, was appointed; he may have had a personal connection with Swine, as he shares a name with at least two of its nuns.[19] In 1311 Walter de Kelk was asked, by the archbishop, to take care of the 'majora negotia' (greater business) of Swine – and the prioress and convent were to recompense him from the goods of their house 'juxta merita sua' (according to his merits); and in 1315, at the request of the prioress and convent, the archbishop appointed Hugh, rector of the chapel of Nuttles, to take care of their temporal goods.[20] In 1352 the rector of Kirkby Misperton bequeathed a silver cup and a maple chest to John de Norton, master of Swine.[21]

The evidence considered so far seems to suggest that the master, who might be a canon, cleric or layman, was responsible for the administration of the external affairs of the priory, and the diversity of their places of origin or occupation is quite striking. This raises the question: why, if the community of Swine comprised canons as well as brothers, was there need for a master? Here the analogy with Sempringham breaks down, for Gilbert, and after him Roger of Malton, were masters of the order, not of one house, and the Gilbertine institutes carefully laid down the chains of authority within individual houses, and the roles of the priors, and the three prioresses who worked on a rota system.[22] The editor of the *Victoria County History* associated the appearance of a master at Swine with the decline of the canons, and suggested that the appointment of Robert, canon of Croxton, as master in 1287 marked the withdrawal of canons from the community.[23] However, there appears to have been a sequence of masters from the time of the foundation; moreover, the continued presence of canons in the community was envisaged in 1287, for, as we have seen, the canons were bidden to profess obedience to Robert. The absence of reference to canons, or literate brothers, in visitation decrees of 1298 and 1319 may be significant;[24] however, the role of the master – for whatever reason – was deemed to be distinct from that of the canons, or clerics. Perhaps an answer to our question might be suggested by the evidence for the status and role of the canons and lay brothers within the community, and for the balance of power between the men and the women.

Here surviving thirteenth-century visitation returns yield valuable insight. On 13 January 1268 Archbishop Giffard visited Swine, and on 15 March issued injunctions which provide some indications of the makeup of the community, and the intended contact between the male and female components.[25] There were evidently two sets of men at Swine: canons and lay brothers (*conversi*). Giffard noticed a possible danger of contact between the men and women of Swine – the window house, which was a distinctive feature of Gilbertine houses.[26] At Swine, as in Gilbertine houses, there appear to have been two windows through which food and drink were passed to the canons and *conversi*. These, it was claimed, were not as well guarded by the two nun-janitors as they should have been, and the men and women were suspected of having conversations.[27] A second danger point was the door which led into the church. This, too, was not guarded well enough: it was in the charge of a secular boy, who at sunset let the canons and *conversi* enter the church so that they might speak to the nuns and sisters: this was, so it was claimed, a far cry from the days when the door was guarded by a faithful *conversus*. Finally, a hint of tension comes in the accusation that the canons, being intimidated by Robert de Hilton who, in addition to wandering around the convent at will, seized its goods under the pretence of guarding them, 'bought him off' with a barn full of grain – and this without the consent of the convent, which should have been required. This suggests a usurpation of the rights of the nuns, and that disposal of property by the canons without the consent of the nuns was not the normal pattern.

Indeed, the prioress appears to have been a woman who enjoyed authority, even if in 1268 her position was undermined both by her own character defects (she was suspicious, untrustworthy and inconsistent), and by the (alleged) conspiracies against her by three 'sisters in the flesh', Sibyl, Bella and Amia, who persuaded others to join them in their defiance.[28] These were, however, personal shortcomings and problems, and the power of the prioress was also apparent in the accusations that she retained money intended for such purposes as pittances, instead of entrusting it to two honest nuns. She was responsible for the punishment of misdemeanours, although her erratic penalties provoked complaints from the nuns' families. As with the men, there were two sets of women, nuns and lay sisters (simply referred to as *sorores*). One problem which the archbishop detected was that the lay sisters were striving to be equal to the nuns, and to wear their black veil 'quod in aliis ejusdem religionis domibus esse dicitur insuetum' (which in other houses of their religion is said to be unaccustomed).[29]

A similar pattern of female authority emerges in a decree following a further visitation by Archbishop Giffard in 1273.[30] The prioress was to be obeyed by the nuns, and was to ensure that she was always present and presided over the daily chapter. In any absence Swine was to be ruled by a subprioress, and mature and careful nuns were to be appointed to the offices of cellarer and subcellarer. All obedientiaries were to render their accounts twice a year, individually, so that their hard work, and faults, could be noted. Two copies of account rolls were to be drawn up, one to be kept in the treasury and the other in the possession of the prioress. All money was to be kept by two or three elected nuns, and the seal of the house was to be in a chest in which the muniments of the priory were kept, and its three keys were to be in the possession of the prioress and two nuns.

These injunctions all have counterparts in decrees issued to other nunneries, and they seem to point to a high level of executive and financial control and authority on the part of the prioress. Yet in the case of Swine this was not due to the absence of men, who were clearly still there in force. One is named: Giffard enjoined that Brother Thomas carry out the internal and external business of the house 'loco magistri' until another master should be appointed, provided that on all major matters he sought the consent of the convent. Thus, it would not be necessary for the prioress to leave the house except when any business demanded her personal attendance. The archbishop's decrees continue: 'alii autem fratres litterati divinis intendant officiis sicut eis incumbit' (the other literate brothers shall attend to the divine offices as is their duty), and they were not to go outside the gates or the church, or wander in the court, unless there was some good reason for them so to do. This suggests that there were a number of literate brethren, presumably canons, and the expectation was that the discharging by one of them, Thomas, of the duties of master would be temporary. There were lay brothers in the community as well: they were to perform the duties laid on them 'horasque suas quoad oraciones et jejunia secundum ordinis statuta conservent' (and they shall keep their hours for prayers and for fasts according to the statutes of the order).[31] The same injunction to the *conversi* is included in the decrees of 1298, but the canons, or literate brothers, are not mentioned.[32] It may be, therefore, that their disappearance is to be dated between 1287 and 1298. Lay brothers are mentioned, by name, in 1320 and 1335, but no canons occur in the priory records after the last decade of the thirteenth century.

That the nuns were in charge of their own affairs, and had a high profile within the priory, is suggested in a number of ways. The charters of the house give prominence to the nuns. Even when there was clearly a master, and a male component in the house, charters were still issued by the prioress and nuns, or the prioress and convent, rather than by the master, or by the canons.[33] In addition, as we have seen, there are references in visitation returns to the prioress's activities, and responsibilities. These contrast with those of Gilbertine prioresses, whose power and authority were severely limited and restricted to the women's part of the monastery. Significantly, the visitation of Swine in 1298 decreed that the office of third prioress – a phrase which is reminiscent of Gilbertine practice – recently created contrary to ancient custom, was to be removed.[34] Returning to the question raised earlier, that is, why the master was chosen from outside the convent when there were men within the community, it can be argued that it was to the advantage of the nuns to have an outsider whose authority was over external affairs – a man who would not undermine, or try to usurp, female authority within the house. External male assistance allowed women a measure of control over their own affairs, which Gilbertine women lacked.

The nunnery of Swine originated in the grant, to the nuns, of the parish church of St Mary, and thereafter the church was shared between the monastic community and the parish. There is a variety of evidence to suggest how this relationship worked in practice. The church was appropriated to the nuns, and the nature of their responsibility is suggested by the finding in 1308 that they had failed to appoint a vicar.[35] At the Dissolution the church is described as 76 feet in length and 21 feet in breadth, with the dimensions of the choir 54 feet in length 'with xxxvi goode stalles alle alonge bothe the sydes of waynscott bourdes and tymber for the nonnes'. There was one altar in the choir, and two 'benethe in the body of the churche'.[36] A number of wills suggest the popularity of Swine as a burial place for the local gentry. Isabella Salvain requested burial in the choir in 1409, as did Peter de Buckton, lord of Buckton, in 1414.[37] Robert Hilton, knight, desired to be interred in the south of the chancel of the parish church (1429), and his widow preferred burial in the choir, on the north side (1432).[38] Thomas Hedon of Marton in Holderness wanted his tomb to be 'befor þe rode of pety'.[39] The sharing of the church created tensions from time to time, and relations between the nuns and the parishioners were not always trouble free. Evidence from the register of Archbishop Greenfield indicates that in June 1308 the archbishop commissioned an enquiry into a building known as 'le Northcrouche' in the church of Swine, which, as he had found during a visitation, was built onto the north wall of the parish church.[40] Its purpose was evidently in dispute. The prioress and convent, described as rectors of the parish church, asserted that the building was their property, to use and dispose of as they wished. They had, they claimed, stored their wool there from time immemorial.[41] The parishioners, on the other hand, claimed that the building was part of the parish church, and in it there was an altar dedicated to St Andrew. The nuns' use, so they claimed, had been temporary: long before, the priory had been destroyed by fire, and the parishioners had allowed the nuns to construct a solar, or upper storey, in the building in order to store their wool, but mass had continued to be celebrated at the altar. Now, on account of the dispute, the building was roofless and ruined. In January 1309 the proctor of the nuns, Stephen de Wytheton, and William West of Coniston for the parishioners, appeared to present their cases, and the judgement was that the building was part of the parish church of Swine, and the parishioners were therefore responsible for its repair and upkeep.[42]

The initiative here appears to have been entirely with the nuns. There is no mention of any canons, literate men or *conversi*, or even a master, acting on their behalf, apart from their proctor. This could have been because the male component within the convent had declined – as evidence for the canons suggests by the end of the thirteenth century – but it might also be that the nuns had always held the reins of power at Swine. To test this hypothesis we return to the thirteenth century, and look at how the community of Swine acted in relation to its powerful neighbours.

The close proximity between Swine and Meaux suggests that their paths were bound to cross.[43] A problem which faced monasteries and nunneries in areas where monastic expansion had been rapid and successful was that they shared patrons and benefactors, which could lead to the acquisition of lands in the same area, and disputed estates and boundaries. An early example concerns the grange of Bealeys (Lockington), which was granted to Meaux by William Fossard, at or shortly after its foundation in 1151, but was lost to the nuns of Swine.[44] A further point of tension occurred in the abbacy of Hugh, fifth abbot of Meaux (1210–20). For reasons of financial exigency the monks had been dispersed, but then recalled on All Saints' Day 1211.[45] In the meantime they had received certain benefactions, and four named men, including

Amandus 'pincerna', as well as free tenants in Arnold, Rowton, and Benningholme, granted the monks licence to make a dyke (Monkdyke) through the middle of their land between Arnold and Benningholme. The monks undertook not to impede or divert the water, and permission seems to have been given by all – except the nuns of Swine. Amandus is recorded by the Meaux chronicler as having granted further lands to the monks, including three tofts in East Benningholme, with his body for burial. However, when Amandus died, and was duly buried at Meaux, the nuns of Swine 'per violentiam' snatched his body, and brought it to Swine, where they reburied it, with the help of Saer de Sutton. To add insult to injury (and we must remember that it is a later abbot of Meaux who is recording these events), the nuns dug turves in the marsh between Wawne and Swine – in Meaux's own back yard. All these actions led to a long-standing dispute, at the conclusion of which judgement was in favour of the nuns: the body of Amandus was to remain at Swine. Another point addressed was Monkdyke, and we now learn the reasons for the nuns' objections. They claimed that before the monks had constructed the dyke the water coming from Lambwath between East and West Benningholme flowed without hindrance through their grange of Fairholme to Wawne marsh, and through Forthdyke into the river Hull, and that the monks had impeded the flow of water, to the nuns' detriment. The monks were adjudged to owe the nuns twenty marks in compensation, and the water was to be divided equally for the use and convenience of both houses. The monks moreover quitclaimed to the nuns the rights which they had in the granges of Bealeys and Fairholme and the dyke from Fairholme to Benningholme, and thence to Swine wood.

The nuns of Swine had successfully stood up against their more powerful neighbours to prevent being sidelined, territorially, by the monks' aggressive grange policy.[46] It may be that the lack of reference to any action by the men of Swine reflects the situation at the time Abbot Burton was writing, in the early fifteenth century, rather than in the early thirteenth. On the other hand, the apparent lead role of the women is consistent with evidence discussed above. That further disputes between the monks and Saer de Sutton are recorded suggests that the nuns might, on the occasion of the litigation with Meaux, have been acting in concert with one of their benefactors and protectors, but this did not prevent them from taking an independent line at other times.

A rather later cause of contention was the church of Drypool, granted to the nuns by Saer de Sutton. In 1226 Saer quitclaimed the church in return for the prioress's undertaking to find a chaplain and clerk, at the expense of the convent, to celebrate divine service for Saer and his successors in the chapel of St George, Ganstead.[47] Ten years later the possession was again disputed, and once more the prioress was successful.[48] The Meaux Chronicler claimed that the nuns then appropriated the church, and took the monks to court concerning the tithes of animals pastured at Southcoates, within the parish, which the monks resisted paying.[49] The monks claimed the liberties of their order – that they should be free from the payment of tithes on lands which they cultivated themselves – and appealed to the pope. However, local ecclesiastical opinion was in favour of Swine: the official of the archbishop excommunicated the abbot and convent, and of the chapters of York and Lincoln all but three men declared themselves in favour of the nuns. The abbot, however, obtained letters to papal judges delegate to investigate the case, against Hamo, canon of Healaugh Park, master of the nuns of Swine, the nuns themselves, and the official of York.

The nuns' response was marked by a consistent failure to appear in court. Eventually their proctor, Stephen, appeared, but was promptly excommunicated; the abbot claimed damages of 500 marks, and the nuns were fined 20s expenses for that day, and twenty marks for their previous non-appearance. The nuns refused to pay the fine, and the prioress was excommunicated in her own church:

Cum vero per officialem Estridingensem et magistrum monialium de Kyllynge, executores ad solutionem dictarum 20 marcarum, super solutione praedicta memoratae moniales coram testibus requisitae fuissent, executoribus quoad solutionem praedictam parere contempserunt. Unde post mensem, candelis accensis et pulsatis campanis, in ecclesia propria de Swyna ejusdem loci priorissam memorati executores excommunicaverunt et per totum archidiaconatum Estridingensem excommunicatam denuntiaverunt.[50]

(When the said nuns, in the presence of witnesses, were required by the official of the East Riding and the master of the nuns of Nunkeeling, executors for the payment of the said twenty marks, to answer concerning payment of the same, they refused to pay. Therefore, after a month, with candles extinguished and bells rung, in her own church of Swine, the executors excommunicated the prioress of the place and announced the excommunication throughout the archdeaconry of the East Riding.)

This did not, however, have the desired effect. The prioress and nuns still failed to pay or to appear in court. Stephen, their proctor, was again excommunicated, and Hamo, their master, was suspended for contumacy. The judges now awarded Meaux the chapel of Marton in Holderness in compensation. Still the nuns failed to recognise the authority of the judges-delegate, and the prioress, subprioress, precentrix, cellaress and sacrist were all suspended and banned from entering the church. The archdeacon of the East Riding was ordered to seize goods of the priory to the value of the fine, but this did not move them either. The nuns then attempted to prevent the transfer of Marton chapel to the monks, and, as a result, the parish church of Swine and all its chapels were placed under interdict. At the same time it was ordered that six *conversi* from Swine be cited to appear before the judges for impeding the transfer of Marton chapel to the monks of Meaux – direct action had been taken. Hamo – who had been reinstated temporarily – was suspended 'ab officio administrandi in dicta domo' (from his post as administrator of the said house), and he and his accomplices were excommunicated.

Once again the nuns failed to appear in court, and so 'ecclesiam conventualem ipsarum monialium, cum ecclesia conversorum eidem ecclesie contigua [adjacente] a celebratione divinorum suspenderunt' (they suspended the conventual church of the nuns themselves, with the church of the *conversi* lying beside it, from the celebration of divine service).[51] Moreover, the judges decreed that two canons and seven *conversi* from Swine should be denounced for impeding the seizures from being carried out. This passage, which as far as I know has not been commented on before, suggests that the physical arrangement of Swine Priory may have been akin to that of Gilbertine Watton, with a separate church for the men lying alongside that of the nuns. In commenting on the architectural evidence from Swine, Roberta Gilchrist has suggested that there was a western nuns' choir, as at Marrick, and that the 'brethren occupied the eastern part of the church, which transferred to parochial control upon their removal, although . . . the parish may have taken over the eastern nuns' church at the Dissolution'.[52] But might this eastern part always have been used by the parish, and the men accommodated in a second church, lying alongside that of the nuns?[53] *Contigua/adjacente* might refer to a part of the church physically separated by a wall or screen from the nuns' choir, but the possibility of a second church cannot be ruled out.[54]

The dispute over the tithes of Drypool was one battle that the nuns were not to win. The nuns, canons and *conversi* failed once more to appear in court, and the judges now put the monks in possession of Drypool church. They also wrote to the archbishop stating that Hamo had been excommunicated and removed from his office at Swine, and to the prior of Healaugh Park, stating that Hamo should be shunned as an excommunicate. However, the women and men of Swine made one last gesture of defiance: four nuns, three *conversi* and several 'seculars' tried to prevent the transfer of Drypool to the monks by entering through a broken wall and occupying the church. The churches of Drypool and Ganstead were now suspended from performance of the sacraments, and a further round of excommunications was ordered, including all the workmen (*mercenarii*) of the nuns. Eventually the nuns agreed that their proctor should appear in court, and an amicable enough arrangement was reached. The Cistercians' privileges were upheld, and the nuns relinquished their claims to the tithes of Drypool.[55] Indeed, they agreed to pay 200 marks in expenses and damages to Meaux, twenty marks down and the rest at a rate of forty marks per annum. For fifty of the marks the nuns offered instead land in Hayton, and when they were down to the last twenty marks the monks waived the remainder. With the consent of the archbishop of York an annual rent of 30s was set aside to provide linen cloth for the nuns and sisters, the chronicle hinting that poverty had forced the nuns to sell the leftovers of their tables – which should have been distributed to the poor – in order to provide yarn for spinning. The rent came from lands in Hornsea, Burton and Beeford, and, anxious to keep their part of the bargain, the nuns promised the abbot and convent that if ever the 30s rent were lost or alienated, they would be obliged to pay back the remaining twenty marks. This is an intriguing snapshot of the pressures on small communities of religious women in the Middle Ages.

The conflict in the third or fourth decade of the thirteenth century between the nuns of Swine and the monks of Meaux suggests that by then the canons might have been outnumbered by *conversi*; this decline, however, was not – as has sometimes been thought – the occasion for the appointment of an external master.[56] On the contrary, the evidence suggests that the master was a consistent feature of life at Swine throughout the twelfth and thirteenth centuries. The Book of St Gilbert, from an early thirteenth-century perspective, stated that Gilbert had introduced the canons into his houses as 'scholars for their skill in ruling others, clerks in order to exercise authority over the church in accordance with law; men to look after women; scholars to open the way of salvation to both men and women, and clerks to supply the pastoral office to all'.[57] The evidence from Swine does not suggest that the canons were there in order to occupy positions of authority, but rather to provide spiritual succour and literacy. Consistently, it appears to be the women who were in charge of affairs within the cloister, and women who took the initiative; and the strong-minded actions of at least some of the prioresses continued until the last decades of the priory's existence. They evidently acted as record-keepers for some of the local gentry, and between 1498 and 1500 Prioress Beatrix Lowe was taken to court by the heiresses of the late Peter Twyer and their husbands, for the non-return of evidences belonging to Peter; a similar action was brought against Prioress Helen Deyne, who was elected in 1521 and was still in office in 1537.[58] The prioresses and nuns of Swine were on occasion acting under acute financial pressures, and the way in which they responded somewhat redresses the picture of medieval religious women as unable to act for themselves. The master of Swine assisted the nuns in external matters; but he does not appear to have intervened in the prioress's running of the community, and – as events at Drypool indicate – she did not feel her actions outside the priory to be constrained by his existence.

This paper began by drawing attention to the Gilbertine 'Chariot of Aminadab' whose four wheels were strictly controlled and driven by the written constitution of the order, and to the evidence for a similar fourfold arrangement at Swine. Certain aspects of the history of Swine – notably the architectural features of the window house and the probable separate church for the men – also bear comparison with Gilbertine houses such as Swine's near neighbour at Watton. But there the similarities seem to end. Where Watton was locked into the male-dominated organisation of the Gilbertine order, Swine illustrates some of the flexible and experimental arrangements, powers and structures of command and authority which were often to be found in female houses. Watton was – on one level – more successful than Swine. It was larger, with a community of forty-one nuns in 1539 against Swine's twenty, and because it appealed to patrons it was also wealthier, with an annual value in 1535 of just over £360, in contrast to Swine's £83.[59] Yet, looked at from another angle, the women of Swine may have been less constrained than the nuns of Watton, and this comparative freedom may have owed much to the fact that the priory was not part of an order. Swine's structure provided the male support that the women wanted: practical back-up from the *conversi* and spiritual guidance from the canons. But it allowed its women a freedom of movement, a part in the decision-making process and a sense of leadership. Utopia it was not, but for a group of women in the medieval north the nunnery of Swine provided opportunities and openings which were denied to many.

NOTES

1. For the latest treatment see Brian Golding, *Gilbert of Sempringham and the Gilbertine Order c.1130 to c.1300* (Oxford, 1995); see also R. Foreville and G. Keir (ed. and trans.), *The Book of St Gilbert*, Oxford Medieval Texts (Oxford, 1987).

2. *Book of St Gilbert*, pp. 50–3; for commentary on this verse (Song of Songs 6:11), see ibid., pp. 336–7.

3. The Gilbertine rule survives in a single manuscript of thirteenth-century date. It is a composite text, with additions to 1238: Golding, *Gilbert of Sempringham*, p. 455.

4. W. Stubbs (ed.), *Gervasii Cantuariensis Opera Historica*, 2 vols., RS (1879–80), II, pp. 420–41 (*passim*).

5. D. Knowles and R. N. Hadcock, *Medieval Religious Houses: England and Wales* (2nd edn, Cambridge, 1971). See S. P. Thompson, *Women Religious: the Founding of English Nunneries after the Norman Conquest* (Oxford, 1991), pp. 100–2 (on Gervase), and 'The Problem of the Cistercian Nuns in the Twelfth and Early Thirteenth Centuries', in D. Baker (ed.), *Medieval Women, Studies in Church History*, Subsidia 1 (Oxford, 1978), pp. 227–52 (p. 246); see also Janet Burton, *The Monastic Order in Yorkshire, 1069–1215* (Cambridge, 1999), pp. 147–52.

6. *Early Yorkshire Charters (EYC)* vols. I–III, ed. W. Farrer (Edinburgh, 1914–16), vols. IV–XII, ed. C. T. Clay, *Yorkshire Archaeological Society Record Series*, extra series (1935–65), III, no. 1360.

7. W. Dugdale, *Monasticon Anglicanum (Mon. Ang.)*, 6 vols. in 8, ed. J. Caley, H. Ellis and B. Bandinel (London, 1817–30), V, p. 494.

8. On the foundation of Meaux see Burton, *Monastic Order in Yorkshire*, p. 121.

9. On the foundation of Watton see Golding, *Gilbert of Sempringham*, pp. 214–17, and Burton, *Monastic Order in Yorkshire*, pp. 137–8.

10. For a confirmation to Watton see J. E. Burton (ed.), *English Episcopal Acta*, vol. V, *York, 1070–1154* (British Academy, 1988), no. 129, witnessed by Abbot Adam of Meaux. Henry Murdac also placed in the nunnery the young girl who was to achieve (anonymous) notoriety as the 'nun of Watton': Burton, *Monastic Order in Yorkshire*, pp. 175–6.

11. *EYC*, III, no. 1361.

12. *Calendar of the Charter Rolls Preserved in the Public Record Office*, 6 vols. (1903–27), III, pp. 61–2; *EYC*, III, no. 1363.

13. John A. Nichols, 'The Internal Organization of English Cistercian Nunneries', *Cîteaux* 30 (1979), 23–40 (28–30); see also Coburn V. Graves, 'The Internal Organization of an English Cistercian Nunnery in Lincolnshire', *Cîteaux* 33 (1982), 333–50 (336–8).

14. *EYC*, II, no. 808 and III, no. 1308; W. T. Lancaster (ed.), *Abstracts of the Charters and Other Documents Contained in the Chartulary of the Priory of Bridlington* (Leeds, 1912), p. 195; J. C. Atkinson (ed.), *Cartularium Abbathiae de Rievalle*, Surtees Society 83 (1889), no. 132.

15. There was an unnamed master involved in a lawsuit with Saer de Sutton in 1223: *Curia Regis Rolls*, XI (1955), p. 14 (no. 76) and p. 193 (no. 956).

16. On Hamo, see below, pp. 35–6.

17. W. Brown (ed.), *The Register of John le Romeyn, Lord Archbishop of York, 1286–1296*, 2 vols., Surtees Society 123 and 128 (1913–17), I, pp. 203–4.

18. Ibid., I, pp. 209–11, 217, 219–20, 344.

19. Ibid., II, p. 222. For Elizabeth Darrains, nun of Swine in 1290, to whom the prioress was ordered to restore the veil after her repentance, see ibid., I, p. 216, and for Helewise Darrains, sent from Swine to Wykeham Priory 'for a certain reason', in 1293, see ibid., I, pp. 177, 225. So that the prioress of Wykeham would not be at a financial disadvantage, the archbishop ordered that a nun of Wykeham be sent to Swine in exchange for Helewise.

20. W. Brown and A. Hamilton-Thompson (eds.), *The Register of William Greenfield, Lord Archbishop of York, 1306–1315*, 5 vols., Surtees Society 145, 149, 151–3 (1931–40), III, pp. 203, 263–4.

21. J. Raine (ed.), *Testamenta Eboracensia*, vol. I, Surtees Society 4 (1836), pp. 63–6.

22. Golding, *Gilbert of Sempringham*, pp. 101–7.

23. See W. Page (ed.), *VCH, York*, vol. III (1914), p. 180.

24. *Reg. le Romeyn*, II, 222–4; York, Borthwick Institute of Historical Research, Reg. 9A (register of Archbishop Melton), fo. 331r–v (new foliation). See below, p. 31 and note 32.

25. W. Brown (ed.), *The Register of Walter Giffard, Lord Archbishop of York, 1266–1279*, Surtees Society 109 (1904), pp. 146–8 (*comperta*) and 248–9 (injunctions).

26. Golding, *Gilbert of Sempringham*, pp. 127–8. For comment on Swine, see Janet Burton, *The Yorkshire Nunneries in the Twelfth and Thirteenth Centuries*, Borthwick Paper 56 (York, 1979), p. 31.

27. The Gilbertine window house was guarded by two nuns on the women's side and a canon on the men's side.

28. 'tres sorores carnales et spirituales' (*Reg. Giffard*, p. 147). The clustering of women of the same families in nunneries is noted in Janet Burton, 'Yorkshire Nunneries in the Middle Ages: Recruitment and Resources', in John C. Appleby and Paul Dalton (eds.), *Government, Religion and Society in Northern England 1000–1700* (Stroud, 1997), pp. 104–16.

29. On the Gilbertine lay sisters see Golding, *Gilbert of Sempringham*, pp. 119–26 (especially p. 122 on the significance of veiling). Cistercian and Gilbertine lay sisters were not allowed to become nuns.

30. This is entered in a later register: *Reg. Greenfield*, III, pp. 135–8.

31. Ibid., pp. 137–8.

32. *Reg. le Romeyn*, II, pp. 222–4 (p. 224).

33. See the examples given by Burton, *Monastic Order in Yorkshire*, pp. 176–7, and by G. Duckett, 'Charters of the Priory of Swine in Holderness', *Yorkshire Archaeological and Topographical Journal* 6 (1881 for 1879–80), 113–24; and compare with Golding, *Gilbert of Sempringham*, pp. 101–11, 133–7.

34. *Reg. le Romeyn*, II, pp. 222–4 (p. 223). On the Gilbertine prioresses, see Golding, *Gilbert of Sempringham*, p. 106.
35. *Reg. Greenfield*, V, pp. 198–9.
36. William Brown, 'Descriptions of the Buildings of Twelve Small Yorkshire Priories at the Reformation', *Yorkshire Archaeological and Topographical Journal* 9 (1886 for 1885–6), 197–215 and 321–33 (328–30). It is interesting to note the suggestion of stalls for 36 nuns; there were 19 nuns and the prioress at Swine in 1539.
37. *Testamenta Eboracensia*, I, pp. 360–1, 418–19.
38. J. Raine (ed.), *Testamenta Eboracensia*, II, Surtees Society 30 (1855), pp. 16–17, 23–5.
39. J. Raine (ed.), *Testamenta Eboracensia*, IV, Surtees Society 53 (1869), pp. 224–5.
40. 'quoddam edificium, ecclesie parochiali de Swyna in pariete boriali ejusdem ecclesie quasi sub eadem contignacione conjunctum' (a certain building connected to the parish church of Swine, on the north wall of the church, as it were part of the same structure): *Reg. Greenfield*, III, pp. 134–5, and V, pp. 232–3. The cloister lay to the south of the nuns' church: Brown, 'Descriptions of the Buildings of Twelve Small Yorkshire Priories', 328–9.
41. On the sheep-farming activities of Swine, see Burton, *Monastic Order in Yorkshire*, pp. 270–1.
42. *Reg. Greenfield*, V, pp. 232–3. Coniston lies just over a mile to the south-east of Swine.
43. Though not that relations between the two communities would be as close as that alleged between two of their residents. In 1310 Robert de Merflet (Marfleet, four miles south of Swine), monk of Meaux, was charged with incest with Elizabeth de Ruda (Routh, about two miles north of Meaux), nun of Swine: *Reg. Greenfield*, III, pp. 188, 190.
44. *EYC*, III, no. 1381; E. A. Bond (ed.), *Chronica Monasterii de Melsa*, 3 vols., RS (1866–8), I, pp. 103, 110 ('nobis ablata, modo est monialium de Swyna').
45. For the episode which follows, see *Chron. Melsa*, I, pp. 354–7.
46. On which see Burton, *Monastic Order in Yorkshire*, pp. 257–61.
47. J. Parker (ed.), *Feet of Fines for the County of York, from 1218 to 1231*, Yorkshire Archaeological Society Record Series 62 (1921), p. 97, no. 377.
48. J. Parker (ed.), *Feet of Fines for the County of York, from 1232 to 1246*, Yorkshire Archaeological Society Record Series, 67 (1925), p. 43, no. 776. This time Saer granted eighty acres of marsh in Bransholme (in Sutton on Hull), next to the thirty he had already granted to the nuns, with permission to enclose as the prioress wished: and the prioress added the right to have a chapel in Southcoates manor, with a free chantry, saving the right of Drypool church.
49. For this episode see *Chron. Melsa*, II, pp. 12–22.
50. Ibid., II, p. 16, note.
51. The two manuscripts have the variants *contigua* and *adjacente*.
52. Roberta Gilchrist, *Gender and Material Culture: The Archaeology of Religious Women* (London and New York, 1994), p. 103; Glyn Coppack, *Abbeys and Priories*

(London, 1990), p. 151: 'the eastern arm of the priory church survives in use by the parish'.

53. Certainly the evidence discussed above (pp. 32–3) suggests parochial use of the church from the early fourteenth century if not earlier. Indeed, the fact that the priory was founded in an existing parish church suggests that part of the priory church was parochial from the very beginning.

54. Coppack, *Abbeys and Priories*, p. 151, notes that part of the priory complex lies under later farm buildings.

55. The church was evidently returned to the nuns. In 1308 they were summoned for failing to appoint a vicar (*Reg. Greenfield*, V, pp. 198–9), and at the Dissolution the nuns paid a chaplain to serve the church: *Mon. Ang.*, V, p. 495.

56. See p. 29 above.

57. *Book of St Gilbert*, pp. 44–7.

58. J. S. Purvis (ed.), *Monastic Chancery Proceedings*, Yorkshire Archaeological Society Record Series 88 (1934), pp. 136–8; Claire Cross and Noreen Vickers, *Monks, Friars and Nuns in Sixteenth Century Yorkshire*, Yorkshire Archaeological Society Record Series, 150 (1995 for 1991 and 1992), p. 590.

59. Cross and Vickers, *Yorkshire Monks*, pp. 394–406 and 589–94.

CHAPTER 3

Godliness and good learning: ideals and imagination in medieval university and college foundations

R. N. Swanson

'Universities, as we are all immediately aware when we leave them and sometimes when we are within them too, are in many ways the most strange, illogical and exotic human communities of all.'[1] Yet universities, and their sometimes stranger, more illogical, and more exotic components, the colleges, have always reflected and sought to influence the concerns and ideals of their societies. For the pre-Reformation institutions, these aspirations are chiefly articulated in papal bulls of foundation and related documents, and in college statutes.

For the universities, such material becomes available as formal processes of foundation evolve in the thirteenth century, their primary document being a papal bull. While validating the foundation, this also commented – briefly – on the ideals behind the new creation, although practical considerations were also significant imperatives.[2]

The idealisation of learning swiftly found voice. In 1289 Pope Nicholas IV, supporting the University of Montpellier, lauded that learning which illuminates the hearts of men and impels them towards virtue, driving away the shadows of ignorance and the fog of error so that men might act in the light of truth.[3] This was explicitly a social role, reiterated at length in Boniface VIII's bull founding Avignon university in 1303, and more succinctly by Alexander V for the University of Aix in 1409. Such study would augment the catholic faith, enhance justice, deal usefully with public and private matters, and increase the prosperity of the human condition.[4] A claim that study would augment the faith and extend justice became almost commonplace, the wording of papal bulls being sufficiently similar to raise doubts about whether the idealism can be taken seriously, or should be discounted as stock phrasing.[5] However, repetition need not invalidate: the aspirations might be as real, and as transferable, as the phrases. There is no reason to dismiss the claim that an insufficiency of learned men caused 'many inconveniences and dangers . . . to public matters in spiritual and temporal affairs'.[6]

The papacy acted from above, and from a distance; those seeking to establish a local university had their own concerns. Here idealism is conveyed in the foundation documents issued by rulers, addressing matters both secular and intellectual. One major aim was to improve the cadres for government. In July 1483, Louis XI of France acknowledged the difficulty of trying to govern 'sans tenir de gens norris en littérature, discipline, doctrine et science', and praised Dole's graduates for their work 'tant en administration de justice que en prédications et aultres exercices licterez'.[7] Princes were not concerned solely with administrative matters. From 1400 faculties of theology became increasingly common in universities across Europe.[8] Theology was the prime science: Henry VI supported the creation of a faculty at Caen in 1437, 'considérans la science de théologie estre très utile et requise a l'instruccion et exaltacion de la saincte foy catholique, et celle des ars est très nécessaire et à acquérir toutes sciences quelzconques premier et principal fondement'. Universities, even though increasingly considered a mark of nationhood or political maturity (as the Dauphin Louis noted with regard to the University of Valence in 1462), remained essentially ecclesiastical institutions. Advocacy of theological study was explicitly concerned with cure of souls, although sometimes the advocates got carried away. In March 1432 Charles VII of France rhetorically asked where orthodoxy was upheld, if not at universities?[9] Paris's tradition of defending orthodoxy certainly sustained doctrinal stability, but experience of Wycliffism and Hussitism at Oxford and Prague rather undermines his case.[10]

University foundation documents and statutes reflect an ideal; but a successful foundation required practical more than verbal support.[11] The location had to be suitable, as one essential element. Naturally, every university town was allegedly appropriate, enjoying an ideal climate and perfect conditions, as itemised in Henry VI's 1432 charter for Caen University.[12]

Caen, like other late foundations, also had to face the fact of competition: older universities sometimes felt threatened by new institutions. In this case, it was Paris which felt challenged, and which mounted a vigorous campaign of opposition. In November 1433, Paris claimed that the Caen foundation was unnecessary, and might indeed prove positively harmful. Paris took its case to the Council of Basle, challenging Caen as a threat to the catholic faith, rather than a support. Nevertheless, Pope Eugenius IV did eventually authorise the new foundation.[13]

Statements about the students likewise sometimes reflect elevated ideals. The statutes of Montpellier's law school, issued in 1339, lauded the scholars as self-exiled; rich made poor in their search for the pearl of learning; men who for the love of learning laboured day and night so that, learned in both mind and tongue, they could ornament the Church; and who, like cultivators of newly farmed land, would by their labours earn a hundred-fold harvest.[14] The reality of student experience was often different. Medieval universities lacked resources of their own. They faced major tasks in accommodating students, in maintaining discipline, and in ensuring continuity in teaching. Students in the higher faculties faced particular difficulties with funding. Few could undertake years of study in law, medicine, or theology with no assurance of financial support. Such circumstances generated the college movement, starting in the late twelfth century and evolving thereafter.[15] College foundations responded to varied personal imperatives and motivations,[16] but all offer glimpses of an ideal, and idealised, picture of a community of scholars. European-wide, but with regional characteristics reflecting differing responses to similar difficulties, the movement's full range cannot be considered here. Discussion therefore focuses on the colleges at Oxford and Cambridge, which by 1550 effectively dominated their respective universities.[17]

The idealism and priorities behind the Oxford and Cambridge colleges have to be gleaned primarily from their statutes.[18] Arguably, college foundation provided the key context in which educational idealists could hope to put their ideals into practice. Their patronage could alleviate the mundane concerns which otherwise distracted scholars from their learning. Their munificence would overcome the financial pressures which particularly discouraged study in the higher faculties, to ensure that appropriate educational priorities were maintained. Such aspirations lead into a realm of imagined communities, and their imagined operation and integration.[19] What matter here are the intentions, not the actuality; for once the body actually existed, different aspirations came into play. Whether the colleges fulfilled their founders' aspirations, or obeyed their statutes, is not the issue.

While the colleges differed from the universities, overlap was unavoidable, possibly more than is acknowledged in the documents. In 1359, for instance, the statutes of Clare College, Cambridge, declared that the foundation was expressly to increase divine service, for the public benefit, and for the advance of scholarship which had suffered from the recent onslaught of plague. Moreover, echoing the formulae of papal documents, the college would allow the pearl of knowledge to be divulged even beyond the university, to draw the wider populace out of the shadows of ignorance.[20] Likewise, at All Souls, Oxford, theology was praised as mistress of the sciences, while canon and civil law were considered useful and necessary for politic rule.[21] Princely involvement and aspirations are also allegedly voiced in the platitudinous comments occasionally contained in the letters patent licensing the foundations.[22]

The process of college foundation – complex, arduous and time-consuming – is irrelevant here.[23] Yet the motivations and aspirations are not easily elucidated. The early statutes are themselves problematic. Their formulation could be a drawn-out process, reflecting assorted influences and tensions. Attempts to define the underlying aspirations are impeded by the co-operative nature of the process, as founders took advice and followed precedents. Some founders appear so reluctant to lose control that they delayed the grant of statutes for years. If left too long, death might supervene, allowing another to give form to the aspirations – possibly not as originally intended. Delay might have unfortunate consequences if the college had gained its own unregulated momentum. The formal imposition of statutes – for they were imposed, not evolved by the body – might produce a clash of aspirations when the fellows found themselves bound by rules not of their making.[24] Moreover, ostensible and actual founders may differ: there is a difference between providing the funds (or other support), and providing the inspiration. Hugh Oldham, bishop of Exeter, allegedly diverted Richard Fox, bishop of Winchester, from his original scheme to establish a monastic college at Oxford. John Fisher, bishop of Rochester, was the intellectual driving force behind Lady Margaret Beaufort's involvement at Christ's and St John's, Cambridge; the former was a reinvigoration of the earlier God's-house, and St John's was actually established after Lady Margaret's death.[25]

To lump all the secular colleges together (the monastic houses are excluded here, even though not exclusively monastic in population)[26] is also somewhat artificial. Their foundation dates range from the thirteenth to the sixteenth centuries, with changing imperatives. At first, the main concern was to house poor clerks; but with the Black Death of 1349, and the plague's impact on learning, the colleges became also a means of recovery. Now major concerns were to restore the universities and increase the availability of clergy; this was further refined after 1400 when defence of orthodoxy gained prominence. Then, as the fifteenth century gave way to the sixteenth, the impact of humanism, and support for humanistic studies, is reflected in some foundations. The statutes also mirror a developing concern to make them work: the initially brief statements for bodies like Michaelhouse, Cambridge, give way to grandiose and expansive codes (as at King's, Cambridge, or New and Corpus Christi Colleges, Oxford)[27] and to meticulous concern with detail and practicality, partly to ensure that the foundation did not founder. Yet despite problems with the material, some generalisations can be drawn.

Although collegiate foundations required considerable investment, surprisingly few founders used their statutes to clarify their aspirations, or to justify their actions at length. These are generally utilitarian codes, concerned with the actual workings of the institution, not its validation. Yet an idealism is there, in the justification of particular points, in the concerns which the statutes address and the anticipated difficulties which they seek to evade, and in the structures which they create. The statutes often appear not primarily as prescriptive towards an end, but as erecting safeguards against its distortion.

The precise models on which the founders drew remain uncertain. One might be the regular convents (perhaps emphasising mendicant over monastic precedent); there is certainly considerable similarity between collegiate and conventual life.[28] However, the similarities must not be pushed too far; while the founders consciously established communities, few identified the principles guiding their codes. The frequent borrowing from earlier college statutes (once these were available) shows that founders rarely worked independently from first principles. Precise numerical analogy with Christ and the apostles appears at Queen's College, Oxford, but only there. Other founders had grander (or lesser) ambitions; most recognised that their provisions were contingent on financial resources, which might decline (*quod absit!*), or be augmented by additional donations. Yet some guiding structural principle is often implicit, prescribing a form of government (via the master) and practical support (via the college servants and administrators) to allow the commoners to devote themselves to study, and to the liturgical duties imposed by their founders. In the late fifteenth century, some founders do invoke guiding patterns for their colleges. In 1506 and 1507 the statutes from Christ's, Cambridge, and Balliol, Oxford, used the well-worn image of the body politic, giving each rank its place, with the servants as the feet. More exotically, the statutes of Corpus Christi, Oxford, issued in 1528, draw parallels with a bee-hive.[29]

Both conceits (and, possibly, the parallel with Christ and the apostles) presume monarchy:[30] the master is the head, the queen (or, following the medieval understanding, king) bee, the *Vicarius Christi*, to govern as prince and father.[31] This monarchical evolution, elevating the head's status in the house, may also be reflected in specific privileges conceded to such heads, giving them additional servants, special commons, increased salaries, and authority to hold benefices with unrestricted income (provided that they remained resident). This process reaches its peak in Wolsey's draft statutes for Cardinal College. His dean is very much a man with dignity, to be so upheld that he is relieved from extensive participation in the collegiate common life, lest excessive familiarity undermine his status. This is a far cry from provisions of earlier codes. That for Peterhouse, Cambridge, suggests that the head was being compensated for abandoning his studies for the good of the community, rather than being raised to a post of power and dignity; while at New College, Oxford, the warden had his separate establishment to avoid disturbance to the fellows and scholars.[32] The image suggested by Wolsey's code is certainly monastic, but of a monastery whose abbot lived very much apart, with much internal administration being left in the hands of obedientiaries.[33] Despite the monarchical bent, many statutes also seek to limit the head's power, to preclude too much monarchy. Most codes contain provisions requiring that extraordinary business – like major court cases which might affect college revenues – have the approval of the rest of the college, or at least of an aristocracy of senior fellows and office holders who, like cardinals around the pope, share in the *pars solicitudinis*, and who in extreme cases might act to depose the head.[34]

The head was to govern precisely so that the college could act as a centre of study. At the heart of the statutes, even if not looming large in terms of word count, lies a concern with maintaining academic life, and assuring academic progress. Striking here is the lack of personal choice allowed to inmates. The colleges become academic machines, their members obliged to follow a prescribed route once they have accepted their posts. The stages of their courses are often mapped out in detail, their choice of faculty dictated, their progress regularly checked. Current emphases on appraisal and quality control are clearly not new ideas. Moreover, the colleges appear increasingly introverted, as the academic focus shifts from the university schools to college-based teaching and lecturing.[35]

College finances were necessarily a major concern, if the colleges were to fulfil their prime function of enabling men who were already engaged in study to continue their labours at university. These scholarships – generally postgraduate scholarships – were not given unconditionally, or (usually) as the recipient's sole life-long income. Some colleges enjoined resignation at a specific age, regardless of status; most imposed means tests requiring resignation when personal income reached a decreed level, from inheritance, or from church benefices. At New College, Oxford, the maximum patrimony which could be held without resignation was 100s. This was not excessive, but still well above the minimum level which generally provided a title to ordination. At ten marks (£6 13s 4d), the benefice income which triggered resignation was below the amount generally considered as the minimum to make a rectory economically viable in the period. Acceptance would normally have forced the holder to leave Oxford to serve the cure, certainly if it was derived from a vicarage or chantry outside the university.[36]

The statutory means tests for fellows in post possibly created an ambivalence. The contention that the holders of college places 'would be able to resist the temptation of fat benefices' seems unsustainable.[37] Such provisions probably focussed minds precisely on those benefices, for only they would provide sufficient funds to permit continued non-residence and study. Founders also expected their protégés to move on: at Queen's, Oxford, the statutes decreed expulsion for those who rejected lay or ecclesiastical incomes to remain in college.[38] Ill-paid benefices, especially those demanding residence, would not be worth having (those not formally requiring residence would be too poor to fund a hired substitute). Chantry work might boost incomes if allowed (several codes permitted it inside the college, but not outside);[39] but such employment was often insecure and would only provide a temporary income.

Ostensibly, founders were concerned to support poor clerks; but while the provision of commons and housing was a charitable act, an academic variant on the Corporal Acts of Mercy,[40] the recipients were rarely true paupers. If, as at Gonville Hall, Cambridge, non-beneficed candidates were to be preferred to beneficed at elections, and the poor before the rich,[41] the poverty thus tackled was relative. Entrants might swear that their income was below a set sum, but that lower income was allowed, and perhaps additional income was generally assumed. Such an assumption underlies statutory provisions allowing college members to pay for extra clothing, for guests, or even for servants, from their own resources.[42]

The problem of unequal poverty within the colleges was occasionally recognised in the statutes. At Trinity Hall, Cambridge, the regulations for the common livery aimed to prevent the poor being pushed into spending beyond their means. The amount to be spent on clothing should be agreed annually by at least two-thirds of the fellows, 'consideratis pauperiorum et impotentiorum viribus'.[43] Similar awareness of differences in wealth occasionally appears in statutes which sought to limit spending on academic celebrations,[44] and offered limited subsidies so that college members could take higher degrees. At New College, Oxford, and King's, Cambridge, the amount allowed for this might reach £20 a year.[45]

One clear concern, clearest in the later codes, was to ensure that England had a sufficiently educated priesthood, able to face the challenges of heresy and maintain traditional theology.[46] Some statutes prescribe that, apart from age, all prospective entrants should be qualified for ordination (including lack of physical defect). Disabilities which could be routinely dispensed might be overlooked: Oriel, Oxford, countenanced men of illegitimate birth. At Christ's, Cambridge, even pupil scholars – undergraduates – had to be intending ordinands. In some codes, priesthood was also the projected destiny for some of those not elected to full fellowships, who were to quit their posts when aged twenty-five, at just the right age.[47]

The clerical emphasis is constant, even though a college's inmates would not all be in holy orders. Ordination might be banned to non-masters. However, at Lincoln, Oxford, and Michaelhouse and Christ's, Cambridge, new fellows had to be priests already, or be ordained within a year, so imposing the commitment to celibacy associated with an ecclesiastical career.[48] At New College, Oxford, and King's, Cambridge, the rate of progress to ordination varied with faculty; but all permanent fellows were to be ordained eventually, and refusal brought expulsion.[49] Priest-fellows sometimes received extra payments, partly compensating for their extra duties, partly to encourage others to take orders.[50]

Even for those not actually ordained, a clerical culture of community permeates the statutes, and the institutions. It was reinforced by making Latin the normal language between college members (some early statutes permitted French; those influenced by the later humanistic trend allowed Greek).[51] The code for Peterhouse, Cambridge, cites Archbishop John Stratford's decree, *Exterior habitus*: the fellows were to maintain their clerical clothing and tonsures, were to act decently, were denied beards, and were not to wear rings.[52] At Trinity Hall the requirement was more general: the priest-fellows were to live according to the canons, so that they might be fit daily to celebrate mass.[53] Such injunctions match those issued to religious houses at visitation: very similar issues arise, about internal discipline, accounting and behaviour. Monastic injunctions regularly ban ownership of dogs and birds, carrying of weapons, and illicit games; so do college statutes. The ban on pets was partly to prevent misuse of funds: charity should not be wasted. At Peterhouse, Cambridge, it was further justified by the discord which might result. If one fellow had pets, all would want them, and disquiet (albeit unvoiced) might arise, distracting from study. Chess and similar games were routinely prohibited, lest they likewise distract from study, disturb the peace, and incite swearing and riotousness. Equivalent prohibitions of such unclerical recreations appear elsewhere, notably in chantry foundations. There was also a practical concern: ball games, and throwing contests, might damage the buildings, especially windows.[54]

Beyond living clerically, college members were to study in preparation for serving the Church. At least, most were: with some exceptions, fellows were generally to study theology, after the arts course.[55] The set leaving age for those not undertaking higher studies may envisage a rapid through-put of men who would not become theologians, but who might become parish clergy. The emphasis on theology must be set in a broader context. While educated parish clergy were required, the parochial utility of a theology degree is questionable: at parish level the prime necessity was pastoral care, not mental abstractions. Yet some practical outcome of theological study was anticipated, by educating preachers and assisting the struggle against heresy.[56]

Ex-fellows were perhaps expected to join the elite of the late medieval Church, as prebendaries of cathedrals and major collegiate churches. Graduates held an increasing percentage of cathedral prebends in the fifteenth century, although theologians were consistently outnumbered by lawyers. This says nothing of active involvement in cathedral life, where changing patterns of residence, and the entrenchment of small cliques of canons residentiary, limited most canons' participation.[57] The role of theologians in such cliques remains to be assessed.

While life in a university college superficially matches a monastic existence, with the communal life, livery, liturgical demands, probationary periods and oaths of admission, the parallels are imprecise. Similarities with other bodies – secular collegiate churches, and fraternities – are also important. The statutes emphasise the idealised community, its members enjoined to live together in charity and fraternity.[58] Self-discipline was backed by provisions enforcing the disciplinary regulations, even to expulsion, to ensure that individuals met their statutory obligations and that a single errant sheep did not infect the entire flock;[59] but there is no insistence on an apostolic life. Communality was sometimes made visible: common liveries (sometimes shared with the servants) identified the members as a body, and thereby commemorated the founder's generosity.[60] Communality also eased the administrative and disciplinary burden; despite idealisation, it was perhaps a means to achieve the foundations' educative and charitable aims, not the end in itself. The administrative and disciplinary advantages of a communal structure also appear in some non-university collegiate foundations, especially in the provision of colleges for vicars choral and chantry priests at some cathedrals.[61] The avoidance of separate prebends in the university colleges also precluded problems of personal responsibility for dilapidation, and limited the risk of eroding a divided endowment by individual mismanagement.

Parallels between the probationary periods for fellows and monastic or mendicant novitiates are also illusory. Probation was precisely that, to prove that the candidate was of the required standard and motivation, and was committed to the society and its communal life. Probationers generally had no part in college government and elections; rejection at the scrutiny ending the probationary period was envisaged as a real possibility.[62]

One major concern was to ensure continuity, and renewal of personnel.[63] The colleges were to be perpetual; they required adequately qualified candidates to fill vacant posts. While founders often assumed that such people would be found at the university, others either augmented their establishments with junior scholars (even if only choristers) with some pre-emptive claim to later election to a higher rank, or established ties with feeder institutions. The classic instances were the links between Winchester College and New College, Oxford, or between Eton College and King's, Cambridge. Other schools, like Archbishop Thomas Rotherham's foundation at Rotherham, and William Waynflete's at Wainfleet, meshed into the geographical preferences decreed for election to college places. Thomas Wolsey envisaged an array of feeder schools for Cardinal College, but his grandiose scheme came to naught. Beyond the native pride and self-commemoration manifest in such links, some also convey a sense of the local boy who made good repaying his natal community, most evocatively in Thomas Rotherham's foundation of Jesus College, Rotherham.[64]

For most of those affected, college membership was temporary. Setting aside those who were expelled, or who left voluntarily, others were required to withdraw at twenty-five, presumably joining the working clergy.[65] However, progress through holy orders after 1350 usually took between six and twelve months, so those leaving at that age need not have committed themselves irrevocably to a celibate clerical career. The common statutory termination of support on marriage suggests that some founders (especially of later foundations) envisaged lay careers for some of their beneficiaries.[66]

Short-term support did not mean short-term obligations. Several statutes required recipients of a founder's charity to support the college however they could, even after leaving. This lifelong obligation extended to court cases, continuing a responsibility imposed during membership: they could not aid the college's opponents or, often, opponents of bodies connected with the foundation. Such demands sometimes cut across other allegiances. At Trinity Hall, Cambridge, the original statutes were altered in 1354, eliminating that obligation in cases involving close kin, or a pre-College patron – although active assistance against either the bishop or the prior and convent of Norwich in cases involving those people was still banned. Founders might also ban links with other colleges: the tie of patronage and dependence was to be exclusive, and binding – although it might be relaxed to permit election as head of another house.[67]

Self-administering and self-disciplinary, the colleges were effectively autonomous. Yet they lacked full sovereignty: founders balked at total independence. Almost all created ties with an external authority, to confirm appointments of heads, to resolve disputes, to exercise ultimate oversight through visitation. Most imposed oaths against challenging disciplinary decisions (especially expulsions) by appeal to secular or ecclesiastical courts, and proscribed dispensations (even papal) from statutory obligations and limitations. All placed their foundations under a patron, although the extent to which the patron was allowed to intervene in college matters was variable.[68]

While much in the college statutes appears formulaic and mundane, they are permeated by a sense of the founders' personal involvement, and determination to ensure the foundations' survival. A founder might well retain some oversight whilst living, even when the college was up and running. Marie de St Pol claimed the right to amend the statutes of Pembroke College, Cambridge, while she lived, on the blunt grounds that 'cuius est condere eius est etiam interpretari'. Legislative autonomy came only at her death.[69] Similar comments appear elsewhere: visitors might interpret, but not amend. Few founders were as generous as Walter de Merton in allowing future change on the grounds that all eventualities could not be foreseen.[70]

However unrealistic a ban on change might seem, from the founders' perspective it appeared justified, to prevent perversion. The lengthier codes aimed to cover all contingencies, making future change unnecessary. To the founders, aware of institutions which had deviated from the original plans, such a ban was hard-headed realism.[71] Moreover, the founders had to address their own concerns, spiritual, familial and geographical. Hence the considerable emphasis on chantry obligations.[72] Hence provisions (curiously limited to Oxford colleges) giving 'founder's kin' pre-emptive rights to college places, and other privileges.[73] Hence, also, the delineation of catchment areas, to enhance and continue existing geographical relationships. These bound the colleges into contemporary structures of patronage and good lordship, as components of bastard feudalism.[74] The sense of reciprocity, of mutual benefit, was concisely expressed by Edmund Dudley in the early sixteenth century, when he urged individual patronage of students, 'for a better Chantree shall ye neuer founde'.[75] In the network of relationships established by their statutes, and the links between mundane provision and spiritual return, the Oxbridge colleges firmly institutionalised that maxim.

The colleges of the statutes might be imagined communities, but the functioning institutions were definitely not imaginary. The statutes had to address very real issues, if only to ensure survival. Frequently, reality and ideal diverged, as statutes were breached, finances failed, or political change undermined support.[76] In that respect, university colleges were as subject to contemporary forces as any other foundations. What matters, here, is the ideal, the imagined community. To set these colleges – fraternities of like-minded individuals, devoted to learning and divine service, liberated from mundane concerns by a master who sacrificed his own scholarly advancement to assure the sustenance of the fellows – in universities motivated by the ideals of social improvement embedded in papal and princely foundation charters is indeed to enter a world of ideals and Utopias. The college model survived the Reformation, despite threats, and with due adaptation to new circumstances, to provide an ideal of its own: 'it was one of the virtues of . . . Lord Robbins's Report on Higher Education of 1963, that it occasionally dared to suggest the value of medieval Oxford and Cambridge Universities as models to emulate rather than eschew'.[77] Their statutory ideals and aspirations were not always achieved, but they should not be ignored.

NOTES

1. R. B. Dobson, '*Preserving the Perishable': Contrasting Communities in Medieval England, an Inaugural Lecture Delivered in the University of Cambridge on 22 February 1990* (Cambridge, 1991), p. 27.

2. W. Rüegg, 'Themes', in H. de Ridder-Symoens (ed.), *A History of the University in Europe*, vol. I: *Universities in the Middle Ages* (Cambridge, 1992), pp. 14–23.

3. M. Fournier, *Les statuts et privilèges des universités françaises depuis leur fondation jusqu'en 1789*, 4 vols. (Paris, 1890–4), II, p. 17.

4. Fournier, *Les statuts*, III, pp. 309 (Avignon), 1 (Aix).

5. Compare Eugenius IV's bulls for Poitiers (1431), Caen (1437) and Bordeaux (1441): ibid., III, pp. 149, 283–4, 337.

6. Ibid., III, p. 149. Cf. the University statutes, ibid., pp. 152–3.

7. Ibid., III, p. 130.

8. J. Verger, 'Patterns', in de Ridder-Symoens (ed.), *Universities in the Middle Ages*, pp. 59–60.

9. Fournier, *Les statuts*, III, pp. 148, 362, 285.

10. J. M. M. H. Thijssen, *Censure and Heresy at the University of Paris, 1200–1400* (Philadelphia, Pa., 1998); J. I. Catto, 'Wyclif and Wycliffism at Oxford, 1356–1430', in J. I. Catto and Ralph Evans (eds.), *The History of the University of Oxford*, vol. II: *Late Medieval Oxford* (Oxford, 1992), pp. 175–261; H. Kaminsky, 'The University of Prague in the Hussite Revolution: the Role of the Masters', in J. W. Baldwin and R. A. Goldthwaite (eds.), *Universities in Politics: Case Studies from the Late Middle Ages and Early Modern Period* (Baltimore, Md, and London, 1972), pp. 79–106.

11. A. Vetulani, 'Les origines et le sort des universités de l'Europe centrale et orientale fondées au cours du XIVe siècle', in J. Ijsewijn and J. Paquet (eds.), *The Universities in the Late Middle Ages*, Mediaevalia Lovaniensia, Series I, studia VI (Louvain, 1978), pp. 148–67; E. J. M. van Eijl, 'The Foundation of the University of Louvain', ibid., pp. 29–41; R. Favreau, 'L'université de Poitiers et la société poitevine à la fin du moyen âge', ibid., pp. 549–58.

12. Fournier, *Les statuts*, III, p. 146.

13. Ibid., III, pp. 147, 149.

14. Ibid., II, pp. 44–5.

15. A. B. Cobban, *The Medieval Universities: Their Development and Organization* (London, 1975), ch. 6; A. L. Gabriel, *The College System in the Fourteenth-Century Universities* (Baltimore, n.d. [1961]). See also Verger, 'Patterns', pp. 60–2; A. Gieysztor, 'Management and Resources', in de Ridder-Symoens (ed.), *Universities in the Middle Ages*, pp. 116–19; H. de Ridder-Symoens, 'Mobility', ibid., pp. 284–5.

16. A. L. Gabriel, *Garlandia: Studies in the History of the Mediaeval University* (Frankfurt am Main, 1969), ch. 10.

17. For the colleges, J. R. L. Highfield, 'The early colleges', in J. I. Catto (ed.), *The History of the University of Oxford*, vol. I: *The Early Oxford Schools* (Oxford, 1984), pp. 225–63; A. B. Cobban, 'Colleges and Halls, 1350–1530', in Catto and Evans (eds.), *Late Medieval Oxford*, pp. 581–633; J. McConica, 'The Rise of the Undergraduate College', in J. McConica (ed.), *The History of the University of Oxford*, vol. III: *The Collegiate University* (Oxford, 1986), pp. 1–68; D. R. Leader, *A History of the University of Cambridge*, vol. I: *The University to 1546* (Cambridge, 1988), pp. 58–84, 225–32, 270–5, 281–91; A. B. Cobban, *The*

Medieval English Universities: Oxford and Cambridge to c. 1500 (Aldershot, 1988), pp. 111–45.

18. The main collections of statutes are *Documents Relating to the University and Colleges of Cambridge*, 3 vols. (London, 1852) (hereafter *Cambridge*); *Statutes of the Colleges of Oxford*, 3 vols. (London, 1853) (hereafter *Oxford*, each college's section is separately paginated). Citations are not exhaustive.

19. This idea is obviously transposed from Benedict Anderson, *Imagined Communities: Reflections on the Origin and Spread of Nationalism* (1983). His definitions offer key starting points: 'Communities are to be distinguished, not by their falsity/genuineness, but by the style in which they are imagined'; '[C]ommunity . . . conceived as a deep, horizontal comradeship . . . [a] fraternity': ibid., pp. 15–16.

20. *Cambridge*, II, p. 121; cf. *Oxford*, I, New p. 2.

21. *Oxford*, I, All Souls p. 12.

22. *Cambridge*, II, pp. 1, 471; III, p. 1; *Oxford*, I, All Souls p. 4; II, Magdalen p. v, Brasenose p. iii, Corpus p. iv, Cardinal pp. 4–5.

23. E. F. Jacob, 'Founders and Foundations in the Later Middle Ages', in his *Essays in Later Medieval History* (Manchester, 1968), pp. 154–74.

24. V. Davis, 'The Making of English Collegiate Statutes in the Later Middle Ages', *History of Universities* 13 (1993), 1–23. And see chapter four below.

25. McConica, 'Rise of the Undergraduate College', pp. 17–18; M. K. Jones and M. G. Underwood, *The King's Mother: Lady Margaret Beaufort, Countess of Richmond and Derby* (Cambridge, 1992), pp. 217–31, 241–9. And see chapter 5 below.

26. Cobban, *Medieval English Universities*, pp. 318–20.

27. A. E. Stamp, *Michaelhouse: Notes on the History of Michaelhouse Published on the 600th Anniversary of the Foundation of the Society by Hervey de Stanton* (n.p. [Cambridge], 1924), pp. 41–7; *Cambridge*, III, pp. 481–624; *Oxford*, I, Corpus pp. 1–117; II, New pp. 1–117.

28. For mendicant parallels, Giulia Barone, 'Les couvents des mendiants, des collèges déguisés? Observations sur les liens entre les écoles des Ordres Mendiants et les collèges (XIII–XIVes.)', in Olga Weijers (ed.), *Vocabulaire des collèges universitaires (XIIIe–XVIe siècles: Actes du colloque, Leuven, 9–11 avril 1992*, CIVICIMA: Etudes sur le vocabulaire intellectuel du moyen âge 6 (Turnhout, 1993), pp. 149–57.

29. *Oxford*, I, Balliol p. 2, Queen's p. 7; II, Corpus p. 1. H. Rackham, *Early Statutes of Christ's College, Cambridge, with the Statutes of the Prior Foundation of God's House* (Cambridge, 1927), pp. 44–5 (see also pp. 94–5, 98–101). Provision for changing numbers appears at e.g. *Oxford*, I, Lincoln pp. 25, 30; II, Magdalen p. 89, Brasenose p. 23; *Cambridge*, II, pp. 20–1, 235, 431.

30. See also *Oxford*, I, Lincoln p. 14.

31. *Oxford*, I, Balliol p. 3; II, Corpus p. 2, Cardinal pp. 14, 150.

32. *Oxford*, I, New p. 33; II, Cardinal p. 91 (cf. p. 95); *Cambridge*, II, p. 11 (similar ideas are suggested at Christ's, Cambridge, in 1506: Rackham, *Early Statutes*, pp. 24–5).

33. J. Burton, *Monastic and Religious Orders in Britain, 1000–1300* (Cambridge, 1994), pp. 172–3; D. Knowles, *The Religious Orders in England*, 3 vols. (Cambridge, 1948–61), II, pp. 253–4.
34. *Oxford*, I, New pp. 28, 32, 80, All Souls pp. 17, 26, 28 (specifically allowing a *pars solicitudinis* to the vice-warden), 57–8; II, Magdalen pp. 11, 57, Brasenose p. 7.
35. Cobban, *Medieval English Universities*, pp. 171–208.
36. R. N. Swanson, 'Titles to orders in medieval English episcopal registers', in H. Mayr-Harting and R. I. Moore (eds.), *Studies in Medieval History Presented to R. H. C. Davis* (London, 1985), p. 244; *Oxford*, I, New pp. 64–5, Lincoln p. 13; P. Heath, *The English Parish Clergy on the Eve of the Reformation* (London and Toronto, 1969), p. 173; R. L. Storey, 'The Foundation and the Medieval College, 1379–1530', in J. Buxton and P. Williams (eds.), *New College, Oxford, 1379–1979* (Oxford, 1979), pp. 18–19; R. N. Swanson, 'Universities, Graduates, and Benefices in Later Medieval England', *Past and Present* 106 (Feb. 1985), 31–2.
37. Gabriel, *College System*, p. 9.
38. *Oxford*, I, Queen's p. 15.
39. *Cambridge*, III, pp. 549–50; *Oxford*, I, Lincoln p. 14 (the income to buy books), All Souls p. 40; II, Magdalen p. 34, Brasenose p. 29 (to buy books), Corpus p. 63 (see also p. 110), Cardinal pp. 80–1.
40. *Oxford*, I, New p. 5.
41. *Cambridge*, II, p. 232.
42. *Cambridge*, II, pp. 430, 494; *Oxford*, I, New p. 94, All Souls pp. 36, 42, 59; II, Magdalen p. 29, Corpus p. 85, Cardinal p. 102. On student poverty see Cobban, *Medieval English Universities*, pp. 303–5; more widely, J. Paquet, 'Recherches sur l'universitaire "pauvre" au moyen âge', *Revue belge de philologie et d'histoire* 56 (1978), 301–53, esp. 306–20.
43. *Cambridge*, III, p. 429. Cf. *Oxford*, I, Balliol p. vi.
44. *Cambridge*, III, p. 429; *Oxford*, I, Balliol pp. vi, 14.
45. *Cambridge*, III, pp. 429, 546–7 (see also II, p. 423); *Oxford*, I, Balliol pp. vi, 14, New pp. 52–3.
46. A. B. Cobban, 'Origins; Robert Wodelarke and St Catharine's', in E. E. Rich (ed.), *St Catharine's College, Cambridge, 1473–1973: A Volume of Essays to Commemorate the Quincentenary of the Foundation of the College* (n.p. [Cambridge], n.d. [1974]), pp. 11–12, 15–17; G. F. Lytle, 'Patronage Patterns and Oxford Colleges c.1300–c.1530', in L. Stone (ed.), *The University in Society*, 2 vols. (Princeton, NJ, 1975), I, pp. 138–42.
47. *Oxford*, I, Balliol p. 9, New p. 7, Oriel p. 133; II, Corpus pp. 20, 61, Cardinal pp. 20, 79; *Cambridge*, II, p. 486; Rackham, *Early Statutes*, pp. 102–3.
48. *Oxford*, I, Lincoln p. 17; II, Corpus p. 62, Cardinal p. 80; Stamp, *Michaelhouse*, p. 42; Rackham, *Early Statutes*, pp. 80–1.
49. *Oxford*, I, New pp. 54–5; *Cambridge*, II, pp. 549–50. See also *Oxford*, II, Brasenose p. 31; *Cambridge*, III, p. 82.
50. *Cambridge*, II, p. 550; *Oxford*, I, New p. 56.

51. French is permitted in *Oxford*, I, Oriel pp. 8, 18, Queen's p. 14; Greek in *Oxford*, II, Corpus p. 47, Cardinal p. 69.
52. *Cambridge*, II, p. 28. For *Exterior habitus*, see D. Wilkins, *Concilia Magna Britanniæ et Hiberniæ*, 4 vols. (London, 1737), II, p. 703; R. M. Haines, *Archbishop John Stratford: Political Revolutionary and Champion of the Liberties of the English Church, ca. 1275/80–1348*, Pontifical Institute of Mediaeval Studies, Studies and Texts 76 (Toronto, 1986), p. 402.
53. Cambridge, II, p. 425.
54. For college recreations, Cobban, *Medieval English Universities*, pp. 360–2; Cambridge, II, pp. 29–30, 542–3; *Oxford*, I, Queen's p. 18, New pp. 41, 48–9, 99–100; II, Magdalen pp. 42–3, Brasenose p. 27, Corpus, p. 68. The restrictions were not always total: *Oxford*, I, Balliol p. 18; II, Corpus pp. 67–9, Cardinal p. 85. For monastic visitations and restrictions elsewhere, Knowles, *Religious Orders*, II, pp. 209–17, III, pp. 64–86; K. L. Wood-Legh, *Perpetual Chantries in Britain* (Cambridge, 1965), pp. 252–3, 255–8.
55. A. B. Cobban, 'Theology and Law in the Medieval Colleges of Oxford and Cambridge', *Bulletin of the John Rylands University Library of Manchester* 65 (1982–3), 60–1, 66–8, 70–2.
56. R. N. Swanson, 'Learning and Livings: University Study and Clerical Careers in Later Medieval England', *History of Universities* 6 (1986–7), 84–5; Cobban, 'Theology and Law', 75–6; *Cambridge*, III, p. 95; *Oxford*, II, Lincoln pp. 7–8. Cf. also *Cambridge*, III, p. 471, 623–4; *Oxford*, II, Magdalen p. v. Heresy is generally a justification for expulsion.
57. Lytle, 'Patronage Patterns', pp. 124–5; T. H. Aston, G. D. Duncan and T. A. R. Evans, 'The Medieval Alumni of the University of Cambridge', *Past and Present* 86 (Feb. 1980), 70–5; D. Lepine, *A Brotherhood of Canons Serving God: English Secular Cathedrals in the Later Middle Ages* (Woodbridge, 1995), pp. 59, 95–100; K. Edwards, *The English Secular Cathedrals in the Middle Ages* (2nd edn, Manchester, 1967), pp. 70–6.
58. E.g. *Oxford*, I, Merton pp. 13–14, 36, New pp. 3, 59; II, Corpus pp. 24, 63–4. The ubiquitous stipulations and oaths against discord also fit in here. The regulations reflecting this concern equate with those governing religious fraternities: B. R. McRee, 'Religious Gilds and Regulation of Behaviour in Late Medieval Towns', in J. Rosenthal and C. Richmond (eds.), *People, Politics and Community in the Later Middle Ages* (Gloucester and New York, 1987), pp. 108–22.
59. *Oxford*, I, Queen's p. 20; the phrase is most appropriately applied to heresy: ibid., Lincoln p. 24. See also Rackham, *Early Statutes*, pp. 48–9.
60. *Cambridge*, II, pp. 229, 536; *Oxford*, I, New p. 41, All Souls p. 42; II, Magdalen pp. 69, 92, Corpus p. 84, Cardinal pp. 100–2.
61. Edwards, *Secular Cathedrals*, pp. 273–85, 297–301.
62. *Oxford*, I, New pp. 16–17, All Souls p. 22; II, Magdalen pp. 18–19, Brasenose p. 10; Cambridge, II, p. 498.
63. *Oxford*, II, Cardinal p. 159.
64. *Oxford*, I, New pp. 5–12, All Souls p. 21, Lincoln p. 13; II, Brasenose pp. 2, 9, Queen's p. 31, Magdalen p. 17; *Cambridge*, II, pp. 24–5, 438, 485–9;

H. Jewell, 'English Bishops as Educational Benefactors in the Later Fifteenth Century', in R. B. Dobson (ed.), *The Church, Politics and Patronage in the Fifteenth Century* (Gloucester, 1984), pp. 152–3; M. Dowling, *Humanism in the Age of Henry VIII* (London, Sydney and New York, 1986), pp. 78, 119–22; Jacob, 'Founders and Foundations', 173.

65. *Oxford*, I, Balliol p. 9; II, Corpus p. 61, Cardinal p. 79.

66. R. N. Swanson, *Church and Society in Later Medieval England* (revised edn, Oxford, 1993), p. 42; *Oxford*, II, Magdalen p. 46, Brasenose p. 30, Corpus p. 72, Cardinal p. 89; *Cambridge*, II, p. 561.

67. *Oxford*, I, Oriel p. 13, New pp. 19, 104–5, All Souls pp. 19, 24–5; II, Magdalen p. 22, Corpus pp. 10, 28, 70; *Cambridge*, II, pp. 35, 131, 237, 433, 606–8; III, pp. 437–8.

68. *Oxford*, I, Merton p. 34, Oriel p. 11, Queen's p. 21, New pp. 25–6, 110–11, All Souls pp. 15, 63–4; II, Magdalen pp. 84–5, Brasenose pp. 38–40, Corpus pp. 8, 11–12, 98; *Cambridge*, II, pp. 231, 236–7, 420–1, 507, 559–60, 614–17; III, pp. 95–6, 98–9; Jewell, 'English Bishops', pp. 151–2; Rackham, *Early Statutes*, pp. 70–3.

69. J. Ringrose, 'The Medieval Statutes of Pembroke College', in Patrick Zutshi (ed.), *Medieval Cambridge: Essays on the Pre-Reformation University*, The History of the University of Cambridge, Texts and Studies 2 (Woodbridge, 1993), p. 123.

70. *Oxford*, I, Merton p. 35; cf. ibid., Oriel p. 12. For explicit prohibitions of future amendments, *Oxford*, I, New pp. 113–14; II, Magdalen p. 87, Corpus p. 108; *Cambridge*, II, p. 618.

71. *Oxford*, I, New pp. 112–13; *Cambridge*, II, p. 617.

72. Wood-Legh, *Perpetual Chantries*, pp. 209–10; Cobban, *Medieval English Universities*, p. 113.

73. G. D. Squibb, *Founder's Kin: Privilege and Pedigree* (Oxford, 1972), pp. 5–11; Lytle, 'Patronage Patterns', p. 138; Cobban, *Medieval English Universities*, pp. 135–7.

74. Lytle, 'Patronage Patterns', p. 138.

75. E. Dudley (ed. D. M. Brodie), *The Tree of Commonwealth* (Cambridge, 1948), p. 63.

76. *Oxford*, I, Merton pp. 40–5; Cobban, 'Theology and Law', 61–5; Cobban, *Medieval Universities*, pp. 157–8; Gabriel, *College System*, pp. 13–14.

77. Dobson, 'Preserving the Perishable', p. 30.

CHAPTER 4

Hugh of Balsham, bishop of Ely 1256/7–1286

Roger Lovatt

No living English medievalist has done more than Barrie Dobson to il-luminate the role of the universities in the history of the Black Monks. Whether in his studies of the two great houses of Durham and Canter-bury – each of which exemplified the tradition of autonomy so funda-mental to the order by founding its own house of study at Oxford – or in his masterly rehabilitation of the general contribution of the monks to the life of medieval Oxford – now matched by a foray into the rel-atively uncharted territory of the place of the monks at Cambridge – or in such more detailed studies as his unravelling of the collective Benedictine foundation at Oxford of Gloucester College, Barrie Dobson has brought to life *le moine universitaire*. Hence an account of the only English monk-bishop to establish a college for secular clerks at Oxford or Cambridge can find an appropriate place in a collection of essays compiled in Barrie Dobson's honour. The fact that this same bishop, of modest origins and elected in the face of fierce and unscrupulous opposition from both the archbishop of Canterbury and the royal gov-ernment, displayed the idealism to found the first college in the nascent and as yet insecure University of Cambridge may also strike a chord with the student of the tales of Robin Hood.[1] And the appetite for historical paradox which is so marked a feature of the writings of Barrie Dobson may draw sustenance from the way in which this monk-bishop, at the very time when his order was becoming increasingly concerned with the need to provide a university education for its most promising young monks, should in fact have chosen to found a college not for his monastic brethren, but for secular clerks.

Not surprisingly, given the circumstances of his election as bishop, Hugh of Balsham played little part in national affairs beyond that which his status made inevitable. He rarely attracted the attention of contem-porary chroniclers, and then normally only in terms of an account of the dramatic circumstances in which he became bishop, followed later perhaps by a note of his death – although by then one chronicler had apparently forgotten his name.[2] Even in the important ecclesiastical councils of the day he is distinguished more by his absence than his presence. As diocesan of one of the most disturbed and recalcitrant areas of the kingdom he was inevitably caught up in the political conflicts of 1258–66 and was certainly suspected, perhaps not without cause, of sympathy towards the baronial party.[3] Later he occasionally appeared on the public stage, but only as the most minor actor. However, such political events were clearly not central to his career as a whole and we may reasonably focus on the three more notable aspects of his life: his election as bishop of Ely, his subsequent role in the administration of his diocese, and his relationship with the University of Cambridge culminating in his foundation of Peterhouse.

Hugh of Balsham's predecessor as bishop of Ely, William of Kilkenny, died in Spain in the course of a royal diplomatic mission on 21 September 1256.[4] His heart was brought back to Ely and there buried under a handsome monument, and he bequeathed 200 marks to the church of Ely to endow the celebration of his exequies in perpetuity. In other respects his legacy to the monks of Ely was a less happy one. The subsequent dispute over the election of his successor involved the monks of Ely and their candidate, the archbishop of Canterbury, the king and the pope himself, and even for a short while changed the canon law of the western church. It also led to the devastation of the monastic estates and massive expenditure for the church of Ely.

Henry III issued his licence to the monks of Ely to elect a successor to William of Kilkenny on 9 November 1256. Four or five days later, acting *per compromissionem*, that is through a small subcommittee of seven of their number, the community elected their subprior, Hugh of Balsham, as bishop and proceeded to seek the confirmation of their choice from the archbishop of Canterbury, Boniface of Savoy. Meanwhile the king made known his own displeasure at the monks' choice. His opposition was essentially based on two associated grounds. In the first place the monks had apparently disregarded his repeated requests that they should elect the royal chancellor, Henry of Wengham. Secondly, Henry argued, Hugh of Balsham was ill-equipped by both temperament and experience for the public responsibilities entailed in governing so potentially unruly a diocese. In the words put into his mouth by Matthew Paris, the king argued that the Isle of Ely was like a castle for fugitives and could not safely be entrusted to 'a simple denizen of the cloister, who was unwarlike and inexperienced in military proceedings, and who had never learnt the shrewdness and sagacity of the court'. The king's views had some foundation both in previous and in subsequent appointments to Ely. Ever since the royal treasurer, Nigel of Ely, had held the see for more than thirty-five years in the previous century the bishopric had been period-ically occupied by senior governmental officials. Four of the thirteenth-century bishops held high administrative office, including both Hugh of Balsham's predecessor and his two immediate successors. Certainly, also, the Isle of Ely was to prove a hotbed of opposition to the govern-ment in the last stages of the Montfortian wars – opposition which it required substantial royal intervention to quell. But another Benedictine monk, Hugh of Northwold, had been a conspicuously successful bishop of Ely for the long period from 1229 to 1254. Similarly it may have been hasty to dismiss as 'a simple denizen of the cloister' the subprior of so rich and influential a cathedral monastery as Ely where, because the bishop was nominal abbot and the prior therefore had substantial public commitments, the subprior became in effect the prior and had the major responsibility for running the day-to-day life of the house. By 1256 Hugh of Balsham would have been a senior monk with substantial administrative experience.

Nevertheless the king's reaction to Hugh's unwelcome election was immediate, and took both physical and legal form. The estates of the bishopric had naturally fallen into his hands during the vacancy and Henry exploited this fact to put pressure on the monks. A royal official, John Waleran, was given the custody of the lands and proceeded to devastate them. To one Benedictine monk, 'It was like entrusting a lamb to a starving wolf.' Forests were cut down, lakes were drained and their fish – the staple monastic diet – removed, farm animals carried off and the inhabitants of the diocese taxed extortionately. At the same time, within about a week of the election, Henry wrote to the archbishop of Canterbury asking him to quash the result on the grounds that Hugh was inadequate for the task and completely useless (*penitus inutilis*), adding for good measure that he was also said to be of servile birth.[5]

The archbishop was therefore faced both with a request from the monks of Ely that he should confirm their election and a request from the king that he should annul it. Despite protests from the royal proctors the archbishop proceeded to undertake the normal examination of the elect's suitability. At this point the king's representatives appealed to Rome. Nevertheless the archbishop continued with his examination, and it was this refusal on his part to stay his hand, even when an appeal had already been made to the curia, that formed the essential grounds of the subsequent case against him. The royal proctors drew the archbishop's attention to their appeal and warned him that he should proceed no further. When he still persisted they renewed their appeal to Rome and were now joined in their action by the representatives of Ely. Behind the appeals by both parties, as well as the archbishop's intransigence, there lay a common concern: that is, the archbishop's intention to reject the claims of both candidates, Hugh of Balsham and Henry of Wengham, and to appoint his own nominee. Accordingly, having completed his examination, the archbishop proceeded to quash the election of Hugh and to appoint instead his own close advisor, the distinguished Franciscan scholar Adam Marsh.

At this point the case was transferred to Rome. In the meanwhile two developments served to simplify the complex of claim and counter-claim. In the first place the chancellor, Henry of Wengham, withdrew, declaring, so it was said, that both of the other two candidates were more worthy of the honour. Soon he was to be consoled with the bishopric of London. More significantly, the king also withdrew his initial opposition to Hugh of Balsham. In February 1257 royal proctors were appointed to represent the king at the papal curia.[6] But by the end of the next month Henry was writing letters to two cardinals and a papal notary at Rome explaining that, although he had appealed to the pope against the election, Hugh of Balsham had since proved his loyalty.[7] That was as it may be, but the real reason for the royal *volte face* is probably to be found in the remaining contents of the letters, in which the king asked his correspondents to canvass support in Rome against the possibility that the pope himself might take advantage of the dispute to quash the claims of both candidates and provide his own nominee to the see of Ely. To add substance to this apprehension Henry pointed out that he had recently suffered in this way with regard to his own candidates for the archbishoprics of both York and Dublin. In other words, the king and his advisers had swallowed their objections to Hugh of Balsham and grudgingly come to the view that he was to be preferred to an unknown papal nominee. As a result the dispute now resolved itself into a straightforward one between the monks of Ely and the archbishop of Canterbury.

When the case eventually came before the pope, the archbishop was represented by his proctor, Master Peter of Limoges, and the monks of Ely by their prior, Walter, although Hugh had also gone to Rome to further his cause in person. The archbishop's case against Hugh was phrased in unusually frank terms even by contemporary standards in such disputes. It was initially asserted that Hugh's election was invalid on account of various procedural irregularities. But the main thrust of the archbishop's argument was directed against the character of Hugh himself, and on proving that he was entirely unfit to hold such a high ecclesiastical office as the bishopric of Ely. It was alleged that he was a drunkard and that his speech became so slurred after a meal that he could scarcely be understood. The archbishop's proctor went on to assert, perhaps in association with the charge of drunkenness, that Hugh was hot-tempered and violent, and even deranged and out of his mind. He had broken all monastic conventions of poverty and had become in effect a businessman presumably while subprior of Ely by buying up wheat, malt and fish cheaply and then selling them at a substantial profit. Finally he was accused of simony, that is, of having obtained election as bishop by promising favours to the electors, the monks of Ely. The arguments went to and fro and there were adjournments for the consultation of legal experts. The prior of Ely neatly rebutted the archbishop's argument that Hugh had violated his vow of poverty and become a profiteer by pointing out that earlier in the proceedings his election had been quashed on the grounds of his unworldliness. Hugh's own presence at Rome also probably went some way to disproving the wilder personal accusations made against him. Certainly the pope eventually decided in Hugh's favour and he was finally consecrated as bishop of Ely by Alexander IV himself on 14 October 1257, nearly a year after the initial election. In his judgement the pope also declared that a disputed episcopal election was a *causa major* and that therefore any appeal on such a matter would cause the issue automatically to devolve on him. Hence Archbishop Boniface's action in persisting with Hugh's examination and then nominating his own candidate, even after an appeal had been made, was null and void. It was a ruling which was briefly to alter the law of the western church until the consequential flood of frivolous appeals caused a later pope to refine his predecessor's judgement.

Hugh returned to England vindicated. His church of Ely was strengthened by various new papal privileges which the Ely delegation had apparently seized the opportunity to obtain. Not the least of these perhaps was the papal concession to the monks that notwithstanding their rule they might wear caps as a protection against the cold weather of Ely.[8] Finally, in January 1258, Henry III restored the confiscated lands of the see.[9] Yet so protracted a dispute was bound to cast long shadows, most immediately in terms of its financial implications. Papal censures against the depredations inflicted by the royal guardians of the vacant see appear to have had little effect, and in November 1258 Hugh was still attempting to obtain redress for the devastation wreaked on the property of the bish-opric while it had been in the king's hands.[10] More serious were the debts generated by the enormous expense entailed in pursuing such an elabo-rate appeal at the papal curia. As Matthew Paris remarked, Hugh 'had given away and promised so much money at the court of Rome . . . that all prudent men were astonished and amazed'.[11] As late as June 1259 the pope was confirming an arrangement by which Hugh undertook to pay for the expenses of his election out of the revenues of the bishopric alone, and hence not from those of the monastery.[12] It may be doubted, however, whether such an undertaking was strictly observed. In August 1265, some eight years after their appeal to Rome, the bishop and the convent of Ely still jointly owed a prodigious sum of money to a group of Florentine merchants, which they were then repaying in instalments, and it is natural to associate this debt with their earlier expenses at the papal curia. Similarly throughout the period of Hugh's episcopate the monks of Ely are to be found paying pensions to various important of-ficials at Rome.[13] All great ecclesiastical corporations found it valuable to maintain their own representatives at the curia at the time, but the events surrounding Hugh's election had made this policy both more es-sential and more expensive. Certainly the monks of Ely were to benefit substantially from having one of their own number as their bishop, and paying a share of his election expenses would come to seem a profitable investment.

Hugh of Balsham was to hold the bishopric of Ely for the unusually long period of almost thirty years. Only two other medieval bishops of Ely held the see for longer. Occasionally he made an appearance at important national events. He witnessed the *Forma Pacis* and its revised version in the parliaments of 1264 and 1265, and he was present at the denunciation of Llewellyn of Wales at the Westminster parliament of 1276.[14] Sometimes he attended major ecclesiastical celebrations, such as the consecration of Robert Kilwardby as archbishop at Canterbury in February 1273 or the translation of the body of St Hugh at Lincoln in October 1280.[15] On at least two occasions he appears to have gone abroad. Towards the end of 1259 he accompanied Henry III to France and, to judge from the charter evidence, did not return to England with the king in April 1260 but remained out of the country until the autumn of 1261. He would also seem to have gone abroad at the end of 1262 and not returned until the autumn of 1263.[16] The purpose of these visits is not entirely clear. Despite his earlier protestations for the benefit of the Roman curia, Henry III may still have suspected Hugh's loyalty and wished to keep him by his side during the political tensions of 1259–60. However it would also seem that Hugh may have visited the pope in both 1260–1 and 1263. At the time of his consecration in 1257 he had given an undertaking to visit the apostolic see every three years, an obligation which was not lifted until 1278. Visits in 1260 and 1263 would have exactly fulfilled this promise. Certainly in 1262–3 Hugh is explicitly described as going abroad on the affairs of his church.[17] But such journeys were uncharacteristic. The overwhelming impression to be gained from his itinerary is that he rarely left his diocese or its immediate neighbourhood, certainly in comparison with many of his episcopal colleagues. It is a revealing indication of this fact that, unlike many of his contemporaries whose public functions dictated frequent absences from their dioceses, Hugh seems to have found no cause to employ a suffragan to deputise for him in his episcopal functions. His favoured residence was his palace at Downham, just two or three miles north of Ely, where roughly half of his charters were given. For the rest, he was naturally often at Ely and also at his other palace some twelve miles away at Doddington, where he was to die in 1286. He also appears spasmodically elsewhere in his diocese, at the important priory of Barnwell, at his palace at Ditton, at Haddenham, Histon or Shelford and once at his own home village of Balsham, where the bishops of Ely also possessed a residence. Remarkably, in view of his concern for the university, he is apparently never to be found in Cambridge itself. At least, none of his charters was given there. His normal pattern of life was centred on the heartland, as it were, of his diocese, between Ely, Downham and Doddington – perhaps the best practical compromise between the demands of his office and St Benedict's denunciation of the *gyrovagus*.

In these circumstances any account of his activities as bishop must be mainly based not on his recorded involvement in public affairs but, given the loss of a presumed register, largely on his charters, texts of rather more than a hundred of which survive. The anomalies inherent in the survival of such evidence can seriously distort the picture. The preservation of a substantial proportion of the Ely archive may lead to the over-representation of material relating to the cathedral priory. The same consideration applies in microcosm to other religious houses, such as Chatteris, whose cartularies have survived. Conversely religious houses in the diocese whose cartularies are no longer extant, such as Barnwell, tend to disappear from view even though other evidence may suggest that the bishop was involved in their affairs.[18] Again, the filing system adopted by the royal government has ensured the continued existence of numerous significations of excommunication even though they presumably represented only a fairly minor administrative concern for the bishop. In similar fashion the *Vetus Liber* of the archdeacon of Ely provides a remarkably detailed picture of parochial life in the diocese towards the end of Hugh's episcopate, while at the same time revealing that the detailed responsibility for such matters had long ceased to attach to the bishop himself.[19] And, of course, material of a more private or transient nature such as correspondence has tended not to be preserved.

Within these limitations Hugh's administration of his diocese would appear in large measure conventional enough. Like so many of his episcopal contemporaries he issued synodal legislation on at least one, and perhaps two, occasions. But this legislation, again like that of his colleagues, was little more than a derivative palimpsest. Much of it is dependent at various removes on the earlier Lincoln statutes of Bishop Grosseteste, or on the 1268 canons of London. Even where apparently original in its actual wording, the legislation is nevertheless entirely conventional in content, insisting that no priest should be admitted to the cure of souls until he had been carefully examined by the archdeacon of Ely or his deputy; laying down basic rules for the conduct of the confessional; encouraging devotion towards the patron saint of the diocese, St Etheldreda; or reinforcing monastic observance.[20] Similarly in the early months of 1262 Hugh is to be found conducting the normal visitation of the religious houses in his diocese, although we know almost nothing of the outcome in the form of his episcopal injunctions, or of any subsequent visitations during the remaining twenty-five years of his episcopate.[21]

In both their form and their content Hugh's *acta* again largely mirror those of his colleagues.[22] They exemplify the commonplace round of formal diocesan administration, testimony to the universality of particular issues rather than to the personal concerns of an individual bishop. Hence he regularly confirms actions taken by others, decisions reached by his officials, grants of land to religious houses, or the foundation of a chantry. He regularly inspects, and hence adds his own authority to, earlier charters. Poor and often defenceless communities within his own diocese, such as the nuns of Chatteris, might understandably seek such reassurances with apparent enthusiasm, but it is hard to see what effective insurance was gained by so powerful and remote a body as the cathedral priory of Durham when Hugh inspected charters issued in their favour by previous archbishops of York.[23] In such cases one may suspect that the charters needed all the authentication that they could obtain. Elsewhere Hugh enters into treaties, as it were, with other important ecclesiastical corporations, such as the monks of Ramsey or Thorney, concerning shared or contested rights within his diocese. He makes small grants, or leases, of land, often to his own servants. He occasionally manumits one of the episcopal villeins or sends routine administrative correspondence to his officials. He hears and resolves disputes in his own court. Licences are issued to prominent knightly families to maintain their own private oratories, and parochial clergy are instituted to livings.[24]

Indulgences loom quite large amongst Hugh's *acta*. Some are almost domestic in character, such as one directed at those who passed a wayside cross near Anglesey Priory, erected to the memory of Walter, vicar of Terrington, and said an *Ave* for the repose of his soul. Another which benefited those contributing to the shrine of St Cuthbert gave support to a cult as famous as it was remote from Ely. A third in favour of those visiting the shrine, at Pontigny, of the recently canonised Archbishop Edmund of Abingdon joined a throng of similar indulgences issued by bishops throughout the western church.[25] Yet this very diversity obscures any obvious underlying theme behind their promulgation. Equally productive of extant written evidence, and perhaps more long-lasting in their effects, were Hugh's appropriations of eight parish churches, and the moiety of another, to various religious communities: a sufficient number to confirm, unsurprisingly, his own sympathy with the regular life. Oddly perhaps, apart from his gifts to Ely, only one of the beneficiaries – Eynsham Abbey – was a Benedictine house.[26] Three of the others were communities of Augustinian canons: Barnwell and the small house of Anglesey in his own diocese, and Merton in Surrey.[27] A fourth appropriation went to his own foundation of Peterhouse, and the moiety to Merton College, Oxford.[28] In almost every case Hugh also made detailed provision for the maintenance of the vicar, often in a separate charter, and he normally also kept in his own hands the right of presentation to the vicarage.

Even allowing for the vagaries inherent in the survival of evidence, Hugh's concern for the well-being of his own monastic community and his detailed knowledge of their circumstances stand out as salient features of his episcopate. His major benefactions to the monks of Ely consisted of the appropriation of the three churches of Foxton, Hauxton and Wisbech.[29] Such appropriations were of course commonplace at the time. What is striking in these cases is the way in which each appropriation was directed towards the particular, almost personal, needs of the Ely community. Hugh assigned the revenues from the church of Hauxton to the monastic chamberlain, whose particular responsibility it was to provide clothes, shoes and bedding for the monks. Similarly the income from Wisbech was to be allocated to the monastic refectory in order to improve the quality of the food supplied to the monks. Such a measure not only met its obvious aim but also improved monastic observance because, as was soon to be pointed out in defence of Hugh's provision, the inadequacy of the diet supplied in the refectory had previously had the effect of discouraging the monks from eating there as a body and conversely of encouraging them to eat elsewhere in small groups, thereby not only breaching the dietary requirements of their rule but also fragmenting the essential unity of the monastic community.[30] Finally, the income from the church of Foxton was to be used for the spiritual, rather than material, benefit of the monks by increasing their store of merit in heaven. These revenues were deployed to enlarge the charitable resources at the disposal of the community's almoner for distribution to the poor and sick at the abbey's gates. In making these appropriations it might be thought that Hugh was merely redistributing resources, from parochial to monastic use, at little or no cost to himself. But, as the monks of Ely carefully noted, in fact Hugh acquired three further advowsons for the bishopric, two certainly by purchase and perhaps also the third, to replace those which he had granted away.[31] Hence, albeit indirectly, these gifts to the monks can be seen as financed from his own resources. On a number of other occasions Hugh also made more immediate, personal donations to the Ely community. Early in his episcopate he gave them his own brewhouse in Ely, and this was followed by occasional grants of individual villeins.[32] However his largest direct gift proved to some degree stillborn. At the outset of their building campaign in the 1270s Hugh apparently promised the monks the quite substantial contribution of 345 marks towards the construction of a large stone house, the total amount to be paid on its completion. In the event the building did not go ahead as planned, and in 1277 he agreed with the monks that in consequence he would be liable for the payment of only 100 marks.[33]

In sum, Hugh's generosity towards the Ely community might seem to contrast unfavourably with the prodigious contribution of several thousand pounds made by his predecessor, Hugh of Northwold, towards the rebuilding of the presbytery of the cathedral.[34] Both bishops were themselves Black Monks and it may seem surprising that Hugh did not contribute in a similarly substantial way to the beautification of the

community's worship. Two reasons may be suggested. At the beginning
of his episcopate he was burdened with the repayment of the immense
expenditure arising from the circumstances of his election. Later he may
have been husbanding his resources, partly to recompense his successors
for the appropriations that he had made earlier and partly to finance
his projected collegiate foundation in Cambridge. Equally the value to
the monks of having one of their own number as their bishop cannot be
measured simply in financial terms. Other concessions made by Hugh
to the community were administrative rather than monetary in nature,
but perhaps no less beneficial. This tone of co-operation is apparent in
the outcome of his only recorded visitation of the Ely community. Consequent upon this visitation, in February 1262, Hugh issued an ordinance
intended to tighten up the procedures by which the monks received their
manorial revenues. Conventional enough in content, the ordinance is
not only unusually described as resulting from extensive consultation
between the bishop and the senior members of the community but also,
again at the request of the convent and with the assent of the prior, is
enforced with the bishop's anathema, and the whole document is sealed
jointly by bishop and prior and chapter. The visitation appears less as an
assertion of authority by the bishop and more as a process of amicable
discussion between colleagues.[35] Another frequent source of contention
in monastic cathedrals lay in defining the respective roles of bishop and
community in the election of a prior. Yet when Prior Leverington died in
1271 Hugh granted the monks the right of free election of his successor,
and this concession was repeated in 1273. The fact that no earlier grants
of this sort are recorded, and that the monks were punctilious in tran-
scribing both of them in their two major cartularies, strongly suggests
that Hugh's concession was the first of the sort to be made in such formal
terms and that the monks regarded it as an important indication of their
bishop's benevolence towards them.[36]

The monks of Ely were entitled to feel that any contribution that they
had made towards the expenses of Hugh's election had proved to be a
worthwhile investment. Indeed there are signs towards the end of his episcopate that Hugh may have become too indulgent towards his *confrères*.
The accusation made in 1283 that the prior himself and other monks had
broken into houses and stolen property at Bergham, in Suffolk, is striking
but unsubstantiated.[37] More serious was the outcome of the metropoliti-
cal visitation conducted in 1285, when Archbishop Peckham summarily
removed from office all the major obedientiaries with the exception of
the prior. Peckham was given to such drastic measures, and we know

nothing of the reasons behind his sanctions at Ely, but they cannot speak well of the state of observance there.[38]

At first sight the character of Hugh of Balsham's long episcopate does little to prepare us for his most remarkable act, the foundation in 1280–4 of the first Cambridge college, the house of the scholars of the bishops of Ely later to be known as Peterhouse. In a broad sense it was perhaps inevitable that, with colleges already established at Oxford in the form of Balliol and Merton, similar foundations should also be made at Cambridge, which followed the model of Oxford in so many other ways. Yet the precise circumstances of the evolution of Peterhouse suggest that Hugh was driven by events as much as realising a developed plan. Certainly its foundation is problematical. Why did Hugh wait before acting until he had been bishop of Ely for more than twenty-two years, and had only some six more years to live, with the result that his foundation was left with incomplete statutes and an inadequate endowment? Above all, why did he, then the most powerful Benedictine monk in the English church, establish an independent college for secular clerks when one of the most pressing issues facing his order at exactly that time was the provision of facilities at university for his fellow monks?

The most obvious reason for the delay might seem to lie in Hugh's financial position. The enormous burden of debt arising from the circumstances of his election clearly overshadowed the first half of his episcopate. He had also been concerned to purchase advowsons to compensate his see for the appropriations that he had made. It may be that it was not until the later 1270s that he had the resources to envisage his own collegiate foundation. Yet his endowment of the college was relatively meagre. It consisted initially of a handful of houses and a rent charge in Cambridge, followed by the appropriation of a church. His one relatively substantial gift of money, to enable his scholars to build a hall, took the form of a bequest made after his death. Such an endowment would scarcely tax the resources of so wealthy a see. Or it may be that Hugh wished to contemplate the final outcome of Walter de Merton's prolonged foundation at Oxford, on which his own college was closely based, and Merton College did not complete its long period of gestation until the third version of the founder's statutes was issued in August 1274. Whatever may have lain behind it, the problem of Hugh's delay in acting is not a straightforward one.

Even more difficult to explain is his establishment of a college whose character seemed to fly in the face of the contemporary preoccupations of his order. For more than forty years the English Benedictine abbots had been concerned that the spectacular growth of scholastic theology at the new universities had not only disparaged the traditional intellectual pursuits of the monks but was also in danger of isolating them from the mainstream of academic development. Hence in 1247 the General Chapter made somewhat tentative provision for daily lectures in theology or canon law to be given in certain houses, and in 1255 they curtailed the liturgy in order to allow monks more time for study. Such concerns reached their climax in 1277, when the General Chapter launched a scheme for a house of studies to be established at Oxford financed by a levy on individual monasteries.[39] This proposal came to fruition in 1283–4 with the establishment of what came to be known as Gloucester College, and as early as 1290–1 the abbot of Westminster was trumpeting the popularity and success of the new foundation as revitalising the whole order.[40] Even the greatest Benedictine communities in England, who rejected the loss of autonomy implied by participating in such a collective institution, were moved by the same concerns, but chose to act independently. Monk-scholars from Durham had found their way to Oxford by 1278, and the community had begun to acquire land for the future Durham College as early as 1286.[41] Similarly the monks of Canterbury, who long remained wary of Oxford and even suffered the indignity of receiving theological lectures from mendicant scholars, were nevertheless sending members of their community to study at the University of Paris by 1288.[42] By the mid-1290s it is possible to identify members of many different Benedictine communities who had studied at Oxford. In 1289–90 a monk of Ely itself had incepted, at an unknown university, and must therefore have begun his studies at least in the early 1280s.[43] Even the members of the Cistercian order, who might have been expected to show a greater reluctance to enter the universities, had in fact anticipated the Benedictines and founded their own Oxford house of studies at Rewley Abbey at the end of 1281 or in 1282.[44] Yet it was at exactly this moment that Hugh of Balsham founded his college, paradoxically, for secular clerks.

His motives must remain ultimately impenetrable. Yet some things are clear. The rush to university did not meet with universal approval, even amongst the monks themselves.[45] There was simple reluctance to pay the levy to support Gloucester College. The daughter houses of Norman monasteries rejected interference from the English General Chapter. Some houses stood aloof from both levy and General Chapter in defence of their traditional autonomy. The bishops felt uneasy that an assertive General Chapter was intruding on their own rights over the houses of the Black Monks. Behind these arguments no doubt there lay the view that a university was no place for a monk. Hugh of Balsham may have shared this attitude. At the same time his sympathetic interest in the affairs of Cambridge University in general is clearly apparent. As early as 1264 he issued the first recorded grant of episcopal privileges to the university. Protesting his devotion to Cambridge, his wish to protect its tranquillity and to preserve and augment its privileges, Hugh decreed that no appeal by a scholar against a verdict by the chancellor should be made in future to the bishop unless it had first been heard by the university as a whole.[46] Some ten years later, again in the interests of preserving peace within the university, he settled a dispute between the scholars and the rector of St Bene't's concerning the ringing of the church's bell to summon convocations.[47] His most important contribution to the structural development of the university was made in 1276, when he precisely defined and confirmed the jurisdiction of the chancellor in his arbitration between the chancellor, the archdeacon of Ely and the Master of Glomery.[48] It was no less than Hugh deserved that in 1291 the university should agree to observe his obit annually 'with filial affection, mindful of one who while living made it his whole endeavour to promote manfully the good and the honour of the scholars'.[49]

Hugh's links with what he came to call 'our' university did not merely consist in the administrative acts of a supportive diocesan. His predecessor at Ely, William of Kilkenny, had bequeathed the sum of 200 marks to support two Cambridge students in theology who were to pray for the repose of his soul, and had entrusted the administration of the bequest to the canons of Barnwell. When the bequest seemed inadequate, Hugh permitted the canons to appropriate the Cambridge church of All Saints by the Castle specifically to ensure that the scholars could continue to be maintained.[50] It was a harbinger of greater support to come, and it is not unreasonable to see this support as also reinforced by the intimate links with the university which existed amongst many of Hugh's closest advisors. Typical in this respect was Master Ralph de Walpole, who was archdeacon of Ely for fourteen years during Hugh's episcopate and whom he later appointed as an executor of his will. Walpole had previously been one of the foremost members of the Cambridge theology faculty, was himself involved in the foundation of Peterhouse, and was later a benefactor of both the college and the university.[51] Another man appointed by Hugh to be his executor was the distinguished lawyer, Master John Lacy. He acted as Official of the Ely diocese for many years during Hugh's episcopate and was also a benefactor of the university.[52]

One of Hugh's earlier Officials, to whom he was particularly closely
attached, was Master Simon de Asceles. After an outstanding career at
Oxford, Asceles had moved to Cambridge and taught there as one of the
earliest regent masters in civil law.[53] Master Hugh de Stanford, who was
described by Hugh as 'our familiar clerk' and also acted at one time as
his Official, was another benefactor of the university.[54] Similarly Master
Andrew de Giselham, who was chancellor of the university at the time
when Peterhouse was being founded, was himself directly involved in
the process and was another benefactor of the university, had previously
been Official of the archdeacon of Ely.[55] These men were all at the very
heart of the administration of the diocese and were the bishop's most
familiar colleagues. They were also all intimately associated with the fortunes of the university. Their influence on Hugh's motivation must be
seen as crucial.

A number of Oxford and Cambridge colleges were more or less explicitly modelled on earlier colleges, but Hugh was unusually forthright
in acknowledging that he had been directly inspired by the example
of Merton. In giving his original assent to Hugh's plans, Edward I
stated in December 1280 that Hugh had conceived the 'praiseworthy
design' of establishing a group of scholars in the Hospital of St John
in Cambridge who were to live together and study 'according to the
rule of the scholars of Oxford who are called of Merton', and the later
statutes of Peterhouse contain frequent injunctions to follow the precedents then existing at Merton.[56] Hugh's links with Merton were both
various and of long standing. Despite their apparently differing political
sympathies it is inconceivable that the two founders, contemporaneously
bishops of Rochester (1274–7) and Ely (1257–86), should not have come
into personal contact. Certainly there were many indirect links. Hugh's
immediate predecessor at Ely, William of Kilkenny, whom Hugh, as
subprior of the monastic community, would have known well, had the
closest of ties with Walter de Merton. They had served together as clerks
in the household of Nicholas Farnham, bishop of Durham, and subsequently Walter seems to have acted as a chancery clerk under William of
Kilkenny and apparently became a member of his household while he
was Keeper of the Great Seal and later Chancellor. Walter de Merton's
sometime Official, leading figure in his *familia* and counsellor to his executors, was William's relation, Master Andrew of Kilkenny.[57] Another
member of the same family was Master Henry of Kilkenny who was not
only Bishop William's executor, and as a result remained involved in the
affairs of the Ely diocese until his death – with his accounts as executor

still unresolved – in 1280, but had also earlier been a party to the property transactions which were to culminate in Merton's acquisition of its estate in Cambridge.[58] This estate, bought by Walter de Merton in 1270, no doubt as an alternative location for his college in case the University of Oxford was obliged to disperse, would have been an immediate reminder to Hugh of Balsham of the existence of his Oxford exemplar. Yet Hugh's direct associations with Merton College actually date from two years before Walter de Merton's purchase of land in Cambridge and coincide with a crucially formative stage in the college's evolution, when the founder's acquisition of the Oxford site had scarcely been completed, building works had probably only just begun and the college still retained its embryonic, hybrid status at both Malden and Oxford. At this point, in October 1268, Hugh appropriated to the Maldon-Merton community a moiety of the rectory of Gamlingay, specifically associating his grant with Walter de Merton's scheme for the maintenance of scholars and stressing the benefit to the whole Christian community which might be expected to flow from it.[59] Then, less than four years later, in April 1272, before the college had achieved complete independence at Oxford, Hugh appropriated the church of Barton, near Cambridge, to Merton Priory, the 'mother house' of Walter de Merton's foundation and a central presence in Walter's own early career.[60] Truly, as the historian of Merton College has observed, 'the small circumference of the circle in which the founders of [the first] English colleges worked cannot be denied'.[61]

The general stimulus of the Merton precedent is clear, yet Hugh of Balsham's plans differed substantially in detail from his Merton model. This is particularly the case with regard to his initial scheme for a joint foundation in Cambridge with the Augustinian Hospital of St John. This notion of a joint community does remotely echo Walter de Merton's original co-operation with the Augustinian canons of Merton, but by far the more obvious precedent would seem to be the Collège des Dix-huit at Paris founded within the Hôtel-Dieu. Many important features of the Merton model are also lacking even in Hugh's revised project for a fully independent college. These include the provision in the Merton statutes for founder's kin, the complement of chaplains and the elaborate collegiate liturgy clearly pre-supposed, the regional preference for election to fellowships, the role of the Warden's deputy, and so forth.[62] Inspired by Merton he may have been, but Hugh was far from being the prisoner of his exemplar. Indeed there is considerable uncertainty about his precise intentions for his new college. Not only did his plans change radically between 1280 and 1284 but there is clear evidence that he tried hard to preserve his original plan for a joint community combining scholars with brethren serving the Hospital, perhaps until even as late as the summer of 1283, and that it was only the irreconcilable differences between the two groups, and their own wish to part company, which eventually induced him – apparently even against his own will – to establish the scholars as an independent body.[63] It was only to be expected that while Hugh should stress the religious and academic purpose of his college, 'ad laudem divinam et eiusdem universitatis incrementum perpetuum', Edward I in giving his support to the scheme should emphasise its public utility, 'perpendentes ex huiusmodi studio per eminentiam sapiencie posse rei publice multa commoda provenire'.[64] One might suppose that all such uncertainties could immediately be resolved by reference to the statutes of Hugh's new college. They would at least provide a clear blueprint of his final intentions.

Unfortunately this is far from the case. The statutes of Peterhouse, as they have survived, were given by Simon de Montacute, Hugh's successor as bishop of Ely, on 9 April 1344, that is, sixty years after the college was founded. These statutes make it clear that Hugh of Balsham had drawn up some rules for his scholars, but they also indicate that these rules were incomplete, or embryonic, and they appear to associate this incompleteness with his early death. Certainly it was the inchoate nature of their rule which subsequently induced the Master and fellows to petition Simon de Montacute to issue a definitive code.[65] This account rings true. Only a few months elapsed between Hugh's abandonment of his initial project and his enforced establishment of an independent college: a scarcely adequate period in which to draw up a completely new code of statutes, and he certainly died little more than two years later. What is more, the details of his endowment of the college suggest that he was then acting with haste and insufficient foresight.[66] Nor need we assume that a college could not function adequately without comprehensive statutes. The examples of Balliol, Clare and Queens' amply demonstrate otherwise. In any case it is clear that Hugh had instructed his scholars to follow the rule of Merton as far as they were able.

So the problem is to distinguish what is Hugh's from what is Simon's, and it cannot be solved with any precision.[67] The statutes themselves imply that Simon's contribution was not trivial and some injunctions can clearly be attributed to him. These include the opening and closing sections of the statutes, the grant of the right of totally free elections to fellowships, the detailed arrangements for the subjects to be studied by the fellows and the precise restrictions on fellows' dress.[68] To these can almost certainly be added the arrangements for electing a Master, the exact quota of fourteen fellowships and the concession that French might occasionally be spoken at mealtimes.[69] It is not even clear that every reference to Merton must derive from Hugh of Balsham. In the chapter defining the duties of the bursars Simon not only directed that they should follow the practice of Merton but added for their further elucidation that he had himself sent a copy of the Merton statutes to his college.[70] Equally the lay-out of the statutes, with a table of contents, each statute numbered and headed and the whole presented in codex form, is characteristic of 1344 rather than 1284.[71] It is possible to identify resonances from the Rule of St Benedict, and hence Hugh's hand, in some clauses, but such resonances are matters of tone and language rather than precise injunctions. In general the statutes may well largely represent Hugh's original intentions, but the evidence does not entitle us to apply this broad assumption to most of the specific provisions.[72] We can only say with reasonable certainty that he founded in Cambridge an independent college – its independence perhaps forced upon him against his better judgement – for poor, secular scholars who were to follow as appropriate the rule of Merton. He seems not to have specified the size of the college but to have wished the number of its fellows to reflect the value of their eventual endowment.[73] There are strong hints elsewhere that he originally planned to keep in his own hands, and those of his successors at Ely, the right of appointment to fellowships and the Mastership. One may also assume that he intended their studies to be largely focussed on arts and theology.[74] Some of his intentions are in fact more precisely revealed elsewhere. The placing of the college adjacent to the church of St Peter and its structural connection with that church are laid down in Hugh's deed separating the scholars from the Hospital. Similarly the exact nature of his endowment is defined in the same deed, supplemented by his simultaneous appropriation of the church of Thriplow to the scholars alone. Later this initial endowment was increased by legacies in his will not only of books from his library but also of the sum of £200, which the scholars used to buy land and erect a hall.[75]

What does emerge strongly from Hugh's own words is his sense of proprietorship towards his college and his association of his college with Ely and its bishops. He describes the scholars repeatedly as 'his' scholars, and they are to be known forever as 'the scholars of the bishops of Ely'.[76] Hence it was fitting that when a monk of Ely compiled an account of Hugh of Balsham shortly after his death he should have stressed these two facets of his episcopate, his collegiate foundation and his devotion to his own community at Ely.[77] The biographer carefully describes the circumstances of Hugh's foundation and his endowment of, and legacies for, 'scolares sui'. But the monk also dwelt in loving detail on Hugh's gifts to Ely, not just the appropriated churches but also in more personal vein a rich collection of vestments, embroidery and plate, much of it redolent of the history and piety of the monastic community. There were 'baudekenes', some 'magni pretii', elaborately ornamented with flowers, birds and animals, and also a fine collection of copes of red, black and green silk, one embroidered with scenes from the life of St Etheldreda, the patroness of the cathedral. Similarly amongst his gift of albs one was decorated with representations of St Etheldreda, another with her shields and a third with scenes from the life of her sister, St Wihtburg. Both saints were buried in the cathedral and their bodies had only recently been translated by Hugh's predecessor, Hugh of Northwold. The monk-biographer also focussed on the exact circumstances of Hugh's burial and it is here, in his death, that we may come closest to him as successively, over some fifty years, monk, subprior and abbot-bishop of the Ely community. His two predecessors as bishop were buried under elaborate and costly table tombs, each bearing an effigy clothed in episcopal regalia. William of Louth, who became bishop four years after Hugh's death, lies under a grandiloquent canopy tomb modelled on no less an exemplar than the tomb of the king's uncle at Westminster. Hugh of Balsham had no such ostentatious memorial. He rested under a simple grave slab yet, unlike the others, this slab lay immediately before the high altar. And his heart was buried separately 'ad tria altaria', that is, adjacent to the chapel in the north choir aisle dedicated to St Benedict.

NOTES

1. For the 'insecurity' of Cambridge at the time, see J. W. Clark (ed.), *Liber Memorandorum Ecclesie de Bernewelle* (Cambridge, 1907), p. 94, and also M. B. Hackett, *The Original Statutes of Cambridge University* (Cambridge, 1970), p. 64.

2. H. R. Luard (ed.), *Annales Monastici*, 5 vols. (RS, 1864–9), III, p. 326.

3. E. F. Jacob, *Studies in the Period of Baronial Reform and Rebellion, 1258–1267* (Oxford, 1925), p. 293.

4. For what follows concerning Hugh's election, see Bodleian Library, MS Laud misc. 647, fos. 154r–6r; Matthew Paris, *Chronica Majora*, ed.

H. R. Luard, 7 vols. (RS, 1872–84), V, pp. 589, 611, 615, 619–20, 635–6, 652, 661–2; Walter Ullmann, 'The Disputed Election of Hugh Balsham, Bishop of Ely', *Cambridge Historical Journal* 9 (1949), 259–68; and A. Maier, 'Notizie storiche del XIII e XIV secolo da codici borghesiani', *Rivista di Storia della Chiesa in Italia* 4 (1950), 171–6.

5. *Calendar of Close Rolls, 1256–59*, pp. 108–9.

6. *Calendar of Patent Rolls, 1247–58*, p. 540.

7. PRO, EI 35/2/23. I am indebted to Professor Nicholas Vincent for the valuable reference to these letters.

8. MS Laud misc. 647, fo. 156r.

9. *Calendar of Patent Rolls, 1247–58*, p. 612.

10. *Calendar of Entries in the Papal Registers Relating to Great Britain and Ireland: Papal Letters*, I, p. 359; *Calendar of Patent Rolls, 1258–66*, p. 48.

11. *Chronica Majora*, V, p. 652.

12. *Cal. Pap. Reg., Letters*, I, p. 365.

13. CUL, EDC 1/B/106, 107, 115 a–c.

14. T. Rymer (ed.), *Foedera . . . et Acta Publica*, 4 vols. (Record Commission, 1816–69), I, pp. 443, 451–2, 535–6.

15. W. Stubbs, *Registrum Sacrum Anglicanum* (Oxford, 1897), pp. 64, 66.

16. *Calendar of Patent Rolls, 1258–66*, pp. 54, 59, 156, 221.

17. *Cal. Pap. Reg., Letters*, I, p. 454.

18. Clark (ed.), *Liber Memorandorum*, pp. 73, 128–9. Simon de Asceles, who was prior during the last half of Hugh's episcopate, had previously been his Official; hence Hugh's pleasure at his election.

19. C. L. Feltoe and E. H. Minns (eds.), *Vetus Liber Archidiaconi Eliensis*, Cambridge Antiquarian Soc., octavo publications 48 (Cambridge, 1917), pp. xiii–xxvii, xxxiii–xxxiv.

20. C. R. Cheney, *English Synodalia of the Thirteenth Century* (Oxford, 1968), pp. 136–8; F. M. Powicke and C. R. Cheney (eds.), *Councils and Synods, with Other Documents Relating to the English Church*, II (Oxford, 1964), pp. 515–23.

21. BL, MS Cotton Julius A.I, fo. 77r. Also S. J. A. Evans (ed.), 'Ely Chapter Ordinances and Visitation Records, 1241–1515', Camden Soc., third series 64 (1940), pp. 4–5.

22. A substantial cross-section of Hugh's *acta* is contained in two Ely cartularies, MS Laud misc. 647, fos. 154r–175r, and CUL, EDR G/3/28 ('Liber M'), pp. 190–203. References to specific *acta* will be separately noted.

23. BL, MS Cotton Julius A.I, fos. 77r, 102r, 105r; Durham, Dean and Chapter Muniments, 2.1. Archiep. 12.

24. For private oratories, see BL, MS Add. 41612, fo. 12r.

25. PRO, E326/1258; Durham, Dean and Chapter Muniments, Miscellaneous Charters 1511; Sens Cathedral, Trésor, H 100.

26. H. E. Salter (ed.), *The Cartulary of Eynsham Abbey*, 2 vols., Oxford Historical Society, 49 and 51 (Oxford, 1907–8), I, pp. 258–61.

27. Clark (ed.), *Liber Memorandorum*, p. 71; PRO, E326/1108; BL, MS Cotton Cleop. C.VII, fo. 218.

28. For these appropriations, see below, pp. 75, 77.

29. MS Laud misc. 647, fos. 160, 162r–163v.

30. Evans (ed.), 'Ely... Visitation Records', p. 16; R. Graham (ed.), *Registrum Roberti Winchelsey Cantuariensis Archiepiscopi, 1294–1313*, 2 vols., Canterbury and York Society 51–2 (1952–6), I, pp. 253–4, 258–9.

31. MS Laud misc. 647, fos. 170r, 173v, 174v.

32. Ibid., fos. 156r, 158r, 164v, 168v; Trinity College, Cambridge, Muns., Box 35, Great Shelford 1.

33. CUL, EDC 1/B/72.

34. P. Draper, 'Bishop Northwold and the Cult of St Etheldreda', in N. Coldstream and P. Draper (eds.), *Medieval Art and Architecture at Ely Cathedral*, British Archaeological Association Conference Transactions 2 (1979 for 1976), pp. 8–27, esp. 26–7.

35. Evans (ed.), 'Ely... Visitation Records', pp. vi–vii, 4–5.

36. MS Laud misc. 647, fos. 160r, 161; CUL, EDR G/3/28, pp. 194, 196.

37. *Calendar of Patent Rolls, 1281–92*, p. 99.

38. D. L. Douie, *Archbishop Pecham* (Oxford, 1952), pp. 156–76, esp. p. 159.

39. W. A. Pantin (ed.), *Documents Illustrating the Activities of the General and Provincial Chapters of the English Black Monks, 1215–1540*, 3 vols., Camden Soc. third series 45 (1931); 47 (1933) and 54 (1937), I, pp. 27–8, 55, 75.

40. Ibid., I, pp. 132–3; R. B. Dobson, 'The Foundation of Gloucester College, Oxford, in 1283', *Worcester College Record* (1985), 12–24.

41. R. B. Dobson, *Durham Priory, 1400–1450* (Cambridge, 1973), pp. 343–4.

42. W. A. Pantin, *Canterbury College, Oxford*, 4 vols., Oxford Historical Soc., new series 6–8 (1947–50); 30 (1985), IV, p. 3.

43. CUL, MS Add. 2957, fo. 17.

44. W. H. Stevenson and H. E. Salter, *The Early History of St John's College, Oxford*, Oxford Historical Soc., new series 1 (1939), pp. 3–9.

45. For what follows, see Pantin (ed.), *Chapters*, I, pp. 119–33; V. H. Galbraith, 'New Documents about Gloucester College', in H. E. Salter (ed.), *Snappe's Formulary*, Oxford Historical Soc. 80 (1924), pp. 336–86, esp. 343–4, 355–6; and C. T. Martin (ed.), *Registrum Epistolarum Fratris Johannis Peckham, Archiepiscopi Cantuariensis*, 3 vols. (RS, 1882–5), I, p. 150. In general, D. Knowles, *The Religious Orders in England*, 3 vols. (Cambridge, 1948–59), I, p. 26; II, pp. 17–19.

46. BL, MS Add. 9822, fo. 91; Hackett, *Original Statutes*, pp. 33–4, 223.

47. CUL, CUA, Collect. Admin. 7 (Markaunt's Book), fo. B. 10v; printed in J. Josselin, *Historiola Collegii Corporis Christi*, Cambridge Antiq. Soc., octavo publications 17 (1880), pp. 56–7.

48. CUL, CUA, Luard 5; printed in slightly abbreviated form, with translation, in A. F. Leach, *Educational Charters and Documents, 598–1909* (Cambridge, 1911), pp. 202–9.

49. Peterhouse Treasury (PT), Cista Communis 4; Hackett, *Original Statutes*, pp. 34–5.

50. Clark (ed.), *Liber Memorandorum*, pp. 71, 94.

51. A. B. Emden, *A Biographical Register of the University of Cambridge to 1500 (BRUC)* (Cambridge, 1963), p. 612. For Hugh's executors, A. R. Dewindt and E. B. Dewindt, *Royal Justice and the Medieval English Countryside* (Toronto, 1981), Part I, p. 261; PT, Reg. Vetus, pp. 27–8, 60; CUL, CUA, Misc. Collect. 4 (Stokys' Book), fo. 26r.

52. Ibid., fo. 27v; *BRUC*, p. 346; Dewindt and Dewindt, *Royal Justice*, Part I, p. 261. For Lacy as Official, see CUL, EDC I/B/110a-m. He held the office *c.* 1274–80.

53. *BRUC*, p. 17; Clark (ed.), *Liber Memorandorum*, pp. 73, 128–9. Hackett, *Original Statutes*, pp. 30–2.

54. *BRUC*, p. 550; PT, Eccl. Cant. A 6; BL, MS Cotton Cleop. C.VII, fo. 218 (as Official in 1272); CUL, CUA, Misc. Collect. 4, fo. 27v.

55. *BRUC*, p. 259; PT, Reg. Vetus, pp. 27–8; CUL, CUA, Misc. Collect. 4, fo. 26v; MS Laud misc. 647, fo. 163v.

56. PT, Coll. Sit. B.1; printed with translation in Leach, *Educational Charters*, pp. 222–5. The relationship between the Peterhouse statutes and those of Merton is conveniently summarised in H. Rashdall, *The Universities of Europe in the Middle Ages*, ed. F. M. Powicke and A. B. Emden, 3 vols. (Oxford, 1936), III, pp. 296–9. See also H. Mayr-Harting, 'The Foundation of Peterhouse, Cambridge (1284), and the Rule of Saint Benedict', *English Historical Review* 103 (1988), 318–38, esp. 337–8.

57. J. R. L. Highfield (ed.), *The Early Rolls of Merton College, Oxford* (Oxford, 1964), pp. 15–16, 18, 34, 39, 58, 83–5.

58. Martin (ed.), *Registrum Epistolarum . . . Peckham*, I, pp. 110–11; J. M. Gray, *The School of Pythagoras, Cambridge*, Cambridge Antiquarian Soc., quarto publications, new series 4 (1932), pp. 11–14, 44, 46. For the ramifications of the remarkable Kilkenny family, see *Report on Manuscripts in Various Collections*, IV (HMC, 1907), pp. 73–4.

59. Merton College Muniments, no. 2355.

60. BL, MS Cotton Cleop. C.VII, fo. 218; Highfield (ed.), *Early Rolls*, pp. 8–10, 21–2.

61. Ibid., p. 68. There is a revealing number of other, more shadowy, links between Hugh of Balsham and Merton College. Ralph de Fotheringay was one of Hugh's executors (see n. 51 above); Henry de Fotheringay was a fellow of Merton by 1284–5, and, for good measure, Walter de Fotheringay was a fellow, and then Master, of Balliol at the same time. Another of Hugh's executors, and previously his Official, was John Lacy; his name appears in the Merton accounts, revealingly, in 1284–5. One of the earliest benefactors of Peterhouse was Robert de Aspale; Geoffrey de Aspale was involved in the preliminary stages of the Merton foundation. A. B. Emden, *A Biographical Register of the University of Oxford to A.D. 1500*, 3 vols. (Oxford, 1957), I, pp. 60–1; II, p. 703; III, pp. 2186–7; Highfield (ed.), *Early Rolls*, pp. 269, 294, 435; St John's College, Cambridge, Muns., D 20.54; P. S. Allen and H. W. Garrod (eds.), *Merton Muniments*, Oxford Historical Society 85 (1926), p. 8.

62. See n. 56 above.

63. For the various attempts to reconcile the scholars and the brethren of the Hospital, including Hugh's own intervention, see PT, Reg. Vetus, pp. 27–8.
64. PT, Coll. Sit. B.1, B.2; Leach, *Educational Charters*, pp. 224–7.
65. PT, Montacute Statutes, caps. 1, 59. Reference is here made to the original statutes; the text printed by the Royal Commission is a later copy which is both inaccurate and seriously incomplete. Its numbering is also one in advance of the original statutes: *Documents Relating to the University and Colleges of Cambridge*, 3 vols. (Royal Commission, 1852), II, pp. 6–42.
66. The detailed arrangements for the appropriation of Thriplow to the college in 1284 were clearly worked out *chemin faisant*: PT, Thriplow A.1, A.2, A.3.
67. What follows differs substantially in emphasis from the account given by Mayr-Harting, 'The Foundation of Peterhouse', 318–38, but I am much indebted to its stimulus and also to many discussions with Professor Mayr-Harting.
68. PT, Montacute Statutes, caps. 1, 54, 59, 60. Any original right of free election seems clearly denied by Archbishop Winchelsey's nomination, under *sede vacante* jurisdiction, of Richer de Aylesham to a fellowship in 1299: Graham (ed.), *Registrum . . . Winchelsey*, pp. 322–3. Furthermore Edward III's rapid, formal confirmation of Montacute's concession (cap. 3) in October 1345 would be unnecessary if free election had originally been granted by Hugh of Balsham: PT, Cista Communis A.1. John Martyn's licence from the bishop of Ely in 1339 to study medicine shows that Montacute's arrangements (cap. 23) for allowing the Master and fellows to permit such studies were newly introduced in 1344: *BRUC*, p. 394. The statutory restrictions on fellows' dress (cap. 34) explicitly refer to Archbishop Stratford's Constitution *Exterior habitus* of 1342–3.
69. The use of the word *deinceps* in cap. 2 clearly implies that Montacute is introducing a new procedure for mastership elections. In any case it seems inconceivable that Hugh of Balsham would have maintained the right to nominate fellows (see n. 68 above) but allowed a large measure of freedom in elections for the mastership. Cap. 1 of Montacute's statutes indicates that the exact number of fellowships had not originally been specified, but that it had subsequently been found that the college's income was sufficient for the support of only fourteen and a Master. This number appears to have been settled in practice by 1339: PT, Collegium A.6. Montacute's concession that French might occasionally be spoken at mealtimes (cap. 39) is much more characteristic of college statutes after 1320 than of thirteenth-century examples, and in fact specifically departs from the Merton exemplar. A. B. Cobban, *The Medieval English Universities: Oxford and Cambridge to c.1500* (Aldershot, 1988), p. 366 and n.; Allen and Garrod (eds.), *Merton Muniments*, p. 22.
70. PT, Montacute Statutes, cap. 15.
71. Compare the lay-out of the Merton statutes of 1274 and the Balliol statutes of 1282; see Allen and Garrod (eds.), *Merton Muniments*, PL. VI and

H. E. Salter (ed.), *The Oxford Deeds of Balliol College* (Oxford, 1913), plate facing p. 277.

72. Mayr-Harting, 'The Foundation of Peterhouse', 318–38.
73. PT, Coll. Sit. B.1; Montacute Statutes, caps.1, 45.
74. This seems to be implied by the wording of cap. 1 of the Montacute Statutes.
75. PT, Coll. Sit. B.2; Thriplow A.1; MS Laud misc. 647, fo. 175r.
76. PT, Coll. Sit. B.2; Thriplow A.1, A.2, A.3.
77. For the account that follows, see MS Laud misc. 647, fos. 174v–175r.

CHAPTER 5

A cruel necessity? Christ's and St John's, two Cambridge refoundations

Malcolm G. Underwood

On 8 April 1511, John Fotehede, Master of Michaelhouse, wrote from Cambridge to John Fisher, bishop of Rochester, formerly spiritual advisor to Lady Margaret Beaufort and now one of her executors, urging faster progress on the buildings of her foundation of St John's College. Fotehede himself had served as her controller of finances in 1504–6, and had presented her statutes to the fellows of Christ's College, her earlier foundation, in the latter year. Both colleges were endowed and built with the resources of the countess's household and estates, and both had transfigured and replaced previous smaller foundations on the same sites. The later educational prestige of the colleges has dwarfed the institutions which preceded them; but for contemporaries there were priorities other than education which weighed equally or even more strongly.

Fotehede's letter mentioned the importance of local opinion in the furtherance of the project; but it was not, according to the writer, an opinion concerned with education. It focussed rather on elements in the old foundation, the thirteenth-century hospital of St John the Evangelist under the patronage of the bishops of Ely, which remained precious to local people. Some headway had been made in negotiations with adjoining King's Hall to secure the southern boundary of the new college, but progress was now held up by the reluctance of the last members of the hospital to surrender a bond in their possession, and the intervention of Dr William Robinson, the bishop of Ely's commissary, was called for. These tiresome matters should be concluded quickly, 'for veryly my lord meny folkes wonder that the Maister is so long un put in, and speke largely by cause in the churche be sum tyme masse and other servyce none. And now the holy tyme [Easter] draweth oppon hand there woldbe sum way that Godes service might be keped, thys holy tyme more specially.'[1] This state of affairs had already caused consternation, for once the brethren had been shipped downriver to Ely the hospital had been left desolate, 'and neither masse ne service be keped therein, many folkes speke thereof . . . '.

For the townspeople remembered the community which had in the recent past celebrated the exequies of two of their number and buried a pauper with a tombstone. At a date after 1498 the organ of the house had been mended and a friar paid for playing 'oftentimes', and a new canopy made for the high altar by one Rose Garlond.[2] The hospital remained under the patronage of the see of Ely. Like other religious houses it had maintained reciprocal obligations of prayer and mutual aid, in this case with the hospital of St John at Ely, and it was natural that the cathedral city should be the first refuge of the displaced brethren. There were earthier points of contact, such as the facts that the brethren had distilled the bishop's *aqua vitae*, a potation for medicinal purposes; that its chapel could be used for episcopal audiences; and that the bishop's official could be accommodated there.[3]

Liturgy, and more specifically intercessory prayer, was not far, either, from the minds of the foundress or her advisors, and figured in another letter from Fotehede to Fisher as chancellor of the University and a former fellow of Michaelhouse, about the dangers of pluralism removing the core of college life. A fellow of Michaelhouse, Robert Cutler, having become provost of Rotherham College, wished to retain his fellowship. Fotehede argued against this, not only because Cutler's income as provost disqualified him from doing so, but because the precedent would be evil: 'it shalbe greet hynderaunce of lerning, dekey [decay] of our service and few or none to tary at home to pray for our founder and to kepe his messes [masses]'.[4] Colleges were grounded as much in requirements to pray for the souls of founders and benefactors as upon the promotion of learning, and ticklish questions arose when they displaced ancient foundations similarly enshrining eternal obligations. Local rites of commemoration defined much of late-medieval society, and if they were disrupted effort had to be put into ensuring their continuation.

Such efforts can be seen clearly in the codes of statutes prepared by Fisher for St John's College. The benefactors of the former hospital were to be prayed for by the fellows, who also continued to serve the hospital's chantry in St Sepulchre's church, across the street in Cambridge. When the college received, through the initiative of Cardinal Wolsey, the endowments of the priories of Broomhall (Berkshire) and Higham (Kent), and of the hospital of Ospringe (Kent), their benefactors were added to the list of those to be remembered. In the code of 1524 tables of benefactors were to be affixed to altars in the college chapel, three specially designated altars being named after the priories and Ospringe Hospital. In 1530 three altars are again mentioned with tables of benefactors affixed, but without reference to a special designation. In both codes Ospringe and Higham were to be endowed from college revenues with a chantry priest, who would also teach grammar to local children, to commemorate their benefactors.[5]

Similar efforts to preserve commemorative continuity, and to enhance spectacularly a chantry function, are to be seen in Lady Margaret's statutes of 1506, at the transformation of God's-house into Christ's College. The fellows of Christ's were to pray principally for their foundress and her royal kindred, but also to maintain the chain of prayer for the founder and major benefactors of God's-house; only they might not be paid to serve as chantry priests for other purposes. The fellows of God's-house who continued in the new foundation, however, were permitted to accept stipends to pray for other souls.

The Christ's liturgy was exhaustively detailed in the statutes. Fellows were to celebrate mass four times on Sunday: a mass of the day, of the Holy Trinity, of the Blessed Mary, and of requiem. From Monday to Saturday the masses of the day were to be celebrated together with those of the Blessed Mary and of requiem. On each day a special mass was added: on Monday that of the Angels, on Tuesday that of the Martyrs, on Wednesday that of the Apostles, on Thursday that of the Virgins, on Friday that of the Confessors, and on Saturday that of All Saints. Thus the whole company of the Church was represented in the Christ's College liturgy in a weekly timetable.

We have besides evidence of the wealth of devotional imagery which was to be found at Christ's. In her will Lady Margaret left both fixed and processional crucifixes, which were in fact calvaries depicting Mary and St John as well as the Saviour. She also left communion vessels and images of the Virgin and Child, St Mary Magdalene, St John the Baptist and St George. Among the altar cloths was one depicting St Gregory's vision of the Passion while he was celebrating mass, and other vestments figured the monogram JHS. Both these embroideries witnessed to the special dedication of the college to Christ.[6]

As educational institutions, Christ's and St John's shared the design of Lady Margaret and John Fisher to make them vehicles for the better training of priests. Their liturgical function continued the work of their predecessors, but were there other signs of continuity? God's-house had as its starting point in 1448 its founder's desire to improve the teaching of grammar, which he had noticed was defective in the Midland areas of England. Training people for this task was a uniquely specialised aim for a college in either university. Grammar was the lowest rung of the arts course, albeit a highly technical discipline with its own lectures and disputations. College graduates were mostly studying for a mastership of arts or entry to the higher faculties. To a large extent the specialised aim was honoured only in the breach. The royal licence to found the college of 1 March 1442 had mentioned instruction not only in grammar but also in the other liberal faculties. The agreement of 1451 by which the lector at God's-house, Ralph Barton, was hired is more geared towards general arts subjects than grammar: the lectures were to be in logic and philosophy, but should there be a lack of scholars to hear these, there must at least be a lecture in grammatical, rhetorical or poetic subjects. The extant statutes of God's-house were not sealed until 1495, and they subjected a career in grammar-teaching to detailed conditions: no one having attained his mastership in grammar was to leave to teach it until assured of a salary and an established school where he intended to teach. This was no invitation to set up new schools; and if the condition were not met the graduate might remain at God's-house until he had incepted as a master of arts and completed one year as a regent, or lecturing, master in the university.[7] The Christ's statutes given in 1506 preserved grammar as an independent subject of study, but extended the range of courses to include the whole arts course and theology. Of the forty-three members of God's-house traced by its historian A. H. Lloyd, seventeen are found mentioned as having degrees in Emden's *Biographical Register* of the University. Of these only three were masters of grammar; nine were masters of arts and five were bachelors of theology. As far as can be deduced from meagre records the statutes of Christ's College merely rationalised the position existing at God's-house.[8]

God's-house was an institution whose early development had depended on co-operation between its founder and his London acquaintances and other benefactors in the 1430s. William Bingham was rector of St John Zachary, in the city of London, and two of the principal benefactors of God's-house were John Brokley, alderman and draper, and Johanna Buckland the widow of Richard, collector of customs in the port of London and treasurer of Calais. The assistance of John Fray, chief baron of the exchequer 1437–48, who acquired on Bingham's behalf land in Cambridge to extend God's-house, smoothed the path for the granting of the revenues of alien priories, an important source of the college's income. Later, Bingham's exertions and the efforts of successive proctors of the house gained the protection of the duke of York while preserving the favour of the Lancastrian king. Henry VI's principal role had been to grant licences for the acquisition of properties, and to facilitate the exchange of Bingham's first site in Milne Street for that of the present Christ's College. By 1500, due to the further good management of John Syclyng, who had used his position as a fellow of Corpus to trade with that college to the advantage of God's-house, its financial base was sound, but only sufficient to continue as a relatively small foundation of a proctor and twenty-five scholars.[9]

Lady Margaret was aware that although Henry VI had licensed the college's foundation and given it power to acquire possessions, he had not provided endowments. Both she and John Fisher saw Henry VII as continuing and completing the work of the last Lancastrian king, who, during the brief period of his restoration, had met Henry and his mother.[10] By buying estates which were then transferred to the new college, she, in the words of the letters patent of 1505, 'finished and stablished' Henry VI's work. She also greatly contributed towards enlarging the buildings. Of the original court, the north wall of the north range, the greater part of the chapel, the master's lodge, and the south range were part of her re-foundation. The complete dependence of the college on Margaret's own assets is shown in a letter from Henry Hornby to John Fisher written after her death. At the request of the Master of Christ's Hornby urges Fisher to transfer money to finish the building works, and at the Malton estate to provide 'bernes wherein corn must nedys be putt', since Christ's had not sufficient ready money. John Scott, fellow of God's-house and of the new foundation, was the accountant for these works, and journeyed to London to render his account to Fisher for the interim money supplied. When the whole was complete, on 15 February 1511, Scott delivered his account book to Fisher, receiving from him £269 10s 8d.[11]

In the case of St John's there was greater transformation, because the hospital had had no statutory educational function. In 1280 it had, however, been chosen by the bishop of Ely as a convenient house within which to locate scholars funded by the hospital endowments augmented by the bishop for the purpose. This idea followed a far older precedent: the Collège des Dix-huit in Paris originated in 1180 with a chamber in a hospital reserved for eighteen poor scholars. The Cambridge experiment had not endured, and the bishop had been compelled to separate the communities and their endowments in 1283, resulting in the independent foundation of Peterhouse, the earliest Cambridge college.[12] Nevertheless the hospital of St John became grafted more closely on to the university during its subsequent history. During the fifteenth century the registers of the bishops of Ely, Norwich and Lincoln show that ordinations were performed on the title of the hospital, in the same way as they could be on the title of a college fellowship. It was a common practice for religious houses and hospitals to give credentials in this way to men claiming the right to orders, and in this case it included Cambridge scholars seeking to embark on a career of clerical preferment. Of the 114 people listed between 1416 and 1508, forty-seven only are traceable in Emden's *Biographical Register*. They were mostly ordained as subdeacons or deacons within a short time of reaching the academic level of Questionist, that is taking part in the exercises required to gain a BA. Some, however, were ordinations of quite senior men, for example entering the study of canon law.[13] In 1471 or 1473–4 the hospital had been officially received with its staff into the privileges of the university, to protect it from legal attacks by unnamed laity. In 1485 university masters were taking lodgings within its precincts.[14]

What of the hospital's charitable functions, apart from intercession? The surviving internal accounts for the hospital, 1484–5, give no indication of support of a number of ailing or poor individuals. The obvious explanation is that there were none, and that the brethren were guest-masters and lodging keepers to a handful of graduates and local clergy. On the other hand it may be that detailed accounts were not kept by the hospital officers. Among payments to staff is 2s 6d to Johanna (or Jane) Howlyn of the almshouse (*de domo elemosinario*). She may have been a pauper-servant; or did she manage the almshouse and look after the casual indigent? It should be remembered that there is practically no surviving evidence about poor or sick inmates of the hospital *at any period*. The evidence is all indirect: one or two grants of bed linen, dispensations recalling the number of poor flocking to the hospital for relief, and provisions of statutes for the kinds of people to be received. Absence of references to this kind of charitable activity cannot therefore be taken as definitive evidence of decline, any more than can the skeleton staff of three brethren and double the number of servants.[15] In 1485 the accounts record 2s 6d expended on bread for the poor on St John the Evangelist's day (27 December) and 2s in wine (but not named as for the poor), and immediately afterwards fourteen ells of cloth for the poor, 4s 2d. There are other trivial sums: 'alms for the poor, 2d'; 'for a pauper, one half-penny'; 'to a pauper for his labour, 3d and 2d'; 'making a tombstone for a pauper, 2d'.[16] The hospital's accounts for the period 1505–10, when the process of dissolution was under way, record no such incidental payments, but rogation procession costs and church expenses at Horningsea continue. The payment for St John's Day occurs until 1508, and once it was fully established the college continued to maintain the St John's Day dole into the second half of the twentieth century. What the college did not do was to provide casual relief, or act as an occasional refuge for lodgers such as Guy Ardern, William Pynchbeck, Master William Gedge, or the bishop of Ely's Official. Titles for orders were granted to its own fellows, but not to the unattached members of the University and other clergy for whom the hospital had furnished this necessary qualification. Signs of the immediate local contacts of the brethren with their neighbours in payments 'for the exequies of Henry Somer', 'to Richard Fysher his wife, to bury him withal', were replaced by the grander chantry duties for college benefactors, mostly from areas remote from Cambridge; although the college did take on important local responsibilities at the church of St Sepulchre and at Horningsea. It is hard to say whether the college immediately abrogated the liturgy for townsmen, with which they had been so much concerned in April 1511.[17]

The earliest account of the course of events which led to the foundation of St John's was written up between 1524 and 1535 in the college's register, the Thin Red Book. There Fisher himself is credited with having steered Lady Margaret's bounty away from Westminster Abbey and in the direction of Cambridge University, resulting in the foundation of Christ's. Once this had been achieved, the narrative continues, some doctors of Oxford endeavoured to enlist her services, pointing out the priory of St Frideswide as ripe for conversion into a college, but Fisher again drew her attention to the neglected condition of St John's Hospital in Cambridge.[18] Contact between Margaret and the hospital had taken place soon after she became actively involved in launching Christ's, licence to endow which was granted on 1 May 1505. In the same year are entries in the hospital's accounts concerning payments for petitions and journeys to Lady Margaret and the archbishop of Canterbury when the master of the hospital, William Tomlyn, resigned. The next year payments occur for a visitation by the archbishop and by the bishop of Ely, Richard Redman.[19] To judge from expenses in the accounts for journeys by the brethren to see the master, negotiations proceeded with him at a distance. Writs of subpoena were issued against him to appear to give an account of his administration, before his official deposition in February 1507; and the hospital administration was vested in the hands of Henry Hornby, Fotehede, Dr Robinson and Richard Dyklond, who had received his commission from the archbishop.[20]

The charges in the deposition were the usual ones of corrupt administration, but on what were they founded? It has been shown that the hospital in 1490 was 'maintaining a tight but viable balance of income and expenditure' like most similar medieval institutions. Its income and expenses were then both around £70 a year. At that date it had recently acquired land at Great Bradley in Suffolk, and come to an agreement with the rector and freeholders to enclose a field in two blocks. For this transaction the brethren had presented a cope to the village church. The land became the nucleus of a much larger estate there acquired by the college.[21] In 1505 revenues had sunk to £38, rising to £50 in 1510. In 1510–11 Robert Shorton, the first Master of the college, recorded the names of those who had paid nothing that year because the college was in their debt. The 'debt', amounting to £29, consists in some cases either of vacant property or property taken in hand, but in others like that of the tenant of Clavering (Essex), John Steward, or the farmer of Horningsea (Cambridgeshire), the entry is simply noted *pro debito*. A startling change occurs in 1511–12, when the receipts total £100, farms had been raised, and the debts discharged. Lady Margaret's executors' accounts included repeated sums paid to Shorton for the buildings and other necessary charges. There had been a lack of determined exploitation and of resources to make a speedy recovery, rather than actual spoliation of the revenues. Plate of the hospital had to be redeemed by a succeeding Master, Alan Percy, from the hands of Dr Robinson to whom it had been pledged; but since he was one of the persons who had taken control of the administration in 1507, money advanced by him was presumably part of the effort to restore the hospital's fortunes.[22]

There were however, more serious indications. The executors had to discharge the large sum of £63 6s 8d to redeem a perpetual annuity granted by Tomlyn out of the hospital revenues to Thomas Stuteville, and another smaller life annuity. The brethren had also engaged in fairly large-scale borrowing: John Steward, the tenant at Clavering, had loaned them £20 on 2 February 1503, for which they had mortgaged the property to him and his heiress. He was apparently not satisfied and did not relinquish the tenement, withholding rent until the college settled with him in 1512 for £25. This case, however, may be more complex than it appears. The holding had been leased to Steward in 1501, a condition being that within two years he should make substantial additions to the dwelling house, on pain of payment of £20. Steward must either have met his obligations and loaned the brethren exactly the same sum as the penalty, or have reached a financial accommodation with them. The loan coincided with an outlay by the hospital of the same sum on the purchase of an estate at Upware, Wicken (Cambridgeshire) on 28 May 1503. In this, as in other matters concerning the hospital, Dr William Robinson, the bishop's commissary, was involved: as the executor of John Girton, clerk, he had executed the sale. The affair points to a situation in which a small religious house had become indebted to an over-mighty tenant, while continuing to sustain and increase its landholding.[23]

William Tomlyn, the offending Master, left an undated but full account of various repairs undertaken by him, intermixed with a number of other miscellaneous expenses. It may be that this account, which runs continuously for sixteen pages without any classification, was an attempt by Tomlyn under pressure to make a case for his conduct. Nevertheless it reveals a conscientious adherence to the details of maintenance: roofing and repairs to buildings at Horningsea church and parsonage, St John's Barns in Cambridge, and at Cottenham (Cambridgeshire); two houses bought at Chesterton and Newnham, and three built in St Clement's parish, at Newnham, and at Great Bradley (Suffolk); usual farm expenses in maintaining barns, hedging, and purchase of livestock. In the midst of one page is a note:

memorandum that I William Tomlyn bought to the said Collage an house of one John Baly sumtyme dwellyng in Horningsey, for xxs., the whiche house was this pore places before and sold oute by my predecessore for iiij li., withoute the consent of our foundere [i.e. the bishop of Ely] and felowes at that tyme beyng; the whiche house is letyn for xl yere yeldyng yerely viiis and the whyte [i.e. quit] rent payd as it specyfieth in certeyn endentours betwix Herry Hart and us dwellyng in Hornyngsey.[24]

The bishop of Ely had found the hospital useful as a base in Cambridge for his own affairs, as a body capable of furnishing ordinands with titles for orders, and as a religious community in confraternity with the hospital of St John at Ely which also did him the personal service of distilling his *aqua vitae*. Reluctance to abandon a part of the patronage of his see understandably led to his hesitancy after Lady Margaret's death to honour his agreement with her to surrender the hospital for transformation into a college. If such transformation had to be, he wanted to make the best bargain he could, and he had the support of a number of legal advisors and officials. The bishop's commitment to the livelihoods of the three brethren of the hospital is apparent from his letter to them on 15 December 1510: 'accordinge to my promise made unto you at your last being with me I have endevoured myself to doo the best for you that may lye in me. How be it I now perceyve that suche bulles be obteyned that whether I will or not meanes will be found that ye shalbe removed from your house . . . '. He goes on to assure them that he has arranged good pensions, which indeed continued to be paid in all three cases until the spring of 1513, in two until the autumn, and in one case, that of Christopher Wright, until 1531. Possession of the house was officially granted by the bishop's agent to Henry Hornby, representing the executors, on 20 January 1511, but Fisher had to write to one of the witnesses, Dr Robert Barray, to surrender an obligation which was preventing possession being taken. Barray was summoned to appear before him at Lambeth, with Robert Shorton the newly appointed Master of the college, who had complained. When all obstacles had been surmounted, the bishop finally settled for preservation of his ordinary jurisidiction in his rights as Visitor, with the benefits of the fellows' prayers, and the right to nominate one fellow of the college.[25]

The impression left by the admittedly fragmentary records of the hospital's last years is that of insufficient administrative power rather than dire insolvency or determined spoliation. Lady Margaret's executors inherited lands, a very small quantity of plate, and a collection of seventy-five vestments and chapel furnishings, including an 'olde myghter of Saynt Nicholas' and an image: 'one table of Saynt Johns hedd of alabaster'.[26] They brought in a concentration of wealth and connections denied to the brethren, and by redeeming pledges and discharging debts they were able to remove immediate problems, and make the most of the still solid landed resources which the hospital bequeathed to the college. In much the same way, modern take-overs often presuppose the basic soundness of the concern being absorbed: otherwise there would be little profit in the exercise. The essential fact was that Lady Margaret's agents were able to transcend the local dimension; but the hospital still commanded local affection. Edith Chamber in 1498 granted a tenement to Michaelhouse for the fellows to perform chantry duties for her and her kindred; but she hedged her grant with the precaution that should they fail the duties were to devolve upon the Hospital of St John.[27] Like God's-house it could have continued performing on a restricted scale duties not exactly those intended at its foundation: little evidence exists to show that the late-medieval hospital succoured great numbers of the poor and sick, just as few grammar masters seem to have proceeded from God's-house. Yet the one provided religious services,

corrodies and confraternity for a few individuals, and the opportunity
of some casual relief for the local community, and the other graduates
in arts and theology who took a full part in the life of the University.[28]
What was also of importance to people in the early sixteenth century, as
to their predecessors, was the existence of a house capable of sustaining
intercessory prayers for its benefactors. This obligation was recognised
by the successors, Christ's and St John's Colleges, and formed a large
part of the concerns of their founders.

NOTES

1. St John's College Archives (SJC), DI 05.106.
2. SJC DI 05.105, 22 March; M. Rubin, *Charity and Community in Medieval Cambridge* (Cambridge, 1987), pp. 176, 181, 188 and notes; organ and canopy mentioned in the accounts for repairs by the last Master, William Tomlyn (1498–1507), SJC DI 06.2, p. 11.
3. Rubin, *Charity and Community*, p. 294 ; SJC DI 05.104, DI 02.3, for mention of *aqua vitae*; in the latter, pp. 34, 47–8, recipes for ink and medicines are given.
4. SJC DI 05.102, 6 November ?1508.
5. J. E. B. Mayor (ed.), *Early Statutes of St John's College* (Cambridge, 1859), pp. 274, 310, 337–8; cf. p. 94 (1530).
6. H. Rackham (ed.), *Early Statutes of Christ's College* (Cambridge, 1927), p. 89.
7. Agreement for lectures: printed in A. H. Lloyd, *The Early History of Christ's College, Cambridge* (Cambridge, 1934), pp. 375–7; Statutes: Rackham, *Statutes of Christ's*, p. 27.
8. Lloyd, *Early History of Christ's*, pp. 380–3; A. B. Emden, *A Biographical Register of the University of Cambridge to 1500* (Cambridge, 1963), *passim*.
9. For the details of the acquisitions and defence of properties, and Syclyng's negotiations with Corpus, see Lloyd, *Early History of Christ's*, pp. 46–8, 151–5, 171–88, 208–14. For Bingham's personal connections, see pp. 383–400.
10. For this meeting and its later elaboration, see M. K. Jones and M. G. Underwood, *The King's Mother: Lady Margaret Beaufort, Countess of Richmond and Derby* (Cambridge, 1992), p. 52.
11. F. Woodman, 'Godshouse-hunting', in S. Gorley Putt (ed.), *Christ's College Magazine* 67 (1978), 30–2; Jones and Underwood, *The King's Mother*, pp. 219–26; Hornby to Fisher, SJC DI 05.89, 15 June, n.y.; Accounts for the works, SJC DI 06.1, fos. 19v, 44v.
12. For the origins of Peterhouse see C. Hall and R. Lovatt, 'The site and foundation of Peterhouse', *Proceedings of the Cambridge Antiquarian Society* 78 (1989), 5–46, and see chapter 4 above.
13. SJC ARCH6.12 (references to ordinations by the bishops of Norwich 1416–27 extracted by R. F. Scott, and by the bishops of Lincoln, 1473–1508 extracted by Rev. Canon Foster); ordination lists from the registers of Bishops

Fordham, Bourchier, Grey and Alcock in the *Ely Diocesan Remembrancer*. See on the question of titles to orders, R. N. Swanson, 'Titles to Orders in Medieval English Episcopal Registers', in H. Mayr-Harting and R. I. Moore (eds.), *Studies in Medieval History presented to R. H. C. Davis* (London, 1985), pp. 233–45.

14. Rubin, *Charity and Community*, p. 182. It has been dated *c.*1470: the narrower dating is based upon the fact that the privilege is granted by Thomas Rotherham as chancellor of the university, bishop of Lincoln and keeper of the privy seal. He was bishop 1471–80, chancellor in 1469–71, 1473–9, and keeper 1470–4.

15. SJC D106.9, fo. 5. From the period after the Black Death the normal number of brethren was five, and in the fifteenth century three: Rubin, *Charity and Community*, p. 174.

16. SJC D106.9, fos. 9, 10.

17. SJC D106.9, fo. 5, D102.3, p. 11, D106.2, p. 15. Singing breads in large quantities and wine continued to be bought for the chapel, but the phrase *parochianis nostris* found once in the hospital's accounts for 1485 (D106.9, fo. 8v) does not recur, either in the hospital's accounts 1505–10 or in those of the college. Ardern and Pynchbeck were feoffees of property at Horningsea which was granted to the hospital in 1483 (D26.115–19). Arden cannot be identified for certain with the former fellow of King's Hall, rector of Strethall, Essex 1470–84 and of Upminster 1484–6, nor William Gedge with a fellow of Peterhouse of the same name and period.

18. The Thin Red Book, fos. 61–4, especially 62–3. A fragment of a letter, not dated or signed, but bearing the signet impression of Henry Hornby, survives in St John's College Archives. It is part of a report to Fisher about the condition of the hospital, evidently still relatively unfamiliar to the writer, for it is described as 'the priory or house of St John': SJC D56.30.

19. *Calendar of Close Rolls, 1500–9*, pp. 227–8; *Calendar of Patent Rolls, 1494–1509*, p. 415; SJC D106.10, fos. 5, 12.

20. D106.10, fos. 12, 19; D3.75, deed of deposition, 3 February 1507.

21. Rubin, *Charity and Community*, p. 234; licence to enclose, recorded in a copy of court roll also recording the gift of the cope 1 December 1489, attached to a sealed deed, 26 May 1491, SJC D51.244.

22. SJC D107.1, pp. 1–20; the plate, in various vessels, weighed 154 oz. and was redeemed for £20 10s 8d, ibid., p. 157.

23. Accounts of the executors of Lady Margaret, printed in C. H. Cooper, *Memoir of Lady Margaret, Countess of Richmond and Derby*, pp. 194, 196; Steward's loan: SJC D39.38, 39, 41. No. 39 is a bond to pay Steward £100 on 2 February 1505, without condition, also dated 2 February 1503.

24. SJC D106.2, p. 2. A lease of the property in 1498 states that it had been given away by the Master, Robert Dunham, and the brethren: D26.123.

25. Jones and Underwood, *The King's Mother*, p. 243, n. 38; Fisher to Barray, SJC D56.2; the bishop to the brethren, SJC D105.96; statutes of the college, 1516, Mayor, *Early Statutes of St John's*, p. 394, and statutes of the college

1580, printed in *Fifth Report of the Select Committee on Education* (House of Commons, 1818), p. 460. The right of nomination endured until 1860.

26. Jewels found in St John's College, at the Master's first coming, SJC c7.11, fo. 4v; certain ornaments belonging to the chapel of St John's in Cambridge of the old foundation, ibid., fos. 44–5.

27. SJC d20.61.

28. Syclyng was senior proctor of the University, 1491–2, 1500–1, and proctor of God's-house 1496–1506, and the refoundation was a matter of negotiation between him and Fisher: Emden, *Biographical Register*, p. 572; Lloyd, *Early History of Christ's*, pp. 281–3.

CHAPTER 6

Coventry's 'Lollard' programme of 1492 and the making of Utopia*

P. J. P. Goldberg

At the Michaelmas session of the 1492 leet court of the city of Coventry a series of ordinances were enacted which culminated in the provision that no 'senglewoman' below the age of fifty and capable of working should live by herself, but rather should 'go to seruice till they be maried'. This ordinance appears to be unique to Coventry. The purpose of this present paper is to explore and explain the context in which this legislative programme and this particular ordinance arose. Of no small importance are the broader economic conditions prevailing in later fifteenth-century Coventry, a city experiencing deep recession culminating in the early sixteenth-century crisis made famous by Charles Phythian-Adams's magisterial monograph.[1] Equally important, however, are the changing religious mores, cultural values and gender ideologies of the city's magistrates or leet jurats, members of what turns out to be a divided and embattled mercantile oligarchy. It is our contention here that the Michaelmas 1492 programme, revised and extended at Michaelmas 1495, represents a radical reform manifesto associated with one particular faction characterised by marked Lollard sympathies. The ordinance directed at single women was thus a key plank in a utopian vision of a godly and ordered society in which all knew their place and all worked to the common good.

Constraints of time and space necessarily limit our exploration of the broader cultural and socio-economic contexts of the 1492 legislation. Phythian-Adams has observed, for example, that the 1492 ordinance concerning single women 'was part of a campaign against harlots in the city'.[2] We might also consider broader shifts in attitudes to sexuality and sexual morality. Similarly we should consider the changing role of civic government and the civic elite's self-perception of their responsibilities as magistrates.[3] Our preliminary discussion focusses on but one facet of this last, viz. the impact of a contracting economy on the sexual division of labour. This allows us to explore the ideologies of gender that follow from such a division and are reflected in the regulation of work. More specifically, it allows us to recover the gender ideology of Coventry's rulers in 1492 and 1495.

Economic contraction during the later fifteenth century led to increased competition for employment. Women in particular seem to have been disadvantaged.[4] This marginalisation of women within the 'public' economy of towns is most conspicuously reflected in guild ordinances designed to restrict the employment of women within workshops or the capacity for widows to manage workshops in their own right. Such regulation is unusual, but where it was deemed necessary demonstrates that the *status quo ante* allowed women a much fuller scope. Ordinances designed to outlaw the employment of women within the workshop are in fact largely confined to weavers' guilds and reflect the particular vulnerability of the industry to the changing economy of the second half of the fifteenth century. This was certainly true of Coventry. Of interest here is the language used to justify the regulation. Best known is the Bristol ordinance of 1461 which claimed that the employment of 'wyfes, doughtours and maidens' had the result that 'many and divers of the Kynges liege people, likkely men to do the Kyng seruis in his warris and in defence of his lond, and sufficiently lorned in the seid Crafte, gothe vagaraunt and vnoccupied and may not haue ther labour to ther levyng'. A discourse of 'common profit' is thus deployed to justify radical action, though pragmatically wives of current members were exempt.[5] Within this discourse, unemployed weavers are represented not as the able-bodied indigent, but as manhood wrongly deprived of labour. The implication here already is that to 'haue ther labour to ther levyng' is the prerogative of the male, not the female gender. The equivalent provision at Coventry in 1453, likewise directed at wives, daughters and female servants, states merely that their labour 'is a geyn all goode order and honeste'.[6]

The rationale for the 1511 bar on women in the Norwich worsted weaving craft was that 'thei be nott of sufficient poure to werke the said worsteddes as thei owte to be wrought'.[7] A 'common profit' implication lurks behind this assertion, for the supposedly unsatisfactory workmanship of such workers implicitly explained the decline in trade, but the gender implications are also similar; men are naturally suited to physical labour, women are not. Whether such a notion would have been really credible only a few decades earlier – in 1446 Elizabeth Baret had been admitted in her own right to the city's franchise as a worsted weaver – is questionable.[8] The assertion would still have helped shape subsequent thought and belief at least among the guild's (now exclusively male) members and the city governors with whom the ordinance was registered. Probably it was already credible at the time it was made.

As more and more occupations were deemed appropriate only to men, women's work identity narrowed; women became increasingly associated with the 'domestic', itself in part an invention of the later fifteenth century. Even so far as women did find employment within the 'public' economy, much of their work could be understood as an extension of the domestic.[9] This was true of the laundress, the huckster supplying foodstuffs and household essentials such as candles, the upholder or vendor of second-hand clothing, the tapster (loosely translated as barmaid), the seamstress, the spinster, the midwife, and even the sexworker.[10] The spinster is a particularly telling case since her labour was so essential to the textile industry, yet her position within the economy was rendered so marginal. We may understand this on a number of levels. Spinning was *par excellence* woman's work and the distaff a manifestation of her gender; when Adam took up his spade to delve, it was to her distaff that Eve turned. Because so much part of their gender identity, medievals saw spinning as *natural* to women; proverbially spinning, weeping and deceit were all part of a woman's birthright.[11]

The spinster then was viewed not as skilled worker, but specifically as woman. Her conditions of employment were safeguarded by no guild. Rather civic government attempted to protect her from the worst excesses of exploitation very much as a work of charity. The logic for this is not hard to determine. The woman who supported herself by spinning necessarily lacked a husband. Because her labour was proper to her gender, it was honest. Consequently she both merited and was in need of a guardian, a role that civic governors seem willingly to have adopted. The Worcester civic ordinances of 1467, for example, outlawed the payment of truck wages to spinsters and other poor textile workers.[12] The authorities in Coventry repeatedly attempted to regulate the weight of the wool that constituted the spinsters' piece-rate. We find ordinances in 1449, 1451, 1513, 1518 and 1530; on these last three occasions truck wages were also prohibited.[13] Employers from the same level of society as provided the civic government can also be found leaving bequests to their spinsters as if a work of charity. Alice Chellow, a York merchant's widow, left 4d in 1466 to 'each poor women who served me in the past (*antea*) by spinning'.[14] Substantial bequests of spinning wheels to support poor women can likewise be found in early sixteenth-century Coventry.[15]

Other indicators of women's exclusion from a whole range of remunerative employments are more oblique. Female servants are regularly found employed alongside male in a whole variety of households in the first part of the fifteenth century; through the second half of the century female servants are increasingly confined to mercantile rather than craft households. In the last part of the century craft households came to be characterised by the employment of male servants, mercantile households by the employment of female servants.[16] This suggests a change in the nature of female service. The exclusion of women servants from craft workshops denied younger, unmarried women exposure to work skills that might subsequently be useful in marriage. The confinement of female service to mercantile households, moreover, changed its meaning; it ceased to fulfil so clear an economic function, but took on instead domestic and status meanings. For mercantile employers, the possession of numbers of female servants was a mark of social rank. Indeed it is precisely because these servants had no significant economic function beyond the household, and hence were comparatively costly to employ, that they came to take on this role. It may also follow that by employing numbers of female servants, these well-to-do male households were protecting their own wives from any physical contribution to housework. Female service would thus have become domestic service, and domestic service, menial service. Conversely, the artisanal workshop became a very masculine place.[17]

Widows also became increasingly unlikely to continue to run workshops or businesses previously managed jointly with their husbands, a process that appears a consequence of social pressures rather more than actual regulation.[18] The underlying logic was that, within a stagnant market, widows by continuing to run workshops deprived skilled young men access to the same. The widow's years of practical experience came to count for nothing when set against the formal craft training of the male ex-apprentice. The implications are as we have seen in relation to servants. A binary gender ideology was being forged in which domestic labour was women's work; labour for the market and for profit was men's work.

These changes are also manifest in the built environment. The creation, in more well-to-do urban households during the course of the fifteenth century, of a multiplicity of rooms beyond the basic structure of hall, parlour and kitchen permitted space to be allocated to more specific purposes.[19] The effect was to create social distance and even perhaps the renegotiation of roles within the household. Thus servants could be assigned their own room or rooms and so need no longer share the same sleeping space as their employers. If we are to believe *The Italian Relation* then in the most well-to-do households at the end of the century servants were eating separately and partaking of plainer fare.[20] At the same time, the shop, the location of manufacture within the artisanal household, might become more physically detached – by the erection of solid walls or partitions – from the family's living space. As a consequence, we may suggest, female members of the household became more marginal to the activities of the shop, more obviously associated with 'domestic' activities, and less publicly visible.[21] Such an understanding of service as an appropriate form of women's work underpins the provisions of the 1492 Coventry ordinance that single women should go into service.

Thus far we have attempted to suggest something of the gender ideology of Coventry's governors in respect of work. The context of economic recession has already been outlined by Phythian-Adams. He describes a long history of economic and demographic contraction, a consequence of falling demand for textiles, going back to at least the middle of the fifteenth century. The early 1490s appear to stand at the end of one phase of recession, though this would hardly have been obvious to contemporaries. For them the city was characterised by vacant and derelict buildings and falling rental values.[22] It is now necessary to consider the political context of the 1492 ordinances. We have already suggested that Coventry was politically divided during the later years of the fifteenth century. This was manifested in a long-running dispute over enclosure that has been chronicled by Mary Dormer Harris.[23] It is worthy of note that it was the city council of 1495 that effected the final ruination of Laurence Saunders, the principal critic of the city governors' abuse of their control of the city's commons.[24]

We know a great deal about who governed at the time of the ordinances from the Coventry Leet Book. The mayor that year was one William Rowley, mercer. Shannon McSheffrey has described his wife Alice as 'the most prominent of the female Lollards in Coventry'.[25] Rowley was himself implicated in heresy trials conducted in 1511–12, as were a group of other leading citizens. These were the draper, Thomas Bonde (mayor 1498), the mercers Richard Coke (mayor 1486 and 1503) and Thomas Bayly (mayor 1487), John Wigston (mayor 1491), William Pysford (mayor 1501), Richard Smyth (mayor in 1508), Thomas and William Forde (mayor 1497), and the capper, John Darlyng. To this group of civic magistrates we should add James Preston, vicar of St Michael's, the civic church, between 1488 and his death in 1507.[26] Their heretical leanings would already have been established by this date; it is the contention here that the ordinances mark a governmental coup by a close-knit group of Lollard sympathisers, indeed that the ordinances represent a Lollard programme in the tradition of the Lollard bill of 1410.[27]

There are two reasons for thinking that this group of elite males engineered what amounted to a coup in 1492 and that the ordinances of the Michaelmas leet of that year constitute in effect a radical reform agenda. Firstly, though several seem to have been active in civic government from at least the later 1480s, they came to pack the council chamber as a group specifically at the time of the 1492 ordinances. Thomas Forde is first recorded as an elector in 1481. He was joined by Richard Coke (sheriff in 1480) the next year and Thomas Bayly (chamberlain 1476, sheriff 1478) three years on. William Rowley first appears as an elector in 1485, and Richard Smyth and John Darlyng in 1486. William Forde likewise first appeared in 1491. William Pysford was appointed a jurat only at the Michaelmas leet of 1492 and Thomas Bonde was elected sheriff at the same time.[28] This pattern of appointment to civic office may appear serendipitous rather than the product of calculated political intrigue, but our second piece of evidence suggests otherwise.

In most years it would seem that there was a very high degree of overlap between the mayor's electors and the leet jurats, the two groups constituting the senior part of the Common Council or Forty-Eight. The composition of these two bodies changed only slightly from one year to the next. During the 1480s and first part of the 1490s it was normal for only a couple of new names (as in 1483, 1487, 1489, 1493, and 1494) to be recorded each mayoral year, invariably to fill vacancies created by deaths.[29] Thus in 1484, 1485, and 1486 three new names were recorded, but in 1488 and 1490 only one, and none in 1482. In contrast the composition of these bodies in 1492 is completely aberrant. The electors for William Rowley included five new names and the Michaelmas leet jury included a further six new names. Of these, only two (Roger Sutton and John Matthewe) are named as part of the Forty-Eight in 1484 and hence represented simple promotions from the junior ranks of civic government. Matthewe evidently had a political career for some years after. So too did Sutton (an elector in 1508 and 1510), Thomas Wardelowe (mayor in 1506), Edward Barbour, Richard Jakson (mayor in 1502), Roger Wode (albeit only very briefly as an elector for Jakson), Roger Chambre and William Pysford (mayor in 1501), but all only after an interval of several years.[30] Again this is a departure from the normal pattern that saw men serve as electors and jurats on a regular basis from their first appointment. Of the other 'new' names, William Alen seems to have had a career as the city mace bearer, but John Reynold and Alexander Horsley remained comparatively obscure.[31]

The implication of these observations is that a number of comparatively youthful men were advanced somewhat precociously to civic office in 1492, most of whom had to wait several years before they served again.[32] It is tempting to conclude that these younger and comparatively inexperienced men would have been more willing to support a radical political programme than was necessarily true of more experienced members of the civic government. The particular sympathies of these groups clearly merit further research. Thus if we turn specifically to the composition of the jury recorded for the Michaelmas leet, we may note a number of absences of experienced and long-serving civic magistrates, viz. Richard Colyns, Robert Colman, John Sissell and Robert Smyth. Despite the presence of several senior magistrates and a number of familiar names, the jury of the Michaelmas leet could not, therefore, but have appeared to contemporaries as highly irregular.

The Lollard sympathies of this group have recently been challenged by McSheffrey. In contrast to earlier writers, notably Imogen Luxton, she argues that the accusations of heresy contained in the depositions from the 1511 trials 'are based either on hearsay and rumour or on short conversations about vernacular books', and that these were instead 'men who were active in religious affairs, pious, and interested in vernacular devotion, but who were orthodox'.[33] An alternative reading of the evidence would put less weight on the artificial distinction between heresy, a clerical construct, and orthodoxy, and the apparent contradiction between the alleged interest these men showed in Lollard writings and the apparently orthodox references to Mary and the saints, and to provision for post-mortem masses contained in their wills.[34] 'Lollardy' represents a particular set of values rather than a specific creed, and a pronounced sympathy for these Lollard values need not be incompatible with some provision for orthodox institutions.[35] But there is another dimension to this apparent conflict that McSheffrey does not consider. Suspected Lollards often seem willing to renounce various heretical beliefs when brought before the diocesan, only to revert to their earlier practices once dismissed.[36] There is every reason to believe that the survival of Lollardy to the very eve of the Reformation owed much to the willingness of Lollard supporters outwardly to conform. The suggestion here, then, is that this group of leading citizens in their capacity as householders, and hence public representatives of their households, deflected direct accusations of heresy by outwardly conforming; in at least two cases, those of Alice Rowley and '*Magistra* Cooke', wife to Richard Coke, that conformity did not extend to members of their household.[37] As John Thomson has noted, moreover, such conformity would not have been difficult, since the Coventry sect treated the Eucharist as commemorative and hence objected to the doctrine of transubstantiation rather than the celebration of the mass *per se*.[38] Another reason why the clerical authorities should have held back from launching an attack on prominent figures within the government of this episcopal city is simply that by 1511 many of this group, including Rowley, were already dead. The potential for social disharmony consequent upon an attack on a few remaining elderly and highly respected members of the city's political elite was surely considered too high a price.[39]

The case for believing this group to be sympathetic to Lollard ideas has been most forcefully put by Luxton. The only direct evidence to counter this view is the observation by Joan Warde, a friend and convert of Alice Rowley, that she left Coventry out of fear (*metu*) of William Rowley.[40] Rowley's antagonism to Joan Warde may have been personal – she was of lower social rank – rather than religious, but most likely it was politic. Such a conspicuous friendship between women of different social rank might well have provoked comment and so drawn attention to Alice Rowley's religious sympathies. (Alice was herself clearly suspected of heretical views sometime before the 1511–12 trials.)[41] This would have been potentially threatening to the ambitions of a man about to take office as mayor.

Luxton argues that a marked interest in vernacular scriptures is characteristic of this group more generally. In particular she points to Richard Cooke's bequest of two English bibles and the evidence for Thomas Forde's possession of a book of the Old Testament. McSheffrey is correct to argue that this did not necessarily constitute evidence for heretical beliefs, but this is how contemporaries would have understood it. The choice of reading, moreover, was essentially unlike that of other devout catholic book owners. This then is evidence of clear Lollard sympathies. Interestingly, one member of the group, William Pysford, took his interest in vernacular scripture still further through his patronage of the Corpus Christi Play.[42]

We shall now examine in detail the ordinances of the Michaelmas leet. These begin with an order for the removal of all pigsties from within the city walls. This might appear a simple reiteration or elaboration of an ordinance of 1444, an instrument to enhance the cleanliness and safety of the streets, but essentially unrelated to the provisions that follow.[43] There are two reasons for believing otherwise. First, there is a sense that the group of ordinances from this in respect of pigsties to that addressed to 'senglewomen' forms part of the same legislative agenda. The clue is in the wording. The first begins 'Hit is ordeyned at þis present lete'. The following ordinance commences 'It is also ordeyned'. The subsequent four clauses repeat merely the 'also'. Only with the next ordinance, concerning the hatmakers, is there a return to a version of the original formulation, viz. 'Also at þis lete is ordeyned'. To use an analogy drawn from modern punctuation conventions, the first two provisions are separated by at most a semicolon, the next five only by commas, but there is a full-stop at this point signalled by the repetition of both 'is ordeyned' and 'þis lete'. Second, to the medieval imagination, the subject of all these ordinances is essentially the same; the ordinance against pigsties serves in effect as a preamble to the legislation that follows.

I have elsewhere described the rationale for a York ordinance of 1301 which subsumed within the same paragraph provisions against pigs wandering the streets and prostitutes plying their trade within the city walls.[44] Pigs, within the medieval imagination, were variously associated with the sins of gluttony and lust.[45] It is hard not to conclude that precisely the same mental bracketing operated in Coventry: pigs, like women 'of evell name', constitute a public nuisance by their free passage through the streets. The one constitutes a form of material pollution, the other moral pollution. The remedy effected by the 1492 ordinance was to bar the keeping of pigsties. This is precisely the same remedy as is directed against the category 'senglewomen' living by themselves: 'And that euery such persone resceyve eny such persones, or set them eny house or Chambre, to lese at þe first defalt xx s, at ij^{de} defalt xl s & at þe iij^{de} defalt to be comyt to prison.' These parallel provisions thus sandwich the radical legislative programme of the Michaelmas leet.

The five-point programme is arranged hierarchically. It begins with a clause addressed to 'eny man of worship within þis Citie that hath be Maire ... shirrif or other officer or comiener'. There follows an ordinance directed at guilds employing priests, but which is concerned with the conduct of those priests. The third clause is addressed to householders, but concerns the lodging of 'eny Tapster, or Woman of evell name'.[46] The subsequent clause is directed at these same tapsters, a term that approximates to the modern barmaid, and relates to the receiving of (implicitly male) servants and apprentices. The fifth and final clause addresses 'senglewomen', but concludes, as we have seen, with a provision in respect of 'persons' by which once again householders are implied. We thus have a status hierarchy, viz. civic magistrate, guild, householder, household dependant, woman who ought to be (but is not) subject to household authority. We also have something akin to a gender hierarchy, viz. male, cleric, woman.[47] The point is not so much that these hierarchies were consciously contrived, but rather that they are so deeply embedded within the culture that they inevitably surface as organising principles. Thus the last clause is directed at the single woman, although its intended audience was as much the (implicitly male) householder. The clear intention of these ordinances, then, was a thoroughgoing reformation of Coventry society literally from the top down.

The language of the ordinances is the language of sin. They constitute a sort of lay sermon targeted particularly against the sin of lechery. Usury, drunkenness and, in respect of servants to their employers, disobedience are also noticed, but these are of secondary concern. The lay governors of Coventry thus appropriated a clerical discourse, but more significantly also appropriated the authority of the clergy to exercise jurisdiction in matters of sexual morality. Indeed they claimed this authority not merely over the lay population, but also over guild priests. Guild priests were thus doubly subject to lay control, first through the guilds by which they were employed and second through the civic magistrates who here legislated not just for craft guilds, but for religious confraternities too. This discourse of sin constructs, nevertheless, a specifically lay magisterial understanding of the evils that beset the city.[48] The first ordinance is concerned with the reputation and good name of those who comprised the governing council. The third and fourth ordinances implicitly equate the female vendor of ale (tapster) with the sexworker. The fourth ordinance also sees the tapster as a threat to the authority of the master over his servants, the ideology here being that also articulated in apprenticeship contracts.[49]

Before the final ordinance there is arguably little that is radical about the individual provisions. (The clause relating to guild priests is no more than an injunction and sanctions are not specified.) Their revolutionary nature comes about both from the inclusion of the final ordinance ('Also that no sengelwomen . . . ') and from the fact that, rather than constituting piecemeal and essentially reactive legislation, the whole forms part of a coherent legislative programme.[50] As has already been intimated, this programme is anticipated, and in some ways encapsulated, in the preceding ordinance against the keeping of pigsties within the city walls.

It is metaphorically a programme about cleaning up the city. But it is also a programme about containment and domesticity. Pigs are not to be kept because they cause a nuisance when they escape their confines and run through the city. Guild priests are to be contained, the ordinance directing them 'to kepe the quer dayly'. Tapsters and other women of ill repute are to be contained through being deprived of lodgings (in much the same way as the problem of pigs might be resolved by a ban on pigsties). Servants and apprentices are to be contained: 'no Tapster nor oþer persone frohensfforth resceyue nor fauour eny mannes prentes or seruaunt'. Finally, women are to be contained.

The last ordinance in the sequence decreed that all able-bodied women categorised as 'senglewoman' below the age of fifty 'go to seruice to they be maried'. The force of the term 'senglewoman' here is to describe women who had no ties of dependency to a spouse or parent, implicitly younger women who had left home or were orphaned or older women who had either not married or been widowed – a view strengthened by the substitution of 'Maide & sole woman' in a revised version of this ordinance three years later.[51] The implication is that daughters living at home or married women were already contained by reason of being subject to the authority of a father or husband. It was therefore with the 'ungoverned' woman that the city governors were here concerned. Clearly such women were perceived to be a problem, first because they fell outside the ideal of household government, but second because their activities implicitly threatened the good order of the city. These were women 'in good hele & myghty in body to labour', but they were contained neither within service (a legitimate form of female labour), nor within marriage (where their labour might contribute to the good ordering of the household). In retrospect we can locate this concern within the context of a rapidly contracting economy that was simply incapable of providing adequate paid employment for the working woman, just as we can suggest that the marked imbalance in the numbers of adult males to females recorded a generation later would have meant that numbers of women would have been unable to find marriage partners even had they wanted them.[52] A contemporary magisterial perspective was probably rather different. Just as medicine taught that disease was a product of an imbalance of the bodily humours, so the cankers afflicting Coventry were a product of disharmony within the body politic. The remedy was to restore society to a proper order of social and gender relations, operating according to a puritanical ethic of hard work and clean living.

But disease, to continue the medical analogy, was not solely a product of an imbalance between the humours. Disease was also a product of divine intervention. The Coventry legislation of 1492 was thus designed to restore divine favour, for God watched over the city.[53] The economic and social dislocation that characterised Coventry by this date would necessarily have been seen as a consequence of divine displeasure at sin. This explains the concern of the legislative programme to reform the city from the highest social echelons to the lowest. The mayor and his brother aldermen and councillors had not only to set an example of exemplary behaviour, but also to be seen to set such an example. The mere suspicion of sexual misconduct, rather than the deed itself, forms the basis of the provisions contained within the first ordinance. Just as devout burgesses could be voluble in their criticism of clergy who failed to abide by the Church's own teaching on clerical conduct – and the ordinance directed at guild priests clearly reflects such a concern – so it was important that civic leaders were seen to conform to their own bourgeois standards of sexual morality. Likewise householders had a responsibility to keep orderly households and so were bound to refuse accommodation to suspect women. At the same time, order was to be extended to the ungoverned woman, who could not be trusted to discipline herself, by demanding that all such women find themselves masters. Thus the bourgeois utopian ideal of the well-ordered city was to be restored. The governors governed as godly magistrates; householders headed sober and industrious households; wives were obedient to their husbands; servants were dutiful to their masters; the lowly respected their superiors; the gender hierarchy was observed.

The last, and most radical, of the 1492 ordinances was revised exactly three years later. This suggests, unsurprisingly, that it was difficult to enforce, but it is also evidence for something of a re-enactment of the 1492 coup. It is very striking that most of the more senior jurats at the 1495 Michaelmas leet were the same as had approved the original 1492 ordinances.[54] There were also three of the same significant absences – Colman was a jurat this time – and in the cases of William Taillour and the Lollard sympathiser Richard Smyth, their appointment as jurats on both occasions occurs during an interval of comparative inactivity within otherwise long political careers. To a more modest degree than was true of 1492, the year also saw the elevation of a larger than usual number of new names to civic office as elector or jurat. Of five new names, four served as jurats at the Michaelmas leet, of whom one, John Folshill, is otherwise obscure, and two others, Thomas Bonde and Richard Lansdale, may be identified as Lollard sympathisers from the 1511–12 heresy proceedings.[55] Once again, it must be concluded that the composition of the 1495 Michaelmas leet jury was anything but routine.

The revised version of the 1492 ordinance directed at single women lowered the upper age limit from fifty years to forty, no doubt to exclude numbers of widows of sufficient means who did not wish to compromise their modest autonomy but, more importantly, it required only that the women to whom the ordinance was addressed live with 'an honest persone' who could answer for them. Such women were still to be contained within the household, but the bonds of patriarchy were less rigidly secured. In both instances we see a translation from the home on to the community as a whole of the power relationship between the genders so favoured by well-to-do Lollards. The sort of patriarchal relations found in St Paul's Epistles, owned by William Rowley's widow Alice, or which might be suggested from the ownership of the same Epistles, the Acts, and the Commandments by Richard Lansdale and later his widow Joan Smyth, became the model for society as a whole. This Lollard perspective on gender relations is manifest in the organisation of Coventry's Lollards into three separate conventicles comprising men, married couples and women respectively.[56] It is likewise hinted at in the provisions for the hospitals founded by Thomas Bonde and William Forde. In both instances a number of suitable poor men were supported, but they were looked after by a woman specifically appointed to this task.[57]

The revision of the 1492 ordinance does not occur in isolation even though separated from its original context. Rather it appears as part of a new reform programme of the 1495 Michaelmas leet.[58] This comprises three linked clauses, thus: 'They woll, ordeyn & conferme the ordennance afore tyme made . . . fferther they woll and ordeyn . . . And also þat . . . '. The first two clauses concern office holding and vagrancy respectively. Again the ordering of the material appears not to be accidental reflecting both a social hierarchy – viz. social elite, householders, singletons – and a gender hierarchy. Again the first clause concerns the obligations and responsibilities of the governing class: persons of substance are to serve their city as office holders when called upon to do so. The second clause similarly is as much about the responsibilities of households as it is about vagrants: all 'vacabundes & beggers myghty in body' are to leave the city, and no one is to shelter such persons unless they are able to justify their actions. As with pigs in the 1492 ordinances, the city was to be cleansed by abolishing the problem. The revised clause concerning single women thus once more appears within the context of a cleansing. The very next ordinance, indeed, concerns the making of pavements, an obligation that falls to the householder. The Easter leet had also ordained that shopkeepers in the Drapery should 'swep & make clene wekely before theire shopes'.[59]

The concern with 'vacabundes & beggers myghty in body' was not entirely new; a major drive against 'theves, riottours, vacabundes and suspect persones' was instigated in 1489 in response to a directive from the crown.[60] The emphasis in 1495 was different, however. The king's letter of 1489 was primarily concerned with illicit gaming conducted under the cover of darkness. It made no mention of the sturdy beggar. The 1495 ordinance, however, mentions neither gaming nor illicit activities carried on at night, but is concerned solely with the 'vacabund or begger' and those who harbour the same. We have here then an implicit distinction between those who beg, though capable of work – 'myghty in body' – and those who beg because they are unable to work.[61] The economic imperative of depression and a scarcity of employment is thus seen not as the cause of vagrancy, but rather as a consequence. In a godly city where all who are able labour honestly, prosperity will follow.

There are reasons for believing that some of the younger members of the Michaelmas 1495 leet jury may have been particularly favourably disposed to thinking in terms of this dichotomy. The corollary of chastising the sturdy beggar was to provide for the 'deserving' poor. Thomas Bonde and William Forde were founders of hospitals in 1506 and 1529 respectively. Forde's Hospital, arranged as it is around a very narrow courtyard, represents an unusual plan, but the imposing street elevation makes a very deliberate statement. Forde's foundation was soon after augmented by William Pysford, a Lollard sympathiser, though not present at the 1495 leet, and John Wigston's close kinsman William further altered this foundation.[62] As mayor in 1501 Pysford also established a civic poor box, symbolically placed in the civic council chamber in St Mary's Hall, and to which Richard Cooke was one of the two first donors.[63] The Corpus Christi guild, the junior of the city's two great guilds whose members included younger men within the lower and middling ranks of civic office holding, likewise provided for 'mendyaunts' from its rental income.[64] The 'deserving' nature of the poor to be provided for is clearly demonstrated by the example of Bonde's hospital. The poor men here were to be drawn from the ranks of the Trinity guild, the senior of the city's two elite guilds.[65]

By the end of the fifteenth century urban magistrates were beginning to think more in terms of binary polarities. We see, for example, the creation of social distance between the governing elite and the governed, between master and servant, between resident and outsider. The poor, previously an amorphous group, came increasingly to be categorised as deserving and undeserving. The former were worthy objects of charity, but the latter were identified as disruptive and subject to regulation and discipline. Women likewise became part of this binary view. The gender ideology we may glimpse is one that imagines women to be either virtuous or whores. Such a binary ideology is implicit in the punning reference in an opposition bill of 1495 to Coventry's mythic benefactress Godiva as 'Dame goode Eve'.[66] These binaries were building blocks in a magisterial programme of reform. The case of Coventry in 1492 is exceptional in that it constitutes an actual programme that anticipates by a generation the sort of radical agenda described by Lyndal Roper for Augsburg.[67] As in the latter example, this was a programme enacted by godly magistrates, sure in the conviction that they were doing God's work. Thus in the very year that Columbus (re)discovered the New World for the Old, William Rowley and his Lollard associates were driving out swine in their struggle to build Utopia in Coventry.[68]

NOTES

* I am grateful to Shannon McSheffrey for reading this paper in draft.
1. C. Phythian-Adams, *Desolation of a City: Coventry and the Urban Crisis* (Cambridge, 1979).
2. Phythian-Adams, *Desolation*, p. 87 n. 41. For divergent discussion of civic policy towards prostitution see R. M. Karras, *Common Women: Prostitution and Sexuality in Medieval England* (New York, 1996); P. J. P. Goldberg, 'Pigs and Prostitutes: Streetwalking in Comparative Perspective', in K. L. Lewis, N. J. Menuge and K. M. Phillips (eds.), *Young Medieval Women* (Stroud, 1999), pp. 172–93.
3. For a discussion of changing attitudes to order and discipline see especially M. K. McIntosh 'Local Change and Community Control in England', *Huntington Library Quarterly* 49 (1986), 219–42, and *eadem*, *Controlling Misbehaviour in England, 1370–1600* (Cambridge, 1998). Cf. also B. A. Hanawalt and B. R. McCree, 'The Guilds of *Homo Prudens* in Late Medieval England', *Continuity and Change* 7 (1992), 163–79. For the changing relationship between civic government and craft guilds see H. Swanson, 'The Illusion of Economic Structure: Craft Guilds in Late Medieval English Towns', *Past and Present* 121 (1988), 29–48; P. J. P. Goldberg, 'Craft Guilds, The Corpus Christi Play and Civic Government', in S. Rees Jones (ed.), *The Government of Medieval York: Essays in Commemoration of the 1396 Royal Charter*,

Borthwick Studies in History 3 (York, 1997), pp. 141–63. For indications of increasing parental influence over courtship and matrimony see P. J. P. Goldberg, *Women, Work, and Life Cycle: Women in York and Yorkshire c. 1300–1520* (Oxford, 1992), pp. 203–79; S. McSheffrey, '"I will never have none ayenst my faders will": Consent and the Making of Marriage in the Late Medieval Diocese of London', in C. M. Rousseau and J. T. Rosenthal (eds.), *Women, Marriage, and Family in Medieval Christendom* (Kalamazoo, 1998), pp. 153–74.

4. For a more detailed discussion of much of what follows, see Goldberg, *Women, Work, and Life Cycle*, pp. 82–202, 324–61.

5. F. B. Bickley (ed.), *The Little Red Book of Bristol*, 2 vols. (Bristol, 1900), II, pp. 127–8.

6. Phythian-Adams, *Desolation*, pp. 87–8, 327.

7. W. Hudson and J. C. Tingey (eds.), *Records of the City of Norwich*, 2 vols. (Norwich, 1906), II, p. 378.

8. Norfolk Record Office, NCR Case 17, shelf c, 1.

9. The marginalisation of women workers is part of a broader pattern. Contemporary craft guild ordinances and common petitions likewise attempt to protect the employment of native-born males by excluding aliens.

10. For a discussion of the way in which women who provided sexual services for payment can be understood in these terms, see Goldberg, 'Pigs and Prostitutes'.

11. R. T. Davies (ed.), *Medieval English Lyrics: A Critical Anthology* (London, 1963), p. 135.

12. J. Toulmin Smith (ed.), *English Gilds*, EETS o.s. 40 (1870), pp. 383–4.

13. M. D. Harris (ed.), *The Coventry Leet Book*, EETS o.s. 134–5, 138, 146 (1907–13), pp. 243, 255, 640, 658, 707.

14. York, Borthwick Institute of Historical Research, Prob. Reg. 4 fo. 72.

15. Phythian-Adams, *Desolation*, p. 88 n. 50.

16. This observation is based on a study of wills and poll tax evidence for York: Goldberg, *Women, Work, and Life Cycle*, pp. 194–202.

17. Cf. M. Wiesner, 'Guilds, Male Bonding and Women's Work in Early Modern Germany', *Gender and History* 1 (1989), 125–37.

18. Cf. Phythian-Adams, *Desolation*, pp. 91–2.

19. This is reflected in the evidence of standing buildings and in the listing of rooms in probate inventories.

20. C. Sneyd (ed.), *A Relation . . . of the Island of England . . . About the Year 1500*, Camden Society o.s. 37 (1847), p. 25.

21. This is reflected in the depositions made in the London consistory in 1472–3 (Smyth c. Langtoft): S. McSheffrey (ed.), *Love and Marriage in Late Medieval London* (Kalamazoo, 1995), pp. 59–65.

22. Phythian-Adams, *Desolation*, pp. 33–9. These are conspicuous signs of a contracting population, but, since towns were dependent on attracting migrants to sustain their populations, they are also indicators of a contracting economy.

23. M. D. Harris, 'Laurence Saunders, Citizen of Coventry', *English Historical Review* 9 (1894), 633–51.
24. Ibid., 646–51. The hostility of the 1495 council is implicit in the ruling in favour of St John's Hospital against 'certen evell disposed persones' who had broken up a close belonging to the hospital and 'hit claymen & vsen as their comien'. The jury appointed to rule in this dispute included Richard Lansdale, and the whole matter is recorded in some detail in the Leet Book: Harris (ed.), *Coventry Leet Book*, pp. 570–1.
25. McSheffrey, *Gender and Heresy*, p. 30.
26. He too was implicated in the trials of 1511–12 and, from the evidence of his will, was closely associated with the Fordes, Coke and Pysford: ibid., pp. 37, 39, 43.
27. Heresy had been detected in Coventry in 1486, but Bishop Hales was clearly unsuccessful in rooting it out, since the later trial evidence demonstrates continuity of practice from at least that date. Alice Rowley claimed to have been a Lollard for some twenty years at her trial and this can be corroborated by other evidence that shows her to have been active since at least 1491. The connections between this group, which included ties of marriage and kinship, have been described by Imogen Luxton and Shannon McSheffrey: J. A. F. Thomson, *The Later Lollards 1414–1520* (Oxford, 1965), pp. 104, 108; McSheffrey, *Gender and Heresy*, pp. 31, 37–44; I. Luxton, 'The Lichfield Court Book: A Postscript', *Bulletin of the Institute of Historical Research* 44 (1971), 120–5. See also Harris (ed.), *Coventry Leet Book*, pp. 528, 532, 541–2, 582, 588, 600–01, 619. For the bill of 1410 see M. Aston, '"Caim's Castles": Poverty, Politics and Disendowment', in R. B. Dobson (ed.), *The Church, Politics and Patronage in the Fifteenth Century* (Gloucester, 1984), pp. 54–7.
28. There were two overlapping bodies of twenty-four, viz. the electors, who appointed the mayor, and the jurats or leet jurors. These names are regularly recorded in the *Leet Book* and presumably provide a clue as to whose voices carried most authority within the city's government. Phythian-Adams argues that of these, it was the mayor and aldermen (or former mayors) who had most power. In 1492 this group included William Rowley, Richard Coke, Thomas Bayly and John Wigston: Harris (ed.), *Coventry Leet Book*, pp. xx–xxvi, 419, 424n., 431, 473, 503, 518, 522, 528, 542, 544; Phythian-Adams, *Desolation*, p. 123.
29. The names of all electors and leet jurats in the period 1479–96, together with the names of common councillors in 1484 and 1496, have been analysed: Harris (ed.), *Coventry Leet Book*, pp. 424–79.
30. Barbour and Chambre both served again as electors in 1495. Wardlow was a jurat at the Michaelmas leet that year. Pysford was an elector in 1494: ibid., pp. 553, 563, 567, 600–01, 604, 619, 628.
31. Ibid., pp. 665ff.
32. The mechanism by which jurats were appointed is obscure, but we may surmise that the current mayor enjoyed a degree of patronage. Cf. note 28 above.

33. McSheffrey, *Gender and Heresy*, pp. 39, 42.
34. As mayor in 1491 John Wigston allegedly 'strove against Mariolatry', but, as McSheffrey observes, subsequently served as master of the Trinity Guild: ibid., p. 42 presumably citing the *Coventry City Annal*. Wigston's term of office is important in laying the foundations for Rowley's appointment the following year, but the *Leet Book* fails to record the activities of the leets for that year.
35. For discussions of the nature of Lollardy see M. Aston, *Lollards and Reformers: Images and Literacy in Late Medieval Religion* (London, 1984); A. Hudson, *The Premature Reformation: Wycliffite Texts and Lollard History* (Oxford, 1988).
36. Aston, *Lollards and Reformers*, pp. 96–7, 110–11.
37. Ibid., p. 38; Luxton, 'Lichfield Court Book', pp. 121–2. This situation is parallel to that of the Church papists of the Elizabethan era. I owe this illuminating analogy to Patricia Cullum.
38. Thomson, *Later Lollards*, p. 112.
39. William Pysford and Thomas Forde both survived until 1518. John Wigston likewise lived until 1512, but appears to have returned to Leicester, his family's home town. There appears to be no extant will for Thomas Bayly, but he is last noticed as an elector in January 1510 and may have died shortly after. John Darlyng is last noticed in April 1510. (There is no surviving will register from the Lichfield Consistory before 1516.) Harris (ed.), *Coventry Leet Book*, pp. 628–9.
40. McSheffrey, *Gender and Heresy*, pp. 30–1, 177 n. 50.
41. Thomson, *Later Lollards*, p. 108.
42. He left 6s 8d and a lined cloak to the tanners' pageant in his will: C. Davidson, 'Civic Drama for Corpus Christi at Coventry', in A. E. Knight (ed.), *The Stage as Mirror: Civic Theatre in Late Medieval Europe* (Cambridge, 1997), p. 147. The association between vernacular scripture and Lollard sentiment hardly merits further comment, but interestingly the Elizabethan governors of Chester tried (unconvincingly) to reinvent their Play as the work of a proto-Protestant when faced by clerical opposition: D. Mills, '"None had the like nor the like darste set out": the City of Chester and its Mystery Cycle', in *idem* (ed.), *Staging the Chester Cycle*, Leeds Texts and Monographs new ser. 9 (1985), 5–7; Luxton, 'Lichfield Court Book', pp. 120–4.
43. Harris (ed.), *Coventry Leet Book*, p. 217.
44. Goldberg, 'Pigs and Prostitutes'.
45. These two sins are related since excessive consumption of meat or drink served to unleash carnal desire.
46. The clause actually commences 'that no person within þis Cite', but it is evident that 'person' here implies the householder named a couple of lines on.
47. P. H. Cullum, 'Learning to be a Man: Learning to be a Priest in Late Medieval England' in M. C. Cross and F. J. Riddy (eds.), *Learning and Literacy in the Middle Ages* (Turnhout, forthcoming).
48. The clerk has glossed the third ordinance (directed at householders) 'For Tapsters & harlattes', but this need not be an implicit reference to the Harlot

of Proverbs 7. The *Middle English Dictionary* (Ann Arbor, 1956–) shows that 'harlot' was then more frequently applied to men, and so here could refer either to householders who knowingly lodged female sexworkers or even to their clients rather than to the women concerned. On the other hand, an ordinance of the Michaelmas leet for 1493, which imposed penalties on anyone speaking in support of suspect women, specifically talks of 'eny myslyffyng woman...which is knowen for a harlat'. It may be that text deliberately blurs the difference between the ill-governed woman and her male protector: Harris (ed.), *Coventry Leet Book*, p. 552. I am grateful to Cordelia Beattie for drawing this ordinance to my attention and discussing its meaning.

49. The apprenticeship indenture invariably forbade the apprentice to visit brothels, game or waste his master's goods.

50. Aston, '"Caim's Castles"', pp. 45–81.

51. Harris (ed.), *Coventry Leet Book*, p. 568. Implicitly wives living apart from their husbands would also have been encompassed in this terminology.

52. This markedly skewed sex ratio is itself perhaps a product of the unusual rapidity of the recession in Coventry. It is probable that rather than attracting migrant women in greater numbers than men, the city was in fact losing men as the job market contracted.

53. 'Nisi Dominus custodierit civitatem frustra vigilat qui custodit eum': Psalm 126:1 from the Vulgate. An English rendition of this passage came to constitute the motto of Ripon (Yorks.).

54. All bar two of the jurats present at the Michaelmas 1492 leet who had held office as elector before 1487 participated again at the 1495 leet. The two exceptions were men who had died in the intervening three years. Only one of the 'new' jurats of 1492 (John Matthewe, who had been a member of the Common Council in 1484) was present again in 1495. The 1495 leet also included the Lollard sympathiser William Forde, who had not been present at the earlier leet.

55. Richard Lansdale was the first husband of Joan Smyth. She subsequently married a Padland and lastly Richard Smyth. McSheffrey identifies Joan's second husband as Thomas rather than John, hence we have circumstantial evidence that the mayor in 1495 was also a Lollard sympathiser: McSheffrey, *Gender and Heresy*, pp. 24, 28, 31, 35, 38–40, 42, 44, 71, 122, 211–12 nn. 63–4.

56. Ibid., pp. 25–33.

57. W. Page (ed.), *VCH, Warwick* (London, 1904), II, 112.

58. Harris (ed.), *Coventry Leet Book*, pp. 567–8.

59. Ibid., pp. 565–6, 568–9.

60. Ibid., pp. 538–40.

61. For the emergence of this distinction see P. H. Cullum, 'Hospitals and Charitable Provision in Yorkshire 936–1540', University of York D.Phil. thesis, 1989, pp. 436–47; M. K. McIntosh, 'Finding Language for Misconduct: Jurors in Fifteenth-Century Local Courts', in B. A. Hanawalt and D. Wallace

(eds.), *Bodies and Disciplines: Intersections of Literature and History in Fifteenth-Century England* (Minneapolis, 1996), pp. 102–9.

62. McSheffrey, *Gender and Heresy*, pp. 39, 44, 180 n. 102; Page (ed.), *VCH, Warwick*, II, 112.

63. Harris (ed.), *Coventry Leet Book*, pp. 600–1.

64. Phythian-Adams, *Desolation*, pp. 119–26; M. D. Harris, *Life in an Old English Town* (1898), p. 313.

65. Or failing that from the junior Corpus Christi guild: Page (ed.), *VCH, Warwick*, II, p. 112.

66. Harris (ed.), *Coventry Leet Book*, p. 567. This usage positions Godiva as Eve's antitype in the same way as Mary (greeted by Gabriel with an 'AVE' reversing EVA). The phrase is contained in a bill posted on the door of St Michael's church, critical of the then city government.

67. L. Roper, *The Holy Household: Women and Morals in Reformation Augsburg* (Oxford, 1989).

68. It is beyond the scope of this paper to explore the subsequent influence of the persons who participated in the 1492 programme, but clearly there is an interesting research agenda here. The mayoralty of William Forde (1497), for example, is marked by a concern for cleanliness.

CHAPTER 7

Thomas More's 'Utopia' and medieval London

Sarah Rees Jones

Reading Thomas More's *Utopia* I cannot help but be struck by the impression that this is not just a book written by a Londoner, and set against a London background, but that here is a book written by somebody who was steeped in traditions of writing and reading about London law, and the history, practices and problems of London's administration.

THE BEST STATE OF THE COMMONWEALTH,
THE DISCOURSE OF THE EXTRAORDINARY CHARACTER,
RAPHAEL HYTHLODAEUS, AS REPORTED BY THE RENOWNED FIGURE,
THOMAS MORE, CITIZEN AND SHERIFF OF THE FAMOUS CITY OF LONDON,
BRITAIN.

So Thomas More both began and ended his treatise on *Utopia*, or the best state of the commonwealth, by drawing attention to his status as citizen and sheriff of the city of London.[1] This choice of signature is surely significant. More himself was under-sheriff, not sheriff, of the city of London from 1510–18, but the title in *Utopia* is given, not to himself, but to the character of the same name (in Latin, Morus) who is given the role of narrator in the text.[2] Morus is deployed to report and debate the virtues of the Utopian way of life with Raphael Hythlodaeus, who claims to have found the island of Utopia while exploring the newly discovered Americas. The discoveries of Hythlodaeus provided More with a *tabula rasa* on which to construct a new vision of the ideal society. The use of the character Morus permitted the practicality of this vision to be debated through a critique of the shortcomings of contemporary society.[3] By identifying Morus so firmly as a sheriff of the city of London, More provides a clue that the form of contemporary government uppermost in his mind was not that of a kingdom, but that of a city. This point is further reinforced by locating the discussion of Utopia in Antwerp where Morus is introduced to Hythlodaeus by the bourgeois Peter Giles, 'an honourable man of high position in his home town'.[4] Most importantly of all, the larger part of the discourse on Utopia in book 2, seems in fact to be a description of its capital city, Amaurotum.[5] Only eight paragraphs in the entire discourse relate to agriculture and rural organisation.[6] Just as, elsewhere in his early works, More explored the values of life in the cloister or in the court, so in *Utopia* he was exploring the values of life in the city.[7] Through all these works More explored the ambiguities, and above all the humour, of the compromises he experienced in combining his public responsibilities, as a father, magistrate and ultimately statesman, with the intimate demands of his conscience.[8]

The fact that More was a Londoner 'through and through' has been fully developed in several biographical studies.[9] Yet the works of Russell Ames (1949) and Lawrence Manley (1995) are unusual in relating the utopian philosophy of More to the secular principles and ideals of contemporary urban government and society.[10] Following Engels, both set their interpretations within Marxist models of historical development and located *Utopia* within a period of transition from feudalism to capitalism.[11] Ames, in particular, drew upon the historical studies of Lipson, Pirenne and Unwin, who shared a general view that the origins of modern liberal democracy were to be found in the constitutions of medieval towns and their guilds.[12]

Perhaps not surprisingly, given the substantial modifications and challenges to the classic Marxist historical model, Ames's views of More were widely ignored, and even condemned, in later writing about *Utopia*. Ames's Marxist perspective was criticised both for its historical inaccuracy and naivety[13] and for its 'loss of literary perspective' in viewing the text as an unambiguous blueprint for social reform.[14] Most modern discussion of More therefore avoided placing his utopian philosophy within the context of the ideals and structures of contemporary urban government. Instead the influence of the idealised city-states and laws of pagan classical authors, such as Plato, Aristotle and Seneca, has been much more fully discussed,[15] while other critics have contrasted More's philosophy with that of contemporary secular political theorists who were, however, more concerned with monarchical than civic government.[16] Against these secular influences the Christian elements of his humanism, and indeed of northern humanists in general, have been widely debated.[17] The conclusion that *Utopia* was a deliberately eclectic work, whose ambiguity was intended to engage the reader in an active critique of social idealism, has become the dominant interpretation in recent considerations of the book.[18]

Nevertheless, the argument that More's experiences as a prominent London citizen and magistrate contributed to the development of his political philosophy deserves restating. Surtz regretted the fact that scholars had yet to identify a satisfactory medieval secular context for *Utopia*.[19] This is perhaps because they have looked in the courts and universities of northern Europe and not in the cities, whose contribution to political culture (especially in England) has traditionally been undervalued compared to that of the more independent city-states of Italy.[20] The English civic context of *Utopia* needs to be reviewed in a new light.

Reading *Utopia* as, in part, a reflection of London's history does not require that we lose sight of the intended ambiguity of the literary text. Lawrence Manley's work has demonstrated this very well, but it does not go far enough in capturing the extent to which More was able to draw upon existing genres of civic writing in constructing his utopian vision.[21] For Thomas More's experience of London embraced its textual identity, perhaps more than it embraced the social reality of London's streets and courts. This textual identity had developed in a substantial body of writing by London's medieval administrators about their own government, laws and history, much of which idealised the city's institutions of government. It constituted an existing secular philosophy of civic life, which More was able both to distil, to parody and to elaborate upon in *Utopia*, and it ensured that More's work would find a ready audience among London's elite.[22] Indeed the daily task of administering this established, idealised view of city life may well have been the crucial experience that encouraged More's doubts about the practical limits of social idealism which are at the heart of the dialogue between Hythlodaeus and Morus in *Utopia*.

The civic registers of London were compiled, from the late thirteenth century, to provide a guide to the increasingly diverse privileges and obligations of London's administrators and citizens, and to extract legal precedents from the burgeoning records of the city's courts. They contain statements of civic custom and copies of civic and royal ordinances, copies of legal proceedings, examples of financial records, lists of civic officials and their duties, and notes on events of importance in the city's history.[23] The sheer volume of records produced in the daily administration of London's courts and offices made the compilation of such registers a practical necessity by the fourteenth century, but their compilation also provided the opportunity for their compilers to include more inventive material of a less narrowly

pragmatic kind.[24] While many of the registers were compiled specifically
for the use of civic administrators, other similar compilations were
made for, or owned by, London aldermen, and such compilations were
clearly used as a source for the many chronicles composed in London
in the fifteenth and sixteenth centuries.[25] Among these registers the
Liber Albus, compiled after 1419, was an especially important work
of reference which was still being used in the city courts in the early
sixteenth century.[26] As a member of the London Mercers' Company,
as an under-sheriff of the city, as legal counsel for the city in the
royal courts and as adviser to various city committees, More had
ample opportunity to acquaint himself with such books of city history,
precedents and laws.[27] He described them in *Utopia* as a 'set of laws
that are too many to be read and too obscure for anyone to understand'.[28]

How is this civic writing reflected in *Utopia?* Firstly there is the manner
and language which More uses to construct the text. Robert Elliott has
already observed that, in advancing the virtues of utopianism, More used
the 'negative–positive' structure found in Roman satire, and also used
by Augustine in *The City of God*.[29] This rhetorical form was widely found
in later medieval didactic writing such as sermons, but it was also a style
commonly adopted by the compilers of London's civic registers. Thus
new laws would be justified in relation to the particular abuse that they
were designed to correct. Sometimes the stories of these abuses were
drawn from individual court cases. More often, the need to represent
law as protecting the common good of all the citizens resulted in the
stories being generalised in the form of moral fables, as in the following
preamble to an ordinance on city corn-dealers:

Some buyers and brokers of corn buy corn in the city from peasants who bring
it to the city to sell, and give, on the bargain being made, a penny or halfpenny
in earnest; and tell the peasants to take the corn to their house, and that there
they shall receive their pay. And when [the peasant] comes there and thinks to
have his payment directly, the buyer says that his wife at his house has gone out,
and has taken the key of the room, so that he cannot get his money; but that
the other must go away, and come again soon and receive his pay. And when
he comes back a second time, then the buyer is not to be found; or else, if he is
found, he feigns something else, by reason of which the poor men cannot have
their pay. And sometimes, while the poor men are waiting for their pay, the
buyer causes the corn to be wetted; and then, when they come to ask for their
pay, which was agreed upon, [they are told] to wait until such a day as the buyer
shall choose to name, or else to take off a part of the price; or if they will not do
this, they may take their corn and carry it away: a thing which they cannot do,

because it is wetted, [and] in another state than it was in when they sold it. And by such evil delays on the part of the buyer, the poor men lose half of their pay in expenses before they are fully settled with.[30]

More's negative–positive juxtapositions in *Utopia* at the very least, therefore, employed a style of advocacy familiar from civic texts. But there are more particular ways in which the language of *Utopia* seems to imitate, even parody, the language of London written customs. One example is the care More takes in describing the hierarchy of offices in Amaurotum, the capital city of Utopia:

Once a year, every thirty families choose an official, whom in their ancient language they call a syphogrant, but in their more recent is called the phylarch. Over ten syphogrants with their families there is another official, once called the tranibor but now a protophylarch. The whole body of syphogrants, in number two hundred, having sworn to choose the man whom they judge most useful, by secret balloting appoint a governor, that is to say one of the four candidates named to them by the people, for one is selected out of each of the four quarters of the city to be commended to the senate.[31]

The meaning of these official titles has been much disputed. The editors of the Yale edition of *Utopia* prefer 'head of a tribe' or, ironically, 'fond of rule' for phylarch, 'plain-eater' for tranibor, and 'wise elders' or 'silly old men' for syphogrants.[32] More's use of obscure, semi-comprehensible, titles, and his insistence on recording antiquarian forms which seem to add nothing to their meaning, is amusing, but could he possibly be parodying passages such as the following, by the city's common clerk, John Carpenter, in the *Liber Albus*?

If we look to the etymology of the word Alderman, the more aged were so called. For *alde* in Saxon means old, and *alder* is our word older; and hence, as the judgement is most vigorous in persons of more mature years, the dignitary who among the Romans was known as Consul or Senator, among us is called Alderman. And yet, in the case of Aldermen maturity of mind is to be considered rather than of body, and gravity of manners in preference to length of years: hence it is that in the ancient Laws of King Cnut and other kings in Saxon times, the person was styled Alderman who is now called Judge and Justiciar, as set forth in the *Liber Custumarum*. Yet in several other laws of Saint Edward, the personages who are now styled Justiciars were called *lagemanni*, from the Saxon *lage*, which corresponds with the Latin *lex*, or law; the *lagemannus* being a man of law, such as we now call a lawyer, or, more correctly, a legislator. These Aldermen too, in respect of name as well as dignity, it is evident, were anciently called *Barones*.[33]

If More was having fun with authors like Carpenter, the humour is tempered by the fact that he borrows the historical administrative system of old London for the new Amaurotum, so setting it up as an ideal.[34] The system of syphogrants and tranibors is very like that of the parishes and wards of fifteenth-century London with their parish jurors and constables (syphogrants), who are chosen from among the householders of their communities and who reported to the ward aldermen (tranibors).[35] The electoral council of two hundred syphogrants would also be recognised as London's Common Council, which numbered over a hundred common councillors chosen from the 'wisest and most wealthy' householders of their wards, who were responsible for nominating candidates in mayoral elections.[36] The tranibors are the London aldermen who 'are elected annually but are not changed without good reason'.[37] The Utopian senate would then become the equivalent of London's inner courts of mayor and aldermen, who exercised supreme judicial and legislative powers within the city. In understanding the representative assemblies of Utopia there is no particular need to look to the English parliament, as many commentators on Utopia's political institutions have done. The representative assemblies of England's cities, particularly the Common Council of London, could be just as much in More's mind. In a similar fashion the shadowy founder of Utopia, Utopus, would remind a London reader of the equally shadower founder of London (or 'new Troy'), Brutus.[38]

So many are the resemblances between the political structures of the London of the civic registers and those of Amaurotum that the former seem essential to the construction of Utopian civic philosophy. In particular the emphasis on the central role of householders in the political system is common to both, but is enhanced by More when he gives them, rather than the syphogrants and tranibors (or common councillors and aldermen), the major role in civic elections.[39] Similarly the rhetorical emphasis on the virtues of prudence and wisdom in civic rulers was as important to the compilers of the *Liber Albus* as it was in More's own view of history.[40]

In this way it would seem that knowledge of London's written records seeps into *Utopia* – providing a signal that the aspirations of utopians might find a familiar home in the minds of civic magistrates. Like More we must remember that while these civic registers contain much that might seem incomprehensible and even absurd, they also contain the materials for reconstructing an ambition for civic society which is equal to that of *Utopia*'s own. When More chose to use the obscurer and older Utopian terms, such as syphogrant (wise old man) rather than phylarch (fond of rule), was this an oblique comment on the disparity between the high moral standards claimed in the civic registers for the idealised officials of London's past, and the failings of contemporary office holders in the city? Could the purpose of More's parody be to sort the wheat from the chaff, and to remind Londoners of the higher purpose of their own civic institutions?

If the location, language and context of the utopian discourse indicate a deliberately civic framework for *Utopia*, it is also possible to suggest that some of the ideals of the utopian system also seem to reflect the ideals of London's pre-humanist civic writers. Quentin Skinner has argued that, prior to the recovery and imitation of Greek authorities in the fourteenth and fifteenth centuries, compilers of Italian civic texts and laws in the thirteenth century, such as Brunetto Latini, were already influenced by the ideas of certain Roman moralists, particularly Seneca and Cicero, which had been preserved in medieval *florilegia* and the *ars dictaminis*.[41] A preliminary analysis suggests that a similar argument could be advanced for London civic writers. The over-arching civic virtue of concord, achieved through triumph over discord, or factionalism, in the civic community, was a constant theme of civic writing in London from at least the late thirteenth century. The rebellious and populist mayor Walter Hervey, who championed the cause of the crafts, was accused in 1274 of advancing his own profit against the interest of the common good ('ad lucrum suum proprium et contra communem utilitatem') in terms which could have come straight from the law codes of Siena (1250) or Cicero's *De Officiis*.[42] Similar language, placing the liberties of the city as a whole before those of particular crafts, was still being used to suppress dissidents two centuries later.[43] Likewise the emphasis on prudence, elaborated considerably by More in *Utopia*, has already been noted.[44] Indeed, the fact that the classical 'active virtues' of prudence, justice, fortitude and temperance were personified in stone on the west front of London's newly constructed Guildhall in the fourteenth century underlines the degree to which there was a civic idealism in medieval London which, like that of central Italy, was influenced by classical principles of government.[45] No doubt the sources of this 'pre-humanism' were as eclectic as those of *Utopia* itself. They would repay closer scrutiny. Certainly we should not rule out the possibility of an active interest in civic philosophies of government among London clerks, since in *c.* 1325 a Londoner copied and adapted Latini's treatise on civic government in one of London's registers.[46]

None of this should be taken to suggest that the 'pre-humanist' influences evident in London's medieval civic writing were necessarily the crucial influence in the development of More's own civic humanism. However it does seem legitimate to suggest that More would have recognised the classical virtues which were embedded in much medieval civic writing, and that his experience in applying them contributed to the development of his own critique of classical humanism. It is perhaps no accident that Hythlodaeus, the advocate of Utopian (or idealised London) government, is presented to us as a Senecan philosopher, whose simplistic idealism is challenged by the pragmatic Morus.[47] Morus recognised the inability of contemporaries to live up to their own civic ideals: 'Outside Utopia, to be sure, men talk freely of the public welfare – but look after their private interests only.'[48] But that recognition was surely derived from More's own experience of both the potential of the rhetoric of the common good and its abuse, when he was employed to use it in representing the interests of different interest-groups within the city. One such occasion occurred in 1512, when More was called upon to represent those crafts who assented to the authority of the mayor and aldermen against the Tailors, who refused to do so.[49]

Thomas More certainly shared the earlier civic writers' belief that the highest purpose of government should be the achievement of concord and the preservation of peace, but his experience forced him to recognise the obstacles to this. More signals the nature of this dilemma in his description of Amaurotum's topography which is explicitly modelled on that of the city of London.[50] Amaurotum, like London, was built on the banks of a tidal river, but the bridge across this river was built far enough upstream to allow all ships to reach their mooring safely. The position of the real London Bridge was too far downstream and this had originally presented a real obstacle to shipping and trade.[51] The resulting problems were fully recorded in the city law books and, as a member of the bridge committee, More would have been familiar with them.[52] Indeed they were still considered worthy of note by Stow in the later sixteenth century.[53] More's alteration of the position of the bridge indicates the relationship he intended between real and imagined cities in writing *Utopia*. The principle of the London laws (that of facilitating access by shipping to the city's markets) was laudable, but the location of the bridge made those laws impossible to enforce fairly and they themselves had thus become a source of discord in the city.

If we extend this principle further in a consideration of More's utopian philosophy, it becomes possible to suggest that some of his most radical ideas also dealt with concerns familiar to readers of London's law books, even if his conclusions, taken literally, were a rather abstract expression of those concerns. The central premise of Utopian philosophy was the abolition of private property, the absence of money and the communal ownership of all land. The absence of private property ensured the material equality of all the citizens of Amaurotum and so destroyed Pride, that vice which results not from enjoying the possession of wealth, knowledge or success, but from enjoying the absence of such riches in others.[54] It was this absence of Pride above all which was the basis of Utopia's success as the ideal commonwealth.

The attack on private property is often considered the most radical criticism of the existing values of contemporary secular society. Conventionally, wealth, and in particular the ownership of property, was considered the foundation of all power. The 'big men', the magnates, were not only the most powerful (*potentiores*) but were also the best men (*meliores*) – the best suited to govern. Their very wealth qualified them for office.[55] Wealth gave them the leisure needed for the activities of government. Wealth limited the opportunity for corruption, and wealth enabled men to rise above factionalism and private interest.[56] The reversal of these arguments, with the accusation that it was the possession of property, not its absence, which sowed the seeds of discord and corruption in government, was thus a dramatic reversal of conventional public norms.

But this preoccupation with the necessity of wealth for rulers represents an over-simplification of more complex, indeed contradictory, civic attitudes towards the role of property in maintaining an orderly civic society. When compilers of civic registers viewed government (at least rhetorically) from the perspective of the citizens and the members of the commonalty – the householders – they generally embraced the essential mutuality of civic relations. From this perspective the Utopian attack on the evils of private property is not without precedent in secular civic writing.

In the case of landed wealth, by Thomas More's time a significant change had taken place in the everyday language describing property in towns, which robbed it of an association with power. By the later fifteenth century real estate was referred to as the landowner's *lyvelod*, or simply a means of sustaining a living; the concept of the *fee* and the lordship which pertained to it had been almost entirely lost.[57] At the same time property-based qualifications for citizenship had been largely eroded and replaced by systems of purchase and patronage.[58] By contrast large private estates were often represented as causes of discord in the city. The authority of communal corporations in cities such as London had long been compromised by the private jurisdictions exercised by landlords over the tenants of their town estates, but over the preceding two centuries a war of attrition had been fought against such private landowners. The most protracted struggles were with church landlords, such as the college of St Martin-le-Grand in London, whose precincts provided an infamous sanctuary beyond the reach of civic officials.[59] Thomas More himself witnessed the problems this caused the city when he was sent to confront rioters attacking aliens who had taken refuge in the college precinct on 'Evil May Day' in 1517.[60]

Private property on this scale therefore presented a real threat to the unity and authority of the civic corporation, but at a more prosaic level protracted and seemingly futile disputes over private property were among the most frequent causes of a collapse of good neighbourliness, of which the under-sheriff, More, would have been only too aware.[61] The communal ownership of gardens in Utopia, and the regular redistribution of houses, would have neatly removed the need for litigation over ownership and boundaries.[62]

In both instances it can be seen that the reader of London records, and the practitioner of London law, would find much in the records that opposed the view that private property was necessary to good government. Indeed most citizens owned little property. Less than one quarter of citizen landowners had estates worth more than £10 a year, and all landowners probably accounted for no more than 1% of the population.[63] The property interests of most individuals did not extend beyond the house or rooms in which they lived, and most of these were rented, often from corporate institutions such as the city itself.[64]

London, like Amaurotum, was thus essentially a city of people without property. As a London magistrate, More would have been much impressed by the problems of maintaining order in a property-less society. How do you govern a society where the majority of the residents are without property? These problems were converted by More into Utopia's, or Amaurotum's, chief virtue: the city without private property. But the

idealised solutions he adopted for the running of a such a city were not
without parallels in fifteenth-century London.

Poverty, and the rootlessness and anonymity of so many town inhabitants, were the greatest problems facing urban magistrates. Like
that of most cities, the formal government of London was based on the
idea that its residents could be divided into citizens and non-citizens.
Citizens enjoyed economic and political privileges and in return paid
taxes and took their turn in holding administrative office in the city.[65]
Citizens (or freemen) were in a minority. Probably only about one quarter
of London's adult male residents were fully paid-up freemen in the fifteenth century. Non-citizens (described as outsiders or foreigners) were
neither so privileged nor so obligated. Their families may have been
resident in the city for generations, or they may have been recent im-
migrants from other parts of England. They were not supposed to keep
shop in the city, and one typical image of such a non-citizen would be a
man or woman who worked for a wage for somebody else and who was
constantly on the move. By the later fifteenth century it is clear that this
ideal of a divided society was breaking down, and the city custumals are
filled with complaints against 'foreigners'.[66] Non-citizens competed for
work and regularly kept shop or traded off the streets; and many refused
to abide by the city's rules. Economically, of course, towns thrived on
such mobility and flexibility.[67] But the administrative system, which depended on being able to locate citizens in resident communities of sworn
householders who, as neighbours, would know and pledge each other to
keep the peace, found no way of maintaining the economic privileges of
the resident and sworn citizens against these outsiders or foreigners.

It is true that the development of trade and craft associations offered an
alternative form of protection to the citizen craftsmen.[68] Yet the evolution
of craft rules provoked disputes between guilds, and some guilds grew so
powerful in protecting their members' interests that they too threatened
the corporate liberty of the city itself. Thus disputes between guilds, and
even between guilds and the city, were another prominent feature of the
city law books.[69]

The Utopian solution to the problems of mobility and sectional interest was straightforward. Hythlodaeus simply reasserted the old-fashioned
values of egalitarian citizenship, and the unity of purpose in the commonwealth of citizens.[70] Amaurotum has no craft associations; all citizen
householders are equal, no matter what their craft.[71] The old system
of government by household, parish and ward is reinstated in Utopia,
and all inhabitants are conveniently accommodated within citizen-led

families grouped, for the purposes of dining and the care of infants and the sick, into associations not unlike parochial fraternities.[72] Utopians were not interested in the family as an agency for perpetuating the ownership of private property (as noblemen might be), but in the household as a unit of moral and social control. This, indeed, was the chief purpose of the household in civic society.[73] Like London, Amaurotum does accommodate foreigners, that is to say those people who come to Utopia from elsewhere in search of a better life. However, they are clearly distinguished as slaves.[74] They do the menial and degrading jobs and offer no competition to the citizen craftsmen. They are admitted to citizenship only when the citizens choose to admit them.[75]

Even the abolition of money in Utopia, and the free circulation of the necessities of life, is not so alien if your view of civic society is determined by reading medieval legal custumals and the resulting prosecutions in the city courts. Perhaps the single most important function of civic government, prominent in the senior officials' oaths, was to ensure the fair circulation of good-quality food at fixed prices.[76] Making excessive profit in the sale of food, selling bad or adulterated food, or selling by false measures were among the most common offences to be brought to the city's courts. While regulations in the civic custumals governing the sale of food did not outlaw money, their strict control of prices and profit was inimical to a free market determined by monetary values and not so far from the Utopian dislike of a money-based economy.

By contrast the prices of luxury goods were rarely, if ever, the subject of civic regulation in English towns, although they might be regulated privately within specialist crafts. Thomas More would have found little reference to such goods in the London custumals, except as the objects of theft, tempting men into sin.[77] No doubt this suited his asceticism. Luxuries are absent in Utopia altogether, except as the objects of ridicule or as children's toys.[78]

Space does not permit a fuller study of other aspects of the Utopian system which reflect the civic ideals of later medieval London. As in *Utopia*, so the civic idealism of later medieval London was not entirely secular, but also embraced the ritual and Christo-centric devotions of the later medieval Church. Ackroyd has provided a colourful synthetic picture of London's civic religion, while Brigden's study of pre-Reformation London provides the most profound critique of a civic elite who acted as a godly, rather than a simply pious, community in the regulation of the Church in London.[79] From the evidence of the wardmote courts, the lowest of the city's secular courts, we can see how far this process had developed, even by the early fifteenth century. There, in addition to several clergy presented for moral lapses, one chaplain was even charged with apostasy by his parishioners, so indicating the willingness of the lay community to supervise matters of faith as well as practice.[80] The secular church of Utopia again finds a familiar location in the secular law books of later-medieval London's courts.

But we should end with a joke. The most famous joke in *Utopia* is the recommendation that prospective marriage partners should view each other naked.[81] One of the under-sheriff's responsibilities was judging those accused of prostitution. Prostitution was an offence of common nuisance, and, using a broad interpretation of this offence, many individuals were also presented to the secular courts for offences of adultery and fornication.[82] In *Letter Book I* a list survives of over sixty people (the majority of the men being clergy), who were charged with adultery between 1401 and 1439.[83] In many cases the form of words used was the same: 'Richard Henney, chaplain . . . taken naked with Johanna, wife of . . . who was also naked'. Surely such language appealed to More's sense of humour. If nakedness was the crux of sexual attraction, then what better triumph over the folly of adultery than to promote the folly of a naked viewing before a commitment to an indissoluble marriage was undertaken? The language of marriage in Utopia is juxtaposed with the language of its antithesis, adultery and prostitution, in London. Utopian marriage offers a critique of London's sexual immorality.

The prophetic purpose of *Utopia* lay in revealing the reality of the present rather than anticipating the future. In 1516, when Thomas More completed the full text of *Utopia*, he was already beginning to turn his attention towards employment in the English court. But his subsequent career should not be allowed to obscure his London origins or the urban perspective of *Utopia*. Going to the court did not mean leaving London. While the mentality of the English civic elite had many distinctive features, an opposition to monarchical government was not one of them.

Utopia was the product not just of More's London experience but also of the shared experience of his friends in the cities of the Netherlands with whom he collaborated in producing the book. More's circle shared a belief that philosophy was a useful discipline for the education of civic

administrators, and Lisa Jardine has suggested that the first edition of
Utopia may have been made for John Colet and for his recently founded
school in St Paul's, where it was intended that *Utopia* should be used as
part of a programme of instruction in Greek philosophy.[84] But how much
more useful such a book would be if it drew on materials and ideas with
which its London audience was already familiar! After all the problem of
how to live a good life within a secular, and specifically civic, society was
already the subject of many volumes of London custumals. More's vision
of a utopian 'future' was built upon foundations drawn from London's
idealised past.

NOTES

1. Edward Surtz and J. H. Hexter (eds.), *Utopia*, in *The Yale Edition of the Complete Works of Thomas More*, vol. IV (New Haven and London, 1965), pp. 46/1–7, 247/5–10.
2. The historical author will be referred to as More, the eponymous character and narrator in the book as Morus.
3. It is generally accepted that the larger part of book 2, which contains the main description of Utopia, was written first, while More was in the Netherlands in 1515. Jack Hexter has also suggested that the introduction to book 1 was written at this time. When More returned to London he then composed the Dialogue in book 1, and the Peroration and Conclusion of book 2. Thus More first constructed his utopian vision and only later wrote the dialogue between the two characters, Hythlodaeus and Morus, which permitted a philosophical debate as to whether such an idealised state was either desirable or possible. J. H. Hexter, *More's "Utopia", the Biography of an Idea*, History of Ideas Series 5 (Princeton, 1952); *Utopia*, pp. xv–xxiii; Alistair Fox, *Thomas More, History and Providence* (Oxford, 1982), pp. 52, 60.
4. *Utopia*, 49. Peter Giles was a friend of Erasmus with whom More stayed in Antwerp. As well as being included as a character in the book, Giles was the author and recipient of several letters published in the first edition of *Utopia* commending More's work, and colluding in the account of Hythlodaeus and his travels with Amerigo Vespucci: ibid., pp. 18–44.
5. The distinction between the institutions of Amaurotum and Utopia is not made clear in the text. The two seem to be conflated, further suggesting that More's priority is with Amaurotum, whose form of government is simply to be replicated in the other cities of Utopia. Indeed in later-medieval England the constitution of London was increasingly used as a model for the government of other towns, to which the London model was spread by royal charter and through the nation-wide impact of parliamentary legislation.
6. *Utopia*, pp. 112/33–116/19.
7. *The Life of Pico*, in A. S. G. Edwards, K. Gardiner Rodgers and C. H. Miller (eds.), *The Yale Edition of the Complete Works of Thomas More*, vol. I (New Haven

and London, 1997), pp. 51–127; *Historia Ricardi Tertii*, in Daniel Kinney (ed.), *The Yale Edition of the Complete Works of Thomas More*, vol. XV (New Haven and London, 1986), pp. 313–486.

8. Stephen Greenblatt, *Renaissance Self-Fashioning, from More to Shakespeare* (Chicago and London, 1980), pp. 57–8; Fox, *Thomas More*, pp. 71–4.

9. See especially R. W. Chambers, 'Historical Notes', in N. Harpsfield, *The Life and Death of Sir Thomas More, Knight*, ed. E. V. Hitchcock and R. W. Chambers, Early English Text Society, o.s. 186 (1932), pp. 297–370; R. W. Chambers, *Thomas More* (London, 1935); G. D. Ramsay, 'A Saint in the City: Thomas More at Mercers' Hall, London', *English Historical Review* 97 (1982), 269–88; Peter Ackroyd, *The Life of Thomas More* (London, 1998).

10. Russell Ames, *Citizen More and his Utopia* (Princeton, 1949); Lawrence Manley, *Literature and Culture in Early Modern London* (Cambridge, 1995), pp. 23–62.

11. Frederick Engels, *Socialism: Utopian and Scientific*, ed. J. Rees (London, Chicago and Melbourne, 1993), esp. p. 59; Manley, *Literature and Culture*, pp. 1–20.

12. E. Lipson, *The Economic History of England* (London, 1937); Henri Pirenne, *Belgian Democracy* (Manchester, 1915), *Medieval Cities* (Princeton, 1939); George Unwin, *The Gilds and Companies of London* (London, 1908), p. 7. This position has since been restated: M. Weinbaum, *British Borough Charters, 1307–1660* (Cambridge, 1943), p. xxvii; Barrie Dobson, 'The Crown, the Charter and the City, 1396–1461', in S. Rees Jones (ed.), *The Government of Medieval York*, Borthwick Studies in History 3 (York, 1997), p. 39.

13. *Utopia*, pp. liv–lvii.

14. Dominic Baker-Smith, *More's Utopia* (London, 1991), p. 239.

15. *Utopia*, pp. clvi–clxv; Brendan Bradshaw, 'Transalpine Humanism', in J. H. Burns and M. Goldie (eds.), *The Cambridge History of Political Thought* (Cambridge, 1991), pp. 116–28.

16. J. H. Hexter, *The Vision of Politics on the Eve of the Reformation: More, Machiavelli and Seyssel* (Princeton, 1972); Quentin Skinner, *The Foundations of Modern Political Thought*, vol. I (Cambridge, 1978).

17. Chambers, *Thomas More: Utopia*, pp. lxiv–lxxvii, xcii–cv; Richard Marius, *Thomas More* (New York, 1984); Bradshaw, 'Transalpine Humanism', pp. 101–15.

18. J. C. Davis, 'Utopianism', in Burns and Goldie (eds.), *Cambridge History of Political Thought*, pp. 329–30; Baker-Smith, *More's Utopia*, p. 243; Manley, *Literature and Culture*, pp. 31–2.

19. *Utopia*, p. clxvii.

20. For reassertions of the importance of 'civic' contributions to English political culture in the early sixteenth century see, *inter alia*, J. Barry, 'Bourgeois Collectivism? Urban Association and the Middling Sort', in J. Barry and C. Brooks (eds.) *The Middling Sort of People. Culture, Society and Politics in England, 1550–1800* (London, 1994), pp. 84–112; Manley, *Literature and Culture*.

21. Manley, *Literature and Culture*, pp. 23–62, esp. 25–7.

22. For the reception of *Utopia* in London see M. Todd, *Christian Humanism and the Puritan Social Order* (Cambridge, 1987).

23. The main registers remaining in the Corporation of London Record Office are described in P. E. Jones and R. Smith, *A Guide to the Records in the Corporation of London Records Office and the Guildhall Library Muniment Room* (London, 1950), pp. 22–4; Geoffrey Martin, 'English Town Records, 1250–1350', in Richard Britnell (ed.), *Pragmatic Literacy East and West, 1200–1330* (Woodbridge, 1997), pp. 126–30; H. T. Riley (ed.), *Munimenta Gildhallae Londoniensis*, vols. I–III, (Rolls Series, 1859–62); R. R. Sharpe, *Calendar of Letter-Books A–L*, 11 vols., (1899–1912).

24. J. Catto, 'Andrew Horn: Law and History in Fourteenth-Century London', in R. H. C. Davis and J. M. Wallace-Hadrill (eds.), *The Writing of History in the Middle Ages: Essays Presented to Richard William Southern* (Oxford, 1981), pp. 367–91; D. S. O'Brien, 'London Pride: Citizenship and the Fourteenth-century Custumals of the City of London', in S. Rees Jones *et al.* (eds.), *Learning and Literacy in the Middle Ages* (forthcoming).

25. Sylvia L. Thrupp, *The Merchant Class of Medieval London* (Ann Arbor, 1948), pp. 163, 247–9; A. H. Thomas (ed.), *Calendar of Select Pleas and Memoranda of the City of London, 1381–1412* (Cambridge, 1932), p. 212; Antonia Gransden, *Historical Writing in England, c.1307 to the Early Sixteenth Century* (London, 1982), pp. 227–48; O'Brien, 'London Pride'; C. Barron, 'The Jubilee Book 1376–1387', unpublished paper (2000).

26. *Munimenta Gildhallae Londoniensis*, I, *Liber Albus*, pp. xvii, xxiii, 1.

27. For references see note 10 above.

28. *Utopia*, p. 194/10–12.

29. Robert C. Elliott, 'The shape of *Utopia*', reprinted in Robert M. Adams (ed.), *Utopia* (2nd edition, New York and London, 1992), p. 184.

30. Original language French. *Munimenta Gildhallae Londoniensis*, I, *Liber Albus*, pp. 261–2.

31. *Utopia*, p. 122/9–19.

32. Ibid., pp. 389, 398–9.

33. Original language Latin. *Munimenta Gildhallae Londoniensis*, I, *Liber Albus*, pp. 32–3.

34. For London's medieval constitution see Gwyn A. Williams, *Medieval London from Commune to Capital*, (London, 1963), pp. 26–50; Thrupp, *Merchant Class of Medieval London*, pp. 66–85; Caroline Barron, 'The Later Middle Ages, 1270–1520', in M. D. Lobel (ed.), *The British Atlas of Historic Towns*, vol. III (Oxford, 1989), pp. 43–4. Cf. Manley, *Literature and Culture*, pp. 40–1.

35. *Munimenta Gildhallae Londoniensis*, I, *Liber Albus*, pp. 36–9.

36. Ibid., pp. 20–3, 40–2.

37. *Utopia*, p. 122/21.

38. Like Utopus, the mythological Brutus was not only the founder of London but also first of the kings of Britain. In the mythology (and political practice) of Utopia, as in that of London, urban government need not be opposed to monarchical authority – although in the daily maintenance of order in London the authority of the mayor was infinitely more important.

39. *Utopia*, p. 134/24–5. For discussion of the centrality of the household to urban government see Barry, 'Bourgeois Collectivism?', pp. 95–107; S. Rees
Jones, 'Household, Work and the Problem of Mobile Labour: The Regulation of Labour in Medieval English towns', in J. Bothwell, W. M. Ormrod
and P. J. P. Goldberg (eds.), *The Problem of Labour in Fourteenth-Century England*
(Woodbridge, 2000), pp. 133–53.

40. *Munimenta Gildhallae Londoniensis*, I, *Liber Albus*, p. 36; for More's providential
view of history see Fox, *Thomas More*, pp. 70–1.

41. Quentin Skinner, 'Ambrogio Lorenzetti: The Artist as Political Philosopher',
Proceedings of the British Academy 72 (1986), 5.

42. T. Stapleton (ed.), *Liber de Antiquis Legibus seu Chronica Maiorum et Vicecomitum
Londoniarum*, Camden Society (London, 1846), p. 165; Williams, *Medieval
London*, pp. 243–5; Skinner, 'Ambrogio Lorenzetti', pp. 9–10.

43. Caroline Barron, 'Ralph Holland and the London Radicals, 1438–1444',
reprinted in R. Holt and G. Rosser (eds.), *The Medieval Town: A Reader
in English Urban History, 1200–1540* (London and New York, 1990),
p. 179.

44. Above, note 40.

45. These statues are preserved in the Museum of London.

46. H. T. Riley (ed.), *Munimenta Gildhallae Londoniensis*, II, *Liber Custumarum*,
pp. 16–25.

47. *Utopia*, pp. 48/33–50/3, 98/14–18; Baker-Smith, *More's Utopia*, pp. 127–9.
Hythlodaeus means 'well-learned in nonsense' : *Utopia*, p. 301.

48. *Utopia*, p. 238/1–2.

49. Chambers, 'Historical Notes', p. 312. For earlier episodes of dispute between the tailors and the city see Barron, 'Ralph Holland and the London
Radicals', pp. 160–83.

50. *Utopia*, p. 118/8–18.

51. The public quays at Queenhithe lay upstream from London Bridge, and by
the later fourteenth century their use was declining in favour of the more
accessible quays at Billingsgate, downstream from the bridge. V. Harding
and L. Wright, *London Bridge: Selected Accounts and Rentals, 1381–1538*, London
Record Society 31 (1995), p. xx.

52. As late as the 1460s the city passed ordinances attempting to coerce shipping into using Queenhithe: *Calendar of Letter Books, Letter Book L*, pp. 45–6;
Chambers, 'Historical Notes', p. 313.

53. John Stow, *A Survey of London, Reprinted from the Text of 1603*, ed. C. L. Kingsford
(Oxford, 1908), pp. 2, 8–10.

54. *Utopia*, pp. 242/23–244/2.

55. S. Reynolds, 'Medieval Urban History and the History of Political Thought',
Urban History Yearbook, 1982; S. H. Rigby, *English Society in the Later Middle Ages:
Class, Status and Gender* (London, 1995), pp. 171–6.

56. *Munimenta Gildhallae Londoniensis*, I, *Liber Albus*, pp. 19, 21–2, 33; *Munimenta
Gildhallae Londoniensis*, II, *Liber Custumarum*, p. 18.

57. P. E. Jones (ed.), *Calendar of Plea and Memoranda Rolls Preserved among the Archives of the City of London at the Guildhall, a.d. 1458–1482* (Cambridge, 1961), pp. 5, 6, 33, 109, 134. Similar usage of this term can be found outside London.

58. H. Swanson, *Medieval British Towns* (London and New York, 1999), pp. 68–73; S. Rees Jones, 'The Household and English Urban Government in the Later Middle Ages', in M. Carlier and T. Soens (eds.), *The Later-medieval Urban Household: Italy and North-west Europe Compared* (Leuven, 2001) forthcoming.

59. *Calendar of Letter Books, Letter Book K (tempore Hen. vi)*, pp. xxviii–xxxiv, 151–60, 241–6.

60. S. Rappaport, *Worlds within Worlds: Structures of Life in Sixteenth-Century London* (Cambridge, 1989), pp. 15–16.

61. *London Assize of Nuisance, 1301–1431: A Calendar*, ed. H. M. Chew and William Kellaway, London Record Society 10 (1973).

62. *Utopia*, p. 120.

63. This assumes a population of *c.* 80,000: Thrupp, *Merchant Class of Medieval London*, pp. 125–6; D. Keene, 'Medieval London and its Region', *London Journal* 14 (1989), 101, 107.

64. The city corporation and the trustees of London Bridge were among the largest landowners in London: *London Bridge Accounts*, pp. xvii–xix.

65. R. B. Dobson, 'Admissions to the Freedom of the City of York in the Later Middle Ages', *Economic History Review*, Second Series 26 (1973), 1–22; Rappaport, *Worlds within Worlds*, 29–47.

66. For example: *Calendar of Letter Books, Letter Book L*, pp. 25–6, 57, 119, 154, 156, 186, 197, 200, 203, 211, 217–8, 234, 236, 259, 275, 291, 294, 295, 302, 308; Rappaport, *Worlds within Worlds*, pp. 29–32, 42–9; P. Nightingale, *A Medieval Mercantile Community: The Grocers' Company and the Politics and Trade of London 1000–1485* (New Haven and London, 1995), pp. 539, 547.

67. R. Britnell, *The Commercialisation of English Society 1000–1500* (Cambridge, 1993), pp. 177, 224–5; Rappaport, *Worlds within Worlds*, pp. 76ff.

68. The formation of both craft and trade guilds eventually permitted their members some measure of control over access to citizenship: Rappaport, *Worlds within Worlds*, pp. 31–2; S. Rees Jones, 'York's Civic Administration, 1354–64', in Rees Jones (ed.), *Government of Medieval York*, pp. 131–2.

69. For example: *Calendar of Letter Books, Letter Book L, temp. Edward IV to Henry VII*, pp. 26–7, 120–1, 165, 184–5, 212, 252–3, 310; Barron, 'Ralph Holland and the London Radicals', pp. 160–83.

70. Some twenty years later More, as Chancellor, had the opportunity to reform citizenship in London in a similar fashion, when he backed legislation to widen the franchise to include many foreigners: Rappaport, *Worlds within Worlds*, pp. 47–8.

71. *Utopia*, p. 126/8–19.

72. Ibid., pp. 134/22–9, 136/22–138/26.

73. Rees Jones, 'Household, Work and the Problem of Mobile Labour', pp. 133–53.

74. *Utopia*, p. 184/25–30.
75. Ibid., p. 192/1–2.
76. *Munimenta Gildhallae Londoniensis*, I, *Liber Albus*, pp. 306–8; Britnell, *Commercialisation of English Society*, pp. 91–7, 174–5.
77. For example in the Infangthef proceedings for burglars caught in the act: *Calendar of Letter Books, Letter Book F*, pp. 249–75.
78. *Utopia*, p. 152/3–26.
79. Ackroyd, *Thomas More*, pp. 108–13; Susan Brigden, *London and the Reformation* (Oxford, 1989).
80. A. H. Thomas (ed.), *Calendar of Plea and Memoranda Rolls a.d. 1413–1437* (Cambridge, 1943), pp. 115–41, 150–9, esp. 131. For the establishment of an anti-heretical library in the Guildhall by John Carpenter, common clerk, see Margaret Aston, 'The Bishops and Heresy', in *eadem* (ed.), *Faith and Fire* (London, 1993), pp. 90–1.
81. *Utopia*, pp. 186/33–188/27.
82. *Munimenta Gildhallae Londoniensis*, I, *Liber Albus*, pp. 332, 337; *Plea and Memoranda Rolls a.d. 1413–1437*, pp. 122, 124, 127, 131, 134, 154, 156; Ruth Mazo Karras, *Common Women. Prostitution and Sexuality in Medieval England* (New York and Oxford, 1996), pp. 14–24.
83. *Calendar of Letter Books, Letter Book I*, pp. xlii–xliv, 273–87.
84. L. Jardine, *Erasmus, Man of Letters. The Construction of Charisma in Print* (Princeton, 1993), pp. 178–80.

CHAPTER 8

Social exclusivity or justice for all? Access to justice in fourteenth-century England

Anthony Musson

> For this reason, I will keep myself within the woods, in the beautiful shade;
> There is no deceit there, nor any bad law,
> In the wood of Belregard, where the jay flies
> And the nightingale sings every day without ceasing.

The outlaw, residing in the idyllic 'wood of Belregard', is a powerful and evocative image in medieval literature.[1] Embodying a strong sense of social justice and imbued with utopian qualities, both the outlaw figure and the greenwood can be taken to symbolise the aspirations, or perhaps more appropriately the plight, of those who had no apparent prospect of 'justice', either through lack of access to the legal system or on account of their treatment within it. The apparent difficulties faced in trying to clear one's name are portrayed as stemming from endemic social prejudice and corruption within the legal system. As such, and in what is a recurring theme during the fourteenth century, the outlaw figure presents a picture of social exclusion amounting to a serious indictment of royal justice in late-medieval England.[2]

This chapter seeks to mitigate the stark 'outlaw's view' outlined above (itself a metaphor for the excluded, both literally and psychologically) through an examination of attitudes towards the disadvantaged and by highlighting the structural and administrative factors ameliorating their experience of royal justice in the fourteenth century. The word 'justice' itself has an inherent duality, referring both to the system of rules and procedures within which the law operates and to notions of fairness and procedural propriety. In order to penetrate the aura of social exclusivity supposedly existing around the judicial system, this chapter tests 'accessibility' with regard to *both* the meanings of 'justice'. It examines, initially, the extent to which the royal courts themselves could be inclusive and, more particularly, whether those with the disadvantages of lowly status, lack of wealth and little education were afforded access to legal services.

Access to justice in this sense should be regarded as incorporating three main considerations. First, it involves the opportunity to gain legal advice and (if necessary) representation and the ability physically to initiate private actions in the full hierarchy of royal courts. Secondly, it includes having the funding to obtain the services of a lawyer and to finance all stages of the litigation process. Thirdly, it means the capacity intellectually to understand the basic legal problem and comprehend something of the court proceedings. The chapter then goes on to consider the other meaning of 'justice' and tries to ascertain whether, once within the system, litigants from a humble background were overwhelmingly disadvantaged by their lack of status or if in fact the system (or its guardians) enabled them to avoid undue prejudice. In other words, to what extent did the system work against you if you were poor? Was it possible to obtain a fair hearing? What could a litigant do if he or she felt let down or betrayed by the system?

In responding to these questions, this chapter strikes at the heart of the traditional picture of medieval justice and suggests that there *was* an understanding of the problems faced by the less prosperous would-be litigant and that there *were* definite attempts to ensure that justice was not as socially exclusive and divisive as it has been characterised. While it is recognised as an unfortunate reality of research into medieval history that most judicial, political and literary evidence is inevitably skewed towards the lives and attitudes of the elite, leaving the experiences and responses of the peasantry and townspeople fairly obscure, it will be argued on the evidence of the plea rolls and law reports that the lower echelons of society could in fact be the beneficiaries of royal justice as well as its victims. This contribution highlights the move towards greater accessibility in royal justice during the course of the late thirteenth and fourteenth centuries and examines the theological and moral justifications underlying judicial and governmental attitudes towards access to justice. It also redresses the notion (favoured by some historians) that the supposed new cultural and political values of the post-plague era necessarily brought restriction to the legal system and oppression in the administration of justice.[3] Indeed, far from bringing alienation from the king's courts, the widening scope of royal justice observable over the course of the thirteenth and fourteenth centuries (in terms of opportunities for redress and in the range of legal remedies available) not only provided greater access at the local level, but also catered for the litigious tendencies of at least some sections of the peasant and urban communities.

The availability of judicial sessions in the localities (thus avoiding a journey to the central courts at Westminster) was a necessary prerequisite for accessibility. The general eyre's disappearance from the system of judicial administration following its suspension in 1294 is often regarded as a factor inhibiting access to justice for the lower orders during the fourteenth century. By the later thirteenth century, however, the eyre was hardly a model of availability: its pace had slowed to such an extent that it visited each shire on average only once every seven years. Its responsibility for hearing assizes and delivering gaols had already been superseded by the countrywide circuits of the assize justices, who became an established feature of royal justice. From the early fourteenth century, justices with wide powers to hear and determine offences were periodically to be found operating on circuits covering all the counties in England, while the court of king's bench visited the shires empowered to hear bills and act as an itinerant court of first instance from about the 1320s. The visitations of the latter two agencies dwindled towards the middle of the fourteenth century when 'trailbaston' commissions ceased to be a politically viable option and provincial visits of king's bench were curtailed. The apparent reduction in judicial outlets may have had little significant impact on the initiating of actions, however, since the justices of the peace could accept private suits and they, together with the assize justices, were able to provide sessions on a predictable and regular basis.[4]

The range of business entertained by the royal courts made them an attractive forum to which to bring disputes. The crown was increasingly offering remedies for new situations and expanded the types of writs available from chancery (large numbers were added to the registers during the reigns of Edward III and Richard II in particular).[5] Some writs arose as a result of statute legislation, but others through the appropriation of remedies previously available in the customary courts.[6] These remedies were designed to appeal to and benefit people across the social spectrum. Indeed, Chief Justice Bereford commented on the advantages of replevin over the cumbersome proprietary action *ne injuste vexes*, 'For twenty years past there has not come to England so good a law for poor folk.'[7] A hearing before the king's justices could also be obtained by procedural means: cases could be transferred from a lord's court to the county court using a procedure known as *tolt*; from the county court to one of the royal courts through the writ *pone*; and any case could be reviewed in the court of king's bench following a writ of *certiorari*.[8]

Even with the manifest availability of judicial arenas and legal remedies there were other hurdles to surmount in the pursuit of private
litigation, notably the financial expense. Affordability was obviously an
important consideration for any potential litigant, let alone the less well-
off. In the normal course of events the poor plaintiff might find it difficult
to afford the writs necessary to bring an action, or might be unable to
meet the fees expected for legal advice and assistance (let alone representation in court). Costs could escalate if a suit was unnecessarily
protracted. Moreover, if the plaintiff was unsuccessful or failed to turn
up, he might be liable to pay a fine to the crown for a false claim. There
is nevertheless clear evidence that considerable allowance was made for
the fact that the cost of litigation (with its attendant expenses) might
prejudice potential suits from the lower orders. Indeed, various forms of
'legal aid' existed, and efforts were made by parliament and the judiciary
to ensure that people were not denied an opportunity for justice purely
on economic grounds.

By the fourteenth century, obtaining the services of a lawyer was a vital
factor when pursuing court action. In order to have a chance of success
the plaintiff needed to be appraised of the legal position, had to obtain
the correct writ and follow the necessary procedures. A defendant also
required expert assistance and had to traverse the charges made against
him without omitting a denial or making a verbal error. Finding an attorney was therefore a necessary first step. Legal advice did not usually come
cheap. How were the less well-off able to cope? In the thirteenth century
ad hoc advice and assistance could often be obtained from the clerks of
royal justices travelling in the provinces.[9] By the early fourteenth century,
men of law whose work lay predominantly in the localities were increasingly available for advice or representation and, judging by the number
of suits brought in the court of king's bench by peasants using an attorney
(see below), the fees they charged cannot have been unduly exorbitant
or prohibitive.[10] Although it is difficult to be sure of the prevailing standard fee (if indeed there was such a thing), it has been suggested, on the
basis of a city of London ordinance of 1356, that 3s 4d (roughly two
weeks' wages for an artisan) was a 'reasonable fee' and probably near
enough the amount charged by a late-medieval attorney operating in the
provinces.[11] Payment did not have to be wholly in cash: some attorneys
accepted payment in kind (for example in cheese and butter).[12]

For the majority of litigants, the services of a pleader (arranged
by their attorney) might also be required. In comparison with attorneys, the fee scale for serjeants was generally higher, but they were not

all the grasping fee earners the poet Langland would have us believe:

> Seriantz it semede that serveth at þe Barre
> Plededen for penys and poundes þe lawe
> And nat for love of Oure Lord vnlose here lyppes ones.
> Thow myghtest betre meten myst on Malverne Hulles
> Than gete a mum of here mouth at moneye be shewed.
>   (Prologue to *Piers Plowman*)[13]

Modest remuneration was levied from some litigants and it was not unknown for serjeants to undertake work *pro bono*. In Edward I's reign, for instance, the sum of 3s 4d is known to have been paid to some serjeants operating in the royal courts; a similar sum was payable to serjeants practising in the city of London courts about half a century later. Clients too poor to pay the required amount for legal representation were sometimes assigned a pleader by the justices free of charge. There were several requests in the eyres of the early 1290s.[14] Alan son of Alan Plotman, for example, on behalf of himself and his mother claimed that they were poor folk and asked the justices 'so that they lose not their right' to grant them a serjeant, but the outcome is unknown.[15]

Once the attorney had advised on court action, the economically disadvantaged plaintiff faced further financial barriers. To bring litigation at the assizes or in the court of common pleas a plaintiff required an 'original' writ to initiate proceedings and, once the writ had been returned to court, a series of 'judicial' writs to control later stages. The prospective litigant could qualify for help with these charges if he or she were poor since, in spite of a reputation for over-charging, chancery clerks waived the fee of 6d for an originating writ if the applicant could swear to poverty.[16] In the thirteenth century and into the early fourteenth century no major outlay was usually required for judicial writs. At least prior to 1285 they were probably issued free of charge, and even after the second Statute of Westminster of that year they only cost one penny.[17] By Edward III's reign, however, the fee for a judicial writ had outstripped the cost of an original writ, having risen to 7d; and a further increase of 3d occurred by 1350.[18] Although this inflated price would appear to endorse claims that justice was becoming more exclusive, the cost of litigation did not go uncriticised. The parliamentary commons petitioned for a reduction in the price of original writs to 3d and for a withdrawal of extra charges (often included for land litigation) which were considered to be unreasonable.[19] The commons were unsuccessful in reducing the cost of an original writ, but they managed to secure some concessions, including the proviso that any extra costs would not be levied if the writ were granted as an act of charity or by favour of the court.[20]

Suits could also be brought by purchasing from chancery a special commission of oyer and terminer. Issued under letters patent, they were eagerly sought by litigants of various backgrounds from the late thirteenth century and reached a peak of popularity during the early fourteenth century.[21] The fee paid to chancery was normally £1. Though it represented a one-off payment (and attracted none of the hidden extras characteristic of judicial writs), such a sizeable sum, considerably in excess of the cost of a writ, would appear to have placed the purchase of such commissions beyond the reach of poorer litigants. Interestingly, however, a variable fee scale appears to have operated, (possibly) controlled by the ability to pay. Charges towards the upper end of the spectrum graduated from two marks (equivalent to 26s 8d) through to £2 and could even reach five marks (£3 6s 8d), levels which at times may have scorched the pockets of some gentry families. Towards the lower end applicants were allowed to pay reduced rates, ranging from one mark (13s 4d) to as little as half a mark. While even these lesser sums may have been difficult for members of the peasantry to raise, it is nevertheless clear that the relative poverty of some of those applying for commissions was taken into consideration. Indeed, it is apparent that not infrequently special oyer and terminer commissions were issued 'for God' as an act of Christian charity, and accordingly the requirement for payment was dropped altogether.[22]

The cheapest method of bringing an action was to go before the justices with an oral complaint (*querela*) or present a written bill outlining the injury suffered. It would appear that no charge was payable for this facility and it enabled ordinary people to bring with relative ease their cases before the particular group of royal justices visiting their county.[23] The practice was initiated in the middle of the thirteenth century when the crown encouraged the bringing of complaints before the justices in eyre. It proved a popular form of achieving redress, in that the general eyre was flooded with business in the form of private suits brought by peasants.[24]

The suspension of the eyre in 1294 did not end the opportunity for cheap and easy access to the courts. Jurisdiction over oral complaints and bills passed initially to justices holding general commissions of oyer and terminer and to the itinerant king's bench. Despite the latter's pre-eminent position in the hierarchy of courts, peasants were not inhibited from initiating proceedings in king's bench, as a social analysis of lawsuits coming before the court when sitting in Lincolnshire (1291–1339) has indicated.[25] New cases brought by 'villagers' never accounted for less than 70 per cent of the total business generated in the shire, while the average for the period was an impressive 81 per cent. The comparative frequency with which the court of king's bench visited Lincolnshire (once every eighteen months on average during the sixteen years 1323–39) may have been a relevant factor in encouraging this group not only to use the court, but to continue using it after its departure.[26]

Litigants could also bring bills before the justices of the peace. Though a number of historians have commented that the justices of the peace were forbidden to accept private suits for common-law wrongs after 1332, in actual fact the peace commissioners appointed in 1338 were allowed to do so. Surviving enrolments indicate that they continued to entertain such bills even when (after 1350) the requisite authority ceased to be included in their commissions. Significantly, after 1350 justices of the peace were empowered to receive bills relating to the labour legislation and other statutory offences. This provided another encouragement for the lower-class litigant and, as the evidence of the surviving session rolls shows, the hearing of bills relating to these areas comprised a significant part of the business at the quarter sessions held in the late fourteenth and fifteenth centuries.[27]

In addition to fees for the services of a lawyer and payments to get the case off the ground there were other expenses attendant on private litigation. A person who initiated an action had to be able at the outset to satisfy the court that he or she would turn up and prosecute the case. A claim, therefore, had to be supported by two people who were duly required to ensure the plaintiff's presence in court and who were liable to imprisonment or a fine if he defaulted. Here, again, special consideration was given to those who lacked the necessary economic wherewithal. Complainants who were poor and unable to find anyone to back their claim could take an oath and pledge their faith instead. Suitors who could not find personal pledges were also allowed to substitute items of clothing or property, such as a cloak or a horse.[28] If, at some later date, the claim was not pursued and the plaintiff withdrew his or her suit (perhaps because the case had been settled out of court), or failed to substantiate the whole claim, he or she might then be liable for further expenditure: suffering an amercement for a false claim or having to pay for a licence to come to an agreement. Accepting the financial hardship that would be incurred by a person of slender means, the court might remit the fine where the litigant was poor.[29]

If the outcome of litigation was favourable, some (or all) of the expense involved in bringing the action might be recouped in the damages awarded. Although the justices and their clerks were usually entitled to a share of the sum recovered, the proportion was not fixed. In any case the assignment of a fraction of the award was probably not obligatory for poorer plaintiffs, or necessary when the sum itself was insignificant.[30] Generally defendants were kept in custody until they satisfied the required sum, although in 1300 a losing litigant who had been committed to prison was released when the justices found out that he was penniless.[31] The justices obviously had some sympathy for, or were realistic about the chances of satisfaction from, a defendant with little or no income as there is evidence that the impoverished were excused payment altogether.[32]

When the parties finally arrived in court, how intelligible were events there? Given the somewhat arcane and technical language, court proceedings inevitably took on an air of mystery and exclusivity and litigants faced potential barriers to comprehension, both cognitive and linguistic. The legal records appear to reinforce this: the plea rolls of royal (and even manorial) courts are in Latin; the legal treatise known as *Bracton* employs Latin dialogue in its examples, as does the earliest report of a cross-examination by a judge,[33] while the Year Books, which often seem to be convincing reports of actual proceedings in the eyre and Westminster courts, are in French.[34] Could the informed layperson understand what was going on? Was the poor litigant able to grasp anything of what was occurring?

To answer this we need to consider both the nature and content of trials. The question of comprehension can be broached initially by querying whether it was necessary for a litigant to be fully conversant with the pleadings and procedures. The extent of any personal involvement would have depended upon whether professional representation was appropriate or available, upon the judicial forum and the nature and complexity of the particular case. Suits which revolved around difficult points of law would necessarily require expert presentation; and – certainly after 1259 – obtaining the services of a serjeant was compulsory in pleas of land and of replevin in the city of London courts.[35]

In order to appreciate the extent to which the system possessed (or acquired) an element of 'user-friendliness' we must first distinguish between the language(s) used to record details of the court proceedings and the language(s) actually spoken in court. A further distinction should then be made between the language of the formal pleadings and that used in the later proceedings. Surviving lawyers' manuals show that the rehearsal of issues before the court was carried out in French, rather than in Latin, certainly from the middle of the thirteenth century.[36] This linguistic preference probably continued for at least another hundred years, until it was decreed by the city of London in 1356 that pleadings should be in English,[37] a move that was extended to all courts of law by royal statute six years later.[38] Such a change did not, of course produce instant transparency, or remove the opportunity for confusion arising out of the complexity of legal language. Nonetheless theoretically a measure of accessibility was achieved through the introduction of the vernacular in that it enabled those who were unrepresented and had little or no knowledge of law French to put (as effectively as they could) their claims before the justices.

Focus on the language of pleadings inevitably obscures the extent of language exchange that took place.[39] Jurors presenting their responses to the 'articles of the eyre' at the Kent eyre of 1313–14, for instance, were apparently required to submit orally in English (through their foreman) answers which, before their acceptance by the court and subsequent enrolment in Latin, had to correspond exactly with the words previously recited in French by the court clerk. The oral use of vernacular was not limited to simple statements. Where the mother tongue of court participants was English (and as early as Henry III's reign the judges were native Englishmen) it would be reasonable to suppose – indeed common sense in the case of a poor villager – that the vernacular was used as a means of enabling a meaningful and effective exchange to take place between the bench and parties or witnesses. There is evidence of French and English being used in cross-examinations in the church courts in 1271, and it is unlikely that the royal courts (even the central courts) differed in this respect.[40]

While the full implications of proceedings may have eluded many litigants, their general understanding of events was undoubtedly enhanced during the later fourteenth century by the use of English, in spite of the illusion provided by the surviving records. The opportunity to employ a local man expert in the law to manage the complexities of litigation and steer the case through court was also a powerful means of overcoming both the technical and psychological barriers to bringing litigation in the royal courts. The ability of the lower orders to obtain legal advice and use the judicial system to their advantage has long been underestimated. Indeed, some peasants can be shown to have been experienced litigators, at times bringing cases in the royal courts, at other times pursuing (often lengthy) disputes in the manorial courts.[41]

Even the unfree (who technically had no rights to sue in the royal courts) appear to have employed lawyers and achieved a measure of access, particularly during the later fourteenth century.[42] The fact that the system was so obviously stacked against the unfree does not mean that justice was perceived as a closed shop: access to the royal courts was clearly regarded as an important advantage to be preserved or acquired.[43]

Entrance to the legal system was obviously one thing, but were poorer litigants treated differently once they were inside? To what extent was the system open to abuse in the form of class prejudice, bias and impropriety? Could justice in its moral sense be achieved? Was the system, as the author of *An Outlaw's Song of Trailbaston* suggested, riddled with 'deceit' and 'bad law'? In the final analysis, can we reconcile the contradictory image of outlawry? Was it as fearsome or, conversely, as desirable as was claimed?

Although Magna Carta did not herald a 'judicial Utopia', its provisions set a benchmark against which the operation of the legal system in the fourteenth century was increasingly measured. The twenty-ninth chapter of the 1225 version proclaimed 'to no one will we sell, to no one will we deny or delay right or justice'. Although this was initially directed at a specific group, the tenants in chief, it was arguably interpreted later to have more general application.[44] By Edward III's reign the Great Charter was regularly confirmed in statute legislation and there were additional guarantees that, irrespective of his estate, no man would be condemned or made to answer accusations without the correct procedures being followed.[45] Emphasis was also placed at a judicial level on the fair treatment of everyone regardless of status. The oath taken by a royal justice (from at least the middle of the thirteenth century) affirmed that when acting in a judicial capacity he would 'do justice to the best of his ability to all as well poor as rich . . . [would not] disturb or respite justice against right or against the law of the land either for the great or the rich . . . [and] loyally do right to all according to law and custom'.[46] The crown's continuing desire that justice should be inclusive and benefit equally persons of high and low status was enshrined in the Ordinance of Justices of 1346.[47]

The justices' oath placed on them an onus to intervene and use their discretion where it mattered. A practical manifestation of the judges' role in this respect might be using their discretion to assign counsel to poor litigants and thus counteract any advantage which a litigant of higher status might wield.[48] This might be particularly pertinent in the case of a poor litigant unable to provide the customary gifts for judges and jurors. The capacity to look at an individual's situation and go behind the strict letter of the law to the underlying morality characterised the term in office of several judges of the period, and was a vital factor in the beginnings of 'equity' and the Chancellor's 'court of conscience'. Towards the end of Edward I's reign, for example, royal judges Staunton, Hengham and Howard were quite prepared to override a statute where hardship might result.[49] A couple of years later, Bereford was willing to act likewise 'in the present case, because of the hardship that will ensue'.[50] Staunton refused to let a woman lose her dower through a tenant's deviousness and by distinguishing between the heir's inheritance and his purchase achieved 'justice' for her.[51] Bereford enunciated a similar concern that a plaintiff should bring a case in good faith. He also once urged that there was a moral dimension to law.[52] Although the judges just mentioned were predominantly men of the late thirteenth and early fourteenth centuries, there were others in the middle to late fourteenth century who carried this spirit forward. Mowbray, for instance, believed the law (judicial decisions) needed to be in accord with reason and to remedy 'mischief' (injustice),[53] while Shareshull felt the intellectual tendency towards following 'precedent' (though a concept itself used to ensure uniformity and fairness) should not be allowed to override 'right'.[54]

The crown was not satisfied with the theoretical impartiality and integrity of its officials. An important feature of royal justice was the provision of the opportunity to complain about the workings of justice (including personnel and the courts) and of mechanisms to take action against those who failed to uphold its standards. This was not a purely philanthropic gesture on the part of the government. It was beneficial to the crown that the activities of its officials could be scrutinised by those on the ground. Punishment of the guilty by fines or removal from office both enhanced the effectiveness of the crown's operations and brought in revenue for its coffers. While a side effect of this initiative may have been the generation of malicious complaints, many of them were probably perfectly genuine and contributed significantly to reducing the amount of corruption or self-seeking that was alleged to have flourished. The eyre, of course, had pioneered the crown's acceptance of such complaints. Its judicial successors (as outlined above) continued to investigate the misdeeds of officials involved in the administration of justice, and in particular were concerned to root out concerted abuse of the legal system.

The specific crimes of conspiracy, champerty and maintenance were tackled by judges in the courts and through parliamentary legislation.[55] The problem of jury corruption was arguably eased by a series of special provisions which tightened up on procedures relating to jury trials and brought in safeguards on the composition and conduct of jury panels.[56] The procedure of attaint, whereby a jury decision could be overturned if there was sufficient evidence of perjury, was extended to the poor (for pleas of land) in 1361.[57]

From the late thirteenth century the poor, humble and weak had also recognised the potential of submitting a petition to the king in parliament. Sometimes (as in 1330 and 1341) encouragement came directly from the crown and was clearly politically motivated.[58] Nevertheless, even in the middle of the fourteenth century (by which time the private petition had to a large extent given way to the 'common' petition and had ceased to be enrolled on the parliament rolls) petitioning in parliament remained a potent method of achieving a hearing for judicial problems. Indeed, most of the extant petitions concern matters arising from legal cases.[59] Given all the other means of taking action within the judicial system, it is significant that this method of achieving redress remained alive.

A system for dealing with complaints against royal judges (to be proclaimed in all public places) was instituted by Edward III in the Ordinance of Justices. There is no evidence as to the effectiveness of this system, but the proclamation may have been listened to, assimilated and discussed among local people. Certainly it represents an approach by the crown towards identifying with the needs of its subjects and attempting to remedy them. Nevertheless, if there is some justifiable criticism of restricted access to justice in the later fourteenth century, then it is possibly in the area of complaint mechanisms. It was a problem probably founded on people's perceptions: despite governmental initiatives, people may have believed there were far fewer opportunities to appeal against the misdoings of officials than was in fact the case because the traditional mechanisms were no longer in evidence. Alternatively, their expectations of justice may have grown commensurately with the developing system, resulting in a dissatisfaction with the new legal world – a dissatisfaction that the royal government was forced to acknowledge during the Peasants' Revolt.

Having demonstrated the relative accessibility of the judicial system and its attempts to avoid social exclusivity, we need to ascertain the thinking behind the moves. Was there a distinct attitude or even a policy towards the less well off and the impotent? Who were the poor who came to seek 'legal aid' and on what basis might they have qualified for and received it?

The thinking within government and judicial circles concerning treatment of the indigent at law may have arisen from a heightened consciousness about the poor combined with new attitudes towards the moral character of poverty. From at least the twelfth century there was much debate amongst jurists and theologians (and particularly between the Church and the mendicant orders) on the nature of poverty and how relief might best be given to the poor. This involved identifying what have subsequently been called the 'deserving poor' – those whom it was felt could be distinguished from the general mass of poor folk for the receipt of charity because they were not capable of working (possibly through sickness or injury or other weakness), or had been respectable but were now experiencing difficult times. Donors were advised to avoid giving charity to those likely to resort to crime or sin, or to able-bodied idlers or mere vagrants – an attitude that was echoed in the labour legislation of the mid-fourteenth century. The *pauperes verecundi* or shame-faced poor, however, those who had been used to a measure of comfort but through circumstances were now reduced to poverty, did merit charity. Indeed, they were regarded as doubly needy since they had suffered not only physically, through shortage and need, but also mentally, through social dislocation and the associated shame.[60]

Some examples of bills presented to the justices in eyre seem to bear this out. John Feyrewin told how he had been forced to become a pauper begging his bread 'for God's sake' and ended up by saying 'I have not a halfpenny to spend on a pleader.' William son of Hugh of Smethumilne's request places emphasis on the personal spiritual benefits of allowing aid: 'And I pray you, for your soul's sake, that you will give me remedy for this, for I am so poor that I can pay for no counter.' Edith, widow of Richard Darlaston, makes similar claims, praying 'remedy for your charity and for God's sake, for she is poor'. She may in fact have fitted into the category of shame-faced poor and thus regarded as truly deserving of help, since she claims that 'by these things [the legal misfortunes she relates] she has been brought to beggary'.[61]

While there appears to have been no clearly defined or articulated 'policy' as such, there was definitely a feeling within government and judicial circles and amongst the more privileged members of society that royal justice was an area in which charitable discretion should operate. The parliamentary commons persistently argued throughout the fourteenth century that the royal courts should be equally accessible to the less well off (if not to the genuinely poor). As we have seen, litigants frequently requested help in purchasing writs or special commissions of oyer and terminer and in obtaining legal representation, and were duly awarded them in terms that describe it as an act of charity. Even if by the end of the fourteenth century the emphasis had changed as to who was truly deserving of charity, some bills from Lincolnshire peace sessions in the 1390s demonstrate (though the wording was probably standard form) that there were still requests for remedy 'for the love of God and by way of charity' (*amore dei intuitu caritatis*).[62]

In comparison to most charitable gifts, legal aid (in terms of the money saved in legal fees) would have amounted to a substantial donation. The minimum given in charity seems to have been $\frac{1}{4}$d, while inmates of almshouses probably received about 1d per day.[63] If the price of an original writ (6d) or a special oyer and terminer commission (3s 4d) were waived, together with legal fees of at least 3s 4d and any other additional charges, the litigant was remarkably fortunate. Indeed, someone who regained a piece of land or a disputed inheritance, or who obtained at least a proportion of the damages claimed, would have gained considerably in both financial and (more significantly) social terms.

The very fact that poor people were granted this legal aid must say something about the approachability of the judicial system, but we can only speculate about how they came to seek it in the first place. How did they know that they could receive help to bring a suit unless this was by some means communicated to the lower classes? Perhaps the poor who were given help to settle their problems in the royal courts received information from persons to whom they were connected in some way, either through kinship or friendship or through a link of clientage, as tenants or servants.

The practice of aiding the litigation of poor persons was not confined to the royal courts, but was mirrored in the ecclesiastical courts. Indeed, from the late thirteenth century it was regarded as the ethical professional duty of canon lawyers to act without remuneration for impoverished clients.[64] The first official indication of the English Church's practice appears in a statute of Archbishop Winchelsey of 1295, which provided that it was the duty of the judge presiding in the Court of Arches to grant advocates and proctors to clients who claimed poverty.[65] This was also the tenor of regulations promulgated by the bishop of Durham in 1312.[66] The phenomenon of legal aid, however, was not limited to the English court system, as legislation from northern

Italy demonstrates. What is interesting from this point of view is, first, the capacity of such provision to transcend national and jurisdictional boundaries. Secondly and more significantly, whilst the general duty to aid the poor may have derived from canonist doctrine, the initiative and responsibility did not remain purely with the Church. Statutes from Modena, Bologna and Ferrara indicate a willingness on the part of civic authorities to provide public lawyers for the poor financed out of tax revenues.[67] Although the English state issued no formal, all-encompassing legislation on this issue during this period, it is clear that its more piecemeal and *ad hoc* discretionary measures nevertheless pre-empted considerably the *in forma pauperis* provisions of Henry VII's reign.[68]

In the *Outlaw's Song*, the system of outlawry is paradoxically blamed for putting people outside the law, but revered as enabling its victims to live in an ideal state, unencumbered by legal institutions and traditional concepts of law. The reality was somewhat different. Viewed in its legal context, the onus was clearly on the individual to respond to the accusation against him (either civil or criminal) within the required time period. There was not necessarily anything sinister about it, it was purely the wheels of bureaucracy: the status of outlaw was proclaimed in default of an answer. The outlaw's view also takes no account of the fact that once outlawry had been pronounced there were in fact many ways of reversing it, not least by having a reasonable excuse for not being able to turn up on the final occasion.[69] Moreover, at the time the poem was written (in the first decade of the fourteenth century) the system of outlawry, like the contemporary legal institutions themselves, was in a state of flux. From the government's point of view, up to the late thirteenth century outlawry was a useful process whereby criminals were identified and information about them communicated. Its effectiveness derived from its use of the sanction of exclusion as a means of preventing crime. By the fourteenth century, however, partly as a result of demographic changes, exclusion from the community had become less meaningful to the individual and more difficult to enforce. Consequently outlawry no longer possessed much bite.[70] Alterations in the rules and practices surrounding it over the course of the century also alleviated its direct effect.[71]

The outlaw's identification with the disadvantaged person who has experienced harsh treatment *within* the legal system, as well as the person who has been placed *outside* it, in fact conflates two separate problems. Those who refuse to answer the sheriff's writ because they fear or know they will not be treated fairly may feel forced to 'opt out', but in fact are not doing themselves any favours by doing so. The medieval judicial system, as we have seen, did not operate deliberately to the exclusion of the disadvantaged in society, provided they remained within the boundaries of the legal world. In many ways it went out of its way to make its services available for those with little money or influence and waived fees or abrogated strict rules of procedure when approached. It was keen to make it known that it followed the ideal that justice should be equally favourable to the poor and to the rich and that its officers were bound to uphold this maxim. Although we should not idealise the medieval world, in order for the poor to use and *reuse* the legal system they must have had some confidence in royal justice and in its capacity to embrace all estates. The greenwood may have seemed idyllic, but there was no chance of achieving redress through 'opting out' or betterment by remaining outside the system.

Medieval justice was clearly flexible and accommodating, but did its apparent benevolence rely wholly or in part on the discretion of the personnel involved in its administration, notably the royal justices and other lawyers? Two of the justices named in the *Outlaw's Song* appear to have been respected. They are described in terms of their piety and concern for the poor. They are clearly contrasted with two of their colleagues, whose discretion, it is implied, is unlikely to be exercised in the litigant's favour.[72] Although to some extent benevolence to the poor became institutionalised over the period (because on proof of status benefits were routinely given), there was still a place for judicial discretion. Sometimes it could be exercised favourably towards the less well off; at other times it might fall more harshly. Justice itself, however, is an ideal, for variance in temperament and in execution of the law are characteristic of judges down the ages and not confined to the medieval period.

NOTES

1. R. B. Dobson and J. Taylor, *Rymes of Robin Hood: An Introduction to the English Outlaw* (3rd edn, Stroud, 1997), p. 252 (*An Outlaw's Song of Trailbaston*, c. 1305).

2. Outlawry was an administrative process which occurred automatically if an individual failed to answer a writ of summons or attachment (which was normally followed by a writ of arrest) by the time his or her name had been proclaimed at five meetings of the county court (in other words, after at least five months): M. Hastings, *The Court of Common Pleas in Fifteenth Century England* (Hamden, Conn., 1971), pp. 174–9.

3. See for example: G. L. Harriss, *King, Parliament and Public Finance in Medieval England* (Oxford, 1975), pp. 354–5; R. W. Kaeuper, *War, Justice and Public Order* (Oxford, 1988), pp. 386–7; R. H. Hilton, *Class Conflict and the Crisis of Feudalism* (rev. edn, London, 1990), pp. 49–65, 173–9; R. C. Palmer, *English Law in the Age of the Black Death, 1348–1381. A Transformation of Governance and Law* (Chapel Hill, NC, 1993).

4. D. Crook, 'The Later Eyres', *English Historical Review* 97 (1982), 241–6; A. Musson and W. M. Ormrod, *The Evolution of English Justice: Law, Politics and Society in the Fourteenth Century* (Basingstoke, 1998), pp. 43–54.

5. F. W. Maitland, *Collected Papers*, 3 vols. (Cambridge, 1911), II, pp. 110–73; E. De Haas and G. D. G. Hall (eds.), *Early Registers of Writs*, Selden Society 87 (1970), p. cxxii: about fifty actions were in use in the early thirteenth century; the figure had risen to nearly 900 a century later.

6. P. R. Hyams, 'What Did Edwardian Villagers Mean by "Law"?', in Z. Razi and R. M. Smith (eds.), *Medieval Society and the Manor Court* (Oxford, 1996), pp. 80–2; A. Musson, 'New Labour Laws, New Remedies? Legal Reaction to the Black Death "Crisis"', in N. Saul (ed.), *Fourteenth Century England*, I (Woodbridge, 2000) pp. 73–88.

7. *Year Book 3 & 4 Edward II*, p. 162.

8. P. Brand, *The Making of the Common Law* (London, 1992), pp. 98–101; J. H. Baker, *An Introduction to English Legal History* (3rd edn, London, 1990), pp. 170–1.

9. Brand, *Common Law*, p. 184.

10. P. Brand, *The Origins of the English Legal Profession* (Oxford, 1992), pp. 91–4; B. W. McLane, 'Changes in the Court of King's Bench, 1291–1340: the Preliminary View from Lincolnshire', in W. M. Ormrod (ed.), *England in the Fourteenth Century: Proceedings of the 1985 Harlaxton Symposium* (Woodbridge, 1986), pp. 159–60.

11. *Calendar of Letter Books of the City of London: Letter Book G*, ed. R. R. Sharpe (London, 1905), p. 74; P. Tucker, 'London's Courts of Law in the Fifteenth Century', in C. W. Brooks and M. Lobban (eds.), *Communities and Courts in Britain, 1150–1900* (London, 1997), p. 33.

12. W. C. Bolland (ed.), *Select Bills in Eyre, 1292–1333*, Selden Society 30 (London, 1914), p. 119.

13. William Langland, *Piers Plowman*, ed. A. V. J. Schmidt (London and New York, 1995), p. 19, C text, lines 160–4.

14. Brand, *Legal Profession*, pp. 104–5.

15. Bolland (ed.), *Select Bills in Eyre*, p. 21.

16. J. C. Davies, 'Common Law Writs and Returns, Richard I to Richard II', *Bulletin of the Institute of Historical Research* 26 (1953), 139–42; B. Wilkinson, *The Chancery under Edward III* (Manchester, 1929), pp. 60–2.

17. 13 Edward I (Statute of Westminster) c. 44 (*Statute Rolls*, I, p. 93); Brand, *Common Law*, p. 183 and n. 81: Dr Brand points out that the sum of 7d per writ was paid by the prior of Norwich in 1283, hence the 'rise' may in some cases have been illusory.

18. Wilkinson, *Chancery under Edward III*, p. 60.
19. *Rotuli Parliamentorum*, II, pp. 170, 229–30, 241, 261, 305; A. J. Verduyn, 'The Attitude of the Parliamentary Commons to Law and Order under Edward III' (D.Phil. thesis, University of Oxford, 1991), pp. 133–4.
20. *Rotuli Parliamentorum*, I, p. 376; *Calendar of Close Rolls, 1341–3*, p. 633; Wilkinson, *Chancery under Edward III*, pp. 61–2.
21. R. W. Kaeuper, 'Law and Order in Fourteenth-Century England: the Evidence of Special Commissions of Oyer and Terminer', *Speculum* 54 (1979), 734–84.
22. Based on an analysis of *Calendars of Patent Rolls 1377–99*.
23. The common form and language of some bills suggests that some legally skilled person drafted them; payment might then have been required, but the evidence is lacking.
24. A. Harding (ed.), *The Roll of the Shropshire Eyre of 1256*, Selden Society 96 (1980), pp. xix–xxv.
25. McLane, 'Court of King's Bench', pp. 158–9.
26. The unusually high frequency of visitations may have created special conditions in Lincolnshire which means these findings are not necessarily applicable to the other counties.
27. Musson and Ormrod, *English Justice*, pp. 130–1.
28. A. W. Hopkins (ed.), *Selected Rolls of the Chester City Courts*, Chetham Society, third series 2 (1950), pp. lv, 41, 54; A. Harding, 'Plaints and Bills in the History of English Law', in D. Jenkins (ed.), *Legal History Studies 1972* (Cardiff, 1975), p. 70.
29. PRO, Court of King's Bench, KB 27/272 *Rex* m21 (Northamptonshire – Emma Watecok).
30. Kaeuper, 'Special Commissions', 757; Brand, *Common Law*, p. 184.
31. S. Sheridan Walker, 'Wrongdoing and Compensation: the Pleas of Wardship in Thirteenth and Fourteenth Century England', *Journal of Legal History* 9 (1988), 267–307 (p. 289).
32. For example: PRO, Justices Itinerant, JUST 1/1395 m10: John Whyshele of Abingdon, found to have assaulted Walter Godusglade, was liable to pay one shilling in damages until he was excused.
33. S. E. Thorne (ed.), *Bracton on the Laws and Customs of England*, 4 vols. (Cambridge, Mass., 1968–77); H. Cam (ed.), *The London Eyre of 1244*, London Record Society 6 (1970), p. 134, no. 345.
34. Published in the Rolls Series and Selden Society volumes. Some of the early law reports may not in fact have been based on discussions in the courtroom: P. Brand, 'The Beginnings of English Law Reporting', in C. Stebbings (ed.), *Law Reporting in Britain* (London, 1995), pp. 1–14.
35. Brand, *Legal Profession*, p. 67.
36. G. J. Turner (ed.), *Brevia Placitata*, Selden Society 66 (1947), p. 153; G. E. Woodbine (ed.), *Four Thirteenth-Century Law Tracts* (New Haven, Conn., 1910), p. 162.
37. *Calendar of Letter Books of the City of London: Letter book G*, p. 73.

38. 36 Edward III st. 1, c. 15 (*Statute Rolls*, ii, pp. 375–6).
39. For what follows see M. T. Clanchy, *From Memory to Written Record: England 1066–1307* (2nd edn, Oxford, 1996), pp. 206–9.
40. E.g.: *Year Book 2 Edward II*, pp. 11, 36; *Year Book 12 & 13 Edward III*, p. 274. We should, however, be wary of reading too much into the law reports since some early ones ascribe dialogue to the parties rather than to the serjeants who must have spoken for them: Brand, 'English law reporting', p. 4.
41. P. R. Schofield, 'Peasants and the Manor Court: Gossip and Litigation in a Suffolk Village at the Close of the Thirteenth Century', *Past & Present* 159 (1998), 1–42.
42. Kaeuper, 'Special Commissions', 752; R. Faith, 'The "Great Rumour" of 1377 and Peasant Ideology', in R. H. Hilton and T. H. Aston (eds.), *The English Rising of 1381* (Cambridge, 1981), pp. 43–73.
43. M. K. McIntosh, 'The Privileged Villeins of the English Ancient Demesne', *Viator* 7 (1976), 325–6.
44. J. C. Holt, *Magna Carta* (2nd edn, Cambridge, 1992), pp. 1, 149–3, 327.
45. 25 Edward III c. 4, 28 Edward III c. 3, 42 Edward III c. 3 (*Statute Rolls*, i, pp. 321, 345, 388).
46. Brand, *Common Law*, p. 150.
47. 20 Edward III (*Statute Rolls*, i, pp. 303–6).
48. J. A. Brundage, 'Legal Aid for the Poor and the Professionalization of Law in the Middle Ages', *Journal of Legal History* 9 (1988), 169–79 (p. 173).
49. *Year Book 33 & 35 Edward I*, p. 380.
50. *Year Book 1 & 2 Edward II*, p. 33.
51. *Year Book 4 Edward II*, pp. 25–6.
52. *Year Book 1 & 2 Edward II*, p. xix.
53. *Year Book 15 Edward III*, p. 126.
54. B. H. Putnam, *The Place in Legal History of Sir William Shareshull* (Cambridge, 1950), pp. 115–18.
55. For example in the trailbaston enquiries of 1305–7 and 1341–4 and in the Statute of Northampton (1328) and the Ordinance of Justices (1346).
56. 25 Edward III st. 5, c. 3; 34 Edward III c. 8; 38 Edward III st. 1, c. 12 (*Statute Rolls*, i, pp. 320, 366, 384–5).
57. 34 Edward III c. 7 (*Statute Rolls* i, p. 366).
58. *Calendar of Close Rolls, 1330–3*, pp. 161–2; *Rotuli Parliamentorum*, ii, p. 127 (5).
59. I am grateful to Dr Gwylim Dodd for this communication.
60. B. Tierney, 'The Decretists and the "Deserving Poor"', *Comparative Studies in Society and History* 1 (1958–9), 360–73; M. Rubin, *Charity and Community in Medieval Cambridge* (Cambridge, 1987), pp. 68–74; C. Dyer, *Standards of Living in the Later Middle Ages* (Cambridge, 1989), pp. 236–40.
61. Bolland (ed.), *Select Bills in Eyre*, pp. 6, 44, 47.
62. E. G. Kimball (ed.), *Some Sessions of the Peace in Lincolnshire, 1381–1396*, Lincoln Record Society 49 (Hereford, 1955), pp. 65, 74.
63. Dyer, *Standards of Living*, p. 253.

64. Brand, *Legal Profession*, pp. 153–4; Brundage, 'Legal Aid', 174–5.
65. D. Wilkins, *Concilia Magnae Britanniae et Hiberniae*, 4 vols. (Brussels, 1964), II, p. 206.
66. Ibid., p. 418.
67. Brundage, 'Legal Aid', 174–5.
68. J. M. Maguire, 'Poverty and Civil Litigation', *Harvard Law Review* 36 (1923), 361–404.
69. Hastings, *Common Pleas*, pp. 180–3.
70. H. Summerson, 'The Structure of Law Enforcement in Thirteenth Century England', *American Journal of Legal History* 23 (1979), 313–27.
71. 18 Edward III st. 2, c. 5 (no exigent to go out unless felony or trespass against the peace); 25 Edward III st. 5, c. 17 (process of exigent in debt detinue and replevin); 37 Edward III c. 2 (indemnity for injustices and mistakes because of outlawry) (*Statute Rolls*, I, pp. 301, 322, 378).
72. Dobson and Taylor, *Rymes of Robin Hood*, p. 253.

CHAPTER 9

Idealising criminality: Robin Hood
in the fifteenth century

A. J. Pollard

The urge to speak of Robin Hood by those who never bent his bow remains undiminished. Why therefore yet another voice? There are two answers: one is that a volume such as this would surely be incomplete without a chapter on the medieval outlaw whom Barrie Dobson has made his own, and the other is that, curiously, in all the recent speakings no one has directly addressed what the tales of Robin Hood said to fifteenth-century audiences who heard them in the form in which they were subsequently set down in their earliest surviving versions. There has been endless speculation about a possible original 'real-life' Robin.[1] Much has been written in relation to the context in which the ballads are apparently set, sometime around 1300.[2] Considerable thought has been given to the composition of their audience.[3] The literary qualities, structure and antecedents of the ballads have been exhaustively analysed.[4] Yet not even in the work of Holt, or of Dobson and Taylor, is the content of the tales examined with a view to what they say specifically to a fifteenth-century audience.[5]

This neglect is to some extent surprising, since it is established that the earliest ballads took the form we know in the first half of the century. Dobson and Taylor, in their most recent discussion, judge that the tales began to survive in written form 'no later than the mid-fifteenth century'. Linguistic analysis of the *Gest* has suggested a date of composition as early as *c.* 1400. Professor Knight has proposed a later recording date, but his proposition does not preclude earlier composition. *Robin Hood and the Monk* survives only in a mid-fifteenth-century manuscript version. A fragment of *Guy of Gisborne* has been dated to the end of the century and the surviving manuscript copy of *Potter* to the very beginning of the sixteenth century. Precision is impossible, but together they constitute a corpus of fifteenth-century texts.[6]

However, we know that 'rymes of Robin Hood' were in circulation by 1377; and it is supposed that they were told well before that date since, as is now established, the names Robin Hood and Little John were known before 1300 in such a way as to suggest the outlaws were already legendary.[7] And since, even after they were circulating in print, the stories have continued to change according to the age in which they are told, it follows that they were no less likely to have changed when they were handed down as part of an oral tradition.[8] The tales recorded in the fifteenth century, therefore, are not necessarily in detail the same as any told in the middle of the fourteenth. It is reasonable to suppose that those known to Sir John Paston in 1473 were not exactly the same as those known to Langland in 1377.[9]

Attention given to the specifically fifteenth-century context of the recorded ballads has focussed primarily on the problem of the meaning of the term 'yeoman' to the audience. As Dobson and Taylor noted, 'from the moment he first steps on the historical stage, Robin Hood is presented as a yeoman hero for a yeoman audience'.[10] Since 1958 the significance of this has been keenly debated. On the one hand there is the view, sustained by Professor Holt, that the term is still used in the recorded ballads in the sense of an intermediary household rank, between squire and page, so placing the ballads firmly in the world of aristocratic service and a noble milieu.[11] On the other hand, there is the view, re-iterated by Dobson and Taylor and reinforced in more recent writings, that the word as it came to be used in the fifteenth century refers to an intermediate social status, between gentleman and husbandman. The audience is thus placed in village and town communities rather than baronial halls, and the ballads set in the context of popular rather than gentle culture.[12] This currently dominant view reflects a growing consensus that the fifteenth century witnessed the emergence of a broadly based and distinctive 'middling sort'.

Apart from the problem of the fifteenth-century use of the term 'yeoman', the only other speculation concerning the relationship between the ballads and the era in which they were first set down has been restricted to the political context. Professor Knight has claimed that his dating of the composition of the *Gest* to *c.* 1450 bears directly on any analysis of its meaning, but apart from a quotation from E. K. Chambers in 1945 on 'the chaotic condition of England under Edward IV' (identified as the King Edward of the *Gest*), he concentrates on a more generalised exploration of the manner in which the ballads articulate a symbolic resistance to authority throughout the later Middle Ages.[13] Simon Schama adds that 'it can hardly be an accident that the first . . . printed editions . . . appear at a disastrous moment in English history: the Wars of the Roses in the late fifteenth century' – which, besides implying a decidedly *passé* view of the era, does not expand on why it was no accident.[14]

There is therefore considerable scope for a fuller examination of what the ballads said to their fifteenth-century audiences. This preliminary exploration of what the seven or more tales of Robin Hood woven together in the early texts might have had to say to contemporaries will first focus on the depiction of crime, but will broaden out to comment further on the kind of criminal yeomen Robin Hood and his merry men were, and to suggest finally that the ballads were a vehicle for a popular history of crime as well as popular entertainment.

The ballads transform the crimes of a gang of hardened common highwaymen and poachers, who do not hesitate to kill even innocent children, into jocular, swashbuckling adventurers. But did the criminal world so portrayed in the ballads relate to the actuality of fifteenth-century crime revealed by surviving legal records? How frequently were the same kinds of crime committed? Were the attitudes to law enforcers and officers of the crown similar to those expressed in the stories? In other words, were audiences from places as diverse as the Pennine village of Mickleton in Teesdale and the Somerset market town of Taunton familiar from their own experience with the pattern of homicide, assault, banditry, highway robbery and poaching represented in the ballads?[15]

To begin with crimes of violence against the person, there are nine homicides in the early ballads (eleven if we count the killing of the sheriff twice and Robin's own murder), besides the twelve men killed by Robin as he fights his way out of church in Nottingham. There are three battles with the sheriff's men and two single-handed combats, both lasting a fabulous two hours.[16] Assault, beating people up for the fun of it, is also integral to the outlaws' self-image:

> 'To bydde a man to dyner
> and syth him bete and bynde,
> It is our olde maner', sayd Robyn.[17]

Robin himself has a nightmare in *Guy* in which he dreams that 'they did me bete and bynde'.[18] Yet, curiously, there are very few incidents of actual bodily harm by the oulaws on their victims. Little John, when masquerading as Reynolde Grenelef in the sheriff's service,

> gave the boteler such a tap
> His backe went nere in two.[19]

Having lured the monk into the forest, Little John turns on him, seizes him by the throat and throws him off his horse:

> John was nothing of hym agast
> He let hym falle on his crown.[20]

But this is the prelude to his murder. The outlaws threaten to assault those they kidnap, but rarely do so. The cowardly sheriff when he is captured by the outlaws is in fear of life and limb, but is only made to spend a cold spring night in his shirt and breeches.[21] And indeed in the case of two of their guests, the knight and the king, they honour them. Nevertheless the pervading sense of threat to life and property represented by the outlaws is real. When the outlaws and the king's men ride to Nottingham all dressed in green, the townspeople of Nottingham panic because they think their town is about to be sacked.[22]

The depiction of violence is also casual and matter of fact, nowhere more so than in the murders of the monk and his page:

> John smote off the Monk's hed
> No longer would he dwell;
> So did Moch the littul page
> For ferd lest he would tell.[23]

The killing of a little boy is horrific, but a listener/reader might discern a certain black humour in the throwaway line. Even the killing of Guy of Gisborne, though the details are grisly (Robin decapitates the body, slashes the face, lifts the head by the hair and rams it on the dead man's bow), is a somewhat cursory description.[24] The ballads revel in violence, but it is a violence taken for granted, sometimes leavened by humour.

One is tempted to assume that violence is a matter of fact in the ballads because it was the common, everyday experience of the century. That may be so, but popular entertainment has always dwelt on violence – and in some ages, such as the late twentieth century, a good deal more graphically than in the outlaw ballads. It is not easy to discern the extent to which the incidents and action in the ballads reflect the general experience and level of violent crime in the fifteenth century. Dr Maddern has calculated that in East Anglia between 1422 and 1442 only 6.8% of gaol delivery indictments were for homicide, and a further 5.25% for crime involving assault. Of cases involving violence heard before king's bench, only 4.15% concerned homicide, but 15.25% involved assault. Yet over 35% of crimes recorded in the Shropshire peace roll for 1400–14 alleged violence; and in the superior eyre for Shropshire and Staffordshire in 1414 more than half the indictments were for homicide. But the incidence of some of these crimes ran back as early as 1367.[25] Records for northern England provide equally varied data. In nineteen gaol deliveries in Cumberland between 1335 and 1457 only 5.7% of the reported crimes were homicide. In Durham, in fifteen months in 1471–3, 9.5% of cases presented before the justices of the peace and gaol delivery involved homicide, but as many as 46% violent assault. Of the indictments before king's bench in the six northern counties of Cumberland, Durham, Lancashire, Northumberland, Westmorland and Yorkshire in 1461–85, 17.5% were for homicide and 11% for assault.[26] For the north as well as the midlands and East Anglia the evidence is too little and too flawed for one to be able to draw firm conclusions about levels of violent crime.

Not much is revealed by a comparison of case histories with the action in the ballads. There are many cases of ambush with intent to kill or maim. In 1472 three brothers Hedlam, probably of the armigerous family seated at Nunthorpe in the North Riding, with a gang of sixteen or more waylaid Sir Richard Strangways, his brother and two servants with the bungled intent to kill Sir Richard. Thomas Dennis, an able but shifty East Anglian on the make, lured Walter Ingham into an ambush in January 1454 and inflicted grievous bodily harm on him. Arrested in Norwich, like Robin Hood he made a daring escape. His eventful life came to a sticky end, again like Robin Hood's, when he was himself murdered in 1461. Dennis was on the margins of gentility. In Weardale in county Durham over the winter of 1471–2 there was a spate of murders committed by yeomen. On 8 December 1471 John Redhed of Wotton and four members of the Wilson family, all yeomen, lay in wait at Stanhope and killed John Westwood. A month later Laurence Harper assembled a gang of labourers to attack and murder Richard Ward in Stanhope Park.[27] But there is nothing in these homicides committed by yeomen from Weardale to liken them to the killings committed by the yeomen outlaws of Barnsdale and Sherwood Forest.

There are many known clashes between armed gangs on a scale comparable to those between Robin's outlaws and the sheriff's men. But these were almost always led by rival gentry or lords and they usually derived from disputes over property or were linked to rivalry for local pre-eminence, such as the feud between the Pilkingtons and Savilles which tore apart the royal lordship of Wakefield in the summer of 1478.[28] Such clashes were not usually directed against the king's officers. In 1472, however, sixteen gentlemen, yeomen and labourers led by Henry Vascy

of Newland and William Merlay of Weysil in county Durham were indicted before the commission of the peace for attacking the sheriff, John
Atherton, who had endeavoured to serve a writ on them at Wolsing-
ham on 15 March. In this confrontation the sheriff, unlike his ballad
counterpart, seems to have come out on top.[29]

The life of crime led by John Belsham of Hadleigh, Suffolk, between
1422 and 1439, including three murders and six assaults, has more of
the outlaw feel to it. Several of his victims were officers of the law, including the constable of Hadleigh whom he murdered in 1427. Although
imprisoned from time to time, and outlawed in 1428–32, he was never
condemned for his crimes. Finally brought to trial in 1441 due to the
persistence of William Wolf, a kinsman of the woman he had murdered,
he was acquitted through the duke of Norfolk's influence. But even here
the differences are more significant than the similarities. Belsham passed
as a gentleman; he was not a masterless man living in the wild; and one
of his victims was a woman.[30]

Belsham, Dr Maddern suggests, forfeited sympathy because he defied
the deep-rooted communal respect for the law. Rather than being admired, as was Robin Hood, she argues that he was condemned by local
opinion because of his rejection of one of the key elements in the ordering
of fifteenth-century gentry life, respect for the officers of the law. She may
well be right that he lost the sympathy of his peers and betters, but does it
follow that he was condemned by public opinion at large? Was it the case
that 'the murder of a law-enforcer to facilitate criminal behaviour could
never be justified by fifteenth-century standards of righteous violence,
which demanded the altruistic maintenance of justice and peace'?[31] For
this is exactly what Robin Hood celebrates – righteous violence to maintain true justice precisely when the officers of the law failed. Therein lies
the significance of the killing of the sheriff in two of the stories, and his
humiliation in a third:

> 'Lye thou there, though proude sheriff
> Evil mote thou cheve:
> There myght no man to the truste
> The whyles thou were a lyve.'[32]

The moral is equally clear in *Guy of Gisborne*. In contrast to the good
yeoman Robin, Guy is the bad yeoman. He 'had bene many a mans bane'
and, as he himself boasted, like a later melodramatic villain, 'I have done
many a curst turne'. He is a bounty hunter, a hit-man who has a con-
tract on Robin. He meets his deserved end, as does the sheriff shortly

after.[33] Seen through the looking glass of the ballads, Belsham is more like Robin Hood and the man who brought him to justice, William Wolf, more like Guy of Gisborne. One wonders, therefore, whether one should assume that public opinion held an unquestioning or universal respect for enforcers of the law. The Robin Hood ballads perhaps appealed to a counter-culture, in which sympathy existed for some notorious criminals in their conflict with the law. One might ask with whom that group of yeomen and labourers sided who took to the roads in Norfolk to waylay travellers in 1441 (the same year as Belsham was acquitted), chanting 'We arn Robynhodesmen war war war'.[34]

Robin Hood was more than a murderer; he was a highwayman – as that group of yeomen and labourers knew. There are six robberies or planned robberies featured in the early ballads, of which five are highway robbery. There is no doubt that highway robbery was a frequent occurrence in the fifteenth century and the sums involved were as large as those stolen by Robin Hood. Dr Hayes has revealed a rash of incidents in northern England in the years 1462–72. Five approvers, described as yeomen, grooms, labourers and a hosteler, confessed to a dozen robberies in Durham, Lancashire and Yorkshire, stealing cash and goods from merchants, churchmen and other unidentified travellers to the value of 300 marks, £300, £700 and in one case £1,000. Robberies took place anywhere on the open road, including the Stockton Road leading out of York towards Sheriff Hutton; but two actually took place in, or on the edge of, Barnsdale, near the very spot in southern Yorkshire where the legendary outlaws themselves were wont to intercept their victims. William Robinson, alias Robert Robertson, labourer, and two others held up a canon and stole a casket containing £400 between Pontefract and Wentbridge in May 1472. On 9 September 1466 Alan Greneside and two accomplices lay in ambush at Wentbridge, where they held up a passing jeweller, William Jackson, and relieved him of £20 in cash as well as his stock of silver pieces and jewels to the value of £60.[35]

Northern highwaymen in Edward IV's reign operated in groups of two or three. But then so did Robin Hood's men when delivering invitations to guests to dine with them. It was Little John, Much and Scarlock, 'these yeomen all three', who waylaid the knight. It was the same three who held up the cellarer of St Mary's Abbey and fifty-two men later in the tale; and it was Little John and Much who intercepted the monk. Robin on his own faced the potter, but watched by Little John and others who intervened when they thought the potter was getting the better of him. It was only when Robin faced the king, disguised as a monk, that he stood in the way with 'many a bolde archere'.[36] While, as the audience is reminded from time to time, there were 'seven score of wight yonge men' in the outlaw band, it was their leaders who lay in wait. In this respect Robin's fictional activities were very much in accord with fifteenth-century experience.

There were, however, few if any bands of outlaws numbering 140 men lurking in forests for years on end in the later fifteenth century. The depredations of William Beckwith and his gang in the honour of Knaresborough in the 1390s and those of Richard Stafford, alias Friar Tuck, a decade or more before 1429 in Sussex were, it seems, exceptional. Even in the late thirteenth and early fourteenth centuries, gangs were difficult to hold together and tended to form and melt away again quickly.[37] The two much-cited cases in which riotous companies were likened to Robin Hood and his men – the banditry of Piers Venables and his gang of fifteen named yeomen and 'many other unknowyn' in the neighbourhood of Tutbury in the late 1430s, and the disturbances at Willenhall fair in 1498 in which one gang leader took the name of Robin Hood – are open to many readings. It seems likely that both were unusual events, for the first was the subject of a petition placed before parliament in 1439 and the second brought before Star Chamber. The comparison of Venables's men with those of Robin Hood and his 'menie' in the parliamentary petition is surely a self-conscious literary flourish. It may well be that the comparison was made precisely because bands of outlaws like Robin Hood's menie rarely existed. And, as has been argued, the affray at Willenhall seems to have arisen out of a ritual May Game involving a group masquerading as Robin Hood and his men which went sour. Besides giving testimony to the ubiquity of the Robin Hood legend, the incidents may also testify to the rarity in the fifteenth century of outlaw bands.[38] There were other brigands operating in northern England in the later fifteenth century. The borders were plagued by highland thieves, whose lawlessness, exacerbated in time of war, was a major threat to life and property. In 1522, it was reported to the archbishop of York, Thomas Wolsey, that gangs of up to a hundred men from Tynedale were in the habit of descending on Hexham, in his liberty, every market day. Whether that degree of lawlessness was a phenomenon throughout the fifteenth century is hard to determine. Dr Neville has shown that there was a general breakdown of order in the far north under the early Lancastrians, a lawlessness revived between 1465 and 1469 when the outlaw Sir Humphrey Neville and his followers harassed the inhabitants of county Durham from Hexhamshire.

Humphrey Neville was neither highland thief nor Robin Hood; he was conducting guerilla warfare against the Yorkist regime. Yet perhaps reports of reivers and partisans gave credibility to the tales of Robin Hood to those living far away.[39]

Piers Venables took to the woods and Sir Humphrey Neville to the hills; but Robin Hood rules the forest:

> 'We be yemen of this foreste,
> Under the grene wode tre;
> We lyve by our kynges dere,
> Other shyft have not we.'[40]

The outlaws are professional poachers who live year by year off the fruits of the forest: not just the deer but also every kind of bird, including swans, taken by snares and nooses rather than by hawks.[41] They have denuded the king's northern forests. In the *Gest* the king discovers that the merry men have destroyed all the herds of deer in his Lancashire park of Plompton. For six months he pursues the poachers round his northern forests, but they elude him, all the time killing his deer.[42] Poaching is a different order of crime and more likely than any other to strike a sympathetic chord with rural audiences.

How much organised, large-scale poaching took place in royal and seigneurial forests in the fifteenth century is impossible to tell because of the paucity of the evidence. The fourteenth century witnessed the decline of the forest eyres. The last commission was issued in 1368, but their ineffectiveness was apparent long before the legal process fell into disuse. The decline of the eyre and other aspects of royal administration was but a reflection of the decline of the royal forest itself in the face of seigneurial hostility and pressure on resources. During the fourteenth century a fundamental change took place. Conflict between crown and nobles over the enjoyment of forests ceased. They closed ranks to enforce their privileges against the commons. There was no difference between a royal forest and a seigneurial forest (a chase) for its local inhabitants. They were excluded from both. The statute of 1390, which set in place the modern game laws, confirmed this trend.[43]

Concurrently the process of deforestation and commercial exploitation – in the south often for woodland management and pig rearing, on the northern moors also for cattle ranching – led to a remorseless and irreversible decline in the numbers of wild red deer. The park became by the fifteenth century the main reserve of deer, predominantly fallow, which became the principal quarry. Linda Drury has shown in detail how the forest of Weardale, belonging to the bishops of Durham, was transformed in the later Middle Ages from a hunting reserve to a leased-out pastoral estate. By the end of the century administration had become so lax that the master forester had ceased to present his rolls of the forest for inspection.[44]

Yet hunting remained a popular pastime for all classes of men. No one would claim that it was less popular in the fifteenth century than the thirteenth. Kings continued to hunt, though circumstantial evidence suggests that the Lancastrians hunted rather less than either the Plantagenets before them or the Yorkists and early Tudors after them. Lords and gentry chased deer in forest and park as much as they could. The growing dissemination of the key manuals, eventually printed in English, attests not only to hunting's special role in gentle culture but also to its wider social appeal. Nonetheless, fifteenth-century lords, royal and seigneurial, seem to have shown curiously little anxiety to preserve the game through their forest courts. Surviving swainmote and forest court records reveal a singular lack of prosecution of cases against the venison. There does not seem to have been a corresponding rise in forest prosecutions through common-law process. Five cases under the 1390 statute were presented to the Durham justices of the peace in 1471–3, all concerning yeomen and labourers, most with lands under the value of forty shillings a year, accused of coursing and killing hares in the open fields of different vills.[45] The principal concern of forest courts in the fifteenth century was the vert, and even here it seems that the main interest appears to have been to make sure that no one grazed in the forest without payment, either in advance by agistment, or in arrears by amercement.[46]

It is inconceivable that there was no poaching; poaching was the gentleman's sport and the common man's fair game. From time to time poachers were presented in forest courts, as were Thomas Beckwith and his associates for taking deer from Haverah park in the forest of Knaresborough in March 1460. Others received royal pardons, as did Philip Pagham, gentleman, for his trespasses of venison in the royal forest of Bernwood, Bucks, in 1438–9, and, more Robin-Hood-like, Richard Stafford for his hunting for deer and lesser game in the parks, warrens and chases of the king's subjects in Surrey and Sussex in the reign of Henry V.[47] The real scale of the taking of illegal game, to which perhaps a blind eye was frequently turned during the fifteenth century, is only revealed after the accession of Henry VII. Henry instituted a revival of vigorous royal forest administration with the objective of bringing poaching under control and restoring the numbers of deer. The 1390 statute was reissued in his very first parliament and the forest eyre re-vived. Thanks to the zeal in executing his wishes and the care in keeping records shown by his chancellor of the duchy of Lancaster and co-justice of the forests south of the Trent, Sir Reynold Bray, the evidence of his impact has survived.[48]

At New Forest swainmotes in 1487 and 1488 and at a meeting of the forest eyre held before the two justices of the forest in August 1488 well over a hundred presentments, almost all for offences against the veni-son, were made. Poachers ranged from the knightly through yeomen, butchers, bakers and bucket makers to vagabonds. Most offences were committed by men on their own or with no more than four confeder-ates taking no more than one animal. There were some serial poachers, notably William Holcombe, gentleman, late of Lymington, who in four-teen separate incidents between 25 June 1484 and 30 January 1488 killed eighteen deer, as well as cutting down a large oak for himself in January 1487. With other gentle offenders, he received a pardon at the forest eyre under a bond of £10 for his future good behaviour.[49]

Most damage to the venison in the New Forest seems to have been done under Richard III. It was claimed by the forester of the In Bailiwick in 1488 that at various times during the reign the suspiciously rounded number of 500 deer had been taken by the northern men and their servants from his bailiwick. Some of these men were identified by the foresters of Battramsley and Burley bailiwicks in February 1487, who pre-sented John Hoton esquire, late of Bisterne, and six yeomen servants for killing without warrant, at various times in the first two years of Richard III's reign, no fewer than 190 animals. Hoton hailed from Hunwick, county Durham. He had been granted Bisterne and the keepership of the New Park by Richard III and he and his servants benefited greatly from royal largesse, being the king's officers in the forest. Two of those indicted alongside Hoton were identified as forest officials: Henry Smith, one of the riding foresters, and Robert Vascy, the bailly of Burley. Vascy may well have been the same Robert Vascy, gentleman of Newland, county Durham, who had been indicted in 1472 with his kinsmen for assaulting the sheriff of the county. One may doubt whether Hoton and his foresters truly took deer without authorisation, and one would be even more surprised if they had been viewed sympathetically by the local inhabitants as heroic greenwood outlaws transplanted from their native north. And they did not denude the forest, for in preparation for an early hunting expedition by the king himself 400 deer were driven from the In Bailiwick into the park.[50]

Yet Robin Hood was first and foremost the greenwood outlaw. As such he can be incontrovertibly identifed with the familiar figure of the forester. He was, we are told more than once, a 'yeoman of the forest' – not, be it noted, of the household or of husbandry. The social distinction is both categorical and significant. Robin instructs his men neither to 'do no husband harm that tilleth with his plough' nor to molest 'gode yeoman that walketh by grene wode shaw'. This does not mean simply a yeoman who happened to be strolling in the woods. A walk was the division of a forest in the charge of a forester; walking was the act of patrolling that division. Thus a husbandman working his land and a forester doing his job honestly were not to be molested.[51] Chaucer, in his celebrated description of the knight's yeoman in the General Prologue of *The Canterbury Tales*, makes it explicit that his man was precisely that. He was dressed in green, carried a mighty bow and a horn, and was a man who knew his 'woodcraft' like the back of his hand. He was neither a yeoman farmer nor a yeoman household officer; 'A forster was he, soothly, as I gesse'.[52]

The forester, the yeoman of the forest, was a familiar figure to fifteenth-century audiences. Every forest maintained its full complement of staff. The head of the establishment in the New Forest in the 1480s was the keeper, a sinecure occupied by the earl of Arundel. He employed a lieutenant and a deputy lieutenant. Beneath them came the chief forester, the riding forester, two rangers (*forestarii itinerantes*) and the bowbearer. The bowbearer's title came from his duty to carry the keeper's or king's bow when hunting. But the bowbearer, along with the rangers and the nine foresters assigned to the bailiwicks into which the forest was divided, played a part in the day-to-day administration and protection of the vert and venison. A similar structure existed in the northern, private forest of Wensleydale. The head of the establishment was the master forester (in 1465–6, Thomas Midleton), assisted by a bowbearer (in 1473–4, William Conyers assigned to the 'New Forest' and Arkengarthdale) and no fewer than sixteen foresters responsible for the seven other 'walks', several bearing surnames such as Forster, Hunt and Hunter.[53] Like his fellow legendary outlaw, William of Cloudesley, who, having been pardoned by his king, took up the post of royal bowbearer and chief rider of all the north country, Robin Hood was of their number.[54] Fifteenth-century audiences would surely have recognised the yeoman Robin Hood for what he was: a forester turned poacher and highwayman. Yet the forest was no longer the cockpit of conflict over rights to game that it had been in earlier centuries. In the long history of this conflict the fifteenth century represents something of a lull. It did not become again a socially divisive issue of significance until after 1485, when the ballads began to enjoy a wider distribution in written form through printing. Indeed their continuing popularity in the sixteenth century and early seventeenth century may be linked to an intensification of enforcement of the game laws and the revival of large poaching gangs.[55] While the world of Robin Hood the forester was familiar, paradoxically the conflict in which the legendary figure was involved was, when the ballads were first set down, both a thing of the past and of the future.

In many ways the ballads in their first written form do not reflect the pattern of crime revealed in surviving fifteenth-century legal records. Apart from the general prevalence of crime, there is little about its character in the records which suggests the criminal activity depicted in the ballads. The pattern of violent crime and homicide is not particularly reminiscent of the brutality of the forest outlaws. Poaching was not then the issue it had been or was to become again. Outlaw gangs such as that led by Robin Hood were few and far between. Only perhaps in highway robbery does the fictional world seem to match fifteenth-century life. In respect of crime, the ballads, to a large extent, represented an imagined or remembered world for their fifteenth-century audiences. The greenwood, in which Robin Hood practised his life of crime, was, of course, an established literary convention. The prologue to the *Parliament of the Three Ages* also deploys it. The narrator goes to the greenwood in the month of May to shoot a deer. Having stalked and killed his prey he falls asleep to dream his allegory of the three ages of man. His young man, 'a bold beryn', appears dressed all in green.[56] The greenwood was the conventional setting for the expression of ideal types. It was an appropriate home for a just order maintained by righteous violence, for the imagining of a Utopia which was in reality unattainable.[57] The utopian vision of the ballads is given credibility by being recognisably set in the known world of the forest with a hero readily identifiable as a forester, a liminal figure on the threshold of both gentle and non-gentle society. The placing of Robin Hood so precisely in the forest world provides one answer to Dobson and Taylor's question as to why he is 'so independent, so confidently aware of his yeoman status and so resistant to any authority but that of his king'.[58]

But in their portrayal of the wrongs which Robin puts right in this idealised world, the ballads reflect a world which has passed; one that possibly existed a century or two earlier, rather than one which is present.

The reference to King Edward in the text of the *Gest* is a specific reminder of that age, which can be placed broadly in the reigns of the first three Edwards, between 1280 and 1340.[59] Criminal gangs were more characteristic of the early fourteenth century, and the records of forest eyres reveal continuing conflict over the taking of game in the later thirteenth and early fourteenth century. Professor Bellamy concluded, however, that the *Gest* did not reflect clearly the face of crime in the first three quarters of the fourteenth century. His concern was to demonstrate that the compiler, whom he appears to have assumed was a contemporary, or near contemporary, was more concerned to tell a story about particular events in 1322–23.[60] But, if we accept that the compilation was in fact much later and more complex, another explanation presents itself, which is that the depiction of crime in all the ballads, not just the *Gest*, is blurred because it has been passed down orally over several generations. Dobson and Taylor noted that they reveal to us attitudes to authority and disorder from the past.[61] But it was already the past when the ballads were set down. The Robin Hood ballads preserve an oral historical tradition and in so doing they reveal that audiences were aware of and remembered that past themselves. In the first form in which we now know them, they record a history of crime in circulation in the fifteenth century. The early ballads of Robin Hood draw upon this historical tradition to inform the fantasy of a better world. Like the Matter of Britain, the matter of the greenwood is a once and future world. In a specifically English and secular way too, the ballads are not unlike the great cycles of the mystery plays which similarly entertained, elucidated the history of the world and offered the hope of a better life to come. Through them we glimpse some aspects of what men and women in the fifteenth century knew of their history, especially of how they remembered, not necessarily accurately, past conflict over rights to game and the resistance to law enforcement. In terms of their portrayal of the criminal activities of forest outlaws of a bygone age, they were perhaps a popular history which even then captured the imagination of teenagers growing up in both Mickleton and Taunton.

NOTES

1. The most recent survey of the literature is to be found in the foreword to the second edition of R. B. Dobson and J. Taylor, *Rymes of Robyn Hood* (3rd edn, Stroud, 1997), pp. i–xxxvi, updating the original introduction of 1976. It is their judgement that 'the long search for a historical outlaw actually called Robin Hood in late thirteenth and fourteenth century English documentary sources can now be … brought to a close' (p. xxxi). J. Holt, *Robin Hood*

(2nd edn, London, 1989) also reviews all the writings on the topic in a postscript discussing publications between 1982 and 1989.

2. See, for instance, J. R. Maddicott, 'The Birth and Setting of the Ballads of Robin Hood', *English Historical Review* 3 (1978), 276–99; J. Bellamy, *Robin Hood: An Historical Enquiry* (London, 1985); and B. Hanawalt, 'Ballads and Bandits: Fourteenth-century Outlaws and the Robin Hood Poems', in B. Hanawalt (ed.), *Chaucer's England: Literature in Historical Context*, Medieval Studies at Minnesota 4 (1992), pp. 154–75. Note also Dobson and Taylor, *Rymes*, p. xxxii: the legend relates 'to social conditions of the fourteenth century'.

3. Most recently C. F. Richmond, 'An Outlaw and Some Peasants: The Possible Significance of Robin Hood', *Nottingham Medieval Studies* 37 (1993), 90–101.

4. S. Knight, *Robin Hood: A Complete Study of the English Outlaw* (Oxford, 1994), provides the fullest discussion from the literary point of view.

5. Holt, *Robin Hood*, pp. 109–58, and Dobson and Taylor, *Rymes*, pp. xxxiii–xxxvi, 25–36, range freely over the later Middle Ages in their discussion of the audience. For the suggestion that they should be set in the context of the late-fourteenth century crisis see P. Coss, 'Aspects of Cultural Diffusion in Medieval England', *Past and Present* 108 (1985), 35–79 (p. 74).

6. D. Gray, 'The Robin Hood Poems', *Poetica* 18 (1984), 23; Dobson and Taylor, *Rymes*, pp. xxxvi, 8–9; Knight, *Robin Hood*, pp. 47–9.

7. Dobson and Taylor, *Rymes*, pp. xxx–xxxi. The uneasy relationship between Robin and Little John, and a reference to John having his own men (*Guy of Gisborne*, stanza 12), suggest a merging of tales about different outlaw gangs. See also the discussion in Dobson and Taylor, *Rymes*, pp. xxx–xxxii, and Holt, *Robin Hood*, pp. 187–91.

8. See Coss, 'Diffusion', 66–76.

9. J. Gairdner (ed.) *The Paston Letters*, 6 vols. (Edinburgh, 1904), V, p. 185. And see Holt, *Robin Hood*, pp. 191–3.

10. Dobson and Taylor, *Rymes*, p. 34.

11. For the original articles of 1958–61 see R. Hilton (ed.), *Peasants, Knights and Heretics: Studies in Medieval English Social History* (Cambridge, 1976), pp. 221–72. For Holt see ibid., pp. 236–57, and *Robin Hood*, pp. 117–28.

12. Dobson and Taylor, *Rymes*, pp. 35–6; Coss, 'Diffusion', 73–4; Richmond, 'Outlaw', 98–101.

13. Knight, *Robin Hood*, pp. 47–8.

14. S. Schama, *Landscape and Memory* (London, 1995), p. 149.

15. An assumption, based on the absence of church-wardens' accounts which might have recorded payments made to players of Robin Hood games, is sometimes made that Robin Hood was celebrated only in the south of England (D. Wiles, *The Early Plays of Robin Hood*, Woodbridge, 1981, pp. 3–4), but place names and other references reveal that he is likely to have been as familiar a figure in north Yorkshire as in Somerset: Dobson and Taylor, *Rymes*, pp. 306, 310; Holt, *Robin Hood*, p. 193; Knight, *Robin Hood*, pp. 264, 266.

16. *Gest*, stanzas 168–71; *Guy*, stanzas 37–41.
17. *Gest*, stanza 257; see also stanza 12.
18. *Guy*, stanza 3. The recurring refrain 'bete and binde' seems to echo the legal formula 'verberaverunt, vulneraverunt et male tractaverunt'.
19. *Gest*, stanza 160.
20. *Monk*, stanza 49.
21. *Gest*, stanzas 193–204.
22. Ibid., stanza 429.
23. *Monk*, stanza 52.
24. *Guy*, stanzas 40–1.
25. P. C. Maddern, *Violence and the Social Order: East Anglia, 1422–1442* (Oxford, 1992), pp. 5, 28 (table 2.1), 34 (table 2.3); E. Powell, 'The King's Bench in Shropshire and Staffordshire in 1414', in E. W. Ives and A. H. Manchester (eds.), *Law, Litigants and the Legal Profession* (London, 1983), p. 97; idem, *Law and Society: Criminal Justice in the Reign of Henry V* (Oxford, 1989), pp. 178–80. I have excluded rape from these figures because of the difficulty of definition and because of Robin Hood's own prohibition against harming women.
26. H. Summerson, 'Crime and Society in Medieval Cumberland', *Transactions of the Cumberland and Westmorland Archaeological and Antiquarian Society* 82 (1982), 197–224 (p. 118); C. M. Fraser, *Durham Quarter Sessions Rolls, 1471–1625*, Surtees Society 194 (1991), pp. 47–8; R. C. E. Hayes, 'Ancient Indictments for the North of England, 1461–1509', in A. J. Pollard (ed.), *The North of England in the Age of Richard III* (Stroud, 1996), p. 30.
27. Hayes, 'Ancient Indictments', pp. 37–42.
28. Fraser, *Quarter Sessions*, pp. 47–8.
29. Hayes, 'Ancient Indictments', p. 32; C. F. Richmond, 'The Murder of Thomas Dennis', *Common Knowledge* 2 (1993), 85–98; Fraser, *Quarter Sessions*, pp. 48–9.
30. Maddern, *Violence*, pp. 154–66.
31. Ibid., pp. 163–4.
32. *Gest*, stanzas 13–14, 349.
33. *Guy*, stanzas 7, 34.
34. Maddern, *Violence*, pp. 108–9.
35. PRO, KB9 330/27, 333/23, 334/151, 992/95; Hayes, 'Ancient Indictments', p. 31. See Dobson and Taylor, *Rymes*, pp. 25–7, for further fifteenth-century examples. For the reliability of approvers' appeals see H. Summerson, 'The Criminal Underworld of Medieval England', *Legal History* 17 (1996), 202–3 (221 n. 24).
36. *Gest*, stanzas 17–20, 208–17, 375; *Monk*, stanzas 40–41; *Potter*, stanzas 9–17.
37. J. G. Bellamy, 'The Northern Rebellions in the Later Years of Richard II', *Bulletin of the John Rylands Library* 47 (1965), 255–61; M. Keen, *The Outlaws of Medieval Legend* (2nd edn, London, 1977), pp. 202–3; Summerson, 'Criminal Underworld', pp. 207–8. See also below pp. 168–9.
38. Holt, *Robin Hood*, pp. 148–51; Knight, *Robin Hood*, p. 108.

39. A. J. Pollard, *North-Eastern England during the Wars of the Roses* (Oxford, 1990), pp. 171–2; C. J. Neville, *Violence, Custom and Law: The Anglo-Scottish Border lands in the Later Middle Ages* (Edinburgh, 1998), pp. 107–11.

40. *Gest*, stanza 377.

41. Ibid., stanza 32; R. Almond, 'Medieval Hunting', *Medieval History* 3 (1993–4), 147–55 (pp. 153–4).

42. *Gest*, stanzas 357, 365–6.

43. C. R. Young, *The Royal Forests of Medieval England* (Leicester, 1979), pp. 149–72.

44. Pollard, *North-Eastern England*, pp. 201–2; J. L. Drury, 'Early Settlement in Stanhope Park, Weardale, c. 1406–79', *Archaeologia Aeliana*, n.s. 4 (1979), 139–49; *eadem*, 'More Stout than Wise: Tenant Right in Weardale in the Tudor period', in D. Marcombe (ed.), *The Last Principality: Politics, Religion and Society in the Bishopric of Durham, 1494–1660* (Nottingham, 1987), pp. 71–2, 79.

45. Fraser, *Quarter Sessions*, pp. 41–2, 57, 61.

46. See for instance Bernwood, the forest moots of the lordship of Northallerton, the swanimotes of Wyresdale and Lonsdale in 1478–80, and a surviving forest court record for Middleham in 1450–51: I. M. W. Harvey, 'Bernwood in the Later Middle Ages', in J. Broad and R. Hoyle (eds.), *Bernwood: The Life and Afterlife of a Forest* (Preston, 1997), p. 10; R. C. Shaw, *The Royal Forests of Lancaster* (Preston, 1956), pp. 191–6; C. M. Newman, *Late-Medieval Northallerton* (Stamford, 1999), pp. 39–40; West Riding Archives, DW 568. I am grateful to Steve Moorhouse for showing me a transcript of this document.

47. W. Wheater, *Knaresbrough and its Rulers* (Leeds, 1907), p. 187; Harvey, 'Bernwood', p. 7; Keen, *Outlaws*, pp. 202–3.

48. R. B. Manning, *Hunters and Poachers: A Cultural and Social History of Unlawful Hunting in England, 1485–1640* (Oxford, 1993), pp. 63–4; D. Crook, 'The Records of Forest Eyres in the Public Record Office, 1179–1670', *Journal of the Society of Archivists* 17 (1996), 183–93.

49. D. J. Stagg (ed.), *A Calendar of New Forest Documents: The Fifteenth to the Seventeenth Centuries*, Hampshire Record Society 5 (1983), pp. 1–29, esp. 1–2, 4–5, 7, 11–12, 23–4. The deer taken were almost all fallow.

50. Ibid., pp. 3, 22–3; A. J. Pollard, *Richard III and the Princes in the Tower* (Stroud, 1991), pp. 145–6; R. E. Horrox and P. W. Hammond (eds.), *British Library Harleian Manuscript 433*, 4 vols. (Upminster, 1979–83), I, pp. 185, 243; Fraser, *Quarter Sessions*, p. 25 and pp. 160–1 above.

51. *Gest*, stanzas 13, 14, 221–2, 377.

52. *The Canterbury Tales*, Prologue, lines 103–17. Holt, *Robin Hood*, pp. 116–28, recognises this specific meaning, but only as one among several yeoman roles. I do not wish to imply that the term 'yeoman' did not have other resonances for the audience, for which see Dobson and Taylor, *Rymes*, pp. 34–6 and Richmond, 'Outlaw', *passim*.

53. *New Forest Documents*, esp. p. 18; PRO, SC 6/1085/20; DL 29/648/10485.

54. Dobson and Taylor, *Rymes*, pp. 272–3 (stanzas 162–9). William too was a good yeoman, 'outlawed for venyson' (ibid., p. 261, stanza 4). Robin too was pardoned and entered royal service, although in what capacity is not stated. Unlike William and his wife, who went to court 'as fast as they might hye', he abandoned the court after a year to return to the outlaw life. See also R. L. Almond and A. J. Pollard, 'The Yeomanry of Robin Hood and Social Terminology in Fifteenth-Century England', *Past and Present* 170 (2001), 52–77, which discusses the forest context, the wealth of hunting allusions in the ballads and their implications for our understanding of Robin's 'yeomanliness'.

55. Manning, *Hunters and Poachers*, pp. 45–7, 52, 74, 143–4, 148–9.

56. M. Y. Offord, (ed.), *The Parliament of the Thre Ages*, EETS o.s. 246 (1959), lines 1–135; and N. Orme, 'Medieval Hunting: Fact and Fancy', in Hanawalt, *Chaucer's England*, p. 140. Note, however, that the 'yonge man' of the poem, dripping with jewels, is most decidedly of gentle birth.

57. For the most recent comment on this theme see Schama, *Landscape and Memory*, pp. 149–51; and A. Musson and W. M. Ormrod, *The Evolution of English Justice: Law, Politics and Society in the Fourteenth Century* (Basingstoke, 1998), pp. 168–70.

58. Dobson and Taylor, *Rymes*, p. xxxvi.

59. *Gest*, stanza 353.

60. Bellamy, *Robin Hood*, pp. 58–72. For the most recent discussion of poaching, see J. Birrell, 'Peasant Deer Poachers in the Medieval Forest', in R. H. Britnell and J. Hatcher (eds.), *Progress and Problems in Medieval England* (Cambridge, 1996), pp. 68–88.

61. Dobson and Taylor, *Rymes*, p. xxxiii.

CHAPTER 10

Fat Christian and Old Peter: ideals and compromises among the medieval Waldensians

Peter Biller

In 1321 the inquisitor Bernard Gui was not satisfied with the answers he got from Raimonda about her contacts with the Waldensians. The record shows that he regarded her as not having confessed fully. However, Gui let her go, because she was breast-feeding her little baby.[1] He got a lot further with Raimonda's sister Aignès, whose sharp observation and willingness to confess bequeathed to the inquisitorial record the name of one of the most interesting if enigmatic of all the Waldensian Brothers named by these witnesses, a certain old man called Peter: 'quendam hominem senem . . . Petrum'.[2] During his examination in 1316, another Waldensian follower, Géraut the son of Formont the Burgundian, told the inquisitor how on one occasion someone introduced him to a large and fat man called Christian: 'ostendit sibi quendam hominem magnum et pinguem . . . et vocabatur Cristinus'.[3] Fat Christian was another Waldensian Brother, but less in the shadows than Old Peter, for he was one of the leaders, a *major*,[4] and one with whom many of the Waldensian followers questioned by Bernard Gui had had contacts.

Fat Christian and Old Peter – to whom I shall return – plunge us into the vivid detail provided by inquisition records, and they also introduce two contrasts between the earliest period of the Waldensian movement and later Waldensianism. One is a contrast in the evidence extant from different periods. From the first fifty years there is a miscellany – usually some words in a chronicle, a papal bull, on one occasion a Waldensian letter reporting a Waldensian Council – which supplies quite a lot of data but little sense of the concrete reality of the movement. Then, with the arrival of the inquisition, record-keeping, and some survival of records, there begin to be patches of intense light, where the accumulation of data about followers in a particular area, their names and families, and the names and activities of visiting Waldensian Brothers is such that the historian can write the 'lived religion' of a local heretical community. There is only a little of this in the thirteenth century,[5] which is still mainly darkness, but there is much more in the fourteenth century. In the early decades there are the sentences imposed by Bernard Gui, which include extracts from the confessions of Waldensian supporters who had come from Gascony (including our Géraut and Aignès), and interrogations in Bohemia, Austria and Piedmont, while much survives from the 1390s in German-speaking areas.

The other contrast is between the ideals of the movement at its beginning and the later compromises. Let us begin by considering this theme within the overall course of medieval Waldensian history. The pious layman Valdes started a movement in Lyons in the 1170s, following as a precept the evangelical counsel of poverty, and then preaching penance. Preaching came to include criticism of the clergy, and the group became careless about the need to gain local episcopal licence to preach – the canonical condition which Pope Alexander III had laid down for the Waldensians when welcoming them at the Third Lateran Council of 1179. Excommunication came in 1184. The Waldensians had started out as an apostolic religious movement and if they had not subsided into disobedience and some (but relative to the Cathars not great) heretical doctrines and thereby incurred the Church's ban, they would have formed a mendicant religious Order, resembling the Franciscan or Dominican Orders. In fact, they retained many of the characteristics of such an Order, taking the three monastic vows, engaging in the same pastoral activities, preaching and hearing confessions, and using the typical vocabulary. They called themselves *Fratres* (Friars or Brothers), belonged to an *Order*, and held regular inter-provincial *chapters* or *councils*.[6] They existed like this among their followers, pushed out of some regions but surviving in others, until their conversion to Reform around 1530.

This change came after an extraordinarily long history, and Waldensian survival over the preceding 360 years needs explanation. Or rather, it needs explanation if one assumes historical continuity in the movement. One of the great modern historians of the subject has called into question assumptions of continuity and unity, suggesting that the plural *Waldensianisms* should be substituted for *Waldensianism* when studying the phenomena before us.[7] Given this, I need to state briefly a case *for* continuity and singleness. First, the organisation and beliefs which are revealed by the largest inquisition records, in Piedmont around 1500, in German-speaking areas around 1400 and in Burgundy around 1300, are very similar. Secondly, a spine seems to be provided in these places by the Order of Brothers, their own organisation and continuity, and a common sense of their past history. Consider, thirdly, some of the evidence of ramifications over time and place. A confession in 1393 takes us back to 1319 and beyond, while one in 1320 takes us back to 1275. In February 1393 a widow who was more than ninety years old and still 'compos racionis', as the record of her interrogation notes, told the inquisitor in Stettin about seeing Waldensian Brothers, confessing to them and hearing their sermons over the last seventy-four years.[8] The first sighting and confession had been when she was sixteen. The fact that her parents, who had died before 1333, had both been 'in the sect' probably takes affiliation in her family back into the late thirteenth century. In 1320 Pèire Aymon told an inquisitor about seeing Waldensian Brothers and hearing their sermons over the last forty-five years, beginning, that is, around 1275.[9] Pèire Aymon, who was called 'Burgundian', like many of the Waldensian adherents sentenced by Bernard Gui, came originally from the diocese of Besançon. The Dominican writer Stephen of Bourbon (died 1260/1) tells a story of a Waldensian in the same diocese of Besançon, and he himself, when writing of Valdes, uses personal connections.[10] For he, Stephen, had often seen a priest called Stephen of Anse,[11] who had helped make translations for Valdes and whose connection with Valdes is attested by a still extant will.[12] A description of the Waldensians drawn up about 1300 and almost certainly emanating from the confessions of the Burgundian group to whom Pèire Aymon belongs – the *De vita et actibus Pauperum de Lugduno* – indicates that the Waldensian Brothers of Germany (Alamannia), Lombardy and southern France (Provincia) were linked, holding regular chapters-general in any one of these provinces.[13] One dramatic instance of the link lies in a text written by a Waldensian between *c.* 1335 and *c.* 1350, the *Liber Electorum*, which circulated in romance dialect in the Alps between Piedmont and the Dauphiné, *and* in Latin among German-speaking Waldensians.[14] Another is the survival of a letter written *c.* 1368 by Italian Waldensians to Waldensians in Austria – at a place, St Peter-in-der-Au, where Waldensians had been found in the 1260s.[15] I resort to italics: the *Italian* letter reminisces about an earlier Waldensian martyr of a century or more before – John of *Burgundy* – who may be the John of Burgundy sentenced around 1240 who had been active as a Waldensian since about 1205.[16] The underground existence of the movement and the patchiness of inquisitorial discovery make the extent of such traces of long duration and unity all the more remarkable.

How did this movement survive? Waldensian Brothers and their followers were 'relaxed to the secular arm', as the phrase of the inquisitor's sentence went, and burned to death. In the face of persecution and a grisly death there was a courage which is difficult even to imagine. The attention devoted to this, whether in the piety of Waldensian martyrology and Protestant historiography, the respectful sympathy of the liberal, or the modern morbid interest in 'medieval' horrors, can encourage one to ignore some less dramatic themes. For most Brothers and their followers did not die this way. Most were not made of the stuff of martyrs. Fear of persecution was always there, but not persecution itself. And compromise was the everyday key to survival.

Consider the range of Waldensian compromises. The Order of Brothers faced a need to compromise in one sense of the word which they shared with Franciscans. Their ideal was obedience to the evangelical counsels, taken as precepts: following the perfect life, in absolute poverty – living off alms and taking no thought for the morrow – and preaching. The question was how to keep to absolute poverty and the daily improvisation of life while the movement grew in numbers, spread through different linguistic areas of Latin Christendom, and lasted through time. In fact, like mendicant Orders in the Church, the Waldensians acquired organisation, houses, perhaps even a written Rule, and although the evidence is sparser and trickier than the evidence about comparable Franciscan experience, there are traces of problems with the vow of poverty and the need for money.[17]

The Waldensians' proscription by the Church and the passing of time entailed other compromises. Early Waldensians preached openly in the squares and streets, and those who were converted left property and family to follow the perfect form of the religious life. Gradually there evolved a group of followers who stayed married and working, while sharing the beliefs of the Brothers, listening to their sermons and confessing their sins to them, and providing them with material support. For the first generation there was conversion – and therefore the fervour and conviction of an individual choice. But among later generations faith and accustomed practices were handed down within their families or at least within a local community of such followers. We encountered two sisters questioned by Bernard Gui, Raimonda and Aignès, both followers of the Waldensian Brothers. Their father was the Pèire Aymon whom we have also met, and their mother Martina, both of whom had seen Waldensian Brothers over forty-five years. Their other brothers and sisters were also followers, as were also their spouses and other members of the families into which they married. One of the Aymon sons, Joan (John), married Guilhelma, whose brother, Huguet Garin, was a Waldensian Brother. The Garin parents were Guilhem and Hélis, and these, like other parents, 'instructed their children and inclined them towards love and belief in the Waldensians': 'filios suos informaverunt et inclinaverunt ad amorem et credenciam Valdensium'.[18] Guilhem Garin brought his son Hélias Garin (one of Pèire Aymon's sons-in-law) to confess to the Waldensian Brothers, while we see Ysabela, the mother of another Aymon son-in-law, bringing her children into the faith.[19] In the 1390s the record of interrogation labels some of those questioned by the inquisitor Peter Zwicker as 'born in the sect' ('nata [or natus] in secta').[20] The consequences of such transmission generation after generation are obvious. Adherence to the Brothers and their faith might be merely a matter of conformity to family and neighbours.

Alongside the erosion of time there were the consequences of the necessary covertness of the Brothers' activities. If the evangelical ideal was open and universal preaching – from the rooftops and to the whole world – the Waldensian Brother who wanted to survive was forced to do it only at night-time, only inside a room in the house of a trusty follower, and only to people who were already of his flock. Newcomers there were, but people who were carefully assessed by lay followers and adjured to secrecy – the inquisitor Peter Zwicker stressed the role of women doing this.[21] Recruits were usually not men and women converted by the Brothers, and never those converted by their open and public preaching.

Part of covertness was John Le Carré stuff, cloak-and-dagger. Brothers used disguises when travelling, were met by local guides, stayed in safe houses, had nocturnal meetings in secret rooms, and even used code-words. But most of it was less dramatic than this: most was keeping one's head down and not drawing attention to oneself. Followers lived in parishes and had to behave like ordinary Catholics. In other words, on Sundays and feastdays they went to church, blessing themselves with holy water as they entered, and sat, genuflected, listened to sermons and communicated, and where they were doing things in which they did not believe they did these, they told Bernard Gui, to dissimulate ('ad dissimulandum'),[22] or, as they later told Peter Zwicker, 'ne notentur', lest they be noted.[23] They were baptised in church, confessed to their parish priests, received communion, married, and were buried in the church cemetery.

For the sake of clarity we can distinguish strands in participation in a local church. A clear-thinking Waldensian follower, who had taken in what the Brothers said about material objects not acquiring holiness through blessing or the non-existence of Purgatory, would think a thought – a mental reservation – when dipping a hand into holy water or appearing to join in prayers and offerings for the dead. Since the Brothers preached and heard confessions, these were two areas of direct conflict as well as overlap. The Waldensian follower listening to a catholic sermon heard things to reject, concerning for example the veneration of saints, but also unexceptionable exhortations to correct vice and embrace virtue. Dual instruction could lead to confusion among followers. The ninety-year-old woman we have already met, interrogated in Stettin in 1393, had not only listened to Brothers for seventy-four years, she had also been going to church and listening to parish priests. She took blessed water and believed it was of value in washing away sin, while at the same time and on the instruction of the Brothers she believed that it did not! The inquisitor told her that she had two faiths.[24]

There was full confession of sins to the Brothers and the reception of absolution and a penance of prayer and fasting; and there was confession of sins to the parish priest – omitting details of secret adherence – followed by absolution and the imposition of penance. It is not clear that followers thought that confession to a local catholic priest who was in good moral odour was invalid. Certainly the formulation of the points they made to Bernard Gui and Peter Zwicker – they confessed to the Brothers as though to their own parish priest, and they thought they were absolved from sin as if by their own parish priest or *better* than by their parish priest[25] – suggest the extensive co-existence in their 'lived religion' of the two sets of confession. Finally, they received *the* sacrament – the Eucharist – at the hands of the local priest.[26] There are signs of tension on this point through much of medieval Waldensian history, but in the Waldensianism which is revealed in the inquisition records the Brothers are not priests consecrating and giving communion to their followers. This was done by the local catholic priest.

Let us turn to the Brothers, looking at them in two sets of inquisitorial records, beginning with Peter Zwicker's. Confessing in February 1393, the eighty-year-old man Coppe Sybe said he had first seen them when he was nine or ten, and over his seventy years in the sect he had confessed to a good twenty of them.[27] One elderly widow who confessed in the previous month, Heylewig, had been in the sect for sixty-five years, and she names some of the Brothers: 'first Godeke, second Sibeke and Hans from Poland, Conrad, Claus of Brandenburg, Herman'.[28] The fact that no one else named Godeke and Sibeke and her 'first' and 'second' suggests that these were very early in her experience, perhaps near to her first confession, which was probably around 1328. In Pèire Aymon's

confession the staging of different Brothers over the years is more firm
and precise, even though the more remote dates are given in suspicious
five-year intervals: Joan (John) of Grandval *c.* 1275; Géraut of Provence
and Perrin Favorel *c.* 1280; Joan Chapayron *c.* 1285; Joan Moran in
1290 and earlier; Joan and Pèire of Cernon around 1300; Bertomieu
of Cajarc and Huguet Garin around 1305; Humbert, 1308 or earlier;
Garnier and a companion whose name he could not remember, son of
Danin, around 1314; Arnaut of Cernon in 1319.[29]

What lies behind the succession of different names in these lists over
a short time-span is mainly the Waldensians' policy of changing regularly the Brothers' areas of pastorate.[30] To the villages near Stettin there
came one year a senior Brother called Nicholas and his companion,
and another year another pair would come.[31] Over a longer time-span
underlying the succession of names are the deeper rhythms of ageing, ill-
ness and death. Talking to Peter Zwicker in winter 1392–3, the married
woman Tele recalled confessing to a Brother called Hans, who was an
old and weak man, 'antiquus debilis homo'. Another married woman
told how she had confessed to the companion, because the Brother was
ill.[32] What happened to these elderly Brothers, men like the 'weak and
old Hans', or the 'little old man' ('parvus antiquus homo') glimpsed in
Piedmont in 1335?[33]

We are told about Waldensian Sisters in the *De Vita et actibus*, a description of Waldensians emanating from the milieu of the Burgundian
Waldensians sentenced by Gui. The text implies that during their years
as young and middle-aged women they took care about secrecy, living in
twos and threes in houses with Brothers and pretending to be married
couples or siblings. When they were *antiquae*, however, they lived without
men.[34] When they came to share the age of many widows, presumably,
living alone would no longer attract suspicion. It is frustrating that the
same text, well-informed as it is, says nothing about retired and elderly
Brothers. However, one authoritative description of the Brothers, drawn
up by a late (but pre-Reform) Piedmontese Waldensian, Georges Morel,
does deal with them, however briefly. Morel sketches the life-stages of a
Brother. First there was selection, between the ages of twenty-five and
thirty, followed by a few years of training in the winter-months; then
a pastorate, with one Brother assigned to his master-Brother (and then
presumably with ageing, a Brother taking on a junior companion). During the years of active pastorate, Brothers were not allowed to live more
than two or three years in one place. And then this could be suspended
for the last stage. The old men were allowed sometimes to live in one

place for the rest of their lives: 'senes, quibus datur aliquando in uno loco commorari ad vitam'.[35]

These elderly retired and no longer travelling Brothers cannot have attracted much attention, and in the inquisition records I have found only one candidate. Pèire Aymon's daughter Aignès was alert to age.[36] Her first reference to Brothers is to a pair who came to her house around 1311, the second of whom was young, *juvenis*. The pairing of seniority and youth we have just seen described by Morel. At a later stage she went to the house of a certain woman, in which she had heard that there was a certain man, a Waldensian, Old Peter, as we saw at the beginning of this paper. He was living there in hiding: 'stabat absconditus'. Aignès took him bread and wine, which he accepted, and she heard from him certain general admonitory words. Peter's advanced age and stability in one place – Aignès's visits took place over two years – suggest that he was one of the retired old Brothers described later by Morel.

Brothers were captured in mid-career and faced death, or they converted to Catholicism, or they lived into old age in retirement: in what proportions? One of Bernard Gui's sentences condemns to death the Brother Joan (John) Breyssan, defiant and courageous to the last,[37] while followers questioned by Gui named two other Brothers who had been executed, Huguet Garin and Raimon de la Côte.[38] Another of Bernard's sentences imposes imprisonment on a Brother, Estève Porchier, who repented and converted to Catholicism.[39] In all about fifty Brothers are named in Gui's sentences,[40] and the silence about most of them suggests a peaceful old age in retirement either as converts to Catholicism or as Brothers, surrounded like Old Peter by Waldensian followers. Over fifteen Brothers were named by those followers interrogated in Stettin in 1392–4, and one of them as now living as a catholic priest in Vienna. In 1391 a list had been drawn up of twenty Germanophone Brothers who had converted, five of whom became catholic priests and one a monk.[41] Unknown are the (larger?) numbers of those who escaped notice and lived into retirement, and those who were captured and, refusing to repent, were executed.

All these men had once been young recruits. Then they had had years not just of fear but of hard slogging: long journeys disguised as artisans. A Brother in the Stettin area could come from nearby Poland, but he could also come from Steyer in Austria, hundreds of miles to the south. Two Brothers are glimpsed preaching at the most geographically remote points of the German-speaking world, in Strasbourg in the south-west and near the Baltic in the north-east.[42] Morel hazarded 800 miles as the distance between far-flung communities visited by the Brothers.[43] What then were their thoughts as they looked back over bygone years of long travels?

It is easiest to access the thoughts of the Brothers who became Catholics. Some Germanophone Brothers who converted in the 1360s wrote to their former confreres, attacking their activities and way of life, and some of the resulting exchange of letters survives.[44] The charges were partly about contradiction of the evangelical counsels about preaching and poverty, beginning with the Brothers' contradiction of Christ's instruction to the apostles about preaching. The faith should be preached openly,[45] but the Brothers expressly say that it cannot be preached openly.[46] The Brothers lack the requisite authority and knowledge to preach.[47] They use attacks on bad prelates as a defence, but in doing so they stretch and exaggerate: they compile examples from various sources, and apply one general condemnation to all, allowing for no exception.[48] One converted Brother took his defence of Roman priests further, saying he had never heard one in the pulpit do anything other than condemn vice and encourage virtue.[49] One minor charge was contradiction of poverty: the Brothers preach poverty but accumulate treasure.[50] More fundamental was the point that the Brothers did not administer all the sacraments.[51] Why do they not receive the faith (Roman) where they receive the sacraments (in the Church)?[52]

The converted Brothers also said that they doubted the truth of the historical claims made in the *Liber Electorum*. Somewhere between *c.* 1335 and *c.* 1350 a Waldensian Brother had written this very brief history of the Church and the Waldensians.[53] The claim to imitate the form of life of the apostles had for a long time encouraged a drift towards claiming historical continuity, and here in the *Liber Electorum* the Brothers were set into such a history, in which the order of poor men began with the apostles leading a poor life. In the 1360s an Italian Waldensian letter was to underline the claim, spelling out that Valdes was a reformer of the Order, not its originator. Through calling the Roman Church the 'synagogue', which sometimes contained the poor preaching men and sometimes did not, the *Liber Electorum* managed to super-impose the relationship of the apostles and the synagogue – in which, though it was superseded, there was still worship – on to that of the Waldensian Brothers and the Roman Church. Finally, the *Liber Electorum* divided history into alternating good and bad stages: good periods of fruitful times and peaceful expansion, bad periods of contraction and frightful persecution. The moon was a figure for the holy church, its waning representing a bad time and its waxing a good time. Just as the moon's waning alternated with its waxing, so the current terrible time would be followed ineluctably by a good time.

Here in historical continuity was the basis of the Brothers' pastoral office. For the Brother who wrote this and those Brothers who memorised it and regarded it as having authority, it conjured away what the renegade Brothers saw as contradiction. History established a new angle for the Brothers' position: tacit recognition of the Roman Church's possession of the sacraments, despite its pastoral supersession by the Brothers. Finally, there was the dream of a minority and persecuted group, good times just around the corner.

This dream could be of something more than relief from weakness and the fear of persecution: of prevailing over the persecutors, even wreaking vengeance upon them. It was spelled out in one rumour which was reported to an inquisitor in Piedmont in 1335. A notary called Hugonet had heard two years before that the men of this new faith had so expanded in numbers and would expand so much more that they would drive the priests and clergy out of the country.[54] One inquisitor with experience of Germanophone Waldensians in the 1260s reported the last words of a Brother called Henry, addressing the attendant crowd at Devin (in the Bratislava region) as he was about to be burnt to death. 'You are right to condemn us now. For, if we were not in the weaker position, we would exercise the power of death, which you are now exercising against us, against you – clergy, monks and laymen, the whole lot of you.'[55] If we were strong, we would kill you. The desperation and bitterness and dream of revenge shine through, breaching even the barriers of translation from German to Latin to modern English and the intermission of over seven hundred years.

Some Brothers responded to the compromises by seeing them in sharper terms. The Brothers' life contravened Christ's instructions to the apostles, and receiving Roman sacraments but not Roman faith was illogical. Construing these as contradictions was their rationale for conversion to Catholicism. Other Brothers, who remained inside the Waldensian Order, resorted to history to provide the Order with a basis, and among these some resorted to the dream of ultimately prevailing. These categories probably still leave out the majority and their views.

We know nothing of Fat Christian's later life – there is no trace of capture or conversion. Perhaps he did not engage in the severe fasting for which the Brothers were famous? A *major* among the Brothers ran their houses, as we learn from the *De vita et actibus*, and was one of those who at the annual chapters took part in discussion of the state of the

movement, the allocation of money, recruitment, and assigning Brothers
to their pastoral areas. As a *major* himself, Christian will have had to take
the larger view that leadership entails, and the many practical decisions
demanded by everyday administration. How did he look at things? As
Old Peter lived his final years as a retired Brother, how did he look back
on his pastoral career? Bequeathed to modern historians are the views
of the extremists, the polemicists and the dreamers. The frustration is
that there is only silence from men of probably middling views, such as
Fat Christian and Old Peter.

NOTES

1. P. van Limborch (ed.), *Liber sententiarum inquisitionis Tholosanae ab anno
   Christi mcccvii ad annum mcccxxiii* (Amsterdam, 1692), p. 344. Annette
   Pales-Gobilliard has prepared a new edition of this text, to be published by the Centre National de Recherche Scientifique. I follow A.
   Brenon's *Le petit livre aventureux des prénoms occitans au temps du catharisme*
   (Toulouse, 1992) in the form of southern French forenames (apart from
   Christian and Peter), which appear in Latin in southern French inquisition
   records.
2. Limborch (ed.), *Liber sententiarum*, p. 359.
3. Ibid., pp. 377–8.
4. Ibid., p. 377: 'Cristinum, qui erat major inter eos.'
5. Extracts from confessions, drawn up for sentences imposing penances in
   1241, illuminate some communities in Quercy in the previous decades.
   There were extensive inquisitions in south-east Germany and Austria in
   the 1260s, whose records would have illuminated the German mission,
   which we know to have predated 1218; but they did not survive.
6. See note 13 below.
7. G. G. Merlo, *Valdesi e Valdismi medievali*, 2 vols. (Turin, 1984–91).
8. D. Kurze (ed.), *Quellen zur Ketzergeschichte Brandenburgs und Pommerns*,
   Veröffentlichungen der historischen Kommission zu Berlin 45, Quellen-
   werke 6 (Berlin and New York, 1975), pp. 154–5. She claimed not to have
   had contact with the Brothers for more than seven years, but I follow the
   inquisitor in computing her as having spent '74 annos in secta'.
9. Limborch (ed.), *Liber sententiarum*, pp. 352–3; similar evidence from his wife
   Martina, ibid., p. 365.
10. Stephen of Bourbon, *Tractatus de diversis materiis praedicabilibus*, ed. A. Lecoy de
    la Marche, *Anecdotes historiques, légendes et apologues tirés du receuil inédit d'Etienne
    de Bourbon, Dominicain du XIIIe siècle* (Paris, 1877), pp. 279–80.
11. Ibid., p. 291.
12. Reproduced in P. Biller and A. Hudson (eds.), *Heresy and Literacy in the
    Middle Ages, 1000–1530* (Cambridge, 1994, reprinted with corrections 1996),
    p. 115.

13. G. Gonnet (ed.), *Enchiridion fontium Valdensium*, 2 vols., Collana della Focoltà Valdese di Teologia 1 and 22 (Torre Pellice and Turin, 1958–98), 2, p. 181: 'semel in anno in quadragesima vel circa celebrant concilium vel capitulum generale in aliquo loco Lombardiae vel Provinciae, vel in aliis regionibus . . . Ad quod concilium veniunt tres vel quatuor . . . de Alamannia.' See also Morel's 1530 description of an annual *consilium* [*sic*] *generale*, V. Vinay (ed.), *Le confessioni di fede dei Valdesi riformati, con i documenti del dialogo fra la "prima" ela "seconda" Riforma*, Collana della Focoltà Valdese di Teologia 12 (Turin, 1975), pp. 38 and 40. On the origin and date of the *De vita et actibus*, see P. Biller and J. N. Green, 'Appendice: argent allemand et hérésie médiévale', in M. Aubrun, G. Audisio, B. Dompnier and A. Gueslin (eds.), *Entre idéal et réalité. Actes du Colloque international. Finances et religion du Moyen-Age à l'époque contemporaine*, Institut d'Etudes du Massif Central, Centre d'Histoire des Entreprises et des Communautés, Collection 'Prestige' 5 (Clermont-Ferrand, 1994), pp. 49–56.

14. On the *Liber Electorum*, see my 'Medieval Waldensians' construction of the past', *Proceedings of the Huguenot Society* 25 (1989), 39–54, and note 44 below.

15. P. Segl, *Ketzer in Österreich. Untersuchungen über Häresie und Inquisition im Herzogtum Österreich im 13. und beginnenden 14. Jahrhundert*, Quellen und Untersuchungen aus dem Gebiet der Geschichte, new series 5 (Paderborn, Munich, Vienna and Zurich, 1984), p. 176; I. von Döllinger, *Beiträge zur Sektengeschichte des Mittelalters*, 2 vols. (Munich, 1890), II, *Dokumente vornehmlich zur Geschichte der Valdesier und Katharer*, p. 355. On the Italian letter, see note 44 below.

16. Döllinger, *Beiträge zur Sektengeschichte*, p. 359. The sentence on a Johannes de Burgundia active between *c.* 1205 and 1240 is printed in A. Patschovsky and K.-V. Selge (eds.), *Quellen zur Geschichte der Waldenser*, Texte zur Kirchen- und Theologiegeschichte 18 (Gütersloh, 1973), pp. 56–8. On early Waldensians in Burgundy, see M. Schneider, *Europäisches Waldensertum im 13. und 14. Jahrhundert. Gemeinschaftsform – Frömmigkeit – Sozialer Hintergrund*, Arbeiten zur Kirchengeschichte 51 (Berlin and New York, 1981), pp. 31–3.

17. See my '*Thesaurus absconditus*: the hidden treasure of the medieval Waldensians', in W. J. Sheils and D. Wood (eds.), *The Church and Wealth*, Studies in Church History 24 (Oxford, 1987), pp. 139–54.

18. Limborch (ed.), *Liber sententiarum*, p. 365.

19. The Aymon family web is attested ibid., pp. 339, 340, 343, 344–5, 352, 353, 358, 359, 365–6, 369, 370.

20. Kurze (ed.), *Quellen zur Ketzergeschichte*, pp. 79, 112, 119. Most were born into the sect, and the relative infrequency of the label is probably explained by this – the label was unnecessary.

21. Writing in 1395, in his treatise *Cum dormirent homines:* 'vetulae & mulierculae sunt ministrae tuae'; M. de la Bigne (ed.), *Maxima Bibliotheca Veterum Patrum*, 28 vols. (Lyons, Geneva, 1677–1707), XXV, p. 280d.

22. Limborch (ed.), *Liber sententiarum*, p. 254.

23. For example, Kurze (ed.), *Quellen zur Ketzergeschichte*, p. 86: 'Interrogata, an asperserit se aqua benedicta et crediderit aliquid valere, respondit sic,

et fecerit ne notaretur'. See also a statement from Pinerolo in 1335, edited in G. G. Merlo, *Eretici e inquisitori nella società piemontese del Trecento* (Turin, 1977) pp. 24, 185: 'illi de eorum secta debent ire ad ecclesiam ad eorum excusacionem ne alie gentes propenderent ipsis esse de secta Valdensium'.

24. Kurze (ed.), *Quellen zur Ketzergeschichte*, p. 155.

25. For example, Helyas Garin said that 'fuit confessus peccata sua predicto Arnaldo Valdensi, et recepit absolucionem et penitenciam ab eodem. Item quando confitebatur peccata sua Valdensibus et absolvebant eum et imponebant sibi penitenciam reputabat se absolutum ac si fuisset confessus proprio sacerdoti et absolutus per eum': Limborch (ed.), *Liber sententiarum*, pp. 353–4. Tyde Ermgart said that the Brothers were men 'potentes melius hominibus dimittere peccata quam presbiteros', Kurze (ed.), *Quellen zur Ketzergeschichte*, p. 107 – and a similar statement was made by most of those questioned by Zwicker. Though the formulation came from the inquisitor's question-list (see ibid., pp. 73–4), there is no reason to think that the inquisitor's question distorts any more than a Weberian ideal-type does.

26. See Morel's general statement in 1530, Vinay (ed.), *Confessioni di fede*, p. 42: 'Sacramentorum signa plebeculae nostrae non nos, sed antichristi membra administrant'.

27. Kurze (ed.), *Quellen zur Ketzergeschichte*, p. 143. The Brothers who are attested in 1392–4 visiting villages around Stettin are studied in D. Kurze, 'Zur Ketzergeschichte der Mark Brandenburg und Pommerns vornehmlich im 14. Jahrhundert: Luziferaner, Putzkeller und Waldenser', *Jahrbuch für die Geschichte Mittel- und OstDeutschlands*, 16/17 (1968), 50–94 (78–81).

28. Ibid., p. 138.

29. Limborch (ed.), *Liber sententiarum*, pp. 352–3.

30. This is described in the *De vita et actibus*, Gonnet (ed.), *Enchiridion*, p. 182, and by Morel in 1530, Vinay (ed.), *Confessioni di fede*, p. 40.

31. On annual changes in Stettin, see Kurze, 'Ketzergeschichte', p. 78.

32. Kurze (ed.), *Quellen zur Ketzergeschichte*, pp. 111, 116.

33. Merlo, *Eretici e inquisitori*, p. 208.

34. Gonnet (ed.), *Enchiridion*, p. 180.

35. Vinay (ed.), *Confessioni di fede*, pp. 36, 38, 40.

36. Aignès's sentence is in Limborch (ed.), *Liber sententiarum*, pp. 359–60.

37. Ibid., pp. 207–8.

38. Ibid., pp. 289–90, 340, 345.

39. Ibid., pp. 200–1.

40. Schneider, *Europäisches Waldensertum*, p. 31; J. Duvernoy (ed.), *Le registre d'inquisition de Jacques Fournier, évêque de Pamiers (1318–1325). Manuscrit no. Vat. Latin 4030 de la Bibliothèque Vaticane*, 3 vols., Bibliothèque Méridionale, 2nd series 41 (Toulouse, 1965), I, p. 101 n. 36.

41. Kurze, 'Ketzergeschichte', pp. 79–80; Döllinger, *Beiträge zur Sektengeschichte*, pp. 330–1.

42. Kurze, 'Ketzergeschichte', pp. 70–1, 79–80 and n. 151.

43. Vinay (ed.), *Confessioni di fede*, p. 44.
44. Together with the Waldensian *Liber Electorum*, these were edited in P. Biller, 'Aspects of the Waldenses in the fourteenth century, including an edition of their correspondence', D.Phil. thesis, University of Oxford, 1974. The *Liber Electorum* had been faultily edited in Döllinger, *Beiträge*, pp. 352–5, as also one element in the correspondence, a letter from Italian to Austrian Waldensians, ibid., pp. 355–62.
45. MS Klosterneuburg CC 826, fo. 229r: 'verbum Domini non est in angulis sed publice in montibus predicandum'.
46. Ibid., fo. 242v: 'expresse dicitis quod fides vera in palam predicari non possit'.
47. Ibid., fo. 224v (Waldensians describing the views of their former confreres): they attack us 'primo propter defectum sciencie, secundo propter auctoritatis privacionem'.
48. Ibid., fo. 237r: 'Omnes namque secte et hereses hoc modo, scilicet per prelatorum detestacionem, se adhortari conantur, in erroribus suis aliam causam defensionis non habentes. . . . nulla sit hic personarum excepcio, sed una generalis sentencia de illis omnibus datur, quasi omnes sint mali et nemo iustus'. Fo. 239v: 'de malicia sacerdotum ex diversis in unum conpilatis'.
49. MS St Florian XI 152, fo. 43v: 'In veritate a iuventute usque hodie quociescunque vidi sacerdotem ambonem ascendere nunquam audivi nisi vicia corrigere et virtutes seminare'.
50. Ibid., fo. 42v: 'Predicatis vos pauperes, dum plures ollas seu amphoras ac multum thesaurum auri et argenti habeatis in terra conclusum'.
51. MS Klosterneuburg CC 826, fo. 228r (Waldensians describing the grounds of former confreres' attacks): 'quia sacramenta ecclesiastica non ministramus'.
52. Ibid., fo. 245r: 'Quare ergo isti non suscipiunt fidem ibi ubi eciam suscipiunt sacramenta?'
53. For the following, see the discussion in my 'Medieval Waldensians' construction of the past', 39–54.
54. Merlo, *Eretici e inquisitori*, p. 167: 'illi de fide nova ita multiplicati et ita multiplicabuntur quod expellent sacerdotes et clericos de patria'.
55. Patschovsky and Selge (eds.), *Quellen zur Geschichte der Waldenser*, p. 72: 'Merito nos dampnatis modo, quia, si status noster non esset minoratus, potestatem mortis, quam exercetis contra nos modo, hanc nos exercuissemus contra clericos, religiosos et laycos.' In a later recension of the treatise the last phrase includes *omnes, scilicet*, thus: '. . . hanc nos exercuissemus contra vos omnes, scilicet clericos, religiosos et laicos'; M. A. E. Nickson, 'The "Pseudo-Reinerius" Treatise, the Final Stage of a Thirteenth-Century Work from the Diocese of Passau', *Archives d'Histoire Littéraire et Doctrinale du Moyen Age* 34 (1968), 255–314 (293).

Imageless devotion: what kind of an ideal?

Margaret Aston

In 1955, having unexpectedly arrived at a strange and happy transformation of his life, Isaiah Berlin wrote to his future wife with a musing question. 'Is there some calm deep feeling which is not tied to "images" and goes on in some even, mystical fashion?'[1] Behind those words, whether or not the writer's thoughts were bent that way, lie centuries of theory and practice. Mystical striving towards some 'calm deep' understanding of God was closely connected to the aim of lifting contemplation above and beyond attachment to the visual. Imageless devotion was part of a spiritual ideal of the medieval Church. But was it not also an ideal of the Protestant reformers who denied the very concept of monastic contemplation, and who worked so hard to eliminate dependence on images in religious learning?

Given the amount that we have learnt in recent years, and are still learning, about the role of imagery, actual and mental, in medieval thought and religion, there is a self-evident absurdity in posing this question in the compass of a short essay. But even if the matter can only be barely broached, it must be worth considering whether there are any continuities, or only discontinuities, in the visual methodology and aspirations which, after so many centuries, were fundamentally called in question in the sixteenth century. Perhaps a health warning is in place at the outset. I am in no way trying to suggest that religious imagery was abolished, or that teaching or thinking by visual methods was jettisoned; or that seeing did not continue to play a role in religion. What follows is all to do with ideals, not realities – though the utopian ideas sketched below certainly affected realities, but that is another story.

When the Church, from the time of Pope Gregory onwards, adopted the ancient techniques of the memory system in the service of the faith, it did so with a consciousness of different levels of learning. Minds of all kinds, literate or illiterate (and *illiterati* included those who were on the lower rungs of learning), had to be built up through the visual building blocks of memory. While the learned had to master the methodology of storing their knowledge in the carefully structured edifices and rooms they prepared in their heads, the uneducated could be guided towards making their own storage cupboards for religious recollection by being presented with depictions of scriptural stories and people. 'What the mind of simple people would scarcely be able to capture with its mental eye at least it can discern with its physical one, and what it can barely conceive from hearing it will perceive by seeing.'[2] Pictures, as Bede pointed out and Church theory of later centuries taught, served to 'recall to the memory of the faithful' the crucifixion and sacred stories.[3] Seeing was the highest of the senses, and mental imagery was integral to religious belief and learning.[4]

But 'the reality of the unseen', on which William James lectured at Edinburgh nearly a hundred years ago, posed its own challenge. For if we grant his premise that 'the life of religion . . . consists of the belief that there is an unseen order, and that our supreme good lies in harmoniously adjusting ourselves thereto',[5] we must also accept that for Christians the unseen is ultimately unseeable. And the life of religion, in the sense of those who dedicated themselves to a religious order, consisted at its highest levels in striving to reach that unseeable essence.

At the highest levels, even in the intensely visual period of the medieval Church, internal and external imagery were alike energetically discarded in pursuit of spiritual ideals. St Bernard and the Cistercian order did so on both a theoretical and practical plane. For St Augustine and St Gregory, as later for St Bernard, the ability to empty the mind of corporeal images marked a critical stage in the meditative ascent. 'The mind cannot recollect itself', wrote St Gregory, 'unless it has first learned to repress all phantasmata of earthly and heavenly images, and to reject and spurn whatever sense impressions present themselves to its thoughts . . . So they are all to be driven away from the mind's eye, in order that the soul may see itself as it was made.'[6] The *via negativa* of mystical theology accepted God's divinity as so transcending the whole of creation that he could only be reached by emptying the mind of all vestiges of images and sense perceptions. Just as there was a hierarchy of prayer, rising from verbal to non-verbal, so there was a hierarchy of meditation, rising from contemplation through imagery to contemplation that was imageless, removed from the physical and its representation.

St Bernard allowed that images had an important role in prayer, but he also pointed out their limitations. Notice, he wrote, 'that the love of the heart is in a certain sense carnal, in that it is chiefly moved towards the flesh of Christ and what Christ in the flesh did and enjoined'. Love of this kind made lighter and easier study and recollection and meditation and prayer:

The sacred image of the God-man, either being born or suckled or teaching or dying or rising again or ascending, is present to one in prayer, and must needs stir up the soul to the love of virtue . . . But although such devotion to the flesh of Christ is a gift, and a great gift, of the Holy Spirit, nevertheless I call it carnal in comparison with that love which does not so much regard the Word which is flesh, as the Word which is wisdom, which is justice, which is truth, which is holiness, piety, virtue . . . [7]

Full immersion in contemplation of the Word made flesh was a step towards another Word. To love in the spirit was another gift: to reach an abstraction beyond the desires of worldly glory and physical boundaries. St Bernard proved this capacity himself when (as reported by a contemporary) he rode alongside the Lake of Geneva all day without ever noticing it. He had made himself, as John Ruysbroeck later put it, 'bare and imageless in his senses'.[8]

Yet the incarnation made the facts of Christ's life a legitimate focus for meditation. St Bernard's Sermon on the Nativity of the Blessed Virgin Mary described the human scenes whose contemplation could effect the transformation expressed by St Paul in one of his favourite texts (2 Cor. 3:18) – 'we all, with open face beholding as in a glass the glory of the Lord, are changed into the same image from glory to glory':

He was incomprehensible and inaccessible, invisible and completely unthinkable. Now he wishes to be comprehended, wishes to be seen, wishes to be thought about. How, you ask? As lying in the manger, resting in the Virgin's lap, preaching on the mountain, praying through the night, or hanging on the cross, growing pale in death, free among the dead and ruling in hell, and also as rising on the third day, showing the apostles the place of the nails, the signs of victory, and finally as ascending over heaven's secrets in their sight.[9]

Concentration of this kind on the life of Christ came to be generally accepted as a widely accessible form of spiritual exercise. It was open to lay persons of differing educational capacity, and the *Meditations on the Life of Christ* long attributed to St Bonaventure offered to later generations exactly the kind of meditation described in this passage.

The abbot of Clairvaux did not think of the highest reaches of spiritual meditation as being within the range of those outside the monastic discipline. His ideal of 'imageless devotion' belonged to the monastic life of prayer and meditation, and he accepted that the situation was different for believers living in the world, whose devotion 'we hope to stir up by ornaments of gold and silver' visible in their secular churches.[10] However, while accepting this important distinction, Bernard was not alone in expressing idealistic aspirations for lay people's use of imagery. In 1135, having restored peace and order in Milan, he persuaded the citizens to remove rich ornaments from their churches.[11] Even in the secular world, images might hinder or distract the devotions of the spiritually gifted, but how many lay men or women had the capacity to do without them? As Walter Hilton pointed out in the fourteenth century, 'if all the faithful were strong in this way and instructed by grace as these [well-educated devout] are, it would not be necessary to place images in churches'.[12]

Through its legislation on the arts the Cistercian order demonstrated St Bernard's higher expectation of contemplatives. It was not only in reaction against the excessive ornamentation of the great monastic pilgrimage churches that he inspired within his order a repudiation of artistic ornament and enrichment that constituted an extreme of artistic asceticism. The ban on sculpture and painting and restrictions on coloured glass windows in Cistercian churches have seemed closely to anticipate the work of subsequent purifiers.[13] But there was a critical difference, for these were orders for monastic churches. They accorded with St Bernard's desire to free the contemplative mind from the distraction of externals. He regarded the glitter and lustre of contemporary monastic art as an impediment, not an aid, to the life of prayer. 'I will overlook the immense height of the places of prayer, their superfluous breadth, the costly polished surfaces and crafted representations which, while they distract the eye, impede the devotion of those who should be praying. To me it all savours of the ancient worship of the Jews.'[14]

For the contemplative, whose meditative ascent aspired to moments of oneness with God, the final peak of spiritual union depended on an ability to rise above sensory perceptions, emptying the mind of all bodily associations. 'Look that nought worche in thi wit ne in thi wil bot only God.' *The Cloud of Unknowing* described this process of suppression of the sensory as 'the cloud of forgetting': 'put a cloude of forgetyng bineth thee, bitwix thee and alle the cretures that ever ben maad' since God was further removed 'when thou hast no cloude of forgetyng bitwix thee and alle the creatures'. The physical negation that preceded spiritual oneness involved all the senses, but it was above all the sense of sight whose banishment opened the way to inner illumination. The vocabulary of mystical experience is built on metaphors of light and seeing, just as our vocabulary of intellectual understanding is filled with words relating to sight and illumination. The mystical training of the 'soul's eye' meant countermanding the diurnal pleasures of the physical eye; learning a capacity for not seeing; practising a kind of gazing that was itself a form of blindness. Behind these careful directions of one contemplative to another, as to how the cloud of forgetting might push against the dark cloud of unknowing separating him or her from God, lay the Pseudo-Dionysius. *Deonise Hid Divinite* showed how any aspiration of reaching towards the unseen intangible divinity must call for experience in unseeing; 'alle thoo soules that ben not havyng iyen of mynde' had to close inward eyes in the exercise of 'blynde beholdynges'.[15]

The Cloud lampoons false ways of seeing. The author was particularly wary of those who believed their meditation could be strengthened by thinking of God's kindness, or of our Lady, or of saints and angels. There could be no positive answer to the question of how to think of God. 'But now thou askest me and seiest: "How schal I think on him-self, and what is hee?" and to this I cannot answere thee bot thus: "I wote never".' A 'blynde steryng of love unto God for him-self' must take precedence over the temptation to contemplate and gaze on angels and saints in heaven, or hear the alluring music of the blessed. Some young aspirants pursued their mental fantasies to a point of absurdity, believing in their imaginative power to gaze upwards into the starry firmament:

Thees men willen sumtyme with the coriouste of here ymaginacion peerce the planetes, and make an hole in the firmament to loke in therate. Thees men wil make a God as hem lyst, and clothen hym ful richely in clothes, and set hym in a trone, fer more curiously than ever was he depeynted in this erthe. Thees men wil maken aungelles in bodely licnes, and set hem aboute ich one with diverse minstralsie, fer mor corious than ever was any seen or herde in this liif.[16]

The inability to clear the mind of invasive flitting images bore on concentration in prayer. 'And in thy prayer thou shalt not set thine heart on any earthly thing', Walter Hilton told the enclosed anchoress for whom he wrote his *Ladder of Perfection*, 'but all thy travail shall be for to draw in thy thought from the beholdings of all earthly thing'. It was to be 'made naked and bare' from the burden of all worldly thoughts and affections. This entailed the withdrawal of thoughts from the senses, paying no attention to what was heard, seen or felt, and excluding all imagery from the mind. It required great strength of discipline. For the 'eyes of the soul' to open, other eyes had to be shut. 'For thy ghostly eye is not yet opened, I shall tell one word for all which thou shalt seek, desire and find . . . This word is Jhesu. I mean not this word Jhesu painted upon the wall, or written with letters on the book, or formed by lips in sound of the mouth, nor feigned in thine heart by travail of thy mind.' To reach this spiritual word sensuous distractions had to be obliterated from the workings of the mind.[17] It was the same problem, viewed in a different light, that faced the 'ignorant man' under instruction from a divine in Arthur Dent's *Plaine Mans Pathe-way to Heaven* (1601). 'Whether you never had any bye thoughts in your prayers, and your heart hath not beene uppon other matters, even then while you were in prayer?' was a question put to Asunetus, the plain man, by the catechising Theologus in this dialogue. Not unexpectedly, the answer is affirmative: 'I cannot denie that: for it is a very hard matter to pray without bye-thoughts.' Now, however, this failure ranked as an offence against the second commandment. The straying of the mind (wayward in its picturing of worldly interests) amounted to serving other gods.[18]

That question in *The Cloud*, 'How shall I think on God himself?', was central. It could only be answered in negatives, but the negatives of the mystic were not those of Calvin and others who preceded him in believing it wrong that God should be represented by any visible appearance, including the image of the Trinity.[19] For Hilton and kindred spirits of his age, 'hid divinity' was a mystery that was not affronted by the physical representations of art. These might be transcended by the spiritually gifted, those visionaries whose seeing surpassed visible forms. For others, paintings and sculptures were valued vehicles of devotion, themselves to be thought of as 'meditations' – the term John Lydgate used for a pietà.[20] The diverse ways of 'seeing' included meditation that approached abstraction. 'And aftyr this I sawe god in a poynte, that es in myne undyrstandynge, by whilke syght I sawe that he es in all thynge.' Julian of Norwich expressed her desire for a vision of God in terms of seeing with her own eyes the physical sufferings of the Saviour. The book of her 'showings' describes how that was granted to her, but it also, as these words tell, took her to more abstract levels of religious experience.[21] Most people could not rise so high. For them it was accepted that the abstract had to be envisageable. 'For a thing entirely abstract, of the sort as God, an angel, infinite space, and such matters are, place an image as the painters make it', was Thomas Bradwardine's advice to the practitioners of the art of memory, and he went on to explain how 'the Trinity as it is usually painted in churches' could serve as a mnemonic symbol for the number three.[22] And while the *Spiritual Exercises* of St Ignatius recognised that meditation on the incorporeal differed from that on the corporeal, they still explained how to meditate on the Trinity: 'see and consider the three divine Persons as on the royal seat or throne of the divine Majesty'. God, like Christ and Virgin and saints, entered and occupied minds as contemporary images showed him, with the result (Hilton admitted) that ignorant yet faithful *simplices*, knowing no better, thought of the Trinity as separate persons like three men.[23]

Mental images of this kind came to seem deeply shocking. False images produced false beliefs, and sixteenth-century reformers were scandalised by the many alabasters and other depictions of the Trinity that showed the unshowable Father as an old man. How could people think about God as they should when imagery of this kind was so common? Steps were taken to remedy this situation in the 1530s. The 'Bishops' Book' of 1537 called for teaching to explain 'that God in his substance cannot by any similitude or image be represented or expressed', and that it was only through 'yielding to the custom of gentility' that the church fathers had allowed pictures of the Father of heaven to be placed in churches. This pagan weakness was perceived to have had pagan results. There were self-evident dangers in portraying a divinity who could be heard, but not seen, with the human features of a bearded ancient. So, 'if the common people would duly conceive of the heavenly Father without any bodily representation, it were more seemly for Christian people to be without all such images of the Father, than to have any of them'.[24] In 1538 Archbishop Lee thought fit to embody this teaching in the articles he issued for the diocese of York. Parish clergy were to explain to their flocks 'that although they see the image of the Father represented as an old man, yet they may in no wise believe that the Heavenly Father is any man, or that He hath any body or age; but that He is a nature and substance, above all measure passing the capacity and understanding, either of man's wit or angel's'.[25]

The English Church, for the first time conjoining art criticism with parish instruction, had embarked on a process of mental engineering. Images had to be erased from minds as well as church walls. Archbishop Lee was in effect calling on his clergy to become instructors in the art of 'blind contemplation'. But the York parishioners, just as much as the recipient of *The Cloud of Unknowing*, might have put the question, 'How am I to think of God himself, and what is he?' – to which the answer in their modernising world was, at least in part, a new negative; 'Not as you see him in this sculpture.' Metaphorical descriptions must not be taken literally. To speak of God seated on his throne or to believe in Christ sitting on the right hand of God the Father did not mean it was permissible to think of an old man with hands and feet. God must not be conceived in these human forms, and no image, physical or mental, should ever be made of him. But how were people's devotions to be made imageless? The attempt to drive a wedge between the representation and the beliefs it engendered, to banish from minds as well as eyes the concept of God as a white-bearded ancient, went on. It was a process of rebuilding that involved inner and outer destruction, and the task of reforming mental imagery proved more intractable than the removal of depictions from churches.

Contemplating Christ was different from contemplation of God. The veil of invisibility was lifted by the incarnation. For centuries the faith and the image met in the assumption that a Christian was a person who lived with an image of the crucifixion lodged in his or her breast. By the late fourteenth century, when John Mirk rebutted Lollard questioning of this position, it had long been accepted that the hearts and minds of all believers were fortified by imagery of Christ crucified to the extent that it was impossible to imagine a world without it. Roods were set on high in churches because of man's need 'by ofte seynge to have the sadur mynde of Cristis passion in his hert'. Christ in the heart – inscribed visually within. The crucifixion became familiar by being seen – frequently seen. 'I say boldly that ther ben mony thousaund of pepul that couth not ymagen in her hert how Crist was don on the rood, but as thai lerne hit be syght of ymages and payntours.'[26] Luther said as much. For him it was impossible to hear or think of the Passion 'without forming mental images of it in my heart'. The image of the crucifixion was as inescapable and natural as the mirrored reflection of his own face. 'Whether I will or not, when I hear of Christ, an image of a man hanging on a cross takes form in my heart.'[27]

Yet by the time Luther wrote those words, this attitude could be seen as both wrong and simplistic. How did that understanding of the depiction get there in the first place? For those whose faith rested on the evangelical priority of the word, the image, physical and mental, was both secondary and dangerous. How could anyone grasp the nature of Christ's death on the cross except through the word, teaching and preaching? How could loving through imagery avoid the dangers of the senses which threatened to turn into idolatry? Behind all the theological discussions that went on, and the outpouring of instruction on the teaching of the commandments, was a questioning of traditional views of human perception and learning.

England's determined purifiers certainly had in mind much more than the removal of erroneous imagery. The battle against papal idolatry was a process of purgation, but it was also idealistic. The end-goal was a

cleansed and renewed Church ruled by the word, whose prayer was un-
sullied by irrelevant distractions of painting, sculpture and music. 'We
must shut up our senses that they wander not; our eyes must see Gods
beauty, not gad after vanities, and send teares as ambassadors: Our eares
must attend the word of truth, not delicious tunes of musicall melody.'
These words might seem to recall the 'forgetting' of *The Cloud of Unknowing*, and the mystics' injunctions to rise above sensuous experience.
They in fact appeared in 1629 in Peter Smart's *Short Treatise of Altars*, a
text of tart polemical criticism of the ceremonial practices introduced in
Durham Cathedral by John Cosin.[28] Smart shared Puritan obsessions
about idolatry and popish superstition. But, like earlier Lollard critics
of costly ornaments and gilding of great churches, he harked back to
St Bernard:

> Why then are set before us so many objects of vanity, so many allurements of
> our outward senses, our eyes and eares, and consequently our minds from the
> meditation of Christs death and passion, and our sins which were the only cause
> of all our miseries and his lamentable sufferings. Can such paltry toyes bring to
> our memory Christ and his blood-shedding? Crosses, crucifixes, tapers, candle-
> sticks, gilded angels, painted images, golden copes, gorgeous altars, sumptuous
> organs, with sackbuts and cornets piping so loud at the communion table, that
> they may be heard half a mile from the church? Bernard saith, no. *Orantium in
> se retorquent aspectum, impediunt affectum*: Such glorious spectacles, draw away from
> God the minds of them that pray, they further not but hinder entire affections
> and godly meditations.[29]

The reform of churches and the reform of worshippers were to go hand
in hand. The sensuous delights of angels and organs and altars must go;
at the same time minds would be freed for purer meditation.

The counter-reforming world was divided over internal as well as external imagery – the pictures in devout minds as well as depictions on
walls. The *Spiritual Exercises* of St Ignatius Loyola amounted to a systematic guide to disciplined meditation on the life of Christ in the tradition
of the late thirteenth-century *Meditations on the Life of Christ*. Central to
the method of the *Exercises* was the use of 'composition, seeing the place'.
'Here it is to be observed that in the contemplation or meditation of a visible object, as in contemplating Christ our Lord, who is visible, the composition will be to see with the eye of the imagination the corporeal place
where the object I wish to contemplate is found' – such as the Temple or
the road from Bethany to Jerusalem. This was the detailed application
to meditation on scripture of the *compositio loci* of the art of memory. It
had long been expounded and practised: witness for example the Italian

fifteenth-century *Zardino de Oration*, the *Garden of Prayer*. St Ignatius gave it classic shape by the thoroughness of his exposition. Preparatory prayer was followed by the mind's imagined creation of the physical setting, in which the biblical persons would be seen and heard. 'The first point is to see the persons with the eyes of the imagination, meditating and contemplating in particular their circumstances, and gathering some fruit from the sight.' 'Composition of place', as the 1599 Directory on the use of the *Exercises* explained, 'is nothing else than to picture to oneself' the places of the event to be meditated.[30] The *Exercises* were, as this guide made clear, open to use by others than religious, and it was accepted that all sorts of lay persons would practise and benefit from them. The use of 'the eyes of the imagination' might be particularly helpful in their meditations, but it also had to be watched. Father Richard Gibbons, who in 1610 published an English version of Luis de la Puente's exercises (dedicated to two devout gentlewomen) warned that the imagination 'when it is untamed and disordered, as it notably hindreth Praier; so also it aydeth much, when it can with facilitye forme within it selfe certain figures, or Images of such things, as are to bee meditated':[31]

> Marke in my heart, O Soule, where thou dost dwell,
> The picture of Christ crucified . . .[32]

The parallels between Donne's poetry and the meditative methods of works like de la Puente's have long been recognised. Donne, seeking assurance against the judgemental terrors of the 'world's last night', brushed away idolatry and Hell with the picture in the heart, and the belief that the Saviour's beauty was itself an expression of an all-forgiving mind. But once the religious world had been set in a new direction by Protestant supremacy of the word, radical questioning of the instructive potential of images and the dangers of their sensuous attractions had profound repercussions on the value and use of such mental pictures. The days when one could take for granted a crucifix either in the heart or on the wall were over:

> Since Christ embrac'd the Crosse it selfe, dare I
> His image, th'image of his Crosse deny?[33]

Plenty of purists did, and the loss of the image which Donne deplored had resulted, long before he wrote, in countless crucifixes being removed from churches, broken and burned. Hostility extended to the sign of the cross, and after Donne's death there were those who saw it as 'superstitious vanity' to allow 'Christs picture among us Protestants', since depictions of the Saviour, 'even for civill or morall uses', were 'utterly unlawful'.[34] Cross and crucifix alike came to be regarded by the high-minded as offensive lies, through 'clothing God's essence with an image'. Both offended God's heavenly majesty by 'carnall thoughts'. 'There is that idoll of the heart begotten, which must be as carefully be expelled out of the minde, as any idoll that is externall out of the Temple'.[35] The ideal was a kind of white blankness, an openness to the divine essence untrammelled by physical form. On this view, Donne's position was wholly unacceptable.

The beliefs and actions of Donne and Cosin, and those who could not begin to share the idea – let alone ideal – of imageless devotion, threatened the pursuit of this spiritual goal. In 1639 when the backsliding or reversal of reforming priorities was causing deep anxiety, Edmund Gurney grappled with the facts of human psychology to explain the dangerous attraction of the visual. He looked to inner frames of mind as well as outward representations. Even for gestures of worship (so contentious at the time), there were dangers in the head as well as in the movement of the knees; 'there be many kinds of knees which are not bodily and visible':

Now, whereas voices, and letters, and other means of instruction (which do not wrap up their notions in images) do readily passe through these common senses; and having presented their matter to the inward senses, presently vanish away; these images do not so: but being such kind of things as the fansie and outward senses are apt to be tickled and pleased withall, they dally and play with them, and soke into them.[36]

The faculty of seeing thus enjoyed a particularly influential role, defrauding the 'inward senses' of proper nutriment, and instead feeding them with 'glaring, grosse, impure, fantasticall, and in the end idololatricall notions'. The memory imagery of the mind was therefore intrinsically dangerous; indeed, a principal reason for the 'divinely minded' to abandon images was their claimed ability 'so deeply [to] imprint their notions in the memorie and outward senses'. By their very nature they were incongruous with God. 'While the Lord calleth inwardly, they call outwardly: while the Lord calleth to the centre, they call to the circumference: while the Lord standeth knocking at the doore of the heart, they stand rapping at the doore of the outward eye, and playing upon the ball thereof.' What could be more contrary than God and images?[37]

Gurney's argument comes close to some of the assumptions of the mystical tradition. His emphasis on that ancient theme of the contrast between the brightness and visibility of the images[38] and the invisible God whose secret place was the 'darkness, clouds, and thick darkness', leads us almost to hear echoes of *The Cloud of Unknowing*. Scriptural commonplaces remained the same, but approaches to 'calm deep' understanding of God had profoundly changed. The term 'blind devotion', used in Edward VI's 1547 Injunctions to dismiss the superstitious beliefs of the time, and by John Hooker of Exeter (d. 1601) to characterise the failure of pre-Reformation 'Romish' religion, encapsulates this change.[39] It no longer related in any way to the powerful insight of 'blind seeing'. On the contrary, it now expressed disdainful disparagement, the rejection of eye-service of any kind in the service of God. Hearing came above and before seeing. Faith was essentially a matter for ears.

A strange transference had taken place. An ideal that had once been the prerogative of the spiritually elect had become the religious framework for all church members. Those whose reformed religion was premised on rejection of intercessory prayers by professional contemplatives, applied to the prayers of their day part of the spiritual discipline of that ousted world. It amounted to holding up to believers at large the highest spiritual aspirations of medieval mystics. Alongside the elimination of idols from places of worship more ambitious aims had been tabled. But the aim of visual purgation was now attached to quite altered views of perceptual priorities, and there was deep unease about the iconographic methodology of the ancient system of learning.

As long as it was believed that learning depended on a memory system which worked with mental pictures and symbols and diagrams, dependent above all on the 'ocular gateway to memory and meditation',[40] abstractions of all kinds, mathematical and divine, were inescapably placed on a visual path. In the sixteenth century, however, this was seriously challenged. The priority of ear replaced that of eye for all who believed that 'Faith cometh by hearing.'[41] In some quarters images of all kinds, physical and mental, became suspect as tools of Christian learning, remembering and devotion. The lawgiver whose dominating presence in the commandments spoke afresh to a new generation had to be safeguarded in his pure inaccessibility. Minds as well as churches had to be cleansed. The deep conviction that the religious image was a potential idol, threatening the believer's relationship with God, was tantamount to jettisoning the ancient 'book of memory' as a devotional tool, and applying to all reformed believers expectations hitherto only aspired to by the few. To be imageless was to be open to the Word in all its fullness; it was the passage not to mystical unknowing, but to scriptural knowing. Imageless devotion was no longer a distant, nearly unassailable peak. It was a condition that impinged on all reformed hearts.

NOTES

1. M. Ignatieff, *Isaiah Berlin: A Life* (London, 1998), p. 220.
2. M. J. Carruthers, *The Book of Memory* (Cambridge, 1990), pp. 241–2 (in the course of a very helpful discussion of 'Mental Pictures', pp. 229–42), quoting the twelfth-century Hugo de Folieto ('per picturam mentes aedificare': *PL* 177, cols. 13–14).
3. L. G. Duggan, 'Was art really the "book of the illiterate"?', *Word & Image* 5 (1989), 227–51 (229–30), citing Bede's *De Templo Salomonis Liber, Bedae Venerabilis Opera*, pt 2, ed. D. Hurst, Corpus Christianorum Series Latina 119A (1969), pp. 212–13; *PL* 91, cols. 790–91.
4. In what follows I refer to mental images (pictures in the head or imagination) without further ado, though it should be recognised at the outset that this is to beg critical questions for today's cognitive psychologists. H. Barlow, C. Blakemore and M. Weston-Smith (eds.), *Images and Understanding* (Cambridge, 1990), pp. 4, 297–309, 358–70. See F. Galton, *Inquiries into Human Faculty and its Development* (Everyman, 1907, first pub. 1883), pp. 57–79, for an investigation into mental imagery. Answers to his questions on visualising (pp. 255–6) returned by a hundred men of standing (including nineteen FRSs) led Galton to conclude that 'an over-ready perception of sharp mental pictures is antagonistic to the acquirement of habits of highly-generalised and abstract thought' (p. 60); also 'there is abundant evidence that the visualising faculty admits of being developed by education' (p. 73).
5. W. James, *The Varieties of Religious Experience* ('The Reality of the Unseen', lecture III of the Gifford Lectures on natural religion delivered at Edinburgh in 1901–2) (Mentor edn, New York, 1958), p. 58.
6. C. Butler, *Western Mysticism: The Teaching of SS Augustine, Gregory and Bernard on Contemplation and the Contemplative Life* (2nd edn, London, 1927), p. 99 from Gregory's Homilies on Ezekiel (*PL* 76, cols. 989–90: 'nisi prius didicerit terrenarum atque coelestium imaginum phantasmata ab oculis mentis compescere . . .').
7. *Sancti Bernardi Opera*, ed. J. Leclercq *et al.*, 8 vols. (Rome, 1957–77), I, pp. 118, 120, the *Sermones super Cantica Canticorum* (xx.6,8) – Bernard's 'mystical masterpiece', on which see Bernard McGinn, *The Growth of Mysticism*, vol. II of *The Presence of God: A History of Christian Mysticism* (London, 1994), pp. 164ff., and Butler, *Western Mysticism*, p. 173; S. Ringbom, 'Devotional Images and Imaginative Devotions', *Gazette des Beaux-Arts*, ser. 6, 73 (1969), 159–70 (163); see also *idem, Icon to Narrative: The Rise of the Dramatic Close-up in Fifteenth-century Devotional Painting* (2nd revised edn, Doornspijk, 1984, first pub. 1965), pp. 17–22, on imageless devotion ('the ideal of the Bernardine tradition') in chapter I, 'The Devotional Image', pp. 11–71.
8. *PL* 185, cols. 305–6 (*S. Bernardi Vita Prima*); Butler, *Western Mysticism*, p. 210, n. 3, citing Ruysbroeck's *Spiritual Espousals*; C. Rudolph, 'Bernard of Clairvaux's *Apologia* as a Description of Cluny, and the Controversy over Monastic Art', *Gesta* 27 (1988), 125–32 (126–7).

9. McGinn, *Growth of Mysticism*, pp. 175–6, 492 n. 88, citing *Sancti Bernardi Opera*, V, p. 282 ('In nativitate Beatae Mariae'), lines 19–25 (part of this passage is missing in McGinn's note).

10. J. M. Hamburger, 'The Visual and the Visionary: The Image in Late Medieval Monastic Devotions', *Viator* 20 (1989), 161–82, argues that the increasing use of images led to visionary experiences and contemplative devotions being increasingly expressed in corporeal and pictorial terms, in a manner that might have shocked St Bernard, the 'theoretician of imageless devotion' (p. 175). The continuity of the ideal is not pursued here.

11. B. S. James, *Saint Bernard of Clairvaux: An Essay in Biography* (London, 1957), pp. 55, 120.

12. J. M. Russell-Smith, 'Walter Hilton and a Tract in Defence of the Veneration of Images', *Dominican Studies* 7 (1954), 180–214 (189).

13. On Cistercian legislation on art and architecture see C. Norton and D. Park (eds.), *Cistercian Art and Architecture in the British Isles* (Cambridge, 1986), pp. 54–55, 56–64, 318–93.

14. Bernard's *Apologia ad Guillelmum Abbatum* in *Sancti Bernardi Opera*, III, pp. 104–7 (104). For a full examination of the *Apologia* and Bernard's concerns, see C. Rudolph, *The 'Things of Greater Importance': Bernard of Clairvaux's* Apologia *and the Medieval Attitude Toward Art* (Philadelphia, 1990), including the text (I have borrowed from the translation p. 10) and a discussion of 'Art as a Spiritual Distraction to the Monk' (pp. 104–24). See also the same author's *Artistic Change at St-Denis: Abbot Suger's Program and the Early Twelfth-century Controversy over Art* (Princeton, 1988) for an assessment of the impact of Cistercian artistic asceticism on Suger's art programme. J. Sumption, *Pilgrimage: An Image of Mediaeval Religion* (London, 1975), pp. 155–6, reflects on some wider aspects of the controversy.

15. P. Hodgson (ed.), *The Cloud of Unknowing and the Book of Privy Counselling*, EETS o.s. 218 (1944, repr. with additions 1958), pp. 24, 42, 61, 66, 81; *idem* (ed.), *Deonise Hid Divinite and Other Treatises*, EETS o.s. 231 (1955), pp. 2–3; *The Cloud of Unknowing and other Works*, trans. C. Wolters (Harmondsworth, 1961, 1978), pp. 66–7, 79, 94, 98, 110, 206, 209 ('you put away your physical senses (hearing, sight, smell, taste, and touch)'); R. K. Forman, 'Mystical Experience in the *Cloud* Literature', in M. Glasscoe (ed.), *The Medieval Mystical Tradition in England*, Papers Read at Dartington Hall, July 1987 (Cambridge, 1987), pp. 177–95. D. Knowles, *The English Mystical Tradition* (London, 1961), pp. 23–4, 29–30, and chapter 5 on *The Cloud*, traces the mystical experience of the cloud of darkness from St Gregory of Nyssa and the Pseudo-Dionysius.

16. *Cloud*, ed. Hodgson, pp. 25, 34, 105; trans. Wolters, pp. 67, 73, 129. Hodgson suggests (p. 200) that *The Cloud* was warning against too literal an interpretation of Rolle's teaching. While the sense of seeing dominates the vocabulary of mystical experience, hearing is also present (witness the angelic song in *The Cloud* chapter 57), and was specially important to Richard Rolle: R. Allen, '"Singuler Lufe": Richard Rolle and the Grammar of

Spiritual Ascent', in Glasscoe (ed.), *The Medieval Mystical Tradition in England, Papers Read at Dartington Hall, July 1984* (Cambridge, 1984), pp. 28–54, at 28, 31, 34, 35; Knowles, *Mystical Tradition*, p. 108.

17. Walter Hilton, *The Scale of Perfection*, ed. E. Underhill (London, 1923), pp. 57, 111–12; Walter Hilton, *The Ladder of Perfection*, trans. L. Sherley-Price (Harmondsworth, 1988), pp. 28–9, 56–7, 63; H. P. Owen, 'Christian Mysticism: A Study in Walter Hilton's *The Ladder of Perfection*', *Religious Studies* 7 (1971), 31–42.

18. A. Dent, *The Plaine Mans Pathe-way to Heaven* (1601), pp. 347–8; M. Aston, *England's Iconoclasts*, I (Oxford, 1988), pp. 457–8.

19. A. Hudson (ed.), *English Wycliffite Writings* (Cambridge, 1978), p. 27 (the eighth of the 1395 conclusions); John Calvin, *The Institutes of the Christian Religion*, ed. J. T. McNeill, 2 vols. (London, 1961), I, p. 112.

20. H. M. MacCracken (ed.), *The Minor Poems of John Lydgate*, pt I, EETS e.s. 107 (1911), pp. 268–79, cited by Carruthers, *Book of Memory*, pp. 224–5.

21. E. Colledge and J. Walsh (eds.), *A Book of Showings to the Anchoress Julian of Norwich*, 2 vols. (Toronto, 1978), I, p. 226; Julian of Norwich, *Revelations of Divine Love*, trans. C. Wolters (Harmondsworth, 1966), pp. 63, 80, 85; on the different kinds of sight and 'beholding' in Julian's account see P. Molinari, *Julian of Norwich* (London, 1959), pp. 32–70, 104–39.

22. Carruthers, *Book of Memory*, pp. 284, 287, and the discussion pp. 130ff.

23. W. H. Longridge (ed.), *The Spiritual Exercises of Saint Ignatius of Loyola* (rev. edn, 1930), pp. 89, 305; Russell-Smith, 'Walter Hilton', p. 190.

24. C. Lloyd (ed.), *Formularies of Faith put forth by Authority* (Oxford, 1825), pp. 134–5.

25. W. H. Frere and W. M. Kennedy (eds.), *Visitation Articles and Injunctions of the Period of the Reformation*, 3 vols. (Alcuin Club Collns, 14–16, 1910), II, pp. 44 (no. 3, clergy to obtain, read daily, and expound the Bishops' Book to parishioners), 48 (no. 17); E. Duffy, *The Stripping of the Altars* (New Haven and London, 1992), pp. 413–14.

26. T. Erbe (ed.), *Mirk's Festial*, EETS e.s. 96 (1905), p. 171; A. J. Fletcher, 'John Mirk and the Lollards', *Medium Aevum* 56 (1987), 217–24.

27. Aston, *England's Iconoclasts*, I, p. 437, and as a background to what follows, pp. 452–66 on 'idols of the mind'.

28. P. Smart, *A Short Treatise of Altars* (1641), p. 19 (the text was written in 1629); John Buckeridge, *A sermon preached before His Majestie At Whitehall* (1618), p. 6, where the passage concludes 'The eares must attend trueth, not leasings . . . '. Smart's claim that he was quoting from a sermon John Buckeridge had preached before James I on kneeling at Communion twelve years earlier was both insidious and disreputable, given the false twist he gave to this passage.

29. Smart, *Short Treatise*, p. 19; Smart had earlier (pp. 2–3) cited St Bernard's famous *Apologia* (above n. 14), and these words are quoted from it (*Sancti Bernardi Opera*, III, p. 104).

30. *Spiritual Exercises*, ed. Longridge, pp. 53, 93–4, 136, 304–5, 326, 337. The Directory, which refers to the example of Bonaventure, discusses in chapters 1 and 9 the different kinds of people who could practise the *Exercises*. M. Baxandall, *Painting and Experience in Fifteenth Century Italy* (Oxford, 1972), pp. 45–6 on the *Zardino*. On the *loci* of artificial memory see F. A. Yates, *The Art of Memory* (Harmondsworth, 1969), pp. 18–20, 22–4, 48, 60–1 etc.

31. Luis de la Puente, *Meditations uppon the Mysteries of our holy Faith with the practice of mental praier touching the same*, trans. R. Gibbons ([Douai], 1610), pt 1, pp. 40–1. Puente's is among the Jesuit works of meditation discussed by L. L. Martz, *The Poetry of Meditation* (New Haven, 1954); see especially chapter 2, 'The Method of Meditation', pp. 25–70.

32. John Donne, *The Divine Poems*, ed. H. Gardner (Oxford, 1969), p. 10, from *Holy Sonnets* (1633); commentary p. 71.

33. Donne, 'The Crosse', lines 1–2, in *Divine Poems*, ed. Gardner, p. 26 (placed as an early poem in the commentary, p. 92).

34. John Vicars, *The Sinfulness and Unlawfulness, of having or making the Picture of Christs Humanity* (1641), p. 1.

35. Robert Parker, *A Scholasticall Discourse against symbolizing with Antichrist in Ceremonies: especially in the signe of the crosse* ([Middelburg], 1607), p. 3.

36. Edmund Gurney, *Toward the Vindication of the Second Commandment* (Cambridge, 1639), pp. 86, 116–17.

37. Gurney, *Vindication*, pp. 120–1, 124–6; see Yates, *Art of Memory*, chapters 10 and 12, for suggestive passages on Ramism and 'inner iconoclasm' (p. 231).

38. On the need for the *locus* of the memory to be well lit see Carruthers, *Book of Memory*, p. 131.

39. Frere and Kennedy (ed.), *Visitation Articles*, II, p. 127; R. Whiting, *The Blind Devotion of the People* (Cambridge, 1989), pp. 135, 147.

40. Carruthers, *Book of Memory*, p. 245.

41. 'The air was filled with the word of God', as W. J. Ong put it in *The Presence of the Word: Some Prolegomena for Cultural and Religious History* (New Haven and London, 1967), p. 268 (one of the works which shows up the absurdity of an essay such as this one, which is offered to Barrie as a silent and imageless thankyou).

CHAPTER 12

An English anchorite: the making, unmaking and remaking of Christine Carpenter*

Miri Rubin

In July 1993 Barrie Dobson and I attended the world première of the film *The Anchoress*, directed by Chris Newby, at the Arts Cinema in Cambridge. After the screening Barrie offered a few thoughts to the audience: he was as much at ease talking about the film as he always is in more conventional settings for historical discussion. It is the wide interests, the humour and curiosity about people, the gentle engagement so characteristic of Barrie, which I wish to salute in this article by bringing together two of Barrie's passions: film and late medieval religion.

Joining the new University of York in 1964, Barrie threw his energies and talent into helping to create one of the best medieval history centres in the world. He was a passionate lover of film, yet around him in York, as elsewhere, cinemas were being closed down. Soon after his arrival in York a chance glance at an advertisement in the local newspaper brought Barrie to the York Film Society's Annual General Meeting. At that, his first meeting, Barrie became a committee member, and within a fortnight, the Society's Secretary. Desperate to enliven his new charge, Barrie wrote off to the British Film Institute with a vague hope for some support or advice. Little did he expect the warm embrace in which he became enfolded: his letter coincided with one of Harold Wilson's pet initiatives, a policy for art in the regions which allocated funding and dedicated expertise. Hectic years of activity followed as the York Film Theatre was established, and with the university's support its home was the campus. Barrie continued to serve for the next six years ushering programmes in the heady years of the French New Wave and Italian Realism. Screenings drew students, academics and townsfolk, and such was its success that the descendant of the YFT still exists, within the recently opened City Screen in Coney Street. It is a pleasure to be able to address this continuing interest of Barrie's in the context of 'his century' – the fourteenth.

This is a particularly interesting time to discuss a medieval theme through film at a time when so much medieval scholarship – and especially areas of religion and gender – has been recast in inter-disciplinary frames. Film engages sight and sound and thus challenges the primacy of the written word as the main vehicle of historical truth. Film can act as witness and record of the past, and its treatment collapses disciplinary boundaries between history and literature and history of art. In the United States in particular film has been brought into the class-room in an attempt to attract and familiarise, and to make use of the visual skills and cinematic enthusiasm characteristic of popular culture and its bearers, students and teachers alike. Film has been appreciated as a medium which might mobilise the cultural interests of our students and galvanise their enquiries into the past. It has proved to be an ex-cellent vehicle for the presentation of large bodies of information, as in the epic histories of this century's wars and of the Holocaust; it is perhaps most poignant in introducing subjects which the written word seems inadequate to contain or express.[1] Situation in landscape and re-construction of texture can also produce experiences which are hard to capture in simple classroom situations even through the most careful study of texts.[2] In attempting to bridge the distance into historical pasts, film is increasingly being incorporated into curricula: *The Anchoress* is now part of a well-planned and challenging course entitled 'Medieval Women and their Legacy', taught at two American universities.[3] It provides foci for learning and raises consciousness of pedagogic challenges.[4]

The Anchoress tells the story of a young woman, Christine, of the village of Shere in Surrey who is deemed to be coming of age and ripe for mar-riage to the manorial reeve. Her mother is a strong local character known for her cures and supernatural powers. Christine is shown to be aware that her days working with the maidens of the village are numbered, and while engaged in the late summer works of harvest and gathering she announces her desire to serve the Virgin, whom she has seen in a vision which focussed on the wooden statue in the parish church. The parish priest accepts her desire, to her mother's discontent, and the bishop ar-rives with his entourage to conduct the ceremony of enclosure. Once in her tiny space, Christine enjoys the calm and solitude; villagers start coming to her for advice and consolation. The parish priest becomes frustrated with Christine's spiritual development as her subsequent vi-sions of the Virgin fail to meet his expectations. Christine's mother is denounced and accused of witchcraft by the priest, whose sexual mis-conduct she denounces. Christine digs her way out from her anchorhold, and spends some time in freedom with a young man, ultimately going to the episcopal town to petition the bishop. The end remains disputed among the tens of viewers with whom I have discussed this film; it involves Christine's descent into the cavernous spaces under the cathedral.

The director's need to visualise so many aspects of past lives which historians, for the most part, treat as purely textual entities is both a challenge and an opportunity. In his notes about the film Chris Newby confesses: 'The film is about a poetic eye at work in a barbaric landscape and in its imagery I tried to reflect the sense of someone who sees the whole world in a grain of sand.'[5] In Newby's filmic vision the delicate soul of the anchoress is dangerously poised against a background of physical starkness and social brutality. His direction seeks to detail the 'barbarity' of that world and the poetry of her subjectivity. In situating the film's protagonist in this manner, Newby realises one of the most prevalent visions of the Middle Ages, one of untold difference from the present, of physical hardship, crude manners and inter-personal relations.

Newby's view is only one elaboration of some of the tropes governing thinking about the Middle Ages, and women's religion within it. Moreover, in its eclecticism of style and design, the film shares a practice of cultural production which currently informs much writing about the Middle Ages: it attends to material culture, to relations of power, to landscape and environment as constituents of experience.[6] The film is produced in monochrome; the director of cinematography, Michael Baudour, made extensive use of wide-angle shots, reminiscent of Theo Angelopoulos's landscapes. Silvery and flat, this British-Belgian co-production was filmed in Belgium,[7] in what looks like an arid plain – reminiscent of some of the landscapes used in Ingmar Bergman's *Seventh Seal* (Sweden, 1957) – as different as possible from the undulating, water-rich landscape of Shere in which Christine Carpenter lived, a village situated between the Downs and the Surrey hills, cosily within the Tillingbourne valley. In what follows I shall explore the case of Christine Carpenter – archival and filmic – and I shall then turn to explore the service which visualisation renders to our process of understanding and interpretation.

The idea which gave birth to *The Anchoress* resulted from Judith Stanley-Smith's visit to the parish church of St James of Shere, in Surrey.[8] The fabric of St James's church is mostly of the thirteenth century; its font, in which Christine was probably baptised, is of *c.* 1200, and a few fragments suggest that some attractive stained glass sections were installed in the windows in the fourteenth century.

Approaching the north wall of the church, upon which the anchorhold leaned, one sees a reproduction of the three documents related to the anchoress of Shere of the 1320s, Christine Carpenter, accompanied by English translations.⁹ These three letters, extracted from the episcopal registers of John Stratford, bishop of Winchester (1323–33), formed the core of the fictionalised script with which the film-maker worked. Stanley-Smith and her co-author Christine Watkins were attracted by the paradox suggested by Christine's choice: the need to become enclosed in order to be set free. This paradox pervades the documents of enclosure and re-enclosure:

ad frugem meliorem vite cupiens transmigrare continentiam velit ac sollempniter perpetuam castitatem vovere et in arco loco in cimiterio iuxta ecclesiam parochiale de Shere facere se includi.¹⁰

The writers lamented the absence of Christine's own voice in the surviving documents, and saw in her re-enclosure an attempt by the church to obliterate her memory.¹¹

The letters which brought Christine Carpenter to our attention, and to re-birth in a film some 650 years after her enclosure, are typical examples of the records associated with episcopal scrutiny of those forms of religious life which were outside parochial routines or the frame of monastic and rule-bound existence.¹² The register of Bishop Stratford displays the forms of episcopal initiation of the process which could lead to enclosure. In a mandate to the officials of his archdeacon of Surrey on 21 June 1329,¹³ the bishop requested that Christine, a recent applicant for enclosure, be examined. The officials were to summon Christine to the church in the presence of the rector and parishioners, and in that audience it was to be found whether (1) Christine was of the good life and conversation required of one seeking a more saintly life, and (2) whether she was free of espousal or marriage. The former is clearly a prerequisite in judging the case's merit, and the latter a canonical requirement for any movement into a chaste religious life, for men and women.¹⁴ The opinions of rector and parishioners were similarly to be sought since enclosure was not only a personal act, but also an incursion into the space of the parish church and its cemetery, an additional burden for maintenance of both the fabric and the anchoress's needs. The community was required to agree to and accept the new anchoress who would then dwell close to their church, and in the section maintained by the parishioners.¹⁵ In a similar act of the decade before Christine's enclosure, on 22 July 1315, Richard Swinfield, bishop of Hereford, granted a licence for the enclosure of Isabella de Leye to live as an anchoress in the chapel of Leye, citing the consent of the rector and the parishioners as well as her suitability of character and the support of her friends – and in that period this meant a large group of kin and acquaintances.[16]

By 19 July, four weeks after his initial episcopal mandate, Bishop John Stratford was sufficiently confident of Christine's suitability to issue an episcopal letter addressed to all concerned, present and future.[17] The letter announced that no impediment had been found and that the rector, here named as Matthew (de Redemane), and the parishioners had agreed that Christine, daughter of William the Carpenter, might be enclosed, 'laid aside from public and worldly sights' so that she might serve God better and keep her heart undefiled.[18]

The Anchoress vividly shows how little in the way of material support the anchoress needed, and imagines how modest offerings could have created a constant flow of food and other requisites. The issue of support was addressed by bishops when they considered the viability of an enclosure: together with the candidate's suitability, bishops attempted to ascertain that a suitable anchorhold and adequate support had been made available. For instance, the mandate of William Melton, archbishop of York, on 4 July 1335 authorised the enclosure of Margaret of Acthorp (near Louth) in a house near St Nicholas's church in Nottingham, a house recently built for her use ('in quadam domo juxta ecclesiam sancti Nicholai Nottinghamie de novo pro manso ejusdem constructa').[19] When income was dependent on the payment of rents by tenants the anchoress was poorly situated to enforce her rights; a letter of William Greenfield, archbishop of York, dated 12 August 1315, exhorted Thomas of Cresaker to pay the ten quarters of wheat allocated by the founders of a house of two anchoresses by Doncaster bridge, for the support of the anchoresses.[20] Inasmuch as acts of support were attached to a person and not to a community, they could be of a personal and passing nature. Thus the two acres of arable and an acre of meadow, which had been given in 1203–25 by Robert Bardolf in Great Carlton (Lincs.) for the support of three 'sisters of Carleton', Berlot, Jeva and Emma, was to be held for life, for the support of their enclosed life-style.[21] In a mandate of 1315 Richard Swinfield, bishop of Hereford, expressed the expectation that necessities of food and clothing would be provided by the anchoress's friends and family; the prevailing worry was that the absence of necessities would force the anchoress to leave her cell and thus to apostatise.[22]

Religious houses were often seen as suitable intermediaries charged with the realisation of the enclosure and provision of the anchorite's needs. In 1361 Henry, duke of Lancaster granted two cottages and lands to Whalley Abbey for the care of recluses and their servants who lived adjacent to the parish church of Whalley. In return for their prayers for the souls of the ducal family the anchoresses were to be provided with seventeen conventual loaves of bread, seven loaves of lesser bread (probably for the servants), eight gallons of beer, and 3d in cash. They were also to receive fish, a bushel of oatmeal and another of rye, a gallon of oil for their lamps, tallow for candles, faggots and turf as fuel.[23] The diocese of Norwich boasted houses with long traditions of support for anchorites: Crabhouse maintained an uninterrupted tradition between the twelfth and the fifteenth centuries, and Carrow supported the most famous anchoress, Julian of Norwich, who occupied her cell until her death in 1416–23.[24]

Inasmuch as endowment for pious purposes was attached to these dwellings an issue of patronage was created: mandates for enclosure often specify the *ius patronatus*. In the case of St Nicholas's in Nottingham the right was shared by the archbishop and the prior of Lenton. This institutional scrutiny and promise of provision was aimed at removing a living woman, usually a young one, from life, burying her alive within a narrow and dark space. The image offered by Aelred in his *Institutio inclusarum*, written *c.* 1162 for his sister, and translated and widely disseminated in Middle English in later centuries, was one of death and burial with Christ.[25]

The funerary tones of the ceremony of enclosure were voiced in the church and ended in the dark and narrow space of the anchorhold. The Use of the province of York current from the thirteenth century provides an order of enclosure for a *famula dei*. It begins with the reading of psalms as the priest prostrated himself at the altar, and is followed by prayers and a requiem mass. The woman's profession then follows, with the blessing of the habit and her clothing, and then the blessing of the veil. Images of protection and enclosure are invoked, in relation to the anchoress's virginity, as during the blessing of the habit:

Oratio. Respice, quaesumus, Domine, super hanc famulam tuam ut virginitatis propositum, quod te inspirante suscepit, te gubernante custodiat.[26]

The prayer goes on to beseech God that this virgin be associated with the purest 144,000 children who remained virgins, emphasising the anchoress's purity of intention and of life. As the veil is blessed the priest prays to God to be her tower of strength:

> Salvam fac ancillam tuam.
> Mitte ei auxilium de sancto.
> Nihil proficiat inimicus in ea.
> Esto ei, Domine, turris fortitudinis.[27]

At the end of the mass a procession follows with a litany whose invocations call for support of the new servant of God. The anchoress is led in procession to her habitation and is then left alone to enter it – not before being asked for the last time whether she does indeed wish to enter it.[28]

The anchoress was to wear a veil and a habit, her hair was to be cut four times a year, and she was encouraged to be clean although 'buried'.[29] The funerary association is also reflected in the language of patronage: in the 1390s Alice West and Elizabeth of Loudres of Salisbury renounced the prospect of a sumptuous funeral and transferred sums equal to the cost of such a ritual to the use of anchoresses.[30] In *The Anchoress* the priest proclaims her 'mortua, mortua' and the bishop arms her with two gifts: swiftness (against the rigidity of enclosure) and clear sight (against the darkness of the anchorhold).

Yet the anchoress could not be totally cut off: her own spiritual needs required guidance, her sacramental needs dictated some observances, and the example she was meant to spread had to be, even obliquely, visible. The author of the *Ancrene Wisse* likened the anchoress, who dwells in the eaves of the church, to a night-raven (*nihtfuhel*) who dwells in such spaces;[31] elsewhere she is as an anchor which is unseen and yet stabilises the ship.[32] These needs were accommodated by the provision of small, discrete openings, windows on to the world and in to her cell.

The anchoress's cell usually possessed a small opening on to the world for the passage of food, the *fenestrella*, and a squint for viewing the high altar in those anchorholds attached to a church.[33] Linda Georgianna sees in the reconciliation of the inner life with the view from outside the major challenge to the writers of guidance literature.[34] The statutes for Chichester diocese of 1245–52 stipulated that the anchorhold windows should be narrow and well made (perhaps 'decent') ('Fenestras quoque arctas habeant et honestas').[35] The *Ancrene Riwle*, written by an Augustinian canon *c.* 1220 for three sisters living as anchoresses, specified that there be three openings: one to the church, one to the servant's room and one to the world.[36] But viewing was associated with sin, as it could provide that little leap ('liht lupe') by which sin might enter the anchoress's heart.[37] At Shere there is still to be seen a squint for viewing the high altar and a quatrefoil window for reception of communion; there must have been a window to the outside world in the structure, which no longer survives.

The opening on to the world was necessary, but dangerous. The *Ancrene Wisse* recommended that the anchoress be kind to the maid serving her, inviting her to eat and stay; but she was to be vigilant, as 'no man shall eat in your presence without your director's permission'.[38] In *The Anchoress* Christine Carpenter's curtained window to the world becomes a busy place as offerings of eggs, onions, bread and flour are placed in front of her. Bishops were clearly exercised by the dangers which such 'commerce' raised. The clause on recluses in the statutes of Chichester of 1245–52 emphasised that the people with whom the recluse was to have contact should be of such gravity and honesty as to preclude any suspicion of wrongdoing.[39]

Most anchoresses were probably attached to parish churches near the community that had bred them; such churches had acknowledged the holy intent of the anchoress, and were willing to lend support.[40] Anchorholds were situated within communities, indeed near their designated meeting places – their churches – which were at once sites of worship, ritual, and intensive social and economic exchange. One of the most convincingly rendered themes of the film *The Anchoress* is the touching exchanges between young Christine and those who come to seek guidance and blessing from her. First hesitantly and later in a constant stream, people seek her help and advice about marriage and child-bearing as she is confronted with questions like 'Why do we not have children?', 'Should I dance with the tinker?'– questions related to the life-cycle, to the choice of indulging or containing sexual desire, areas about which – through the charisma which surrounds her own choice – the anchoress is deemed able to judge well. Above all she has to confront her own sister, Meg, now destined to marry the reeve. Like several saints of the later Middle Ages, identified and celebrated in their own communities, Christine's act of separation, asceticism and solitude is shown to inspire devotion and admiration.[41] In the case of an anchoress, the emergent charisma undercut and frustrated the very rhetoric of separation, by creating a desire for contact with her.[42]

What did the anchoress do all day? What type of consciousness could her enclosure engender? *The Anchoress* suggests that at the beginning she enjoyed the calm and quiet, the time away from the violence of her mother's hand, and the disapproval of her fierce tongue. Christine is shown playing with the little light entering her cell; she listens to bird song and notices acutely a rabbit's movement, a fluttering dove. She is able to close the curtain to those, like the reeve, who seek her out, but also to surrender herself to imaginings of a closeness – face to face, eye to eye – with the Virgin whom she can only see through the chink in her cell wall. Christine is given a piece of velvet to embroider and she repeatedly makes and remakes the pattern.[43] But this is light labour compared to the work in which most women were involved. Lest their fingers become too soft and white, the *Ancrene Wisse* recommended that anchoresses should 'scrape up earth every day out of the grave in which they shall rot'.[44] In *The Anchoress* Christine Carpenter does just that, and this penitential scraping leads her, in yet another paradoxical twist, to compulsive burrowing which eventually opens up a tunnel out of the anchorhold.

The anchoress was expected to provide answers, and these were produced through her own imaginative resourcefulness and the ideas developed in the solitude of thought, work and prayer. In *The Anchoress* the Virgin, who has moved Christine to the desire for enclosure and virginity, continues to offer her inspiration. The village girls come up to her; only a few days earlier they were working in the fields together laughing in the sunshine, and now Christine might answer their questions 'How may we see God?' By the thirteenth century texts for the spiritual guidance of anchoresses were available in English in a variety of linguistic registers and pedagogic formats, while texts for nuns tended to be in Anglo-Norman French. The genres considered appropriate for an anchoress were many: they were thought to require hagiographical example, to be desirous of simple instructions on daily routines and in need of exhortative example.[45] Reading and reflection were to fill their days, the custody of their body was to occupy them. The literature for anchoresses is suffused with images of (en)closure – bodies, castles, wombs and cities.[46] The anchorhold was a castle, guarded by the anchoress; according to a Dominican friar's lyric for a maiden dedicated to God, as long as she guarded her castle she would remain sweeter than a flower ('þu art swettre þane eny flur/hwile þu witest þere kastel').[47] Unlike the mystical literature of the later Middle Ages, there is little of the images of annihilation and unmaking of the self, or of spiritual ascent. The method is one of control; of body and routines, of fasts and work, of limited contact with the world, and busying oneself with the work of being Christ's buried bride.

The Anchoress cannot help us to imagine how Christine might have passed her days: she cannot read, and she has no spiritual guide once she falls out of her priest's favour. She displays little interest in liturgy and prayer, but for a while she is taken up with embroidering a piece of velvet with a white silken thread, work which frustrates her as she undoes it again and again. Yet a more integrated existence within the religious life of a parish may have indeed developed in those churches which hosted anchoresses: in Tarrant Crawford (Dorset) fourteenth-century wall paintings are of an age with a group-anchorhold there and may be related to it. The thirteen painted panels tell the life of St Margaret of Antioch, one of the martyrs most associated with anchoritic living.[48] This might suggest that awareness of the anchoritic experience lived in their midst became a token of the community's identity, and thus affected instruction and liturgical practice. Faversham (Kent), which housed anchoresses in the fifteenth century, also boasted wall paintings on the north wall, to which Christ's childhood and his mother's life are central.[49] The literature for anchorites emphasised the anchoress's marriage to Christ, and meditation on Christ's Passion. The Dominican's love lyric, composed for a maiden who may have been an anchoress, offers Christ as the source of light which alone can brighten the dark cell:

> His Sihte is al ioye and gleo,
> he is day wyþ-ute nyhte.[50]

Yet *The Anchoress* persists in making the Virgin Christine's prime inspiration. Christine's Virgin appears to her in red, the colour of the Passion – not in blue, as the rector expected her to do, in keeping with iconographic tradition. Consequently Christine and the rector fall into conflict and the relationship is soured. It is this crisis with her confessor and religious guide which *The Anchoress* sees as the motivation for Christine's escape. We know well just how fervent female devotion to Christ was, even among women of widely differing social backgrounds, and unlettered ones. Yet the creators of *The Anchoress* seize a currently popular conception of the Virgin as a figure more accessible than the male Christ, as being closer to Christine's emotional and devotional world.[51]

In England royal writs supported the effort to capture runaway religious, known as apostates, and these offer an important source for the study of failed religious professions. They yield no material on anchorites, but allow us by comparison to reflect on the circumstances which might have led to abandonment of the anchorhold. This is most useful, since the document of re-enclosure offers not a glimpse into Christine's own story, merely stating that 'she had left her cell inconstantly and returned to the world'.[52] *The Anchoress* suggests a particular narrative underpinning Christine's escape: a charming drover who hovers around the village as part of the semi-permanent fair which grows around Christine's fame. The drover is portrayed not so much as seducer, but as playmate, releasing the young Christine, who manages to (literally) burrow her way out of the anchorhold by digging up soil under the wall and out into the open – like so many prisoners in films about the Second World War, or more recently in *The Shawshank Redemption*. Once she escapes, *The Anchoress* portrays a playful Christine who enjoys nature, climbs trees and runs about laughing; but after a spell of freedom the film leads her to the episcopal city, to the feet of the episcopal throne. The bishop is placed on a high wooden stage, and Christine is obliged to climb a ladder in order to attend him. The space is a grand basilica, of a type which did not exist in medieval England. The bishop quibbles with Christine: 'You are dead, so I can neither hear nor see you.' The reeve wants her punished, violence erupts around her, and in the commotion Christine disappears under the wooden stage and into the church's cavernous foundations.

This ambiguous ending has Christine walking through the vast crypt, the foundation upon which the cathedral is built: its interior is cool, watery, quiet and smooth. The end relates to Newby's view of the underlying struggle between Christianity and paganism, with the Christian surface, evident in the church's edifice, placed upon a deep and preexisting matter and space. Or in his own words: 'Christianity battles with paganism, dogma fights a girl's inner vision.'[53] The film suggests that hers is an escape from doctrine and discipline into nature and its calm beliefs. Here Newby shares the underlying understandings which have sometimes animated work of scholars such as Carlo Ginzburg:[54] that there was a subterranean, indigenous, authentic culture available particularly to rural folk of pre-modern Europe, a culture which could be invoked in rituals and which competed with and offered an alternative to normative Christianity. Such an understanding shows Christine as able to adhere to a pre/non-Christian world which is always within reach, and to turn to it in a crisis.

What probably happened is more intricate and interesting. The Church confronted the problem of religious disenchantment which could lead to the desire to leave or change orders almost as a matter of course. The machinery of the papal penitentiary was oriented towards processing these cases, since excommunication followed *ipso facto*.[55] The papal penitentiaries, who numbered between fourteen and eighteen in the fourteenth century, and who were almost all friars, were experts in the hearing of confessions and the meting out of penance. In the papal chancery they were expected to bring their expertise to the examination of petitions presented from all over Europe, and to grant dispensations from the canonical punishment which would otherwise be forthcoming. Since none of the penitentiary registers of the fourteenth century have survived, Christine

Carpenter's case is known to us only from the copy entered into the register of the bishop of Winchester. Her case offers an interesting instance of a woman of modest social standing, who was directed towards the appropriate canonical process by which she might be allowed to return to enclosure and escape the excommunication which fell upon her at the moment of leaving the enclosure.[56] Christine Carpenter's case is a particularly interesting one, since it offers a glimpse into the working of a system which aimed to reconcile fleeing religious, by recognising and accepting a variety of reasons for the possible collapse of the will or inability to adhere to an extremely demanding life-style. Recent scholarly interest in monastic runaways has revealed the types of pressures and dilemmas which beset those who had chosen a life of religious rigour, especially those who seem to have been directed towards such a life at an early age. The large majority of runaways were men, and the overwhelming number were regular religious; the reason for the collapse of discipline might be an intolerable regime, fear of superiors, indignities inflicted on the supplicant, or molestation.[57] Of the 768 supplications made to the Penitentiary between 1458–64 eighty-nine were cases of apostasy: seventy-seven by men and twelve by women.[58] Christine was clearly advised in the intricacies and forms of her supplication, probably by officials of her diocese, and it met with success. The letter of reconciliation which Bishop Stratford entered into his own letter of 1332 was issued by the Dominican John of Wrotham, an English papal *poenetentiarius*.[59] It was thus possible in the early fourteenth century for a rural English woman, of some local renown, to make contact and seek reconciliation through a papal canonical/penitential process.[60]

The film's end does not see Christine reconciled with the Church, as she probably was in reality. The desire to demonstrate subjugation and ill-treatment, in keeping with contemporary understandings of the 'medieval', led the film's makers to offer a confusing ending. Thus they attached some of the most prevalent conceptions of the Middle Ages – misogyny and religious repression – to Christine's life, and consequently chose to deviate from one of the few facts which we do know about her, that she applied for re-enclosure and was granted it. Instead, the film situates her within cavernous spaces, under-worlds of pagan survival which some scholars have promoted as an 'authentic' medieval cultural frame.[61] The celebration of extreme asceticism and forms of self-denial and bodily testing as creative forms of self-expression stands in a powerful tradition of scholarship about women and the Middle Ages, particularly that inspired by Caroline W. Bynum. The film's makers, like several scholars, are keen to see in asceticism a force which empowers women to rebel against family and community expectations.[62] Yet they also wish to see asceticism as subjected to (male) institutional pressures of the kind which ultimately make Christine dig her way out, and into the embrace of – what? The 'pagan' alternative can have little historical validity or power to persuade.[63]

To understand Christine we need not seek other, alternative religious cultures. Life outside the *saeculum* in exultant seclusion was an option attractive to some young women with an interest and inclination for religious involvement and reflection. The challenges that such a life posed were serious: writers of conduct books for anchoresses clearly tried to help them keep busy and interested, thus sane and stable in their religious quest. Much more contact with the world than the name 'anchoress' suggests was tolerated, even recommended. And when a vocation failed, there was a bureaucratic-pastoral procedure which could lead back into the vows. While the surviving case-documents help us glimpse the operation of this procedure, *The Anchoress* helps us imagine the textures of life, particularly in the solitary scenes within the anchorhold.

When addressing the Anglo-American Conference in 1971 on Film and History, Barrie Dobson considered film as source material for the study of many aspects of twentieth-century history. He was convinced that sitting in the dark and viewing films which were made by people of a certain decade for audiences at that time added a dimension of understanding – albeit incomplete – in a later viewer. What of film and the Middle Ages? *The Anchoress* demonstrates that the Middle Ages offer a stage for powerful expression of contemporary perceptions and concerns. In the 1990s the 'medieval' emerged as a token for the description of horrors of inter-communal strife and war crimes in the Balkans. *The Anchoress* fits in neatly with a view that sees deep communal loyalty, oppressive family pressure, visceral religious sentiment, as belonging to a different era, and having strayed, almost by mistake, into the late twentieth century. The Middle Ages were as complicated and diverse as our times and places; in it resided side by side zones in which violence was checked and those in which it was more erratic. The violence of Bosnia and Kosovo is modern European violence and must be understood as such. The 'medieval' never existed – not then and definitely not now, inasmuch as no social or cultural system is ever as static or amenable to reduction as the Middle Ages are often taken to be.

This is not to say that a filmic vision cannot advance or enhance our explorations. We have already noted the fruitful results of the need to give visual form, acoustic resonance and texture to the past. The poetic evocations of film can illuminate by making connections which are not readily evident through conventional scholarly investigation. In *Blanche* (France, 1971) Walerian Borowczyk offered a brilliant treatment of honour and gender in medieval France, based on a Polish romantic novel, *Mazepa*. Rendering the Middle Ages visual contributes in important ways to our understanding of the temporality and materiality of the lives lived then. To recreate life-spaces, routines, textures is to imagine and to force a critical encounter upon those who know or wish to know better, like historians and their students. Such contact is offered by the coarse cloth of Christine's garment, the joy of sunshine on her face after months of enclosure, the smell (yes, smell) of good apples in autumn, and the temptation which they could pose to a young woman who picked but did not own them. For these, and more, links with the past we must be grateful to thoughtful film-makers such as Chris Newby. Scholars such as Barrie Dobson will make it possible for us to know enough, from the strong testimonies of archival sources, to be able to contextualise and correct; but to view, and thus sense, the loneliness of the night spent in an anchorhold is an experience which even the most professional of medieval historians cannot, should not, do without.

NOTES

* I am most appreciative of the many friendly and scholarly suggestions offered with greatest generosity by Marilynn Desmond. Rosemary Horrox followed the production of this paper with a host of stylistic and substantial suggestions of characteristic incisive good sense. For useful suggestions and comments I am grateful to Richard Pfaff, Helen Philipps, Shulamit Shahar, David Wallace and Patrick Zutshi. For insight into *The Anchoress* I am indebted to the graduate seminar group of 1998 at the Center for Medieval Studies at the University of Connecticut at Storrs. Christopher Fletcher has been most instrumental in researching the cinematic background of the *The Anchoress* and commenting on this paper.

1. I am thinking of projects as varied as *The World at War* and Claude Lanzmann's *Shoah*.

2. The *American Historical Review* has led discussion by devoting a forum in issue 93:5 (December 1988) to Film and History, including an article by the medieval historian David Herlihy, 'Am I a Camera? Other Reflections on Film and History', 1186–92. Since 1994 the journal has included an annual review section on historical films.

3. Ulrike Wiethaus and Jane E. Jeffrey, 'Cinematic Representations of Medieval Women and their Legacy: Film, Text, and Theory to Teach Medieval Women's Culture', *Medieval Feminist Newsletter* 25 (1998), 40–6, see esp. 44; and the special issue *Medieval Women in Film*, Medieval Feminist Newsletter Subsidia Series 1 (2000).

4. Lorraine Attreed and James F. Prior, 'Lessons in the Dark: Teaching the Middle Ages with Film', in S. W. Gillespie (ed.), *Perspectives on Audiovisuals in the Teaching of History* (Washington DC, 1999), pp. 59–68.

5. 'Notes accompanying the film *Anchoress*', BFI Production and Corsan Productions, London, 1993, p. 3.

6. Scholars have commented on the eclecticism of recent work on the Middle Ages: see for example Paul Freedman and Gabrielle Spiegel, 'Medievalisms Old and New: the Rediscovery of Alterity in North American Medieval Studies', *American Historical Review* 103 (1998), 677–704.

7. *La recluse* in French; a co-production between the BFI and Corsan productions by Ben Gibson and Paul Breuls.

8. See the entry, which ignores the remains of the anchorhold (except for the description of the squint) in Ian Nairn and Nikolaus Pevsner (revised by Bridget Cherry), *The Buildings of England: Surrey* (Harmondsworth, 1971), pp. 455–7 (on St James's church).

9. On the association of women with the north, cold, 'sinister' part of churches see Roberta Gilchrist, *Gender and Medieval Culture: The Archaeology of Religious Women* (London, 1994), pp. 128–43.

10. Winchester, Hampshire Record Office, AI/5, fo. 46v. 'In developing Christine's story, we worked with the central paradox of being enclosed in order to be set free': 'Notes to *Anchoress*', p. 13.

11. Ibid. On attempts to recover voices from the medieval past see Sherri Olson, *A Chronicle of All that Happens: Voices from the Village Court in Medieval England*, Toronto, Pontifical Institute of Medieval Studies, Studies and Texts 124 (Toronto, 1996); Anne Clark Bartlett, *Male Authors, Female Readers: Representation and Subjectivity in Middle English Devotional Literature* (Ithaca, NY, 1995).

12. From the thirteenth century synodal statutes reiterated the need for clear authorisation by episcopal licence for enclosure: see the synodal statutes (of an unidentified diocese) of 1221–5: 'Ad hec districtus inhibemus ne inclusi vel incluse constituantur alicubi sine nostra licentia speciali, pensatis sociis, moribus, et qualitate persone, et unde debeat sustentari', *Councils and Synods with Other Documents Relating to the English Church* vol. 1, ed. F. M. Powicke and C. R. Cheney (Oxford, 1964), I, c. 57a (added after c. 57), p. 150. On the relations between bishops and anchoresses see Ann K. Warren, *Anchorites and their Patrons in Medieval England* (Berkeley, CA, 1985), chapter 3, pp. 53–91.

13. Winchester, Hampshire Record Office, AI/5, fo. 46v; David M. Smith, *Guide to Bishops' Registers of England and Wales: A Survey from the Middle Ages to the Abolition of Episcopacy in 1646* (London, 1981), p. 205.

14. For the discussion of impediments to entry into religious life related to previous marriage or a promise of marriage see James A. Brundage,

Law, Sex and Christian Society in Medieval Europe (Chicago, 1987), pp. 296, 375–6.

15. That the proliferation of structures could become an impediment to the parish is seen in the synodal provision for the diocese of Salisbury in 1238–44, in a discussion of edifices in cemeteries: 'si qua vero in quocunque cimiterio inveniantur, nisi fuerint usibus ecclesie vel inclusis deputata, penitus demolliantur. Nova inclusoria fieri prohibemus, vetera decedentibus inclusis dirui precipientes, illis exceptis que auctoritate pontificum ab antiquo sunt constructa, certos et sufficientes redditus ad sustentationem inclusorum', *Councils and Synods*, c. 31, p. 379. On the cells of anchoresses see Warren, *Anchorites and their Patrons*, pp. 15–52.

16. 'Ad devotam instantiam amicorum, et piis devotionis ipsius precibus inclinate... Rectoris capellae praedictae et... parochianorum ejusdem et consideratis circumstantiis universis... cum per ipsam et per amicos ipsius congrue fueritis requisiti, ipsam vice et auctoritate nostra recludatis': *A Roll of the Household Expenses of Richard de Swinfield Bishop of Hereford during Part of the Years 1289 and 1290*, Camden Society 62 (London, 1854), no. 8 (in appendix), pp. 213–14.

17. Winchester, Hampshire Record Office, AI/5, fo. 76r.

18. Although I was unable to approach close enough to measure it, the cell was clearly smaller than that at neighbouring Compton (Surrey) described in Warren, *Anchorites and their Patrons*, p. 29.

19. R. Brockelsby (ed.), *The Register of Archbishop William Melton 1317–1340*, Canterbury and York Society 85 (Woodbridge, 1997), no. 781, p. 186.

20. W. Brown and A. H. Thompson (eds.), *The Register of Archbishop William Greenfield, Lord Archbishop of York, 1306–1315*, Surtees Society 149 (1934), II, no. 1129, p. 221. For the document of enclosure see W. Brown (ed.), *The Registers of John Le Romeyn Lord Archbishop of York 1286–1296 and of Henry of Newark, Lord Archbishop of York 1296–1299*, Surtees Society 128 (1917), no. 361, pp. 322–3.

21. In 1247 the bequest was reallocated to Barlings abbey: A. E. B. Owen (ed.), *The Medieval Lindsay Marsh. Select Documents*, Lincolnshire Record Society 85 (1996), nos. 20–1, p. 48. For similar reallocation of resources from an anchoress after her death see the case of Bisina of Venice: Paulette L'Hermite-Leclercq, 'Le reclus dans la ville au bas moyen âge', *Journal des Savants* (1988), 219–62 (228).

22. 'ne, quod absit, pro defectu victualium ab hujus suo proposito laudabili resilire vel contra votum suum exire cogatur, in animae suae periculum et scandalum plurimorum': *A Roll of the Household Expenses*, p. 214; Warren, *Anchorites and their Patrons*, pp. 43–4.

23. *Calendar of Patent Rolls, 1358–61*, p. 246; Warren, *Anchorites and their Patrons*, pp. 49, 174.

24. Marilyn Oliva, *The Convent and the Community in Late Medieval England: Female Monasticism in the Diocese of Norwich, 1350–1540*, Studies in the History of Medieval Religion 12 (Woodbridge, 1998), pp. 155–6, 130; see also Roberta

Gilchrist and Marilyn Oliva, *Religious Women in Medieval East Anglia*, Studies in East Anglian History I (Norwich, 1993), pp. 75, 98. For some examples from the diocese of Salisbury see Andrew D. Brown, *Popular Piety in Late Medieval England: The Diocese of Salisbury 1250–1550* (Oxford, 1995), p. 206. The enclosure of anchorites and anchoresses tended to be a rural phenomenon in the thirteenth century; it gradually gained an urban following. See the very rough numerical estimates offered in Warren, *Anchorites and their Patrons*, pp. 292–3; see also Gilchrist, *Gender and Material Culture*, p. 177. For an example of combined episcopal and mayoral blessing for an anchorite see Brown, *Popular Piety in Late Medieval England*, pp. 206–7.

25. On the textual history see Ralph Hanna III, '"Meddling with Makings" and Will's Work', in A. J. Minnis (ed.) *Late Medieval Religious Texts and their Transmission: Essays in Honour of A. I. Doyle* (Woodbridge, 1994), pp. 85–94 (pp. 90–1). On the imagery of death see Paulette L'Hermite Leclercq, 'La femme, la recluse et la mort', in E. Serrano Martín (ed.), *Muerte, religiosidad y cultura popular siglos XIII–XVIII* (Saragossa, 1994), pp. 151–62 (pp. 154–5).

26. Cambridge University Library (CUL) Ff. 6.1, fo. 194r; see in W. G. Henderson (ed.), *Liber pontificalis Chr. Bainbridge archiepiscopi Eboracensis*, Surtees Society 61 (1875), pp. 81–3, quote from p. 82.

27. Ibid., p. 83.

28. CUL Ff. 6.1, fos. 197v–198r; *Liber pontificalis*, p. 85. On the requiem of enclosure see Jean Leclercq, 'Solitude and Solidarity: Medieval Women Recluses', in Lillian T. Shank and John A. Nichols (eds.), *Medieval Religious Women*, vol. II, *Peaceweavers*, Cistercian Studies 72 (Kalamazoo, 1987), pp. 67–83 (p. 73).

29. *Medieval English Prose for Women*, trans. Bella Millett and Jocelyn Wogan-Browne (Oxford, 1990), pp. 140–1; it also recommends that they abstain from wearing wimples, pp. 136–7.

30. Brown, *Popular Piety in Late Medieval England*, p. 204.

31. 'þe nihtfuhel i þe euesunges bitacneð recluses; þe wunieð for þi under chirche euesunges. þe ha understonden þat ha ahen to beon of se hali lif', J. R. R. Tolkien (ed.), *Ancrene Wisse Edited from Ms. Corpus Christi College Cambridge 402*, EETS o.s. 249 (1962), p. 74. The *Ancrene Wisse* emphasises the importance of obedience to the religious director, but with some ambivalence: Linda Georgianna, 'The Solitary Self: Individuality in the Ancrene Wisse' unpublished dissertation (Cambridge, 1981), pp. 24–5; Warren, *Anchorites and their Patrons*, pp. 294–8. On relationships of religious guidance between men and women see Elisabeth K. Bos, 'Gender and Religious Guidance in the Twelfth Century', Ph.D dissertation, University of Cambridge, 1999, esp. chapter 4.

32. Tolkien (ed.), *Ancrene Wisse*, p. 74. On these images see Georgianna, *The Solitary Self*, pp. 51–2.

33. On squints see Gilchrist and Oliva, *Religious Women*, p. 76; Gilchrist, *Gender and Material Culture*, p. 178; Warren, *Anchorites and their Patrons*, p. 33.

34. Georgianna, *The Solitary Self*, p. 34.

35. *Councils and Synods*, I, c. 69, p. 465. In this context *honestas* may mean not giving a generous view.

36. Windows are discussed in the section 'On the Custody of the Senses': see for example Charlotte d'Evelyn (ed.), *The Latin Text of the Ancrene Riwle*, EETS o. s. 216 (1944), esp. p. 11; Frances M. Mack (ed.), *The English Text of the Ancrene Riwle*, EETS o. s. 252 (1963), pp. 2–4; in translation, M. B. Salu (ed. and trans.), *The Ancrene Riwle* (London, 1955), esp. Figs. 107–8; in the section on anchoritic living, pp. 183–93.

37. Georgianna, *The Solitary Self*, pp. 61–5.

38. *Medieval English Prose for Women*, pp. 134–5.

39. 'Eisdem etiam cum hiis tantummodo personis secretum tractatum habere permittimus, quarum gravitas et honestas suspicionem non admittit', *Councils and Synods*, c. 69, p. 465.

40. Georgianna, *The Solitary Self*, p. 34. Another type of somewhat restricted living was experienced by vowesses, widows who received episcopal blessing for their state of chastity and charitable living; on this form, which was very popular in England, especially in the fifteenth century, see Mary C. Erler, 'Three Fifteenth-Century Vowesses', in Caroline Barron and Anne F. Sutton (eds.), *Medieval London Widows* (London, 1994), pp. 165–83; Patricia H. Cullum, 'Vowesses and Female Piety in the Province of York, 1300–1500', *Northern History* 32 (1996), 21–41.

41. André Vauchez, *Sainthood in the Middle Ages*, trans. Jean Birrell (Cambridge, 1997), especially book II.

42. On the move to identification of sanctity among the living, and the resulting rise of the lay saint, see Aviad M. Kleinberg, *Prophets in their Own Country: Living Saints and the Making of Sainthood in the Later Middle Ages* (Chicago, 1992), esp. chapters 2, 3 and 4 on Christina of Stommeln.

43. On needlework as anchoress's work see Warren, *Anchorites and their Patrons*, p. 40; on work see also Hanna, '"Meddling with Makings"', p. 92. The 1245–52 Chichester synodal statute on recluses warned against the use of anchoresses as parochial servants in charge of vestments. In cases which required their assistance the greatest care was to be taken lest they be seen by the bearer of the vestments: 'Inclusis vero mulieribus custodia vestimentorum ecclesie non tradatur; quod si necessitas hoc exegerit, ita caute tradi mandamus ut non inspiciantur a tradente', *Councils and Synods*, I, c. 69, p. 465. The *Ancrene Wisse* insisted that the anchoress do only coarse needlework, not in silk or lace. Mending church vestments and the garments of the poor was recommended: *Medieval English Prose for Women*, pp. 138–9.

44. 'hie seolf bihalden hire ahne hwite honden deð hearm moni ancre. þe haueð ham to feire as þeo þe beoð for idlet. ha schulden schrapien euche dei þe eorðe up of ha re þut ha schulien rotien in', *Ancrene Wisse*, p. 62.

45. Bella Millett, 'Women in No Man's land: English Recluses and the Development of Vernacular Literature in the Twelfth and Thirteenth Centuries', in Carole M. Meale (ed.), *Women and Literature in Britain, 1150–1500* (Cambridge, 1993), pp. 86–103, esp. pp. 89–90, 93, 96–7.

46. Nicholas Watson, 'The Methods and Objectives of Thirteenth-Century Anchoritic Devotion', in Marion Glasscoe (ed.), *The Medieval Mystical Tradition in England*, vol. IV (Woodbridge, 1987), pp. 132–53 (138–40); Millett, 'Women in No Man's Land', p. 99. On closure and virginity see Jocelyn Wogan-Browne, 'Chaste Bodies; Frames and Experiences', in Sarah Kay and Miri Rubin (eds.), *Framing Medieval Bodies* (Manchester, 1994) pp. 24–42.

47. Carleton Brown (ed.), *English Lyrics of the Thirteenth Century* (Oxford, 1932), no. 43, pp. 68–74, ll. 151–2, p. 72.

48. See the life of St Margaret in *Medieval English Prose for Women*, pp. 44–85; Millett, 'Women in No Man's Land', p. 93

49. E.W. Tristram, *English Wall Painting of the Fourteenth Century* (London, 1955), pp. 171–2, 255; Gilchrist, *Gender and Material Culture*, pp. 180–1; on the Faversham anchoresses see Anon, 'Anchorites in Faversham Churchyard', *Archaeologia Cantiana* 11 (1877), 24–39 (I am grateful to Nigel Morgan for this reference). For some very interesting later material about women's own devotional artistry see Jeffrey F. Hamburger, *Nuns as Artists: The Visual Culture of a Medieval Convent* (Berkeley, 1997).

50. *English Lyrics of the Thirteenth Century*, ll. 141–2, p. 72.

51. The leading figure in illuminating this area is Caroline W. Bynum, *Holy Feast and Holy Fast: The Religious Significance of Food to Medieval Women* (Berkeley, 1987); *eadem*, '. . . And Woman his Humanity: Female Imagery in the Religious Writings of the Later Middle Ages', in C. W. Bynum *et al.*, (eds.), *Gender and Religion: On the Complexity of Symbols* (Boston, Mass., 1986), pp. 257–88.

52. Winchester, Hampshire Record Office, AI/5, fo. 76r.

53. 'Notes to *Anchoress*', p. 3.

54. Carlo Ginzburg, *The Cheese and the Worms: The Cosmos of a Sixteenth Century Miller*, trans. John and Anne Tedeschi (London, 1980); *idem, Ecstasies* (London, 1992).

55. F. Donald Logan, *Runaway Religious in Medieval England c. 1240–1540*, Cambridge Studies in Medieval Life and Thought ser. 4, 32 (Cambridge, 1996), p. 10; Emile Göller, *Die päpstliche Pönitentiarie von ihrem Ursprung bis zu ihrer Umgestaltung unter Pius V*, fasc. I, Bibliothek des königlichen Preussischen historischen Instituts in Rom 3 (Rome, 1907); on apostasy see especially pp. 133–44.

56. The Penitentiary sources survive from the middle of the fifteenth century and have been studied in Ludwig Schmugge with Patrick Hersperger and Béatrice Wiggenhauser, *Die Supplikenregister der päpstlichen Pönitentiarie aus der Zeit Pius' II (1458–1464)*, Bibliothek des deutschen historischen Instituts in Rom 84 (Tübingen, 1996); on apostasy see esp. pp. 116–24.

57. On reasons for leaving the religious life see Schmugge *et al.*, *Die Supplikenregister*, pp. 119–20, and Logan, *Runaway Religious*, pp. 83–9. Christine Carpenter is included in the list of runaways on p. 267.

58. Schmugge *et al.*, *Die Supplikenregister*, pp. 117–25.

59. For his career see A. B. Emden, *A Biographical Register of the University of Oxford*, III (Oxford, 1957, repr. 1989), pp. 2095–6.

60. On contact with the papal penitentiary see A. D. M. Barrell, *The Papacy, Scotland and Northern England*, Cambridge Studies in Medieval Life and Thought ser. 4, 30, (Cambridge, 1995), pp. 11, 226. On penance enjoined on female apostate religious see Logan, *Runaway Religious*, pp. 53–5.

61. See for example Ronald Hutton, *The Rise and Fall of Merry England: The Ritual Year, 1400–1700* (Oxford, 1994).

62. See the discussion of Caroline Bynum's work in Dominick LaCapra, *Representing the Holocaust: History, Theory, Trauma* (Ithaca, NY, 1994), p. 181.

63. *The Anchoress* also casts Christine's mother as a healer, wise-woman, who is ultimately persecuted by the priest and executed as a witch. Here too, the suggestion of alternative worlds of knowledge is very forcibly made.

CHAPTER 13

Victorian values in fifteenth-century England: the Ewelme almshouse statutes

Colin Richmond

The paper is in seven parts. I have called them: Impeccable Epigraphs; A Proustian Preamble; The Ewelme Workhouse; Parallels and Models; Personalities; Quantity and Quality; Memorials and Modernity. As with all my pieces, explanations will have to wait and readers will have to curb their impatience.

I

The first epigraph is from Jane Austen's *Emma*. We are on Box Hill. Mr Knightly is reprimanding Emma for her behaviour towards Miss Bates:

Were she your equal in situation – but, Emma, consider how far this is from being the case. She is poor; she has sunk from the comforts she was born to; and if she live to old age, must probably sink more. Her situation should secure your compassion.

The second is from George Eliot's *Middlemarch*; it concerns the aptly named Miss Noble:

Pray think no ill of Miss Noble . . . Perhaps she was conscious of being tempted to steal from those who had much that she might give to those who had nothing, and carried in her conscience the guilt of that repressed desire. One must be poor to know the luxury of giving!

And the third and last is item 16e in Ludwig Wittgenstein's *Culture and Value*:

Nearly all my ideas are a bit crumpled: Fast alle meine Gedanken sind etwas verknittert.

2

Ewelme is my Balbec. In other words this short paragraph is about how a name became a place. How one arrives is always important. I arrived one warm spring morning on a bicycle. I had cycled from Reading. It was all of forty years ago. To say that I was entranced puts too blunt a point on what I felt. Here, after all, was England. Here too was my beloved fifteenth-century England: in brick and stone. The late-medieval combination of red brick and white stone, the red of a uniquely faded kind, the white of a texture unimposingly plain, has never failed to engage my imagination since it first encountered such a compelling conjunction at Kirby Muxloe on another spring morning in 1957. There too I had arrived on a bicycle. Most recently I have been at King's Lynn once again: Red Mount Chapel made me realise how inevitable had been the generation of a fifteenth-century historian. I am less certain that it was the tomb of Alice Chaucer in Ewelme church which turned me into an admirer of fifteenth-century tomb sculpture. There had been earlier expeditions to churches with fifteenth-century tombs, some of those expeditions in the company of Bruce McFarlane, whose authoritative taste in such matters was not to be gainsaid by a tyro in the subject. Nonetheless, Alice's effigies, one clothed and the other naked, made an undoubted impact, although in 1961 I was without the knowledge to admire the irresistible skill by which patron and craftsman might have transformed a short and plump old woman into an aristocratically tall and slender elderly lady. Alice's horsey face surely resembles less her own than it does any of the portraits of another master of his craft, Roger Van der Weyden. If all this smacks of romanticism, so be it. I would not be bothering with the Ewelme almshouse statutes in the year 2000 had it not been for seeing the almhouses themselves on that bright spring morning forty years ago.

Not that documents do not matter. Think, for example, of the letters of Proust's mother. In my case it is a document which will not go away which matters, specifically in this instance the Ewelme almshouse statutes. For more than twenty years I have wanted to do something with them. Now there is an opportunity. It is usually an original, and often an unprinted, document which an historian cannot get off his mind; that is not so with the statutes of the Ewelme almshouses. They are printed in a *Report of the Historical Manuscripts Commission*. I have always assumed that they have been published *in extenso*, so have never troubled to consult the original. Or believed I had not, until on looking at my notes find that I have looked at the original at some point in the distant past. The notes say that the *Historical Manuscripts Commission* transcript is accurate. Nevertheless, and unusually, I present a study based upon a transcript which is not mine.[1]

3

We come to the Ewelme workhouse where the living served the dead. I begin by citing what I have written of it elsewhere:[2]

The Ewelme almshouse reminds me of *Utopia*. The 89 clauses of the statutes of the de la Pole almshouse at Ewelme cannot be discussed here; in summary one would say the 13 poor men who suffered as a result of them were as much on the medieval–modern boundary as was Thomas More himself: it is hard to tell whether they were meant to be penitential Carthusians or toilers in a Dickensian workhouse. Was it Alice Chaucer, daughter of a civil servant probably as remarkable as Thomas Cromwell, who meant them to say, *inter alia*, 189 Aves, 69 Pater Nosters, and 15 Creeds every day? I am sure it was: her husband was too busy losing his soul at Westminster – it was his wife who had to concern herself at Ewelme with saving it. There was to be even less idleness in Alice's model society than there was in Thomas More's ideal commune, but both were equally keen on work, and their concept of charity was (as Miri Rubin might have said) calculated if not calculating.

Ewelme was founded between 1437, when a royal licence was granted,[3] and 1448–50, which, because William de la Pole is named as duke of Suffolk in them, has to be when the statutes were drawn up. The date of the statutes is important for the question of who influences whom in almshouse-statute making during the 1430s and 1440s. It is difficult to put into order and summarise eighty-nine clauses. I have done so under four headings: the foundation itself; poverty; the daily programme of prayer; discipline.

First, the establishment. I shall not deal with the Master himself or with the Schoolmaster (the foundation being one of an almshouse and school), only with the thirteen poor men of the almshouse and Alice Chaucer's regime for them.[4] Under the supervision of the Master and the Schoolmaster one of the poor men was to be appointed what was called the Minister; he was to report to the Master on the misbehaviour of the other twelve men (clause 4): 'to present errors and defaultes of the forsayde pore men to the Maystyr withoute fraude or gyle'. Was it unusual, even unique, for the senior bedesman in an almshouse to be given responsibility for informing on his fellows? The Minister was also to be bell-ringer and doorkeeper and he was to have 16d a week (clauses 5 and 13).[5] The other twelve men were each to have 14d a week (clause 14). That was double what most bedesman had elsewhere. Were there other twopence-a-day bedesmen in fifteenth-century England? It is to be noted that Alice paid double the standard labouring rate: the minimum daily wage for an agricultural labourer with a meal was a penny. As we shall see, she consequently demanded twice as much work from her employees.

A bedesman, says clause 5, was to be poor, clean, and gracious of living; he was, says clause 78, to be meek in spirit, poor in temporal goods 'that without relief beyond his own goods he shall not competently live', chaste in body, and 'of good conversation named and trowed [reputed], ybroke in age or else by other manner of feebleness unable to get his living'. In the first instance bedesmen were to have been de la Pole servants and tenants, preferably tenants of the three manors with which the almshouse was endowed, says clause 79.[6] They were to be virtuous and devout: 'and we pray and beseech them most devoutly and meekly', reads clause 80, 'and with all reverence before god charge them as they will answer at the dreadful day of doom, that they will put away all affection and inordinate love, all corruption of prayer and temporal mede'. A bedesman was to be 'no feigned poor man but verily poor and devout'. Alice Chaucer would have shaken her head at the 1909 Royal Commission's definition of poverty as 'a defect in the citizen character'. Or would she? See the next paragraph.

The second heading is poverty. Not just any old and poor man was acceptable at Ewelme. No lepers, madmen, or those with infectious diseases and intolerable sicknesses were to be admitted, says clause 76. Yet, the clause continues, should a bedesman catch an 'intollerable sikenesse' and have to be dismissed the almshouse to prevent him infecting his fellows and 'provoking them to orrour', he was to be put into some 'behovefull place' and was to receive his twopence a day for as long as he lived. The bedesmen were not only to be presentable; they were also to be respectable. Clause 55 states that if a man 'aftyr his admission . . . be promoted, and grow clerly to the some of vi mark [£4] yerly by tityll of heritage or any othir wyse whereby he may sufficiantly live duryng hys lyfe without the almesse of the sayde howse' he was to depart; if, says clause 56, the income he came into was 5 marks [£3 6s 8d] or less it was to be divided equally between himself and the common chest of the almshouse. In other words, if a Ewelme bedesman came into an income which was £1 or more higher than the £3 he received annually as a bedesman he would have to forfeit his place; if he came by an annual income of £3 6s 8d or less he might stay and keep half of it for himself to augment the £3 a year he had as a bedesman. An annual income of between £4 and £5 would place him in the husbandman or artisan class. Was that, indeed, what he was likely to have been? Was it what Alice Chaucer wanted him to have been? It was certainly what she conceived of him as being: not so much a labourer at prayer but a craftsman of prayer. Not, however, and as we shall see, a literate craftsman of prayer. The Minister, after all, does look as much like the master of a workshop as he does a foreman in field or factory. Whatever conclusion on the matter we might arrive at, Ewelme was far from the original Franciscan concept of poverty. The Ewelme bedesmen demonstrate not simply the acceptable poor of fifteenth-century England; they might also be said to represent a poverty that has ceased by any definition to be poverty at all.[7] Any income that a bedesman still enjoyed at his death was to be left to the almshouse (clause 60). In the accounts of 1461–2 there are sums recorded as receipts from the chambers of deceased almsmen, 20s from that of Simon, labourer [sic], 8s 10d from that of John Dauntsey, and an unnamed sum from another which had been put at Alice Chaucer's disposal.

Thirdly, there was the daily grind. The bedesmen got up sometime before 6 a.m., an hour or even two before bedesmen in other foundations rose from their beds. The rooms at Ewelme are set around a courtyard; in those rooms each man was to eat, drink, pray and contemplate, as well as sleep, alone. Moreover, the wording of clause 10 suggests Alice was thinking of her bedesmen as secular Carthusians: they were to 'have and holde a certcyn place by them self . . . that is to sayng, a lytyl howse, a celle or a chamber with a chemeney . . . in the whiche any of them may by hym selfe ete and drynke and rest, and sum tymes attende to contemplacion and prayoure'.[8] Once the men were up they were to kneel by their beds to say three Pater Nosters, three Aves and a Creed; they were to have in mind Henry VI and the duke and duchess of Suffolk, in order that, says clause 16, they might so live as to enter the Kingdom of Heaven: 'desiryng inwardly in theire sowles that . . . Kyng Harry the Sext and wee theire seide fownders . . . mow soo be demeyned in oure lyvyng, that at the last we mow have and opteyne the kyngdom of heven'. At 6 a.m., says clause 17, they were to troop into the parish church, whose west door is directly up a flight of dauntingly steep steps from the almshouse courtyard, for Matins, Prime, Terce, Sext and Nones. At 9 a.m., presumably after breakfast, they were to return to the church for Mass in the Chapel of St John the Baptist. After Mass they had to gather round the tomb of Thomas Chaucer and Maud Bergersh, Alice's father and mother, to say another three Pater Nosters, three Aves and a Creed, as well as to offer up prayers for the king and for the duke and duchess (clauses 18 and 23). The morning's work was not yet over. At 2 p.m., before dinner, they had to be back in church where the Minister was to say 'certeyn bedis', assigned him by the Master, for the church and for the founders, after which he and the almsmen were to get down on their knees again to recite fifteen Pater Nosters, three Aves and a Creed (clause 29). At 3 p.m. Evensong followed dinner; Compline followed Evensong. Possibly the almsmen were allowed a nap after dinner while the Master was saying these services; at any rate their presence at them, so far as I can determine, is nowhere specified, although silence might mean that their attendance was taken for granted. Certainly, immediately after Compline they were to be in church to say three Pater Nosters, three Aves and a Creed, with one of them to say prayers in English for the king and for the duke and duchess; to these prayers all were to answer openly 'Amen' (clauses 18 and 24). They returned to the church for the fifth and final time at 6 p.m. More prayers for the founders were to be said by the Minister, while the kneeling bedesmen were to say a further fifteen Aves for the everlasting quiet and rest of those founders (clause 30).[9]

Fines of 1d and 2d for lateness at services were elaborately set out in clause 32. All excuses for absence, says clause 31, were to be approved by the Master. In addition to the formal routine of prayer, the almsmen, says clause 22, were to go to church every day 'whanne they mowe best therto attende', where they were to say for the king and the founders 150 Aves, fifteen Pater Nosters, and three Creeds, that is, three times 'oure lady psawter, a psawter conteyning thryes Aves with Pater nostris and 3 Credis'. The total of prayers for a day amounted to thirty-nine Pater Nosters, 177 Aves and seven Creeds.[10] There could well have been a sign hung on the almshouse door: No Lazy Beggars Wanted Here.

Fourth, there is the house of correction aspect of Ewelme. The almsmen were not allowed to wander about the village: 'walke muche abowte either in or out of the parish'. If anyone did so without reasonable cause he was to suffer the 'takyng away of hys wages'. They were not allowed to be off the premises for more than an hour without permission (clauses 34 and 35). Absences had to have the approval of the Master, yet even absence on pilgrimage or to visit friends is disapproved of. By the absence of bedesmen, says clause 36, the hours of prayer shall not be properly performed, the performance of them will be reduced ('lassid') by outward aquaintance and worldly occupations, and their seats in the church will be void and unoccupied to the dishonour of the almshouse. Thus, even if they are given permission to be absent their wages are stopped for the time that they are away. When a man was absent for a quarter of a year without the Master's licence he was to be dismissed for good (clause 39).

The almsmen were not to be noisy, they were not to be quarrelsome, scolds, or gossips (clause 40): 'without crying and great noise making, keeping themselves from jangling and chiding, and in especial from foul boastful and ribald talking of things done in days gone by'. Was it John Sainsbury, the long-serving parish priest and first Master, who was responsible for this acute observation of the habits of the elderly? They were not to be drunkards, gluttons, tavern-haunters, nor be 'brigous amonge' their fellows, 'faitours', 'chiders', or 'incontinent' (clause 41). They were strictly forbidden outside the almshouse to discuss in a critical fashion what went on there (clause 42). They were not to work elsewhere, nor were they to beg, especially (says clause 43) of any lord or lady of the lordship of Ewelme in time to come or of their servants. They were to be tidy about the place: gardens had to be weeded, alleyways kept clean and neat (clauses 44 and 45). The stronger were required to help the weaker (clause 46), and any women 'by the which lykly suspicion of sclaundyr myght fall to the seyde howse' were not to enter the chambers of the Master, Schoolmaster or bedesmen (clause 47). For church they were to wear their proper dress, a tabard and a hood with a red cross on the breast (clause 37). The statutes, which every newcomer had to swear to abide by (clause 85), were to be read out in full every quarter by the Master and Schoolmaster 'and understondyngly be expounded', while a number of the rules and regulations 'ytake oute of this hole ordenaunce' were to be read out every month by them (clause 87), 'that the contentis and chapitres of the same mowe the more inwardly be commended to here myndes'. Rebels were to have their wages docked and defaulters were to be disciplined in an ever more shaming manner (clause 33). The first correction was to be by the Master alone; the second was to be by the Master before the Schoolmaster and two almsmen, the slacker to have a week's wages taken from him; the third time the whole company was to be witness to the offender's disgrace and he was to lose a month's wages; thereafter he was deemed incorrigible and obstinate and was to be put out of the almshouse (clause 62).

The founders were strongly aware of the designs of the covetous on the landed endowment of the property of their foundation (clause 7): with good cause, as the contemporary history of Cardinal Henry Beaufort's almshouse of St Cross at Winchester illustrates.[11] They were equally conscious that standards might drop: the founders and their successors were to make a yearly visitation (clause 81). The visit of Alice in July 1458 is recorded. So appalled must she have been that she cut the weekly wage bill by a swingeing fifty per cent: that week the men got 7 s instead of 14 s.[12] It did not always need Alice's intervention for discipline and decorum to be maintained. In 1461–2 15 s 11 d was raised 'de correctionibus', details of which, the accounts declared, were to be found in an attached paper, now inevitably lacking.[13]

4

This section concerns 'Parallels and Models', or rather a parallel and a model. The closest parallel to Ewelme is the hospital at Heytesbury (Wilts.), a foundation of the Hungerford family of pre-1442: a Keeper, a Schoolmaster, twelve poor men and a single poor woman. The statutes, of 48 clauses, are, however, of February 1472 and very much reflect the heart and mind of Margaret Botreaux, widow of Robert, Lord Hungerford (d. 1459).[14] It was therefore the Ewelme statutes which influenced the Heytesbury ones. They do so conspicuously. The differences, nonetheless, are instructive. For example, once admitted 'no poreman . . . was to exercise ne use, ne besynesse, ne handwerke, ne foldewerke', but, 'all thing put a parte', was to 'study and intende to execute and fulfil the charges expressed in the foundacion and statutes . . . with all his power'. The imperative to eschew paid domestic work in the Wiltshire clothing industry and to concentrate on study is an aspect of Margaret's expectation that some at least of her poor men would be literate. They will read their prayers (clause 22), not merely get them by heart as those who are 'not lettered'; if they do not already have them by heart on entry, they are to be taught to get them by heart; they are to be examined in their proficiency quarterly (clause 25). Once a quarter the Keeper is to be read out the statutes 'distinctly and openly' and expound them 'understandyngly', but the poor men who are able to read the statutes for themselves are to do so, in order that they 'may be the more effectually conned and ymprynted in ther myndes' (clause 47). Moreover, once every month the literate are to read out the statutes to the unlettered (clause 22).

At Heytesbury the poor men and the poor woman, who was to be laundress and nurse at 13 s 4 d per annum (clauses 29 and 38), were to live more communally than were the Ewelme bedesmen. The Heytesbury folk were to eat dinner and supper together, and there was to be no improper talk at table (clause 24). Margaret Botreaux also provided for them collectively. They did not have 1 d or 2 d a day; food, drink, clothing, heating, and shaving were costed by the week or year (clauses 36, 37, 39, 40). The poor men of Heytesbury were as Benedictine-like as their brothers at Ewelme were Carthusian-like. Another difference was that the poor men of Heytesbury, who were to be old Hungerford servants and tenants (clause 19) and not to be either lepers or contagiously infected (clauses 25 and 28), were not reckoned to be as financially well off as their Ewelme brethren. If any of them inherited or in any other way came by an income of 4 marks a year he was to leave (clause 27). At Ewelme it had been 6 marks. If the gift was less than 4 marks it was to be divided equally between man and almshouse as at Ewelme, but at his death only half a poor man's property was to go to the hospital (clauses 28 and 32); all of it went at Ewelme.

Equally significant is that there is only a single clause about proper behaviour in the Heytesbury statutes (clause 17), and no clauses at all detailing fines for lateness or disciplinary measures for offenders. Nothing is said concerning cleanliness and tidiness. Nor was Margaret Botreaux to be the visitor of the hospital; that was to be the dean of Salisbury cathedral at 6s 8d a year (clause 6). Although Margaret might dismiss an unsatisfactory Keeper (clause 14), it is notable that at Heytesbury the church was allowed in: it was not at Ewelme. Margaret nonetheless cared almost as little for absence as did Alice. The Keeper might go for a walk of a mile or two for recreation (clause 3), and the poor men could be away for a day (clause 20), which demonstrates that she was a little more relaxed on the matter than Alice, but that was all Margaret was ready to tolerate. She was generally more pernickety about administration in her forty-eight clauses than was Alice in her eighty-nine, especially about the administration of money.

Finally, there is the prayer cycle. At Heytesbury it was not as hectic as it was at Ewelme. On getting up both the poor men and the woman had to say three Pater Nosters, three Aves and a Creed; they were to say the same before going to bed (clause 21). They also had to go to the almshouse chapel after supper to say prayers for the founders and to recite three Paters Nosters, three Aves and a Creed (clause 23). They were expected to attend Mass in the parish church daily if they were fit enough. There was also to be Mass in the almshouse chapel two or three times a week, particularly if there were three or more poor men who were sick (clause 10): it seems that Margaret Botreaux expected some of her bedesmen to be bedridden, an eventuality which appears not to have occurred to Alice Chaucer. That was all as far as communal prayer was concerned – far less than was demanded of the almsmen at Ewelme. Nonetheless, the illiterate poor men of Heytesbury hospital did have to say each day when they could, that is individually and privately, three psalters of Our Lady, 'every sawter three times 50 Aves with 15 Paternosters and 3 Credes', and additionally every day 'onys our Lady Sawter for all Christen soulis'. While the unlettered were busy about these prayers, the literate had to say a psalter of the Virgin, twenty-two psalms and the relevant lessons, as well as Matins of the Virgin, every day before noon; in the afternoon they were to offer prayers for the dead (clause 22). The regime of private prayer at Heytesbury was no less exacting than that at Ewelme; perhaps it was more so, which seems paradoxical given the greater emphasis on communality at Heytesbury. Michael Hicks has written of 'a taxing programme of unbelievable boredom, involving endless repetition of Latin prayers, especially for the illiterate with their 66 Hail Marys, 26 Lords Prayers, and 6 Creeds, but [which] was in no way unusual'.[15] He is surely correct about the normality of the Heytesbury programme. It is the Ewelme programme which is abnormal, being more Victorian than Plantagenet, even more Tibetan than English. At Ewelme, we need to remind ourselves, it was 177 Hail Marys, thirty-nine Lord's Prayers and seven Creeds which were said every day. John Durkan has commented that 'Nowadays, when psychological medicine is coming into its own, these requirements will seem less otiose than they might have done fifty years ago.'[16] We will have to take our pick between unbelievable boredom and psychological medicine. Or should it be between psychological boredom and unbelievable medicine?

Now for the model. Ewelme is probably unique. Nevertheless, Henry Chichele's bedehouse at Higham Ferrers might be added to St George's College, Windsor, as an influence if not a model. The bedehouse at Higham Ferrers was part of the college the archbishop founded at his birthplace in 1427, the year of the royal licence. It was for twelve poor men and a woman; the men and the woman were to have a penny a day. There is not space to make detailed comparisons and contrasts, but one's impression is that while there are certain similarities, overall Henry Chichele was a good deal more generous and tolerant towards his almsmen than Alice Chaucer was to her bedesmen.[17] Chichele's statutes comprise thirty-six clauses. One of the twelve poor men who was sober and wise was to be chosen to be over the others and to be called the Prior. There was also a typical concern for correct behaviour, although any of Chichele's bedesmen who were brawlers or drunkards got four rather than three warnings before they were removed, and only a penny was to be docked from their week's wages at the second and third warnings (clauses 7, 8, 9, 13). No whoremaster was to be in the house; if any was discovered he was to be dismissed at once before two witnesses (clause 5). Is it 'sexist' to note that neither Alice Chaucer nor Margaret Botreaux considered the possibility of a whoremaster in the house? Only clean men were to be admitted: no blotches, blains or boils (clause 17). The men had to be fifty or over, and if at death they had any landed property it was to be left to the almshouse (clause 16). They were to dig and plant the garden in spring under the supervision of the woman (clause 28), who evidently had the task of head gardener to add to her other duties as cook, night-nurse, laundress and cleaner. Visits to friends were tolerated for one week a year and with no loss of that week's allowance (clause 19). Careful consideration was given to the provision of the almsmen's meals, which were to be cooked by the woman; on Sunday and Wednesday there was to be soup and roast meat, the meat to be bought on Saturday by the men and taken to the woman to prepare; on Monday she was to make the left-overs into a potage for their dinner; on Friday she was to bake them good bread (clauses 25 and 26). Monday was wash day, when with hired help the woman was to wash the clothes of the almsmen (clause 27). Every morning she was to rise before them, light a fire and bring warm water to wash in, and every day she was to sweep the house; if any man was ill in the night she was to tend to him, at his cost and charge (clause 29). A barber was to come at noon every Friday to shave the men and dress their heads (clause 20). Any man getting an infectious disease was to go to his friends until cured, when he might return: there was no mention of whether his wages were to be paid while he was absent from the bedehouse (clause 18). One wonders who ruled the roost, the Prior or the Woman of All Work. A most un-Ewelme-like clause is 22, which deals with new entrants: each new bedesman was to be robed with the best robe of the dead man he was replacing and was to make a monetary contribution for the other men 'to make merry withall'.

What of the prayer regime at Higham Ferrers? The men were to be up at 7 a.m. in summer and at 8 a.m. in winter, an hour later than at Ewelme where Alice was exceptional in her desire for an early start; they attended the parish church for an hour, the church at Higham Ferrers being almost as near at hand as at Ewelme or for that matter at Tattershall, Ralph, Lord Cromwell's almshouse of the 1450s.[18] At 2 p.m. they returned to the church for two hours and at 6 p.m. they knelt outside their chambers in the hall to pray for an hour. An hour later at 8 p.m. they went to bed (clauses 11 and 12). What the prayers were is not specified in the statutes. The four hours the bedesmen of Higham Ferrers put in at prayer, with a daily Mass perhaps adding another hour, seems to be about the same length of time those of Ewelme were obliged to spend on their knees. Two hours in church every afternoon will have tested their patience to the limit.

5

What sort of persons were the founders, principally Alice Chaucer, whose preferences, not to say prejudices, seem to be those one discovers in the Ewelme almshouse statutes? Alice was devoted to detail, particularly the details of prayer. She wanted her bedesman to work harder at prayer than they had worked at anything else in their lives, for there were no seasonal lulls in the Ewelme prayer year. In that sense, and only in that sense, the almshouse was more like a factory than it was anything, unless it was like a monastery. Yet she paid double the standard rate to those producing for her a commodity she considered crucial to an eternal existence. Much else might be said about her: her insistence on cleanliness, decorum, respectability, perhaps her obssession with quantity rather than quality – quality at any rate, as defined by the literacy Margaret Botreaux expected some of the bedesmen at Heytesbury to have. It was perpetual intercession, not devotional – let alone theological – understanding, that Alice wished for. Does Alice also exhibit an exceptional preoccupation with self-perpetuation? At any rate self-and husband-perpetuation? In this connection, the images at the Hull Charterhouse have always intrigued me. They were erected according to an agreement made between Alice and the convent in October 1462:[19]

two stone images, one in the likeness of the late Duke and the other in the likeness of the Duchess, each image holding in its right hand a dish, the emblem of bread and baked meats, and in the left hand a jug, the emblem of ale; before which images the Prior and his successors shall every day distribute to two indigent almspeople, one male and the other female, two convent loaves each weighing one and a half pounds, and two jugs of convent ale, each jug containing one pottle, two messes of convent pottage, and two messes of a convent dinner: likewise on Sundays, Tuesdays, Thursdays and Saturdays, four kinds of baked meats properly cooked, and on Mondays and Wednesdays . . . [gap] similarly cooked.

The 'indigent almspeople' are named on the dorse of the document as brothers and sisters of the convent; there are six men, eleven widows, and six poor girls. I have not come across other such 'active' images in England. The Emperor Maximilian I in his will of 1519 requested that his image might be put up in the eight hospitals to which he left money, but they were not to be 'active' in the manner of those in Hull.[20] Alice might well have had in mind a provision of her second husband's will. Thomas Montagu, Earl of Salisbury, declared that 'dilectissima uxor nostra' was to distribute meat, bread, and drink daily to three paupers 'ipsa propriis manibus'.[21] Did she ever do so? A reader of the Paston Letters will find it hard to picture the scene. It is easier to imagine her finding fault with the bedesmen at Ewelme in July 1458 (look at that untidy garden, look at this filthy alleyway) and docking their wages, than it is handing out food and drink to the needy. She seems more like the wife of a Victorian industrialist than the widow of three husbands who had fought in the Hundred Years War. Nor do I see Alice Chaucer as Dorothea Brooke.

6

The title of this part is 'Quantity and Quality'. The sheer quantity of prayer offered up at Ewelme is exceptional; it is also understandable. The more prayers the better. The richer one was, the more prayers one could afford. There might also have been, probably was, an awareness that the richer one was, the more prayers one required. What of the quality of those selected to pray? We have seen that they had to be not only neat and tidy, but also sound in wind and limb, clean of body and mind, and not from the dregs of society. Far from it: the Ewelme bedesmen were likely to have been respected and responsible members of village communities. They might have fallen on hard times, it is true, and the idea of the poor as just that – the respectable who through no fault of their own had descended in society – was an idea with a long history: the deserving poor will always be with us. Nonetheless, the bedesmen at Ewelme were not poor men. They had been and continued to be comfortably off, they had to be fit and well, and they were clean and decent. All they lacked for the good life was a wife. They seem a lot like monks who did not get out much. They seem like it because they were monk-replacements. Monks themselves, unless they were Carthusian monks, were no longer respectable – probably because they were so evidently no longer in the least poor, were not always clean, and were from time to time indecent. How could the prayers of those who behaved like disreputable clubmen be acceptable unto God? To the untheologically inclined and materially orientated, monasticism had depreciated to such a degree that the prayers of monks were reckoned as worth little or nothing. Think of Barrie Dobson's Durham monks with their rest home at Finchale, 'a regular holiday villa'.[22] Look at that extraordinary meat kitchen at Jervaulx. Recollect Barbara Harvey's deep-drinking, heavy-eating, hard-whoring and property-dealing Benedictines at Westminster.[23] Recall Dom William Ingram sitting in his summerhouse in a private garden at Canterbury.[24] Whatever else these fellows were – and how like college fellows some of them were – they were no longer prayerful. Someone had to take their place. The Ewelme bedesmen seem, therefore, to be on that margin of modernity which J. H. Hexter identified Thomas More also straddling (or bestriding). They were the new secular workhorses of prayer, employees of a hard but fair task mistress who was adamant she would have her twopenny worth and for whom the moral probity of her workers was essential to the success of a quasi-commercial, quasi-industrial, quasi-religious enterprise.

Yet was Alice old-fashioned in her emphasis on quantity? The margin of modernity is also a medieval margin. Was she not facing backwards as well as forwards, as those on margins are likely to be doing, even bound to do? Margaret Botreaux was turned more squarely towards modernity because of her literate bedesmen. The desire to know what one was saying, to understand what one was hearing, was one of the impulses behind the changes of the sixteenth century. Already in Alice's time education of that sort was fashionable. What happened to St Leonard's almshouse for old women at St Andrews was typical: in 1512 it was turned into a University College. The reason was put more bluntly than was normally the case with such transformations. The old women, it was said, were giving 'little or no return in devotion or virtue'.[25] How revealing is the phrase, 'little or no return'. It is a thoroughly modern way of putting a medieval preoccupation.

7

Finally: 'Memorials and Modernity'. What distinguishes modern from medieval is the medievalism absent from modernity, and what is missing in modernity is the medieval idea of eternity. All traditional societies, or pre-modern societies, or not-modern societies, are in one fashion or another connected to eternity. They are tuned into it. At the Reformation, the English, the most advanced and progressive people in Europe, turned their backs on what the modernisers of the 1530s called superstition: the elaborate apparatus accompanying, upholding and fulfilling prayers for the dead. Thus, it was the English who began the process of eliminating eternity from time and time-keeping, a process which has culminated in twenty-four-hour shopping every day of the year. Round-the-Clock Capitalism has no time for the Eternal. It is the complete opposite of Round-the-Clock Monasticism, even if, or precisely because, it is a parody of it: not pray now and live later, but buy now and pay later. Modern memorials have, therefore, to be substitutes for eternity just as nostalgia is modernity's substitute for prayer. If we remember, we do so at theme parks, in virtual reality museums, or in front of monuments which have lost their original meanings. We no longer gather in prayerful mode around tombs, as the almsmen went daily to pray at the tomb of Thomas Chaucer and after her death at Alice Chaucer's tomb. If we remember the dead at all it is in a desultory fashion, when someone or something reminds us of them. They are not with us always. At Ewelme the dead were buried; they were not forgotten.

I am unable to conclude a paper in honour of Barrie Dobson without citing Marcel Proust and without mentioning (for the second time) another outsider at Cambridge, Ludwig Wittgenstein. To the tomb of the latter Barrie and I once went to say a prayer for a great twentieth-century soul who assuredly will not be forgotten. Finally, here is Proust: 'We *think* we no longer love the dead because we don't remember them; but if by chance we come across an old glove we burst into tears.' Alice Chaucer was not so romantic; at Ewelme it was remembrance without tears, unless they were those of old men who had to spend too long on creaking knees.

NOTES

1. See *HMC, Ninth Report*, Part I, appendix, pp. 216–22. This contemporary copy of the statutes, which in 1883 was still at Ewelme, is now in the Bodleian Library with the rest of the almshouse archive: MSS DD Ewelme a. 6, A25.
2. 'Ruling Classes and Agents of the State: Formal and Informal Networks of Power', *Journal of Historical Sociology* 10 (1997), pp. 19–20.
3. The licence of 3 July 1437 is in the Ewelme muniments in the Bodleian Library, Oxford, MSS DD Ewelme a. 6, A21.
4. The first Master was to be John Sainsbury, 'late parson of long continuance of time of the parish of Ewelme'. John was preferred to a graduate because of his long and good service, especially his attention to the building of the church and almhouse; after him, however, the Master was to be a graduate of Oxford, thirty or more years old: clause 69. John Sainsbury, rector of Ewelme, died 27 August 1454, according to his brass in the church.
5. John Bostock is named as Minister in the statutes.
6. The accounts of 1461–2, for which see below, show the three manors providing just about enough to cover salaries and wages. These came to around £56 a year. The Master and Schoolmaster had an annual salary of £10 each, while in the 1460s the wage bill of the Minister and the other twelve bedesmen was between £34 and £38 per annum. In 1461 there was £32

in the common chest. The chest was topped up with gifts as well as from the bequeathed income of dying bedesmen, for which see also below: there was, therefore, other money besides annual income available for additional expenses and for maintenance costs. For the conventionally close attention paid in the statutes to yearly accounting and an annual inventory, see clauses 49–54.

7. I suppose I am taking issue with Miri Rubin at this point. She has written that the function of the late medieval almshouse was to relieve society of its unacceptable members: *Charity and Community in Medieval Cambridge* (Cambridge, 1987), p. 120. It is clear to me that Ewelme was designed for the acceptable [poor] for the rather simple reason that only the prayers of the acceptable [poor] were envisaged as effective; the unacceptable [poor] were unacceptable because no one, even or especially God, valued the prayers of nasty down-and-outs and unpleasant drop-outs. It should be recalled that Francis and his ragamuffin bunch had to be made respectable, like the Umiliati and all the rest, before they were accorded recognition, unofficial as well as official. Where I do agree with Ms Rubin is in her description of Sir John Colville's foundation of 1411 at Newton-on-the-Sea, Norfolk; he added to an existing college a chantry and an almshouse: 'it was', says Ms Rubin, 'typical of its time'. I agree with her not because Newton was as she describes it (ibid., p. 146), 'a hospital primarily for the needy', but because it was a chantry with the poor attached as a liturgical appendage to pray for the founder's soul. Newton was like Ewelme, except that at the latter the poor were not an appendix: they were the beating liturgical heart of the establishment.

8. The gardens, however, were not attached to each chamber; they were (and still are) in a plot by themselves between almshouse and school. The Carthusian influence at Ewelme demands consideration, particularly in light of William and Alice's association with the Charterhouse at Hull.

9. There were, of course, special services and celebrations on High and Holy Days, and on the Anniversaries of William and Alice: clauses 26 and 27.

10. Not sixty-nine Pater Nosters, 189 Aves, and fifteen Creeds as my earlier, more wayward arithmetic had it: see the quotation cited previously.

11. See Gervase Belfield, 'Cardinal Beaufort's Almshouse of Noble Poverty at St Cross, Winchester', *Proceedings of the Hampshire Field Club and Archaeological Society* 38 (1982), pp. 79–91; and also Gerald Harriss, *Cardinal Beaufort* (Oxford, 1988), pp. 369–75. In a longer study Henry Beaufort's foundation would have featured in more than a footnote. Unless it was the other way about, Beaufort's statutes of 1445 may have influenced the making of those for Ewelme. It is perhaps worth noting that Beaufort's effigy was on the gatehouse of St Cross; for the de la Pole effigies at the Hull Charterhouse, see below.

12. See the paper cited in note 2, p. 10, fn. 16. The Minister presumably escaped Alice's retribution.

13. The accounts are Bodleian Library, Oxford, MSS DD Ewelme a. 6, A 35 B: 1461–2 is the only year I have looked at.

14. Michael Hicks, 'St Katherine's Hospital, Heytesbury', in his *Richard III and his Rivals* (London, 1991), pp. 120–36. The statutes were published by Rev. Canon J. E. Jackson, 'Ancient Statutes of Heytesbury Almshouse', *Wiltshire Archaeological and Natural History Magazine* 11 (1869), pp. 289–308.

15. Hicks, 'St Katherine's Hospital', p. 130.

16. At St George's College, Windsor, the poor knights were to attend three times a day in choir at High Mass, Lady Mass and Vespers, and to say a total of 150 Aves and fifteen Pater Nosters during those services: A. K. B. Roberts, *St George's Chapel, Windsor Castle, 1348–1416* (Windsor, 1947), p. 150. At the Hospital of St Mary Magdalene, Edinburgh, the bedesmen were to say fifty Aves, five Pater Nosters and a Creed when they heard the rising bell, rung by one of themselves at 6.30 a.m. in summer and at 7 a.m. in winter; the same number at the ringing of the closing bell, rung at 7 p.m. in winter and at 8 p.m. in summer; and the same again on their knees before the high altar of the chapel after supper. Before supper they were to say two psalters of the Virgin, and to do the same again before dinner: John Durkan, 'Pre-Reformation Hospitals', in David McRoberts (ed.), *Essays on the Scottish Reformation, 1513–1625* (Glasgow, 1962), pp. 116–28 (citation p. 127).

17. For Chichele, and Higham Ferrers as 'Chicheleville', see Philip Morgan, 'Of Worms and War: 1380–1558', in Peter C. Jupp and Clare Gittings (eds.), *Death in England* (Manchester, 1999), pp. 119–46 (p. 138); also E. F. Jacob, *Archbishop Henry Chichele* (London, 1967), chapter 7, esp. pp. 88–90; and *VCH, Northants*, II, pp. 177–9. The statutes were printed by John Cole, *The History and Antiquities of Higham Ferrers* (Higham Ferrers, 1838), pp. 75–83: I am grateful to Ms Clare Trend of the Central Library, Northampton, for sending me a copy of the relevant pages the same day I asked for them. Cole justly observes that the statutes 'add life to the mouldering relics [of the bedehouse]'; they were not, however, mouldering in 1958 when I first visited them on one of those eye-opening expeditions into the English landscape organised by the History Department of Leicester University. Although I have never revisited it, the Higham Ferrers bedehouse is a vivid memory: like Ewelme, it can be said to have played a part in the genesis of this chapter. Also not forgotten are those who accompanied us on those expeditions, giving of their time and knowledge to enlighten students about England and English relics: Babette Evans, Rupert Evans, Geoffrey Martin, Norman Scarfe and Jack Simmons.

18. There is not space here to discuss its statutes of 1458–60. They are quite standard and appear not to reflect Cromwell's personality in the way I am suggesting the Ewelme statutes reflect Alice Chaucer's, or for that matter those of Higham Ferrers reveal Henry Chichele's. As the Tattershall statutes date from after Cromwell's death they are, one presumes, the creation of his executors.

19. *HMC, Eighth Report*, appendix, p. 628a. The original is Bodleian Library, Ewelme MS A42; it is badly damaged, but it supplies the additional (and important) information that the two images were to be placed in the refectory.

20. Gerhard Benecke, *Maximilian I, 1459–1519, An Analytical Biography* (London, 1982), p. 121.

21. E. F. Jacob (ed.), *The Register of Henry Chichele, 1414–43*, 4 vols. (Oxford, 1938–47), II, p. 392. The will is dated 20 May 1427.

22. *Durham Priory, 1400–1450* (Cambridge, 1973), p. 310.

23. *Living and Dying in England 1100–1540: The Monastic Experience* (Oxford, 1993), esp. chapter 2.

24. G. H. Rooke, 'Dom William Ingram and his Account-Book 1504–1533', *Journal of Ecclesiastical History* 7 (1956), 30–44 (p. 37).

25. John Gifford, *The Buildings of Scotland: Fife* (London, 1988), p. 386.

CHAPTER 14

Puritanism and the poor*

Patrick Collinson

The puritan response to poverty, which was, or should have been, the dominant concern of anyone with a liability or concern for social policy in the late sixteenth and early seventeenth centuries, combined elements of utopianism and pragmatism, making it a subject especially worthy of inclusion in a collection of tributes to Barrie Dobson. But this is no new subject. Nearly half a century ago, Christopher Hill published an essay on the most representative of puritan divines, 'William Perkins and the Poor'. Hill read Perkins selectively, and suggested that so did Perkins's original readers. They would have filtered out, as he filtered out, the hard things that Perkins, as a representative Puritan, had to say about the spiritual peril of riches, and about the obligation of those with means to do so to give without stint. Hill believed that the sixteenth and seventeenth centuries witnessed a drastic change in social attitudes, one which was favourable to the proto-capitalist ethic. 'To be sure he did not have to invent the fervour with which puritan preachers and writers castigated work-shy idleness. But this was not all that the Puritans had to say on the subject of poverty and how Christians should respond to it, and much of it, as John Walsh has remarked of John Wesley's doctrine and practice in the eighteenth century, was 'not the stuff of which the capitalist ethic is easily constructed'.[2]

It was an obscure Suffolk preacher, Thomas Carew of Bildeston, who first drew me to the subject of Puritanism and poverty. Rather as Thomas Cromwell, according to the late Sir Geoffrey Elton, came out of the archives to grab his attention, Carew of Bildeston plucked my sleeve as I browsed in the Huntington Library in California with his *Certyane godly and necessarie sermons*, published in 1603. The sermons were not so necessary that anyone had ever bothered to look at them. But what caught my eye as I leafed through an otherwise unremarkable body of divinity was the last piece in the collection: *A caveat for clothiers*.[3] At once it was clear that this preacher entertained what David Sheppard, sometime bishop of Liverpool, called 'a bias towards the poor', and against the rich. You tell me that the rich remember the poor in their wills. 'Therefore it might be wished that such rich men would die quickly, that there might be some good done at their deaths, for they do hurt while they live.' In the Bible, the rich were reproved ten times more often than the poor. 'The reason is, because they are most faulty.'[4] But Carew was Carew and no one else, perhaps an exceptional, eclectic case. It was necessary to turn away from Carew to see what other Puritans had to say.

But first we should define our terms. 'Puritanism' is a piece of deference to a troublesome taxonomic convention. It is not meant to suggest the existence of a distinct party with its own views on every matter of public concern, still less that a particular attitude to poverty characterised and defined Puritanism. That was the mistake of a large book called *Religion and Society in Elizabethan England* and it ought not to be repeated.[5] However, Paul Slack, our leading authority on early modern poverty, has discovered distinctive, and even distinctively enlightened, social policies in some early seventeenth-century urban communities, and he finds no difficulty in characterising those policies, and the magistrates and ministers who invented them, as 'puritan', or, at least, 'godly'. 'Puritanism was not necessary for all forms of reforming activity in all places', but 'it was essential in some places', and often had the effect of 'ratcheting up the regular machinery by another notch'.[6]

Such cities on a hill were Dorchester in the days of John White, its famous 'patriarch'; the Salisbury of Henry Sherfield, whose government was described in Star Chamber as 'severe'; and Exeter under its mayor, Ignatius Jordan, memorialised as 'one of those rare examples which the Lord giveth the world now and then'.[7] It would not be reasonable to suggest that social policy in these exceptionally godly places was absolutely different from the generality of social policy in the age which generated the Elizabethan Poor Law. It is not as if in one town they were building gas chambers as a final solution to the problem of poverty, while in another the poor received rent rebates and hot dinners. We are talking about differences of temperature and motivation. Exceptional godliness could have interesting if not quite exceptional social consequences.

And what about 'the poor'? There were different kinds of poverty, or different perceptions of what constituted poverty. It is the first thing you are told by the contemporary literature on the subject, for the minds that made that literature worked with the Ramist rhetorical device of *divisio*, splitting everything in sight into two, and then subdividing the two things divided, a process of progressive binary opposition. So it is that we read of deserving and undeserving poor, able and impotent poor, your own poor and someone else's poor. But William Whately, the preacher of Banbury, offers us a simple definition. 'A poore man is one that wants things needful for him', having them either not at all or in 'scant measure'. Those able to help had 'something to spare'.[8] This dovetails with Perkins's doctrine that man may with a good conscience desire 'goods necessarie', but that if he seeks for what is more than is necessary, he sins.[9] In an unequal society, 'necessity' was, of course, an imprecise concept. The scholar's library, the politician's great house, wardrobe and servants, may all have been 'goods necessary'.

Whately's no-nonsense definition accommodates the labouring poor, persons in work whose wages or other sources of income were incapable of supporting themselves and their families; or who, while willing to work, could not find work, or found it only intermittently. We know from local examples of poor relief that such people were helped, from time to time.[10] But in sermons and treatises they are either absent, or only qualify for relief as the victims of personal accident and misfortune. The phenomenon of endemic unemployment and low pay, as structural features of the economy, hovers only on the margins of the argument. The phrase 'labouring poor' was not in use before the eighteenth century.[11] But unemployment and low wages are precisely the issues which exercised Carew of Bildeston, which makes his *Caveat for clothiers* such an arresting document.

The sermons and treatises which may serve as a backdrop for Carew's more unusual views invariably invoke two or three salient scriptural injunctions. To the forefront are those many places where beneficence to the poor is required, and most often Galatians 6.10: 'While we have therefore time, let us doe good unto all men, but specially unto them which are of the household of faith.'[12] But then comes a text of almost menacing qualification: 'If any would not work, neither should he eat' (2 Thessalonians 3.10). Christopher Hill's friend William Perkins lays the matter out in the most orderly fashion, especially in his *Cases of conscience*. But more extensive treatments will be found in John Downame's *The plea of the poore* (251 pages, 1616), and in Richard Bernard's *Ready way to good works* (486 octavo pages, 1634). All writers[13] use similar, two-part, titles, and conclude, according to rhetorical convention, with the formal confutation of sundry 'objections' – usually the same objections in the same order. Ian Breward, an authority on Perkins, speaks of 'a common fund of ideas approaching the status of moral orthodoxy'.[14]

To relieve the poor is an inescapable duty, which is as far as the Elizabethan preacher Henry Bedel gets: 'We must of necessitie give.'[15] 'All stand bound to give . . . according to his ability.'[16] 'These duties of beneficence are commanded unto all.'[17] Bernard, a migrant from near-Separatism to puritan conformity, and from Nottinghamshire to Somerset, divided 'all sorts of persons' into five classes. Only the fifth and last, 'poor in extremity', were exempt from this obligation.[18] This was hardly puritan doctrine, since Article 38 of the Church of England asserts: 'Every man ought of such things as he possesseth, liberally to give alms to the poor.' But surely my goods are mine own, to dispose as I choose? No. Rich men are 'but stewards in respect of God though owners among men'. The poor have 'title and interest to part of our goods', as bankers for God's talents, 'God's factours'.[19] This doctrine of stewardship I take to be fundamental to Christian social ethics. But I am not able to locate its biblical taproot.[20]

Charity must be discriminating, 'wisdom moderating beneficence'. Sturdy beggars and vagrants are not to be relieved, which was no more than the law of the land. For beggars and vagrants were 'mice, rats and polecats', 'ulcers, scabs and vermin'. To relieve such was actually to lack compassion. 'For those that can work and will not, let them starve', says John Rogers, the famous preacher of Dedham, in a harsh rendering of 2 Thessalonians 3.10. For Michael Sparke, these were people not worth speaking of.[21] Others taught that in cases of extreme necessity, even sturdy beggars must be kept alive, if admonished and punished. Bishop Lewis Bayley, in *The practice of piety*, erred on the side of compassion: 'It is better to give unto ten counterfeits than to suffer Christ to go, in one poor saint, unrelieved.'[22] Yet it would be hard to exaggerate the fear and loathing which these writers expressed for the idle, vagrant, threatening poor. Their vehemence orchestrates the anti-vagrancy clauses in the new Poor Law, so that we may suspect that this legislation may have been influenced by pulpit rhetoric. Bernard reached the topic 'To Whom Not To Give' only after 411 pages (whereas Robert Allen of Suffolk had led off with a savage attack on vagrants); and Bernard prefaced what he had to say with 'I am very loth to enter into this discourse.' But then he launched into the same extravagant language as everyone else.[23] Attitudes had certainly hardened since the middle of the sixteenth century, when Robert Crowley had taught: 'Cease not to give to all, without any regard.'[24]

Excluding the utterly unworthy, further discrimination was to be exercised. We must prefer our own poor to strangers. Perkins says that to reverse that priority would be 'a sinne against the law of nature'. Downame and Bernard quote the age-old proverb: charity begins at home. From home, it moved outward to kindred and neighbourhood.[25] This was consistent with the social policy of the seventeenth and eighteenth centuries: a parochial politics of exclusion.[26]

However, this set of priorities was in potential conflict with Galatians 6.10: 'especially unto those of the household of faith'. John Dod and Robert Cleaver taught their readers not to rely on 'carnal friends' but on 'godly men, for they will proove our surest friends. Vicinite and neighbourhood will faile, and alliance and kindred will faile, but grace and religion will never faile.'[27] That was the voice of Puritanism. Downame insists that we are to prefer 'our spiritual kindred' before 'those who are only a kinne unto us in the flesh...I say only, because if our kindred in the flesh be also vertuous and religious, they are to be preferred before the other.' But if not, not.[28] What was 'the household of faith'? Allen thought that it meant the ministry, whose maintenance should come before poor relief.[29] Sometimes the text was used to support the ordinary distinction between worthy and unworthy. But for Puritans 'household of faith' might mean the visibly godly. Whately says: 'such as show forth holinesse, those chiefly must be relieved'.[30] Charity as choosy as that became a bond to consolidate the peculiar and divisive affinity of the godly, and it reached beyond locality and neighbourhood. Godly towns like Dorchester and Exeter helped each other.[31] Of course, everyone, godly or not, had some obligation to bail out a distant and afflicted individual or community, when encouraged to do so by an official brief from the Privy Council. But when Nantwich in Cheshire burned down in 1583, and a brief duly arrived in Bury St Edmunds, 200 miles away, godly Bury contributed £40, more than anywhere else. [32]

Puritans had mechanisms, in their lectures, fasts and communions, for reaching into their pockets on behalf of total strangers. This was a kind of informal presbyterianism in voluntary action. The monthly communions which we find in some early seventeenth-century London parishes [33] were regular occasions for collecting money. Thomas Cooper speaks of weekly contributions and of offerings given at the sacrament and 'ministered to the saints', to relieve not only the poor of the parish but 'other churches in their afflictions and wants'.[34] And here we may allow Thomas Carew to chip in. Preaching in Ipswich, he urged the need for 'a brotherhood and fellowship in the Church, and they ought to send salutations to one another, although they dwell afar off from the other, as twenty or thirty miles, not only by word of mouth, but also by some remembrance.'[35] One way in which Puritanism transcended ordinary social values was in a godly vision which looked beyond the narrowness of the parish and its legally enforceable social policies.

There was little in this literature which touched the structural causes of poverty, including economic recession and unemployment; although Whately of Banbury includes 'want of work' among the misfortunes of the poor, 'which no labour of theirs could prevent'. And the Yorkshire writer Henry Arthington acknowledges the existence of 'such as are willing to take pains, and cannot get work', as well as others whose labours earn little, and who are to be relieved 'in part'. Downame's characterisation of the deserving poor implies that they include honest labourers who cannot get by, 'not able by the sweat of their face to earne their bread'.[36] However, whereas Christopher Hill leads you to expect an emphasis on the creation of work, and we know that it was not an uncommon practice to create 'stocks' of working materials for the poor, or to sow labour-intensive crops with a charitable intent, there is less said in these texts about such benign if inadequate devices than about the abuse of wilful unemployment – idleness.[37] Slack suggests that in social practice, the provision of work for the able-bodied and deserving was the weakest pillar of the Elizabethan Poor Law. He also finds 'a fundamental and damaging lack of fit between puritan perceptions of poverty and the facts'.[38] Top marks for Thomas Carew.

When it is the consciences of the poor themselves that are the object of attention, they are usually told to be content with their lot, and to 'keep a good tongue though men deale not very well with you . . . Carry yourselves dutifully and humble towards the rich and all your superiors . . . not saucy, surly, ill-tongued'.[39] Some preachers rubbed it in. Philip Jones of Cirencester believed that the poor man was really better off than the rich man. He was so exhausted by his day's toil that he had no trouble in getting to sleep at night, whereas 'the satietie of the riche will not suffer him to sleepe'. The poor man was so used to hunger, disease and want of money that these things no longer troubled him. And death was simple and welcome. The only advice Jones had for the pauper was that he should elevate his mind in some heavenly meditation: 'to take, as it were, a spiritual view'.[40] Puritans (Jones was not a Puritan)[41] were more compassionate and down to earth. Rogers of Dedham insisted on the need to visit the poor in person, a long-established practice in his township. Downame took the same line. Those who entered the hovels of the poor would see for themselves 'their provision, hungrie fare, thinne cloathes and hard lodging: the children crying for hunger, and the parents out crying them because they have no food to give them; some lying in straw for want of beddes, others drinking water in stead of drinke'.[42]

The message was often formally double-edged. Preaching to the Northamptonshire magistrates in the aftermath of serious disturbances in the Midlands in 1607, Robert Wilkinson condemned rebellion outright. Nothing could excuse it. And yet it was hardly to be wondered at that these 'mutineers' had buried their patience even as they had buried the hated hedges of enclosure. 'Desperate estates breed desperate minds.' Preachers might exhort to obedience until they were blue in the face. But 'in case of extreame hunger men will not be persuaded, but they will have bread'. Wilkinson's text was 'man shall not live by bread alone'. But man must have bread. 'And let it be a lesson for all states generally, not to grind the faces of the poor.' The lord lieutenant of the county was instructed to have ' a religious respect of the poore'.[43] In this not quite even-handed indictment of both 'the oppression of the mighty' and 'the rebellion of the many', Wilkinson echoes the controversial pronouncements of Martin Luther in the Peasants' War, and he carries us forward towards Richard Baxter's *The poor husbandman's advocate*,[44] and to Wesley. The whole discursive strategy within the continuities of this literature was for the preacher to insert himself and religion, as a critical and hopefully not impotent force, between property and poverty – which was to claim for religion agency and even power. These norms of Christian doctrine are more in evidence than sports like Thomas Carew.

It is time to bring Carew centre stage. There is no doubt about Thomas Carew's credentials as a Puritan.[45] In the 1580s he was the sharpest of all thorns in the side of that pioneering anti-Puritan, John Aylmer, bishop of London: an Essex preacher who refused to conform, took it upon himself to excommunicate the many church papists in his parish, defied his bishop's suspension and endured imprisonment 'sundry times'. He told Aylmer that whatever he might have learned at the university 'ye have not so learned Christ'. Forced out of the diocese of London, Carew took refuge in Ipswich, where his nonconformity persisted, and where he preached flagrantly presbyterian doctrine. When his past caught up with him, the great and the good of Elizabethan East Anglia rode to the rescue and found him a berth in Bildeston, where he arrived in 1591 and was never in serious trouble again. Bildeston was one of the better livings in the archdeaconry of Sudbury. There were forty acres of glebe with a good mix of arable, pasture and woodland, and a ten-roomed rectory, which Carew and his wife Margaret proceeded to populate with children, of whom, by 1602, there were nine.[46] Bildeston was a town with impeccably protestant, and even puritan, credentials, its most recent minister a nonconformist who had rivalled Carew himself as a puritan barrack-room lawyer.[47] But in Bildeston Carew discovered a new agenda – if we are to speak anachronistically, a christian socialist agenda.

Perhaps it was Bildeston which dictated that agenda. Like other Suffolk cloth towns on the cusp of the seventeenth century, it had its problems.[48] Described disparagingly in the eighteenth century as 'a town in a bottom' (Carew's church stood on a hill, half a mile away), it was just far enough away from the larger Hadleigh to maintain a distinct economic existence. The subsidy returns from the earlier sixteenth century suggest great disparity of wealth. The rich, a tiny minority, were assessed at sums of £40, £30 or £24, whereas no less than fifty-eight inhabitants, two thirds of the tax payers, were assessed on wages, put at a nominal £1. This tells us nothing about the majority who failed to reach even this tax threshhold.

Bildeston lived from cloth (which may explain the very uneven distribution of wealth), a small model of proto-industrialisation. While the labour force of carders, spinners, weavers and other operatives may have owned the hardware proper to their trades and have worked in their own 'shops', they took in the raw materials from enterpreneurial clothiers, returned the finished articles, and were paid, not always very promptly, wages for their labour. Carew describes these people as 'work-folks', 'under' their employers.

The mainstay of the industry was, or had been, the manufacture of cloth in the strict sense, the famous Suffolk 'true blues', 'dyed in the wool'. But by Carew's time cloth was giving way to the so-called 'new' and lighter draperies, generically referred to as 'stuffs', which in Bildeston included some pretty rough stuffs, such as coarse blankets, but also 'dormick', a fabric containing some linen and used for curtains and other hangings. In the early seventeenth century, Bildeston was forced to find a subsidiary role in the production of yarn by wool-combing, called 'kembing'. This was women's work, and it supplied looms in other places, especially Norwich. By 1622 it was reported that in twenty towns in the region, 4453 broadcloths with a total value of £39,282 remained unsold, and that bankruptcies had cost the local economy £30,415. The Privy Council was understandably anxious to prevent 'tumultuous and disorderly assemblies'. So Carew preached his social gospel in a minor industrial town on the verge of depression and facing industrial unrest, and at the end of a decade of low wages and high food prices.

It was in these depressing circumstances that Carew chose to look inside the Suffolk cloth industry, and in particular into its employment and wages practices. Robert Reyce, who almost at the same time wrote his *Breviary of Suffolk*, praised clothing for maintaining in work large numbers of the poor who would not otherwise know how to live. Carew put his own spin on this conventional wisdom. 'The poor must work for little rather than sit still for nothing.'[49]

Carew took his text from the fifth chapter of the Epistle of James: 'Go to now ye rich men, howl and weep for the miseries that shall come upon you.' Why, asked Carew, had he applied his text exclusively to clothiers, for some considered that the apostle's words were intended for landlords? He explained that the congregation to which the sermon was preached consisted of clothiers, and that clothiers were absolute bastards, the most unconscionable of all employers.[50] 'It is a thing monstrous and strange that any should be so void of religion and humanity as to defraud the poor of their wages.'[51] Carew explained that he was not against the clothing industry as such, which was 'a necessary, a commendable and profitable trade'. He did not blame all clothiers. He did not know all clothiers. But he could not excuse those he did know. The abuse was not isolated but general, and so demanded 'a public reprehension'.[52]

Carew could turn a pungent phrase. But his sermon is notable less for rhetorical effect than for its deployment of facts and figures, almost in the manner of a nineteenth-century blue book. The bottom-line contention that the workforce in the broadcloth industry was paid less than a living wage was substantiated in minute detail.[53] Other tradesmen, such as carpenters, masons, thatchers, even labourers – speaking only of 'the sorriest workmen' – could hope to earn 4d a day with food and drink provided, 8d without it. A more skilful workman could hope to earn a shilling. How did this compare with wages in the clothing industry, where meals were not provided? The spinners, dexterous women, got 3d or 4d a day, which was no more than they could earn as midwives or in haymaking and harvesting, occupations which provided subsistence. (Barmaids in London got 6d or 7d.) As for children, whose labour was indispensable, 'children have children's wages'. Weavers were paid by the piece. And 'mark that the clothiers set the price'. By the time the earnings had been split three ways, between the two men and a boy needed to operate a loom, weavers earned 6d, and for that had to work from four in the morning until eight o'clock at night, three hours more than in most occupations. Tailors earning 4d a day with meals were better off. The clothiers claimed that weavers did not wear out their shoes and clothing like labouring men, and that they needed less to eat. Carew believed that weaving in fact took a heavy toll in hose and doublets, and he believed that weavers were less healthy than labourers, and died at an earlier age.[54]

Turning to the shearmen, with their teasels and giant shears for finishing the cloth, Carew pretended ignorance. 'I am not privy to their wages.' Here he was on a sticky wicket, since shearmen were thought to be well off, earning perhaps 10d a day. But Carew said that he had yet to meet a rich shearman. Their hours were long, the capital outlay heavy, and the work very seasonal.[55]

And now Carew began to play the economist on the edge of the socialist theory of labour value. The profit enjoyed by the clothiers was made possible by low wages. It could be expressed as 3d or 4d out of every weaver's pocket, 2d from each spinner, a penny or halfpenny from every working child, amounting to 10s of value added to every cloth made. If the annual output from a single clothier was 500 cloths, which in some extreme cases it was, then here was a tidy profit of £250 a year. Clothiers might argue that their profits were made by clever dealings in the market place. Carew doubted that, but asked, if that were the case, what was that but usury? But there was no doubt in his mind that the employers drew their large profits from cheap labour, 'which is miserable gain, as if a man should rob the spittle house'.[56] The result: some clothiers worth twenty thousand pounds, some weavers, after twenty years of toil, worth twenty groats. This was 'the enriching of two or three in a town . . . the impoverishing of many'. For the poor, life was lived on the edge, and survival depended upon good health, no child at the breast, and a cow or two.[57]

At this point, Carew became very technical and explained in detail that he had in his sights only the 'blue men', not those involved in the new 'Dutch' work of bays and says. 'You may see that those that spin for clothiers do four knots in every penny more than those that spin Dutch work.' And so he went on, proving rather than merely alleging that conditions in the new draperies were more benign.[58] Now if the new draperies predominated in Bildeston (which perhaps they did), and if the sermon was preached at Bildeston (which is far from certain), then perhaps the *Caveat* was not as close to the local bone as it may appear at first sight to have been.

Finally Carew put the moral and religious boot in. It was said that clothiers were charitable to the poor. 'They bid their poor work-folks at Christmas to a dinner.' But what was it to leave five or ten pounds to the poor at death, compared with what had been extracted in life? Let the clothiers pay decent wages and forget their charity! Clothiers were also said to be religious, 'the specialest men' in their towns. But pray, what was religion? The Apostle James came back, quick as a flash. 'Pure religion and undefiled before God is this, to visit the fatherless and widows in their adversity.'[59]

Can Carew really have preached his sermon as it was printed, with all those facts and figures? Perhaps. He explains: 'Because some clothiers have showed deaf ears in hearing it, I would see if they had better eyes to read it.'[60] But what good could it have done? Carew's motive is inaccessible. He went on living among the clothiers and weavers of Bildeston for another fifteen years. When he died, in harvest time 1616, he left nothing to the poor but was concerned about his wife's interest in his still unharvested corn. And indeed Margaret Carew seems to have had few pennies to rub together by the time she died a few years later. By then, only one of those nine children was mentioned in her will. We do not know what happened to the offspring, except for the eldest son, George, who went to Oxford and became a London clergyman.[61] Perhaps Carew had gone out of his way to be helpful to the poor in his lifetime.[62] And the same may be true of the Bildeston clothiers, whose surviving wills left little or nothing to charitable uses, rather less than Carew had suggested was the norm.[63] None of the Bildeston employers remembered their own 'work folks' in their wills. But to look only through the eyeglass of wills is to suffer an almost certain optical illusion, and we know nothing about the practical, casual, day-to-day charity of such people in life.

What of the ascertainable facts of the economy and society of Bildeston otherwise? (And we cannot be sure that Carew's sermon was preached in, or directed at, Bildeston.) I have published my findings elsewhere.[64] The evidence of wills and inventories suggests that the town was by no means as polarised as Carew's sermon alleged. Some weavers, and some shearmen, were possessed of property and had interests which makes one hesitate to call them a proletariat. Indeed, the semantic distinction between 'clothier' and 'clothworker' proves on examination to be hard to sustain. To use a Victorian analogy, it is not clear that those who made jam and those who ate it already lived in different places. But no doubt there was biting poverty in Bildeston, which we should not expect a few wills to disclose; and that poverty would worsen as the successive industrial recessions of the seventeenth century bit deep.

Nor should we forget that from no later than 1565 the inhabitants were subjected to a regular poor rate, which was effectively involuntary, and became legally compulsory with the passage of the Elizabethan Poor Law.[65] Those parishioners who remembered the poor in their wills usually made arrangements through 'collectors' – after 1597, 'overseers'. Private and a kind of public charity were tending to merge, as personal donations were administered by representatives of the community. That being the case, the concentration of the puritan literature on the voluntarism of individuals, rather than the legal responsibilities of communities, looks dated. Carew seems to have thought that the poor rate amounted to peanuts. But recent work on Hadleigh, a mere seven miles from Bildeston, based on a continuous series of collectors' accounts running from 1579 to 1596, demonstrates on the contrary that private charity in the form of testamentary bequests was of minor significance in comparison with the very substantial funds derived from the poor rate, which came to as much as £180 in a single year, disbursed to some 120–130 needy persons, mostly pensioners.[66] As for statistics for the totality of the resources devoted to social security, nationally and in Bildeston, expressed as a percentage of the Gross National (or parochial) Product – figures which the Thomas Carews of this world would love to deploy – that is an unattainable pot of gold at the end of the rainbow.

Did godly religion assist the poor? It seems to have done so in some places, and, according to the preachers, it ought to have done so. But Hadleigh, John Craig tells us, was not an especially godly town.[67] And yet Marjorie McIntosh's Hadleigh did very well, perhaps exceptionally well, by its poor. The prescriptive literature on this subject, like the literature on domestic relations or child-rearing, is a better guide to certain perceptions and attitudes than to social reality. Contemporaries thought that the yeomen of England were an endangered species, when they were more numerous than ever before. John Stow believed that charity in Elizabethan London was dead – which, as with Mark Twain, was an exaggeration.[68]

But Thomas Carew is different and takes some explaining. Godly religion in post-Reformation Suffolk has been seen as a uniting and ameliorating bond, providing opportunities for the energies of yeoman and clothier elites, harmonising such interests with those of the ruling gentry and their preachers, the famous alliance of 'magistracy and ministry'.[69] But perhaps this was at the expense of the poor, in a society in which the widening gap between the haves and the have-nots began to count for more than the traditional gradations in the social hierarchy. Carew is almost alone in telling us that in Elizabethan Suffolk, the 'social miracle' (to borrow a phrase from John Bossy) may have been a hollow sham.[70] And he is the more convincing for supplying us with facts, informing us, for example, that for the poor Sunday was a day for washing clothes and fetching firewood, rather than for going to church.[71] Well, yes, it must have been so.

If Carew was a lone voice for the poor, communicating with them and not down to them, I have no idea what made him such a voice.[72] The enigma reminds me of the case of a Calabrian christian socialist priest of our own century, Don Carlo de Cardona. Jonathan Steinberg tells us that he cannot explain Don Carlo, why he should have become a priest or his brother an active communist, why this particular bourgeois family 'should have a burning commitment to social justice'. And then Steinberg extrapolates, 'it takes an astonishing amount of evidence to "explain" the smallest historical event'. And he quotes David Hume: 'Nothing is more requisite for a true philosopher than to restrict the intemperate desire of searching into causes.'[73] Well, Thomas Carew had a cause, and in the absence of an astonishing amount of evidence, we cannot know what it was. But since historians are not philosophers, that will not stop us wondering.

NOTES

* I acknowledge the profit derived from discussions of this essay at the Cambridge Church History Seminar, a Lilley Colloquium held at the National Center for the Humanities, NC, with Professor Peter Lake and colleagues at Princeton University, and from the suggestions of Professor John Rilling of the University of Richmond, Virginia.

1. Christopher Hill, 'William Perkins and the Poor', *Past & Present* 2 (1952), 32–50. See also 'The Poor and the Parish', chapter 7 of Hill's *Society and Puritanism in Pre-Revolutionary England* (London, 1964).

2. John Walsh, 'John Wesley and the Community of Goods', in K. Robbins (ed.), *Protestant Evangelicalism: Britain, Ireland, Germany and America c. 1750– c. 1950. Essays in Honour of W. R. Ward*, Studies in Church History, Subsidia 7 (Oxford, 1990), p. 36.

3. In full, *A caveat for craftsmen and clothiers*. Hereafter *Sermons*. For a fuller treatment of Carew's *Caveat* and its gestation and context than is possible on this occasion, see my 'Christian Socialism in Elizabethan Suffolk: Thomas Carew and his *Caveat for clothiers*', in C. Rawcliffe, R. Virgoe and R. Wilson (eds.), *Counties and Communities: Essays on East Anglian History Presented to Hassell Smith* (Norwich, 1996), pp. 161–78.

4. Carew, *Sermons*, Sigs. o5v, s8v–Tr.

5. R. L. Greaves, *Religion and Society in Elizabethan England* (Minneapolis, 1981).

6. Paul Slack, *Poverty and Policy in Tudor and Stuart England* (Harlow, 1988), pp. 149–56; Paul Slack, *From Reformation to Improvement: Public Welfare in Early Modern England* (Oxford, 1999), chapter 2, 'Godly Cities'.

7. David Underdown, *Fire from Heaven: The Life of an English Town in the Seventeenth Century* (London, 1992); Paul Slack, 'The Public Conscience of Henry Sherfield', in J. Morrill *et al.* (eds.), *Public Duty and Private Conscience in Seventeenth-Century England: Essays Presented to G. E. Aylmer* (Oxford, 1993), pp. 151–71; Ferdinand Nicholls, *The life and death of Mr Ignatius Jurdaine* (1655).

8. William Whately, *The poore mans advocate, Or, a treatise of liberality to the needy, delivered in sermons* (1637), pp. 4, 105, 101.

9. William Perkins, 'Cases of Conscience: Sect. 2, Concerning the Moderation of Appetite in the Uses of Riches', in *Workes*, vol. II (1617), 125b.

10. Patrick Collinson, *The Religion of Protestants: The Church in English Society 1559–1625* (Oxford, 1982), p. 219n.

11. Slack, *Poverty and Policy*, p. 27.

12. Thus the Geneva version, following Tyndale. The Authorised Version of 1611 is responsible for the more familiar (and less urgent) 'as we have opportunity'.

13. In addition to Perkins, Downame and Bernard, and Whately's *The poore mans advocate*, and in chronological order of publication, Henry Bedel, *A sermon exhorting to pitie the poore* (1571); H(enry) A(rthington), *Provision for the poore, now in penurie* (1597); Robert Allen, *The oderifferous garden of charitie, A treatise of christian beneficence* (1600, 1603); Thomas Cooper, *The art of giving. Describing the true nature and right use of liberality* (1615); John Rogers, *A treatise of love* (1632).

14. Ian Breward, *The Work of William Perkins* (Appleford, Abingdon, 1970), p. 75.

15. Bedel, *A sermon*, Sig. Biv.

16. Allen, *The oderifferous garden*, p. 39.

17. Downame, *The plea of the poore*, pp. 10–11.

18. Bernard, *The ready way*, pp. 19–20.

19. Perkins, *Workes*, II. 126b, 198b; Rogers, *A treatise of love*, p. 188; Downame, *The plea of the poore*, p. 36.

20. John Walsh suggests a patristic basis ('John Wesley and the Community of Goods', pp. 35, 38–41).

21. Whately, *The poore mans advocate*, p. 108; Bernard, *The ready way*, p. 412; Perkins, *Workes*, II. 144b–145a; Rogers, *A treatise of love*, pp. 213–14; Michael Sparke, *The poore orphanes court, or orphans cry* (1636), Sig. B.

22. Bayley quoted by Hill, *Society and Puritanism*, p. 289.

23. Bernard, *The ready way*, pp. 411–21; Allen, *The oderifferous garden*, Epistle, pp. 126–7.

24. Slack, *Poverty and Policy*, p. 20.

25. Perkins, *Workes*, II. 145b; Downame, *The plea of the poore*, Epistle, p. 130; Bernard, *The ready way*, p. 398.

26. Steve Hindle, 'Exclusion Crises: Poverty, Migration and the Limits of Parochial Responsibility in English Rural Communities, *c.* 1560–1660', *Rural History* 7 (1996), 125–49.

27. Quoted in Patrick Collinson, *Godly People: Essays on English Protestantism and Puritanism* (London, 1983), p. 547.

28. Downame, *The plea of the poore*, p. 133.

29. Allen, *The oderifferous garden*, p. 46.

30. Whately, *The poore mans advocate*, p. 110.

31. Collinson, *The Religion of Protestants*, p. 262.

32. Christopher Kitching, 'Fire Disasters and Fire Relief in Sixteenth-Century England: The Nantwich Fire of 1583', *Bulletin of the Institute of Historical Research* 54 (1981), 171–87.

33. Arnold Hunt, 'The Lord's Supper in Early Modern England', *Past & Present* 161 (1998), 51–4.

34. Cooper, *The art of giving*, pp. 17–20. See Collinson, *The Religion of Protestants*, chapter 6, 'Voluntary Religion: Its Forms and Tendencies', and *idem*, *Godly People*, pp. 467–98, 527–62.

35. Depositions in the Consistory Court of Norwich *c.* 1590, 'super articulos contra Thomam Carew clericum', Norfolk Record Office, DEP 24, fos. 251v–58v.

36. Whately, *The poore mans advocate*, p. 109; Arthington, *Provisions for the poore*, Sigs. B2v–3r; Downame, *The plea of the poore*, pp. 39–40.

37. Hill, 'William Perkins and the Poor'; Hill, *Society and Puritanism*, pp. 267–8; Slack, *Poverty and Policy*, chapter 7, 'Projects and Policies, 1570–1660', and pp. 27–32; Joan Thirsk, *Economic Policy and Projects. The Development of a Consumer Society in Early Modern England* (Oxford, 1978).

38. Slack, *Poverty and Policy*, pp. 128, 153.

39. Rogers, *Treatise of love*, p. 237.

40. Philip Jones, *Certaine sermons preached of late at Ciceter in the countie of Glocester, upon a portion of the first chapter of the Epistle of James* (1588), Sigs. DV, E3r–5r, A4r.

41. Evidence from the dedicatory preface to *Certaine sermons*.

42. Rogers, *Treatise of love*, pp. 224–5. See the orders drawn up by the ministers and 'ancients' of Dedham in the 1580s in R. G. Usher (ed.), *The Presbyterian Movement in the Reign of Queen Elizabeth as Illustrated by the Minute Book of the Dedham Classis 1582–1589*, Camden third series 8 (1905). Downame, *The plea of the poore*, pp. 56–60, rather spoils the effect by remarking that if we would sometimes visit the poor at their houses, 'they would not so often have occasion to visit us at ours'.

43. Robert Wilkinson, *A sermon preached at North-Hampton the 21. day of Iune late past before the Lord Lieutenant of the County and the rest of the Commissioners there assembled vpon occasion of the late Rebellion and Riots in those parts* (1607), Sigs. D2, D3r, Epistle.

44. Richard Baxter, *The poor husbandman's advocate* (1691), ed. by F. J. Powicke as *The Reverend Richard Baxter's Last Treatise* (Manchester, 1926).

45. For the details, see my 'Christian Socialism in Elizabethan Suffolk', pp. 161–3.

46. West Suffolk Record Office, Bildeston terrier, 24 September 1627, Bildeston Parish Register, FB 79/D1/1.

47. References in my 'Christian Socialism in Elizabethan Suffolk', p. 163, nn. 27–31.

48. For what follows, see ibid., pp. 163–4.

49. *Suffolk in the XVIIth Century: The Breviary of Suffolk by Robert Reyce 1618 . . . with Notes by Lord Frances Hervey* (London, 1902), pp. 21–3; Carew, *Sermons*, Sig. v8R.

50. Ibid., Sigs. T6v–7r, Y2r.

51. Ibid., Sig. T3v.

52. Ibid., Sigs. N3r–4r, T2, T7r, X3r.

53. Ibid., Sig. T7v.

54. Ibid., Sigs. T8, vr–4v.

55. Ibid., Sigs. v3v–4v.

56. Ibid., Sigs. v4v, v6r. Carew's 'socialist' insight was not quite unique, but was anticipated in a petition from neighbouring Hadleigh in 1539: W. Page (ed.), *VCH, Suffolk*, vol. II (1907), p. 259.

57. Carew, *Sermons*, Sig. v6.

58. Ibid., Sig. X. A petition of 1615 supports Carew's analysis (PRO, S.P. 14/80/13). But, according to George Unwin, 'this happy state of affairs' did not last (*VCH, Suffolk*, II, p. 267), while by the 1620s farmers' wives were competing for a limited amount of employment as spinners, taking bread out of the mouths of the poor (BL, MS. Add. 39245, fo. 65).

59. Carew, *Sermons*, Sigs. x6v–Y.

60. Ibid., Sig. T7r.

61. West Suffolk Record Office, IC 500/1/75 (119), IC 500/1/85 (26); Joseph Foster, *Alumni Oxonienses, 1500–1714*, 4 vols. (Oxford, 1891–2), I, p. 237.

62. As, allegedly, did a more famous preacher whom he plagiarised, Richard Greenham of Dry Drayton: Samuel Clarke, *The lives of thirty-two English divines* (1677), pp. 12–13.

63. There are nine surviving wills made by Bildeston men who described themselves as clothiers. Three left nothing to the poor, six something. But what was the £20 left to the poor by William Wade, the most generous legacy, when his total estate far exceeded £2000? (Details in Collinson, 'Christian Socialism in Elizabethan Suffolk', pp. 169–70.)

64. Ibid., pp. 167–9.

65. F. S. Growse, *Materials for a History of Bildeston in the County of Suffolk* (privately printed in 25 copies, 1902), extracting from a set of churchwardens' accounts no longer extant.

66. Marjorie McIntosh, 'Networks of Care in Elizabethan English Towns: The Example of Hadleigh, Suffolk', in Peregrine Horden and R. M. Smith (eds.), *The Locus of Care: Families, Communities, Institutions, and the Provision of Welfare since Antiquity* (London, 1998).

67. John Craig, 'Reformers, Conflict, and Revisionism: The Reformation in Sixteenth-Century Hadleigh', *Historical Journal* 42 (1999), 1–23.

68. Ian Archer, 'The Nostalgia of John Stow', in David L. Smith *et al.* (eds.), *The Theatrical City: Culture, Theatre and Politics in London, 1576–1649* (Cambridge, 1995), pp. 17–34.

69. Diarmaid MacCulloch, *Suffolk and the Tudors* (Oxford, 1986), chapter 11, 'Alternative Patterns of Politics'; Patrick Collinson, 'Godly Preachers and Zealous Magistrates in Elizabethan East Anglia: the Roots of Dissent', in E. S. Leedham Green (ed.), *Religious Dissent in East Anglia*, Cambridge Antiquarian Society (Cambridge, 1991), pp. 20–5.

70. 'Almost only': but see another whistle-blowing sermon preached as the Clare lecture by Bezaleel Carter, *Christ his last will, and John his legacy* (1621), discussed in Collinson, 'Christian Socialism in Elizabethan Suffolk', pp. 170–1.

71. Carew, *Sermons*, Sig. v6v.

72. But for the half suggestion that Carew's supposedly gentry class connections may have inclined him to look down on mere clothiers, and bishops, see Collinson, 'Christian Socialism in Elizabethan Suffolk', p. 161.

73. Jonathan Steinberg, 'The Poor in Christ: Peasants, Priests and Politics in the Consenza General Strike, November 1920', in Derek Beales and Geoffrey Best (eds.), *History, Society and the Churches: Essays in Honour of Owen Chadwick* (Cambridge, 1985), pp. 257–78.

CHAPTER 15

Realising a utopian dream: the transformation of the clergy in the diocese of York, 1500–1630

Claire Cross

The Utopians expected their priests to be 'of extraordinary holiness' and in consequence they possessed 'very few'. After Luther had shattered the unity of western Christendom and Sir Thomas More rallied to the defence of the Catholic Church, in *A Dialogue concerning Heresies* the latter repeated his conviction that excessive numbers had largely been responsible for the failings of the English secular clergy:

And as for me touchynge the choyce of prestys, I coulde not well devyse better provysyons than are by the lawes of the chyrche provyded all redy, if they were as well kept as they be well made. But for the nomber, I wold surely se suche a way therin, that we sholde not have suche a rabell . . .

The authorities, he believed, needed to implement a far more selective ordination system to redress the abuse: 'yf the bysshops wolde ones take unto presthed better ley men and fewer . . . all the matter were more than halfe amended . . .'[1]

The diocese of York certainly bears out More's assertion that men had been flocking to enter the Church in the early sixteenth century. The whole process, however, was reversed in the 1530s, when the dissolution first of the monasteries and then of the chantries greatly reduced the demand for priests and the numbers seeking ordination fell accordingly. All evidence of ordinations at York in the middle of the sixteenth century has disappeared, but when ordinations re-emerge in the archiepiscopal registers at the beginning of Elizabeth's reign the numbers stay at the level to which they had sunk in the early 1540s. Though scarcely cause and effect, hand in hand with the reduction in ordinands from about 1570 there begins a steady improvement in their educational qualifications which reaches its culmination in the reign of James I. Within less than a century the transformation More had sought, but could not realistically have hoped to have seen, had been achieved, though in a Protestant and not, as he would have wanted, in an English Catholic Church. This analysis of York ordinations between 1500 and 1630 sets out to chart and explain the change.[2]

In the early sixteenth century more northerners were entering the Church than ever before. In the *annus mirabilis* of 1508 alone the archbishop of York's suffragan admitted 444 candidates to the priesthood. Ordinations never approached this level again; usually during Savage's archiepiscopate the annual number of priests oscillated between 200 and 300. Under his successor, Christopher Bainbridge, priestly ordinations remained constant at around an average of 250 a year. During Wolsey's term of office the figure declined somewhat to between 150 and 270, though his suffragans ordained as many as 204 priests in 1528. These figures were very high on any reckoning, and exceeded the number of priests being ordained in a comparable diocese such as Lincoln, and possibly in the majority of dioceses elsewhere in England in the generation before the Reformation.[3]

Normally, though not invariably, the York archiepiscopal registers state the educational qualifications of these ordinands. Some sixty-five priests – a tiny fraction, around one per cent, of something in excess of 6,700 priests ordained at York between 1500 and 1528 – seem to have studied at a university. (The number rises to just over a hundred if those who became acolytes, subdeacons or deacons, but not priests, at York are included.) About two thirds of the sixty-five had graduated from English or (in some cases) continental universities, twenty as bachelors of arts, ten as masters of arts, ten as bachelors of civil or canon law (usually both), two as doctors of laws and one, perhaps significantly a foreigner, as doctor of medicine. Some of these clergy later went on to take degrees in theology, but none had obtained these qualifications on ordination. Of the third who probably attended Oxford or Cambridge but did not proceed to a degree, two gave their title as St Edmund's priory in Cambridge, while no fewer than eleven cited St John's House, in the process of being converted into a college by John Fisher, and three Barnwell priory just beyond the town. At Oxford, but on nothing like the same scale, one or two priests had obtained sponsorship from St Frideswide's priory or Osney abbey.

Career-minded clergy had long been aware that an academic degree opened the gate to mobility and promotion in the Church. Of the forty-three graduates ordained priest at York in the first third of the sixteenth century three, Thomas Stanley, John Bell and Francis Malet, ended their lives as bishops. Stanley, an illegitimate son of Edward Stanley, Lord Mounteagle, apparently studied at Oxford and on the continent, but did not take a degree before he was ordained deacon and priest at York in 1517. In addition to possessing the rectories of Badsworth and Barwick-in-Elmet in Yorkshire, and Winwick, North Meols and Wigan in Lancashire, he held the bishopric of Sodor and Man from 1530 to 1545, when he was deprived by Henry VIII, and then again from 1555 until his death in 1570.[4]

The Stanleys had come to regard the see of Sodor and Man as a family preserve, but it is noteworthy that by the sixteenth century a member of the clan felt it necessary to attain at least a tincture of higher education before claiming his hereditary right. The other two graduate priests to achieve a bishopric seem to have risen more through academic merit than social background. This certainly seems to have been the case with John Bell, LLB, somewhat surprisingly (since he seems to have had no previous or subsequent connection with the diocese) ordained subdeacon, deacon and priest at York in 1504. A native of Worcestershire and educated first at Balliol College, Oxford, and then at Cambridge, Bell acted as vicar general to the bishop of Worcester before entering royal service and actively furthering Henry VIII's divorce. Consecrated bishop of Worcester in 1539, he resigned his see in somewhat mysterious circumstances in 1543 and lived in retirement in Clerkenwell until his death thirteen years later.[5]

The third graduate priest advanced to the episcopate, on the other hand, originated in Yorkshire. Francis Malet of Normanton, made priest at York in September 1526 when already a Cambridge MA, went on to take the degrees of BD in 1534 and DD in 1535 and as a client of Cromwell became Master of Michaelhouse and served as vice-chancellor of the university in both 1536 and 1540. A chaplain to Princess Mary, he fell foul of the council of Edward VI, being imprisoned for a time in the Tower, but came into his own in Mary's reign. Having been made dean of Lincoln on Cranmer's deprivation in 1554, he was nominated bishop of Salisbury in October 1558, but was never consecrated because of the queen's death the following month. He conformed under Elizabeth, and, though suspected of Catholic leanings, retained the deanery of Lincoln till his death in 1570.[6]

Although on occasions employed for diplomatic or propaganda purposes by the central government, some of the graduates ordained priest at York in the first part of the sixteenth century essentially remained within the university world for the whole of their lives. Robert Wakefeld, MA, ordained subdeacon, deacon and priest at York as a fellow of St John's, Cambridge in 1520, illustrates the long-established tendency of educated northern clergy to make their career in the south. Probably a native of Pontefract, after graduating in arts at Cambridge, with Fisher's encouragement he then went to the continent to study biblical languages. Having taught Hebrew briefly at Louvain, he moved to Tübingen University before being recalled to England in 1523 to lecture in Hebrew at Cambridge. Later in the decade he helped promote the royal divorce. At the request of Oxford University he was dispatched to teach Hebrew there in 1530 and appointed to a canonry at Christ Church, which he held until his death in 1537. Learning and languages clearly ran in the family: in 1540 his brother and executor, Thomas Wakefeld, became the first Regius Professor of Hebrew at Cambridge.[7]

Other Yorkshire graduates besides the Wakefeld brothers seem to have seen their academic qualifications as a means to geographical mobility. Gilbert Haldesworth, of Halifax, LLB of Oxford when ordained subdeacon, deacon and priest at York in 1500, acquired the Sussex livings of St Thomas at Cliffe, Lewes in 1506 and Ringmer in 1511. Giving St John's House as his title when ordained priest in 1505, Richard Sharp had a rather longer career in the university, rising to be Master of St John's College in 1515. Fisher, to whom he was chaplain, seems to have been responsible for his move to the diocese of Rochester, where he obtained the rectory of Chislehurst in 1520 and that of Bromley in 1523. He died in Kent in 1528. William White of York followed a very similar path. Ordained deacon and priest at York in 1506 and 1507, with Balliol College as his title, he supplicated for the BTh degree in 1516 after sixteen years' study in logic, philosophy and theology, and held the mastership of Balliol from 1525 to 1539. He also secured the livings of Oddington in Gloucestershire, Gresford in Denbighshire and St Lawrence, Jewry, London, where he died in 1546. John Bicardike, MA, of Bolton Percy, made acolyte, subdeacon, deacon and priest at York in 1521 and 1522, took his first degree at Oxford, but then moved to Cambridge before being admitted vicar of Walton on Thames, Surrey, in 1528.[8]

The inclusion of clergy who received lower orders at York, but did not return for ordination as priests, yet further emphasises the loss of native graduates to the region. Already an Oxford MA and fellow of Balliol when made an acolyte at York in December 1525, George Cottes of Leeds seems to have had little further contact with the West Riding. After a long academic career, during which he proceeded MA, BTh and DTh and in 1539 as Cromwell's nominee was elected Master of Balliol, he became bishop of Chester in 1554. A very similar route brought Owen Oglethorpe of Newton Kyme to the ecclesiastical heights. An Oxford MA when granted letters dimissory as a subdeacon from York in 1531, he also stayed in the university for many years, in this case as President of Magdalen. Consecrated bishop of Carlisle in 1557, he refused to take the oath of supremacy on Elizabeth's accession and so forfeited his see. Perhaps in recognition of the crucial part education had played in his career, at his death late in 1559 he endowed a school and hospital at Tadcaster.[9]

Despite this overall drain of graduates away from the diocese, not all who came back to York for ordination permanently abandoned the county of their birth. The son of John Staneley, and both born and ordained priest in York with St Edmund's priory in Cambridge as his title, William Staneley took in succession the degrees of BA in 1504, MA in 1507, BD in 1522 and DD in 1524. In addition to the rectory of Ellington in Huntingdonshire, which he held from 1517 until his death in 1536, he appears to have been for the last four years of his life vicar of Otley. Already treasurer of the church of St John in Beverley when he received the orders of acolyte, subdeacon, deacon and priest in 1508 and 1509, William Tate, LLD, also of York, obtained the livings of Everingham and Thwing in Yorkshire before becoming treasurer of York in 1522 and canon of Windsor from 1534 until his death in 1540. John Brandesby, MA, ordained priest in 1517 with a title from Watton priory, in addition to prebends at Lincoln, Southwell and York and the living of Wittering in Northamptonshire possessed at different times during his clerical career the Yorkshire livings of Sproatley, Sutton in Holderness, Settrington, Kirby Wiske and Beeford, and died in York. Gregory Grice, a fellow of Magdalen College, Oxford, ordained subdeacon, deacon and priest in York in 1520 and 1521, was in 1535 appointed rector of the free chapel of Thirsk.[10]

Damp and low-lying, the two English universities cannot have been very healthy places to study in the early sixteenth century, and some York ordinands did not live to reap the rewards of their labours. Laurence Litster, BA, of Yorkshire, ordained priest at York in 1501 to the title of St Edmund's priory in Cambridge, took his MA in 1504 and then died in the university in 1508, a fellow of St Catharine's Hall. Citing his fellowship at Balliol as his title when ordained subdeacon, deacon and priest at York early in 1506, Peter Waide, BA, was buried in Oxford the following year. Alexander Lake, BA, made priest at York in April 1503, had just proceeded MA on his death in Oxford in January 1509. Giving Balliol College as his title when priested at York in September 1522, Edward Burton, BA, spent seven years as a fellow of his college and accumulated a library of over forty books before he died in 1529.[11]

For the universities, as for the English Church at large, the Henrician Reformation marked the end of an era. The numbers of students slumped as the demand for clergy fell, and a degree was never again the passport to high office in quite the way it had been in the later Middle Ages. The period 1542 to 1560, for which no ordination records survive, constitutes a dark period in the history of the diocese of York. For one and perhaps two decades former monks, friars and chantry priests may well have supplied the majority of candidates for livings, though it seems unlikely that Holgate undertook no ordinations at all, while a novel cache of clerical testimonials indicates that Heath's suffragans were almost certainly performing ordinations in the Marian period. All, however, is conjecture until the ordination lists reappear soon after Elizabeth's accession, to reveal a cataclysmic decline in numbers from the first three decades of the century. Whereas from 1500 to 1528 between 200 and 300 priests were ordained in the diocese every year, from 1561 to 1575, that is during the archiepiscopates of Thomas Young and Edmund Grindal, they only once (in 1566) reached fifty-six and in most years hovered at around half that figure. Young and Grindal ordained approximately the same number of priests: Young 159 priests over seven years, Grindal 131 over six years. As death took its toll of the clergy from the pre-Reformation period, Young appears to have accepted for ordination all the candidates who presented themselves, to alleviate the ministerial shortfall. His successor, in contrast, pursued a new and consciously reformist policy. While Young and his suffragans ordained no graduates at all, Grindal, in addition to the highly educated beneficed clergy he succeeded in attracting to the diocese in his six years at York, ordained nine graduates and five *literati* to the priesthood. Around the same number of graduates were becoming priests as in the 1520s, but now they formed a far higher proportion of a much smaller whole.[12]

In the aftermath of the Rebellion of the Earls and the attempt to reinstate the old religion, these graduate ordinands played a major role in Grindal's campaign for the protestant evangelisation of the north. The most highly qualified academically of these new clergy, and probably the most influential, was Edmund Bunney. The eldest son of Richard Bunney of Bunny Hall in Wakefield, one-time treasurer of Berwick, who had suffered for his Protestantism under Mary, Edmund Bunney proceeded BA at Oxford in 1560. At this juncture his father, having intended that he should become a lawyer, deprived him of his inheritance when he insisted upon entering the Church. He nevertheless continued at Oxford, taking the degrees of MA in 1565 and BD in 1570. Grindal then brought him back to the north as his chaplain, appointing him subdean of York Minster in 1570 and ordaining him priest in July of the following year. The archbishop in addition collated him to the prebend of Wistow and the rectory of Bolton Percy in 1575. For over a quarter of a century Bunney utilised these livings to finance itinerant preaching throughout the diocese, for good measure publishing an impressive range of protestant books which included *The Whole Summe of Christian Religion*, an abridgement of Calvin's *Institutes*, *The Coronation of David*, *The Scepter of Judah* and an expurgated version of Robert Parson's *Christian Directory*.[13]

Christopher Shute, MA, admitted to the diaconate in 1572 and the priesthood in 1575 and made vicar of Giggleswick by Grindal the following year, similarly lived the life of a model protestant pastor. Licensed to preach throughout the province, he fulfilled his obligations regardless of his auditory, of whom at least one thought it 'a shame for him to tarry so longe in the pulpytt'. In addition to founding a remarkable clerical dynasty, with five sons all following their father into the Church, during a ministry of almost fifty years he furthered the preaching exercises around Gargrave and established a tradition of radical Protestantism which persisted in Craven to the Civil War and beyond.[14]

Grindal also made it possible for two generations of the Whitacres family to promote the Protestant cause in Yorkshire for almost three quarters of a century. Edward Whitacres, a Cambridge MA admitted priest by the archbishop in 1575, served from 1578 until his death in 1612 as rector of Thornhill. His son, Gamaliel, another Cambridge graduate, returned to the West Riding in 1609 as an assistant to his father and then in 1615 acquired the living of Kirk Burton, where he remained until 1643.[15]

Thomas Utye, *literatus*, who matriculated as a sizar from Christ's College, Cambridge, in 1571, but did not study long enough in the university to obtain a degree, was ordained by Grindal deacon in 1574 and priest in 1575. In 1578 he became vicar of the important town parish of St Mary's, Beverley, where in the 1590s he introduced regular monthly communions in accordance with the practice of the continental Reformed churches.[16]

Unlike the majority of the graduates ordained at York in the earlier part of the century, most of this little band of university-educated ordinands stayed in the diocese, if not in the county, for the rest of their lives. Robert Blackwoode, BA, made deacon and priest on 14 April 1574, and admitted in November 1576 to the vicarage of Walesby and a year later to that of Rotherham, on both occasions on the presentation of the earl of

Shrewsbury, ended his life as rector of Kirton in Nottinghamshire, where he died in 1603. Promotion came equally quickly to John Campyon, BA. Made deacon and priest on 12 July 1571 by letters dimissory from the diocese of Chester, he became Master of the Hospital of St Mary Magdalen in Ripon in July 1573. Described as a student at Oxford at his ordination as deacon and priest at Bishopthorpe on 13 September 1574, William Bucktrowte received on the very same day the vicarage of Aberford from the president and fellows of Oriel College. He then used the income from his living to finance his university studies, not taking his BA degree until March 1578.[17]

Preferment, however, did not come so rapidly to all these university-educated clergy. Robert Gylmyn, *literatus*, had to wait six years after his ordination before obtaining in October 1581 the rectory of Kirby Underdale. An even longer interval elapsed before Richard Webster, *literatus*, ordained at York in 1574, became rector of Adel on the out-skirts of Leeds in 1581. Christopher Parkinson, who had worked his way through Cambridge as a sizar at Clare College, taking his BA in 1574, his MA three years later, and being ordained deacon and priest in York in 1575, only acquired the rectory of St Nicholas *alias* Holme in Beverley in March 1582.[18]

Not even Grindal in this intermediate period could ensure that all the graduates he ordained went on to employ their talents in the diocese. In the earlier part of his career John Sykes appears to have had a very tenu-ous connection with the region. A sizar from Jesus College, Cambridge, admitted BA in 1571, he was made deacon at York in May 1575, but priest at Ely in the succeeding autumn at the canonical age of twenty-five. He then acquired the Cambridgeshire living of West Wratting in 1577 before moving in 1603 to the rectory of Kirton in Nottinghamshire, where he died in 1622.[19]

Richard Richardson, BA, ordained deacon and priest at York in 1574 before he went on to take his MA at Cambridge in 1576, seems never to have held a Yorkshire benefice, settling instead in the diocese of Lincoln, where in 1576 he became rector of Saxby and in 1578 vicar of Barnetby. Yet while some of these graduates may have failed to exercise their min-istry in the diocese, only Thomas Story, BA, seems to have fallen short of the standards expected of a protestant minister. Presented to Scaw-ton by Sir William Fairfax immediately after his ordination as deacon by Grindal in 1575, he resigned the rectory for that of Addlethorpe in Lincolnshire in 1577, where he was subsequently reported not to reside and to be living as a pluralist in the diocese of Chichester.[20]

On Grindal's translation to the archbishopric of Canterbury in January 1576 his successor, Edwin Sandys, vice-chancellor of Cambridge in 1553 and a fellow Marian exile, almost certainly continued the policy of attracting university graduates into the church, but no evidence of his ordinations now survives. When the ordination lists begin again under his successor, John Piers, early in 1589 the former strategy re-emerges with even greater clarity. In five and a half years at York Piers ordained a mere twenty-nine priests, but of these no fewer than twenty-five were graduates and one *literatus*. Matthew Hutton, archbishop from March 1595 until his death in January 1606, ordained many more priests than Piers: around twenty a year till the turn of the century, rising to over thirty in 1604. Given the increase of candidates he understandably failed to emulate Piers's achievement of almost 100 percent graduate ordinations, but still maintained a predominance of university men. Of the twenty priests ordained in 1600 eight were graduates, four *literati*; of the twenty ordained in 1602 twelve were graduates, one *literatus*; even more remarkably in 1604, when thirty-one men were admitted to the priesthood, eighteen were graduates, three *literati*. Then under Archbishop Toby Matthew an ideal pursued for more than a generation finally came to fruition. In an archiepiscopate which lasted from 1606 to 1628 he ordained only five priests who had apparently not received a university education, and this at a time when his ordinations were far more numerous than those performed by Piers, and significantly above those conducted by Hutton. In 1618, for example, when Matthew ordained thirty priests, twenty-nine were graduates, one *literatus*; when ordinations of priests rose to thirty-two in 1619, all were graduates. Even when the number of priests increased from an annual average of around thirty to a record fifty-two in 1625 and forty-eight in 1627, the very high level of graduates continued: forty-eight graduates and two *literati* in 1625, thirty-six graduates and twelve *literati* in 1627. By the reign of James I the archbishops of York were successfully implementing an all-graduate recruitment policy which would have been inconceivable in the earlier part of the sixteenth century.

To prevent them from becoming a charge upon the Church, medieval canon law required candidates to provide a guarantee of future clerical employment before ordination; but, as More realised, they could easily circumvent the regulations by citing their patrimony or, much more commonly, an assurance of support from a religious house. For a short time after the dissolution of the monasteries York ordinands supplied pledges from local noblemen and gentlemen; this expedient then lapsed, with the result that by Elizabeth's accession the ordination lists contain no information whatsoever about candidates' nominal or actual destinations. Once again the situation changes during Matthew's archiepiscopate when fuller record keeping makes it possible for first time to evaluate systematically the career opportunities of all York ordinands.[21]

For most of the years between 1608 and 1628, loose sheets of ordination particulars inserted into the Institution Act Books provide details of the posts to which the candidates were proceeding. On 25 September 1608, for example, when Matthew ordained eight priests at Cawood, three went straight to permanent livings: John Ronison, MA, to be parson of Thornton, Thomas North, MA, to be vicar of Firby and John Savage, MA, to be parson of Gotham. The remaining five had to content themselves with temporary employment: Francis Allott, M.A., with a curacy at Hemsworth, Henry Jeffray, BA, with a curacy at South Stainley, and Thomas Stephenson, MA, with a curacy at Warter, while John Hancock, MA, and Thomas Watt, MA, progressed to assistantships at Sheffield and Bubwith respectively. At a comparable ceremony in Bishopthorpe chapel ten years later, at which Matthew admitted another eight candidates to the priesthood, only one, Marmaduke Constable, MA, secured a clerical freehold (the rectory of Toft Newton); six others obtained curacies in Yorkshire and Lincolnshire parishes and one, Thomas Fryer, BA, a teaching post at Great Barugh. As the number of academically well-qualified candidates for the ministry increased, more and more found it necessary to serve an apprenticeship before they could hope to obtain a charge of their own.[22]

The English universities, which by the early seventeenth century were supplying this stream of graduates for the Church, have often been criticised for not providing a directly vocational education. Virtually all graduates presenting themselves for ordination at York as at other dioceses had followed an arts degree either to the BA or MA level, and scarcely any had gone on to study theology. Only through obligatory attendance at college chapels and university sermons supplemented by voluntary bible study in some of the more forward colleges would they have been exposed to the teaching and liturgy of the established Church. Consequently these assistant curacies, when properly supervised, could supply a very necessary stage of preparation for pastoral ministry.[23]

Whereas in the Elizabethan period in the diocese of York graduates could expect to obtain incumbencies, if not immediately on ordination like Edmund Bunney, at least within a reasonably short time thereafter, with the rapid rise in the number of graduates in the later sixteenth and early seventeenth centuries competition for livings became much more severe, and many ordinands without influential backing had little choice but accept a series of temporary posts in the hope of eventually reaching their goal. Particularly from the beginning of the seventeenth century a number regarded teaching as the first rung on the ladder.

Early in the reign of Charles I a few ordinands became tutors to the gentry, doubtless in the expectation that their patron might in the course of time advance their career in the church. In 1625 alone Francis Robinson, BA, went to Mr John Dawney's family and Thomas Phillipps, BA, joined Sir John Stanhope's household, while Matthew Stanton, BA, became schoolmaster to Sir Henry Slingsby's children. If they had entertained hopes of rapid promotion, they met with disappointment, for not one of the three seems to have secured a living in the diocese.[24]

Less susceptible to aristocratic oversight, Yorkshire grammar schools regularly furnished a number of established posts for newly ordained clergy. In 1619 John Belwood, a Cambridge MA, went as a deacon to be a schoolmaster in the city of York; another Cambridge graduate, William Smith, BA, in 1622 acquired a position at York free school; and in 1626 Abraham Dyson, *literatus* from Gonville and Caius College, also left Cambridge for a York school, apparently situated in St Saviour's parish. Belwood had to wait twelve years before he obtained the living of Dalby; Smith quickly transferred to Otley grammar school, where he remained for sixteen years and seems never to have left teaching. Other ordinands took appointments in schools in Skipton, Bingley, Knaresborough, Pocklington, Howden, Wakefield, Barnsley, Rotherham, Doncaster and Retford.[25]

Graduate inflation even forced some clerics to seek a livelihood in village schools. In 1618, for example, Edward Hodgson, BA, came from Trinity College, Oxford, to be a schoolmaster at Halsham in Holderness; in 1619 William Allerton, BA, forsook Peterhouse for Long Marston school; William Barker, BA, went from Trinity College, Cambridge, to teach in Brafferton in 1625. Of the three clerics only Allerton succeeded in gaining a living in the diocese, in 1626 securing the rectory of Goxhill, which he held until his death in 1661. These graduate clerical schoolmasters in their turn fed the stream of students proceeding to the universities in the first part of the seventeenth century, and further reinforced the presumption that a university education now constituted a necessary qualification for any post within the church.[26]

Some newly ordained clergy like Thomas Charter, in 1621 described as schoolmaster and curate of Thorpe Salvin, or Thomas Rawson, BA, who during his long teaching career at Sheffield grammar school served at least for a time as a curate in the nearby village of Dore, combined teaching with assisting in pastoral work. Others soon made the leap from school teaching to an assistant curacy. Roger Atey, BA, ordained deacon in December 1621 as a schoolmaster at Linton on the Wolds, gave a curacy at Bulmer as his title when priested in December the following year. William Calverley, schoolmaster at Haworth when made a deacon in September 1627, had become the curate at Thornton in Bradford parish when ordained priest only two months later.[27]

Many of these young clerics, moving like indentured servants from parish to parish at the year's end, discovered that they had to take on a succession of curacies before they could hope to gain a permanent cure. William Appleyard, BA, an assistant at Gargrave when made deacon in March 1612, had taken a curacy at Carleton in Craven when ordained priest less than a year later. Between May and September 1619 John Bewe, BA, went from being curate at Birkin to a curacy at Kirby Misperton. Curate at Sutton on Derwent in September 1625, John Barker, BA, had become curate at Goodmanham by the autumn of 1627. Such rapid changes at the beginning of a cleric's career seem to have been the norm in the diocese in the early Stuart period.[28]

For the fortunate few in the right place at the right time a curacy could lead to a permanent living. John More, BA, progressed from being curate of Humbleton in March 1609 to becoming vicar of the parish by the autumn of the same year, but such transitions seem to have been rare. A transfer from a curacy in one parish to a living elsewhere seems to have been rather more common. Curate at Holme on Spalding Moor when made a deacon in 1618, Henry Skinn, BA, had acquired Sherburn vicarage by the time he was ordained priest the next year. John Storr, BA, similarly moved from a curacy at Cayton in the spring of 1622 to an incumbency at Helperby the following autumn, while between March and June 1622 Leonard Moyser, MA, exchanged a curacy at Lockington for the vicarage of Pocklington.[29]

Birth and family ties undoubtedly accelerated promotion, and despite the greatly increased competition some graduates still managed to obtain a permanent living in the diocese immediately on ordination. Marmaduke Constable, MA, perhaps the son of William Constable of Drax, who in 1618 went directly from Queens' College, Cambridge to the rectory of Toft Newton, and his possible relative, Charles Constable, son of John Constable of Lazenby, gentleman, already the recipient of the rectory of Danby Wiske on his ordination as deacon in 1620, seem both to have benefited from family influence. His social status appears to have helped Samuel Phillipps, MA, in a similar way. Described as a gentleman from Yorkshire when he matriculated at Oxford aged twenty-one in 1610, he had secured the living of Slingsby before his admission to the priesthood in February 1619. Ecclesiastical connections as well as descent facilitated the progress from St John's College, Cambridge to the rectory of Badsworth in 1625 of Edward Dodsworth, MA, the grandson of Simon Dodsworth of Settrington and son of Matthew Dodsworth, LLB, chancellor to Archbishop Matthew.[30]

Clerical networks in their turn eased the path of other ordinands as they had done from time immemorial. Coincidence of name suggests that William Crosthwaite, BA, who obtained the living of Lofthouse in the same year as he took priest's orders in 1619, was related to the earlier William Crosthwayt, MA, appointed the incumbent of the same parish in 1573. The clearest case of preferential treatment, however, occurred in the Thurscross family. In 1625 Henry Thurscross, MA, archdeacon of Cleveland and rector of Stokesley, vacated the vicarage of Kirkby Moorside in favour of his son Timothy Thurscross, MA, on his return to the North Riding from Magdalene College, Cambridge. Subsequently also succeeding to his father's archdeaconry, Timothy Thurscross astonished his contemporaries in 1638 by resigning both posts, 'being much troubled in his conscience for having obtained them through simony'.[31]

After the accession of James I the competition for livings in the north of England was intensified yet further by a new phenomenon, the incursus of Scots. More than twenty Scottish graduates from the universities of Edinburgh, Aberdeen, and St Andrews, together with a solitary graduate from Trinity College, Dublin, sought ordination from archbishops of York between 1613 and 1628. Their prospects, at least initially, seem to have been even worse than for their plebeian English counterparts. By 1619 John Hepborne, MA of St Andrews, had moved from a curacy at Kirkleatham to a curacy at Glaisdale. Another Master of Arts from St Andrews, John Gibson, became a schoolmaster at Acomb near York in 1620; he left in 1621 for a similar teaching post at Aldbrough. Francis Barcley, MA of Aberdeen, in 1627 went from one curacy at Rock in Northumberland to another at Bishopton. Only two of this group attained a clerical freehold early in their careers. Patrick Meanes, MA of St Andrews, a curate of Holy Trinity, Micklegate, York when ordained deacon in 1613, had secured the rectory of St Mary, Bishophill Senior, in the city when priested a year later. His compatriot John Innesse, MA of Aberdeen, a schoolmaster at Snaith when admitted deacon in 1618, on his ordination as priest in 1619 had become vicar of Water Fryston.[32]

Although the diocese of York had not yet gained an all-graduate clergy by the death of James I, by the archiepiscopate of Toby Matthew, in line with the metropolitan diocese of London and ahead of the somewhat more remote dioceses of Gloucester and Lichfield, a university education had become a requirement for all ordinands whatever their social standing or family and professional connections. This constituted an immense change from a century earlier, when only a tiny number of graduates had presented themselves for ordination at York and when virtually the only graduate clergy resident in the diocese were confined to the chapters of cathedral and collegiate churches. Both the clergy and the laity deserve credit for the transformation, which their predecessors could scarcely have imagined. Protestant archbishops like Grindal and Matthew had striven tirelessly to attract and promote educated protestant clergy. That sector of lay society which before the Reformation had established permanent and temporary chantry foundations and commissioned masses and prayers at their deaths, by the turn of the sixteenth century had discovered an appetite for preaching. Decades before the Civil War the towns of York, Leeds and Hull had all created civic lectureships, and popular clerics like Thomas Wincop and Andrew Marvell, the father of the poet, could accumulate as much as £50 a head in bequests for funeral sermons. The social origins of these clergy are notoriously difficult to gauge, but the majority seem to have worked their way through the university as sizars, and high-born ordinands seem to have been more the exception than the rule.[33]

While as a convinced Catholic deploring the means by which it had been achieved, Thomas More would surely have approved the reduction in the number of clergy in the sixteenth century. Whether a much smaller but far better educated clerical estate created a priesthood which was also more holy remains a matter for speculation. Unlike some of his more optimistic fellow humanists, More never subscribed to the belief that learning in itself had the power to make men good. Although willing to justify so many of the practices of the old Church when necessity demanded it, he had nothing but condemnation for educated but immoral clerics: 'without vertue the better they be learned the worse they be'.[34] Human nature may well not have improved in the diocese of York, and the clergy may have been no more meritorious at the end of the period than at the beginning; but there can be no doubt whatsoever that between 1530 and 1630 the educational qualifications of ordinands had changed out of all recognition.

NOTES

1. E. Surtz and J. H. Hexter (eds.), *Utopia, The Complete Works of St Thomas More*, vol. IV (New Haven and London, 1965), p. 227; T. M. C. Lawler, G. Marc'hadour and R. C. Marius (eds.), *A Dialogue concerning Heresies, The Complete Works of St Thomas More*, vol. VI, pt. I (New Haven and London, 1981), pp. 295, 301.

2. This analysis is based upon Borthwick Institute of Historical Research, York (BIHRY) Abp. Reg. 23 fos. 466r–468r (14 Mar. 1499/1500–4 Apr. 1500), *Sede Vac.* Reg. 5A fos. 527v–532v (13 June 1500–10 Ap. 1501), Abp. Reg. 25 fos. 108Br–141r (5 June 1501–29 May 1507), *Sede Vac.* Reg. 5A fo. 578r–605v (18 Sept. 1507–23 Sept. 1508), Abp. Reg. 26 fos. 99r–126v (23 Dec. 1508–17 Dec. 1513), *Sede Vac.* Reg. 5A fos. 620v–623r (23 Sept. 1514), Abp. Reg. 27 fos. 166r–215v (22 Dec. 1514–11 Apr. 1528), *Sede Vac.* Reg. 5A fos. 669r–671v (25 Mar. 1531–8 Apr. 1531), Abp. Reg. 28 fos. 184r–201v (30 Mar. 1531 [?1531/2]–16 Ap. 1541), Ord. Reg. 1 fos. 1r–6v (?1542–23 Sept. 1542), Abp. Reg. 30 fos. 35r–162r and Inst. AB 2 fos. 4r–82v (6 July 1561–12 Nov. 1575), Inst. AB 3 fos. 215v–510v (24 June 1589–21 Feb. 1618/19), Inst. AB 5 pp. 5–176 (23 May 1619–9 Mar. 1527/8) and Inst. AB 6 p. 11 (23 Sept. 1632).

3. C. Cross, 'Ordinations in the Diocese of York 1500–1630', in C. Cross (ed.), *Patronage and Recruitment in the Tudor and Early Stuart Church*, Borthwick Studies in History 2 (York, 1996), pp. 1–19; J. A. Hoeppner Moran, 'Clerical Recruitment in the Diocese of York, 1340–1530: Data and Commentary', *Journal of Ecclesiastical History* 34 (1983), 19–54; M. Bowker, *The Henrician Reformation: The Diocese of Lincoln under John Longland 1521–1547* (Cambridge, 1981), p. 40.

4. R. B. Dobson, 'The Residentiary Canons of York in the Fifteenth Century', *Journal of Ecclesiastical History* 30 (1979), 145–174; J. Taylor, 'The Diocese of York and the University Connection, 1300–1520', *Northern History* 25 (1989), 39–59; A. B. Emden, *A Biographical Register of the University of Oxford A.D. 1501–1540* (Oxford, 1974), pp. 535–6; *DNB*, XVIII, p. 937.

5. J. and J. A. Venn, *Alumni Cantabrigienses*, 4 vols. (Cambridge, 1922–7), pt. I, vol. I, p. 128; *DNB*, II, pp. 165–6.

6. Venn, *Alumni*, pt. I, vol. III, p. 129; *DNB*, XII, pp. 874–5.

7. Venn, *Alumni*, pt. I, vol. IV, p. 312; Emden, *Oxford 1501–1540*, pp. 599–600; *DNB*, XX, pp. 446–7.

8. A. B. Emden, *A Biographical Register of the University of Oxford to A.D. 1500*, 3 vols. (Oxford, 1957–9), II, pp. 853–4 (Haldesworth), III, p. 2036 (White); Emden, *Oxford 1501–1540*, p. 37 (Bicardike); Venn, *Alumni*, pt. I, vol. IV,

p. 50 (Sharp); J. Taylor, 'The Diocese of York and the University Connection', 45.

9. Emden, *Oxford 1501–1540*, pp. 140 (Cottes), 423–4; *DNB*, XIV, pp. 942–3 (Oglethorpe).

10. Venn, *Alumni*, pt. I, vol. I, p. 205 (Brandesby), vol. IV, pp. 148 (Staneley), 201 (Tate); Emden, *Oxford 1501–1540*, p. 249 (Grice).

11. Venn, *Alumni*, pt. I, vol. III, p. 90 (Litster); Emden, *Oxford 1501–1540*, pp. 87 (Burton), 337 (Lake) 598 (Waide).

12. BIHRY Ord. Papers 1 (letters testimonial 1 Aug. 1554–7 Mar. 1557/8).

13. J. Foster, *Alumni Oxonienses*, 4 vols. (Oxford, 1891), pt. I, vol. I, p. 210; *DNB*, III, p. 271–2; BIHRY Inst. AB 3 fos. 85v.–86r.; P. Collinson, *Archbishop Grindal 1519–1583* (London, 1979), p. 208.

14. Venn, *Alumni*, pt. I, vol. IV, p. 71; BIHRY Inst. AB 3 fo. 95r; R. A. Marchant, *The Puritans and the Church Courts in the Diocese of York 1560–1642* (London, 1960), p. 278; Collinson, *Grindal*, p. 208.

15. Venn, *Alumni*, pt. I, vol. IV, p. 384.

16. Venn, *Alumni*, pt. I, vol. IV, p.292; BIHRY. Inst. AB 3 fo. 124r; D. Lamburn, 'Politics and Religion in Early Modern Beverley', in P. Collinson and J. Craig (eds.), *The Reformation in English Towns 1500–1640* (London, 1998), p. 67.

17. Marchant, *The Puritans and the Church Courts*, p. 296 (Blackwoode); BIHRY Inst. AB 3 fos. 32r (Campyon), 60v (Bucktrowte), 101r, 112v (Blackwoode); Foster, *Alumni*, pt. I, vol. I, p. 206 (Bucktrowte).

18. BIHRY Inst. AB 3 fos. 153v (Gylmyn), 182r (Webster), 156r; Venn, *Alumni*, pt. I, vol. III, p. 311 (Parkinson).

19. Venn, *Alumni*, pt. I, vol. IV, p. 195; Marchant, *The Puritans and the Church Courts*, p. 312–13.

20. Venn, *Alumni*, pt. I, vol. III, p. 453 (Richardson); vol. IV, p. 171; BIHRY Inst. AB 3 fos. 74r, 113r (Story).

21. Cross (ed.), *Patronage and Recruitment*, pp. 6–7, 10–11.

22. BIHRY Inst. AB 3, inserted sheet at fo. 394r, inserted sheet at fo. 499r.

23. R. O'Day, *The English Clergy: The Emergence and Consolidation of a Profession 1558–1642* (Leicester, 1979), especially chapter 10.

24. BIHRY Inst. AB 5 pp. 127, 130, 140, 166 and inserted sheets; Venn, *Alumni*, pt. I, vol. III, pp. 375, 469; vol. IV, p. 150.

25. BIHRY Inst. AB 5 pp. 16, 57, 125, 146, 156 and inserted sheets; Venn, *Alumni*, pt. I, vol. I, p. 133; vol. IV, p. 113.

26. BIHRY Inst. AB 3 fo. 495r. and inserted sheet, Inst. AB 5 pp. 5, 124–5, 140 and inserted sheets; Venn, *Alumni*, pt. I, I, pp. 21, 88; Foster, *Alumni*, pt. I, vol. II, p. 725.

27. BIHRY AB 5 pp. 13, 50–1, 52, 63, 166, 167, 175, 176 and inserted sheets; Venn, *Alumni*, pt. I, vol. I, p. 51, vol. III, p. 426.

28. BIHRY Inst. AB 3 fos. 413v, 418r, Inst. AB 5 pp. 5, 13, 130, 167 and inserted sheets; Venn, *Alumni*, pt. I, vol. I, pp. 86, 147.

29. BIHRY Inst. AB 3 fos. 396r, 402r, 497r, and inserted sheets; Inst. AB 5 pp. 5, 55, 57, 59, and inserted sheets; Venn, *Alumni*, pt. I, vol. III, pp. 205, 225; vol. IV, pp. 85, 170.
30. BIHRY Inst. AB 3 fos. 497r, 499r, 500r, 501v, and inserted sheets; Inst. AB 5 pp. 35, 50–1, 59, 140, and inserted sheets; Venn, *Alumni*, pt. I, vol. I, pp. 380, 381; vol. II, pp. 52, 53; Foster, *Alumni*, pt. I, vol. III, p. 1159.
31. BIHRY Inst. AB 3 fo. 427v and inserted sheet; Inst. AB 5 pp. 5, 130 and inserted sheets; Venn, *Alumni*, pt. I, vol. I, p. 427; vol. IV, p. 239; Marchant, *The Puritans and the Church Courts*, p. 284.
32. BIHRY Inst. AB 3 fos. 423v, 431r, 495r and inserted sheets, AB 5 pp. 5, 13, 35, 52, 146, 166 and inserted sheets.
33. O'Day, *The English Clergy*, pp. 135–6, 138–9; C. Cross, *Urban Magistrates and Ministers: Religion in Hull and Leeds from the Reformation to the Civil War*, Borthwick Paper 67 (York, 1985), p. 23.
34. Lawler, Marc'hadour and Marius (eds.), *A Dialogue concerning Heresies*, p. 301.

Bibliography of Barrie Dobson's published works

(A) BOOKS, EDITIONS AND LECTURES

Selby Abbey and Town (Leeds, 1969).

The Peasants' Revolt of 1381 (London, 1971, 2nd edn 1983).

'*Mynistres of Saynt Cuthbert*': *The Monks of Durham in the Fifteenth Century* (Durham Cathedral Lecture, 1972).

Durham Priory, 1400–1450 (Cambridge, 1973).

The World of the Middle Ages (with M. J. Angold) (London, 1974).

The Jews of Medieval York and the Massacre of March 1190 (Borthwick Institute, York, 1974, 2nd edn 1996).

Rymes of Robyn Hood (with J. Taylor) (London, 1976, 2nd edn Stroud, 1989, 3rd edn Stroud, 1997).

(ed.) *York City Chamberlains' Accounts, 1396–1500*, Surtees Society 192 (1980).

The History of Clementhorpe Nunnery (with S. Donaghey) (York Archaeological Trust, 1984).

(ed.) *The Church, Politics and Patronage in the Fifteenth Century* (Stroud, 1984).

'*Preserving the Perishable*': *Contrasting Communities in Medieval England*, inaugural lecture (Cambridge, 1991).

Church and Society in the Medieval North of England (London, 1996).

(ed., with Peter Biller) *The Medieval Church: Universities, Heresy and the Religious Life: Essays in Honour of Gordon Leff*, Studies in Church History, Subsidia 11 (Woodbridge, Suffolk: Boydell & Brewer for the Ecclesiastical History Society, 1999).

(ed., with Michael Lapidge) English translation of André Vauchez (ed.), *Encyclopaedia of the Middle Ages*, 2 vols. (Cambridge, 2000).

(B) ARTICLES ETC.

'Richard Bell, Prior of Durham (1464–78) and Bishop of Carlisle (1478–95)', *Transactions of the Cumberland and Westmorland Antiquarian and Archaeological Society*, new series 65 (1965), 182–221.

'The Foundation of Perpetual Chantries by the Citizens of Medieval York', *Studies in Church History* 4 (1967), 22–38.

'The Last English Monks on Scottish Soil: The Severance of Coldingham Priory from the monastery of Durham, 1461–78', *Scottish Historical Review* 46 (1967), 1–25.

'The Election of John Ousthorp as Abbot of Selby in 1436', *Yorkshire Archaeological Journal* 42 (1968), 31–40.

'The First Norman Abbey in Northern England: The Origins of Selby', *Ampleforth Journal* 74 (1969), 161–76.

'The Medieval Origins of the Robin Hood Legend: A Reassessment', *Northern History* 7 (1972), 1–30 (with J. Taylor).

'Admissions to the Freedom of the City of York in the Later Middle Ages', *Economic History Review*, second series 26 (1973), 1–22.

'German History, 911–1618', in M. Pasley (ed.), *Germany: A Companion to German Studies* (London, 1974; 2nd edn 1982).

'The Later Middle Ages, 1215–1500', in G. E. Aylmer and R. Cant (eds.), *A History of York Minster* (Oxford, 1977), pp. 44–110.

'Oxford Graduates and the So-Called Patronage Crisis of the Later Middle Ages', in *The Church in a Changing Society*, CTHEC Conference in Uppsala (1977), pp. 211–16.

'Urban Decline in Late Medieval England', *Transactions of the Royal Historical Society*, fifth series 27 (1977), 1–22.

'The Decline and Expulsion of the Medieval Jews of York', *Transactions of the Jewish Historical Society of England* 26 (1979), 34–52.

'The Residentiary Canons of York in the Fifteenth Century', *Journal of Ecclesiastical History* 30 (1979), 145–74.

'Cathedral Chapters and Cathedral Cities: York, Durham and Carlisle in the Fifteenth Century', *Northern History* 19 (1983), 15–44.

'Robin Hood of Barnesdale: A Fellow Thou Has Long Sought', *Northern History* 19 (1983), 210–20 (with J. Taylor).

'The Risings in York, Beverley and Scarborough, 1380–81', in R. H. Hilton and T. H. Aston (eds.), *The English Rising of 1381* (Cambridge, 1984), pp. 112–42.

'Mendicant Ideal and Practice in Late Medieval York', in P. V. Addyman and V. E. Black (eds.), *Archaeological Papers from York presented to M. W. Barley* (York, 1984), pp. 109–22.

'The Foundation of Gloucester College, Oxford, in 1283', *Worcester College Record* (1985), 12–24.

'Yorkshire Towns in the Late Fourteenth Century', *Publications of the Thoresby Society* 59 (1985), 1–21.

'Recent Prosopographical Research in Late Medieval English History: University Graduates, Durham Monks and York Canons', in N. Bulst and J.-P. Genet (eds.), *Medieval Lives and the Historian: Studies in Medieval Prosopography* (Kalamazoo, Mi, 1986), pp. 181–200.

'The Bishops of Late Medieval England as Intermediaries between Church and State', in *Etat et église dans la genèse de l'état moderne* (Casa de Velásquez, Madrid, 1986), pp. 227–38.

'Richard III and the Church of York', in R. A. Griffiths and J. Sherborne (eds.), *Kings and Nobles in the later Middle Ages* (Gloucester, 1986), pp. 130–54.

Introduction to A. R. Myers, *Crown, Household and Parliament in Fifteenth Century England* (London, 1986), pp. ix–xix.

'The City of York', in Boris Ford (ed.), *Cambridge Guide to the Arts in Britain*, vol. II (Cambridge, 1988), pp. 200–13.

'Beverley in Conflict: Archbishop Alexander Neville and the Minster Clergy, 1381–88', in C. Wilson (ed.), *Medieval Art and Architecture in the East Riding of Yorkshire* (British Archaeological Association, 1989), pp. 149–64.

'Contrasting Chronicles: Historical Writing at York and Durham in the Later Middle Ages', in I. Wood and G. Loud (eds.), *Church and Chronicle in the Middle Ages: Essays Presented to John Taylor* (London, 1991), pp. 201–18.

'John Taylor: A Tribute', ibid., pp. xi–xx.

'English Monastic Cathedrals in the Fifteenth Century', *Transactions of the Royal Historical Society*, sixth series 1 (1991), 151–92.

'The Historical Role of the Archbishops of York during the Reign of Edward I', *Thirteenth-Century England* 3 (1991), 47–64.

'Citizens and Chantries in Late Medieval York', in D. Abulafia, M. Franklin and M. Rubin (eds.), *Church and City, 1000–1500: Essays in Honour of Christopher Brooke* (Cambridge, 1992), pp. 311–32.

'The Role of Jewish Women in Medieval England' (Presidential Address), in D. Wood (ed.), *Christianity and Judaism*, Studies in Church History 29 (1992), pp. 145–68.

'Two English Cathedrals: Exeter and York', in H. Millet and E. Mornet (eds.), *I Canonici al Servizio dello Stato in Europa, Secoli XIII–XVI* (Modena, 1992), pp. 15–46 (with D. N. Lepine).

'The Church of Durham and the Scottish Borders, 1378–88', in A. Goodman and A. Tuck (eds.), *War and Border Societies in the Middle Ages* (London, 1992), pp. 124–54.

'The Religious Orders 1370–1540', in J. I. Catto and R. Evans (eds.), *The History of the University of Oxford*, vol. II, *Late Medieval Oxford* (Oxford, 1992), pp. 539–79.

'The Jews of Medieval Cambridge', *Jewish Historical Studies: Transactions of the Jewish Historical Society of England* 32 (1990–2), 1–24.

'The Prosopography of Late Medieval Cathedral Canons', *Medieval Prosopography* 15 (1994), 67–92.

'The Monks of Canterbury in the Later Middle Ages, 1220–1540', in P. Collinson *et al.* (eds.), *A History of Canterbury Cathedral* (Oxford, 1995), pp. 69–153.

'The Ballads of Robin Hood', in Kevin Carpenter (ed.), *Catalogue of the International Robin Hood Exhibition* (Oldenburg, 1995), pp. 35–44 (with J. Taylor).

'William Sellyng, Prior of Canterbury Cathedral, 1472–94', *Canterbury Chronicle* 89 (1995), 15–21.

'The Educational Patronage of Archbishop Thomas Rotherham of York', *Northern History* 31 (1995), 65–85.

'Politics and the Church in the Fifteenth-Century North of England', in A. J. Pollard (ed.), *The North of England in the Age of Richard III* (Gloucester, 1996), pp. 1–17.

'A Minority Ascendant: The Benedictine Conquest of the North of England, 1066–1100', in S. J. Ridyard and R. G. Benson (eds.), *Minorities and Barbarians in Medieval Life and Thought*, Sewanee Medieval Studies 7 (1996), pp. 5–26.

'A Minority within a Minority: the Jewesses of Thirteenth-Century England', ibid, pp. 27–48.

'Merry Men at Work: The Transformation of the Medieval Outlaw into the Heritage Hero', *Northern History* 33 (1997), 232–7 (with J. Taylor).

'The Black Monks of Durham and Canterbury Colleges: Comparisons and Contrasts', in H. Wansbrough and A. Marett-Crosby (eds.), *Benedictines in Oxford* (London, 1997), pp. 61–78.

'Craft Guilds and City: the Historical Origins of the York Mystery Plays Reassessed', in A. E. Knight (ed.), *The Stage as Mirror: Civic Theatre in Late Medieval Europe* (Cambridge, 1997), pp. 91–106.

'The Crown, The Charter and the City, 1396–1461', in S. Rees Jones (ed.), *The Government of Medieval York: Essays in Commemoration of the 1396 Royal Charter*, Borthwick Studies in History 3 (University of York, 1997), pp. 34–55.

'Urban Europe', Chapter 6 in C. Allmand (ed.), *The New Cambridge Medieval History*, vol. VII, *c. 1415–c. 1500* (Cambridge, 1998), pp. 121–44.

'The Monastic Orders in Late Medieval Cambridge', in Peter Biller and Barrie Dobson (eds.), *The Medieval Church: Universities, Heresy and the Religious Life: Essays in Honour of Gordon Leff*, Studies in Church History, Subsidia 11 (Woodbridge, Suffolk: Boydell & Brewer for the Ecclesiastical History Society, 1999), pp. 239–69.

'Claire Cross: A Tribute', in D. Wood (ed.), *Life and Thought in the Northern Church, c. 1100–c. 1700: Essays in Honour of Claire Cross*, Studies in Church History, Subsidia 12 (Woodbridge, Suffolk: Boydell & Brewer for the Ecclesiastical History Society, 1999), pp. 1–9.

'English and Welsh Monastic Bishops: The Final Century, 1433–1533', in B. Thompson (ed.), *Monasteries and Society in Medieval Britain*, Harlaxton Medieval Studies 6 (1999), pp. 348–67.

'Robin Hood: The Genesis of a Popular Hero', in T. Hahn (ed.), *Robin Hood in Popular Culture: Violence, Transgression and Justice* (Cambridge, 2000), pp. 61–77.

'The Later Middle Ages, 1300–1540: General Survey', in D. M. Palliser (ed.), *Cambridge Urban History of Britain*, vol. I, *600–1540* (Cambridge, 2000), pp. 273–90.

'Aliens in the City of York during the Fifteenth Century', in J. Mitchell (ed.), *England and the Continent in the Late Middle Ages: Studies in Memory of Andrew Martindale*, Harlaxton Medieval studies 8 (2001), pp. 249–66.

Index

Aberdeen, 271
Abingdon, Edmund of, archbp of Canterbury, 68
Acthorp, Margaret of, 208
adultery, 16–17, 129
Aelred, 209
Aix en Provence, 43
Alexander III, pope, 27, 175
Alexander IV, pope, 64
Alexander V, pope, 43
Allen, Robert, 245, 246
All Souls College, Oxford, 46
almshouses, 85, 89, 92, 109–10, 149, 224–38, 263, 266
Americas, 111, 117
anchoresses, 192, 204–17
Ancrene Riwle, 210
Ancrene Wisse, 210–11, 212
Anglesey Priory, 68
Antwerp, 117, 129
apostasy, 129, 213, 214–15
appropriations, 68–9, 71, 73, 75, 77
Arthington, Henry, 247
Asceles, Simon de, 74
attorneys, 139–40
Augustinians, 16, 26, 28, 68, 75, 210
Aumale, William of, earl of Yorkshire, 28
Austria, 175, 176, 181, 184
Avignon, 43
Aylmer, John, bp of London, 248
Aymon, Pèire, 176, 177, 178, 179–80, 181

Bainbridge, Christopher, archbp of York, 260
Balliol College, Oxford, 47, 71, 76, 261, 262, 263
Balsham, Hugh, bp of Ely, 60–78, 88
Barlings Abbey, 219
Barnsdale, 22, 160, 162
Barnwell Priory, 66, 68, 73, 260
Basle, council of, 44

Baxter, Richard, 248
Bayly, Thomas, 101, 102
Beauchamp, Richard, earl of Warwick, 20–1
Beaufort, Henry, bp of Winchester, 230
Beaufort, Margaret, countess of Richmond, 46, 84, 86, 88, 90, 93
Beauvale Priory, 23
Beckwith, William, 163
Bedford, duke of, *see* John, duke of Bedford
beggars, 109–10, 148, 245
Bell, John, bp of Worcester, 261
Belsham, John, 161, 162
Benedictines, 12, 15, 19, 20, 21–2, 23, 60, 66, 68, 71–2, 231, 236–7
Bereford, William, 138, 146
Bergersh, Maud, 228
Bernard, Richard, 244–5, 246
Bernwood Forest, 165
Besançon, 176
Beverley, Yorks, 28, 263, 265, 266
Bicardike, John, 262
Bildeston, Suff, 242, 248–9, 251, 252
Bingham, William, 86–8
Black Death, 46, 137
Blackwoode, Robert, 265–6
Bohemia, 175
Bonde, Thomas, 101, 102, 108–9, 110
Boniface VIII, pope, 43
Botreaux, Margaret, 231–2, 234, 235
Bradwardine, Thomas, 193
Brandesby, John, 263
Bray, Reynold, 166
Brinton, Thomas, bp of Rochester, 24
Bristol, 98
Brokley, John, 87
Broomhall Priory, 85–6
Buckland, Joanna and Richard, 87
Bucktrowte, William, 266
Bunney, Edmund, 264–5, 268
Burgundy, 175, 176, 180
Burton, Edward, 263

Burton, Ernegata de, 28
Bury St Edmunds, abbey, 20, 21–2; town, 246

Caen, 44
Calvin, John, 193
Cambridge, colleges *see individual entries*;
    St Edmund's priory, 260, 263; St John's
    hospital, 74, 75–6, 77, 84–6, 88–94,
    260, 262; university, 5, 43–54, 60, 73,
    84–94, 260–71
Campyon, John, 266
canons, regular, 29–30, 36, 37; *see also*
    Augustinians; residentiary, 51, 272
Canterbury, archbps of, 90, *see also*: Abingdon,
    Edmund of; Chichele, Henry; Kilwardby,
    Robert; Peckham, John; Savoy, Boniface
    of; Stratford, John; Winchelsey, Robert;
    priory, 60, 72, 237
Canterbury Tales, 12, 14–17, 19, 23, 167
Cardinal College, Oxford, 48, 52
Carew, Thomas, 242–3, 244, 246, 248–54
Carlisle, bp of, *see* Oglethorpe, Owen
Carpenter, Christine, 204–17
Carpenter, John, 121–2, 135
Carrow Priory, 209
Carthusians, 18, 23, 226, 228, 235
Cathars, 175
chantries, 49, 51, 52, 54, 85–6, 90, 93, 209,
    228–9, 237, 239, 259, 264, 272
Charles VII, king of France, 44
Chatteris Priory, 66, 67
Chaucer, Alice, duchess of Suffolk, 225–38
Chaucer, Geoffrey, 11, 12, 13, 14–17, 167
Chaucer, Thomas, 228, 238
Chester, bp of, *see* Cottes, George; city, 114;
    diocese, 266
Chichele, Henry, archbp of Canterbury,
    233
Chichester, diocese, 210, 211, 266
Christ's College, Cambridge, 46, 47, 50,
    84–94, 265; *see also* God's-house
Cicero, 123
Cistercians, 26–8, 37, 72, 189, 191
Clare College, Cambridge, 45–6, 76, 266
Cloud of Unknowing, 191, 192, 193, 194
Coke, Richard, 101, 102, 104, 110
Colet, John, 130
Colville, John, 239
Constable, Marmaduke, 268; family,
    270–1
Corpus Christi College, Cambridge, 88
Corpus Christi College, Oxford, 47
Corpus Christi plays, 104, 169
Cosin, John, bp of Durham, 196, 198
Cottes, George, bp of Chester, 262

Court of Arches, 149
Coventry, bp of, *see* Hales, John; city, 97–111;
    diocese *see* Lichfield
Crabhouse Priory, 209
Cranmer, Thomas, 261
Craven, Yorks, 265
Cromwell, Ralph, lord, 234; Thomas, 226,
    242, 261, 262
Croxton Priory, 28
Cutler, Robert, 85

Dance of Death, 18–19
Darlyng, John, 101, 102
Darrains, William, 29
deadly sins, 13, 106, 125
Dedham, Essex, 245
deer, 164–6
de la Pole, William, duke of Suffolk, 226, 228,
    235
de la Puente, Luis, 197
Dennis, Thomas, 160
Dent, Arthur, 193
Dissolution, 13, 23, 36, 259, 267
Dodsworth family, 271
Dominicans, 175, 212, 213, 215
Doncaster, Yorks, 208
Donne, John, 197–8
Dorchester, Dorset, 243, 246
Downame, John, 244, 246, 247
Drypool, Yorks, 34–5, 36–7
Dublin, archbp of, 63; Trinity College, 271
Dudley, Edmund, 54
Durham, bps of, 149, *see also*: Cosin, John;
    Farnham, Nicholas; Puiset, Hugh de;
    priory, 2, 60, 67, 72, 236
Durham College, Oxford, 72

Edinburgh, hospital, 240; university, 271
Edward I, king of England, 74, 76, 140
Edward III, king of England, 82, 138, 145,
    147
Edward IV, king of England, 157
Edward VI, king of England, 261
Ely, archdeaconry, 67, 73, 74; bps of, 84, 85,
    89, 92–3, *see also*: Balsham, Hugh;
    Kilkenny, William of; Louth, William of;
    Montacute, Simon de; Nigel; Northwold,
    Hugh of; Redman, Richard; cathedral,
    69–70, 78; hospital, 85, 92; Isle of, 61, 62
Erasmus, Desiderius, 130
Eton College, 52
Eucharist, 104, 178–9, 246, 265
Eugenius IV, pope, 44
Ewelme, Oxon, 224–38
excommunication, 35, 37, 67, 175, 214, 215

Exeter, bps of, *see*: Hooker, John; Oldham, Hugh; city, 243, 246
Eynsham Abbey, 68

Fairfax, William, 266
Farnham, Nicholas, bp of Durham, 74
Faversham, Kent, 213
film, 204–5, 216–17
Fisher, John, bp of Rochester, 5, 46, 84, 85, 86, 88, 90, 93, 260, 262
Florence, 65
Forde, Thomas, 101, 102; William, 101, 109, 110, 116
forests, 136, 164–8
Fotehead, John, 84, 85, 90–1
Fountains Abbey, 28
Fox, Richard, bp of Winchester, 46
Foxton, Cambs, 68–9
Franciscans, 175, 177, 228, 239
Fray, John, 87
friars, 12, 56, 72, 148, 175, 214, 264; *see also individual orders*

gaol delivery, 138, 159, 160
Gascony, 175
general eyre, 138, 140, 141, 144, 146
Germany, 175, 176, 184
Giffard, Walter, archbp of York, 30, 31
Gilbertines, 26–7, 28, 29–30, 32, 37–8, 39
Giselham, Andrew de, 74
Gloucester, diocese, 272; duke of, *see* Humphrey, duke of Gloucester
Gloucester College, Oxford, 20, 21, 60, 72
God's-house, Cambridge, 46, 86–8, 93; *see also* Christ's College
Gonville Hall, Cambridge, 49
graduates, 51, 260–72
Gratian, 13
Great Carlton, Lincs, 208
Greenfield, William, archbp of York, 33, 208
Grice, Gregory, 263
Grindal, Edmund, archbp of York, 264–6, 272
Grosseteste, Robert, bp of Lincoln, 67
Gui, Bernard, 174, 176, 178, 179, 181
guilds, 98, 106–7, 110, 123, 127
Gurney, Edmund, 198
Gylmyn, Robert, 266

Hadleigh, Suff, 249, 253
Haldesworth, Gilbert, 262
Hales, John, bp of Coventry, 113
Hatfield Broadoak, Essex, 20
Hauxton, Cambs, 68–9
Healaugh Park Priory, 28, 35
Heath, Nicholas, archbp of York, 264

Hedlam family, 160
Henry, duke of Lancaster, 208–9
Henry II, king of England, 28
Henry III, king of England, 61–2, 63, 64, 65–6
Henry V, king of England, 19, 21–2
Henry VI, king of England, 44, 88, 228
Henry VII, king of England, 88, 150, 165–6
Henry VIII, king of England, 261
Hereford, bp of, *see* Swinfield, Richard
heresy, 44, 50, 51, 101–2, 103, 113, 135, 259; *see also* Lollardy, Waldensians
Hexham, Northumb, 163
Heytesbury, Wilts, 231–3, 235
Higham Ferrers, Northants, 233–5
Higham Priory, 85–6
highwaymen, 158, 162–3, 168
Hilton, Robert de, 30; Walter, 191, 192–3
Holgate, Robert, archbp of York, 264
Hooker, John, bp of Exeter, 199
Hornby, Henry, 88, 90–1, 93
Horningsea, Cambs, 90, 91, 92
hospitals *see* almshouses
Hoton, John, 166
Hull, Yorks, charterhouse, 235; city, 272
humanism, 46, 50, 118, 123–4
Humphrey, duke of Gloucester, 21
Hungerford, Robert, lord, 231
hunting, 15–16, 165–6
Huss, Jan, 44
Hutton, Matthew, archbp of York, 267

images, 188–99, 213
indulgences, 68
Ingram, Walter, 237
inquisition, 174–5, 176–7, 178, 179, 183
Ipswich, Suff, 246, 248
Italy, 119, 123, 150, 176, 182

Jervaulx Abbey, 236
Jesus College, Cambridge, 266
John, duke of Bedford, 20
Jones, Philip, 247
Jordan, Ignatius, 243
Julian of Norwich, 193, 209
justices of the peace, 138, 142, 159, 160, 165

Kilkenny, William of, bp of Ely, 61, 73, 74
Kilwardby, Robert, archbp of Canterbury, 65
king's bench, 138, 139, 141–2, 159, 160
King's College, Cambridge, 47, 50, 52
King's Hall, Cambridge, 84
Knaresborough, Yorks, forest, 165; friary of St Robert, 29; honour of, 163
Knighton, Henry, 16

Lacy, John, 73
Lake, Alexander, 263
Lancaster, duke of, *see* Henry
Langland, William, 11–14, 23, 24, 140, 157
Lansdale, Richard, 109
Latini, Brunetto, 123–4
lawyers, 44–5, 136–51
Lee, Edward, archbp of York, 194
Leeds, Yorks, 272
Leicester Priory, 16
Lenton Priory, 209
Le Romeyn, John, archbp of York, 28
Leye, Isabella de, 207–8
Lichfield, diocese, 272; *see also* Coventry
Lincoln, bps of, 89; *see also* Grosseteste, Robert;
    cathedral, 65, 261, 263; diocese, 260
Lincoln College, Oxford, 50
Litster, Laurence, 263
Llewellyn, prince of Wales, 65
Lollardy, 97–111, 195, 196
London, bps of, *see*: Aylmer, John; Wengham,
    Henry of; bridge, 124–5; city, 117–30,
    139, 140, 143, 144, 246, 253; diocese, 67,
    272; guilds, 21, 124, 127; St John
    Zachary, 87; St Martin le Grand, 126; St
    Paul's, 130
Louis XI, king of France, 44
Louth, William of, bp of Ely, 78
Luther, Martin, 195, 248, 259
Lydgate, John, 11, 17–21, 193
Lyons, 175

Magdalen College, Oxford, 263
Magna Carta, 145
Malet, Francis, 261
Marton in Holderness, Yorks, 32, 35–6
Marvell, Andrew, 272
Mary, queen of England, 261
Matthew, Toby, archbp of York, 267–8, 271,
    272
Matthewe, John, 102
Maximilian I, emperor, 235
May games, 163
Meaux Abbey, 27, 28, 33–7
Melton, William, archbp of York, 208
memory, 188–9, 193, 196
Merton, Walter de, bp of Rochester, 53, 71, 74
Merton College, Oxford, 68, 71, 74–5, 76–7,
    81
Merton Priory, 68, 75
Michaelhouse, Cambridge, 47, 50, 84, 85, 93,
    261
Mirk, John, 195
monks, 11–23, 50–1, 60, 70, 71–3, 190–1,
    236–7, 264; *see also individual orders*

Montacute, Simon de, bp of Ely, 76–7
Montagu, Thomas, earl of Salisbury, 236
Montpellier, 43, 44–5
More, Thomas, 4, 117–30, 226, 237, 259, 272
Morel, Georges, 180, 181
Murdac, Henry, archbp of York, 28, 39

Nantwich, Ches, 246
Neville, Humphrey, 163–4
New College, Oxford, 47, 48, 49, 50, 52
New Forest, 166, 167
Newton-on-the-Sea, Norf, 239
Nicholas IV, pope, 43
Nigel, bp of Ely, 62
Northwold, Hugh of, bp of Ely, 62, 69, 78
Norwich, bps of, 53, 89; city, 98, 160, 249;
    diocese, 209; priory, 53, 152
Nottingham, 22, 158, 159, 208, 209
Nun Cotham Priory, 27
Nunkeeling Priory, 27, 35
nuns, 13, 19–20, 26–38, 67

Oglethorpe, Owen, bp of Carlisle, 262–3
Oldham, Hugh, bp of Exeter, 46
ordination, 49, 50, 89, 259–73
Oriel College, Oxford, 50, 266
Osney Abbey, 260
Ospringe, Kent, 85–6
outlaws, 136, 150–1, 156–69
Oxford, Christ Church cathedral, 262; colleges
    see individual entries; St Frideswide's priory,
    90, 260; university, 43–54, 60, 72, 75,
    260–71
oyer and terminer, 138, 141, 149

Paris, 16, 18, 44, 72; Collège des Dix-huit, 75,
    88; Holy Innocents, 18; Saint-Denis,
    16–17
Paris, Matthew, 61–2, 65
Parkinson, Christopher, 266
parliament, 65, 122, 130, 140–1, 147, 148–9,
    166
Paston, John, 157
Peasants' Revolt, 4, 147
Peckham, John, archbp of Canterbury, 70–1
Pembroke College, Cambridge, 53
penitentiaries, 214–15
Percy, Alan, 91
Perkins, William, 242, 244, 245–6
Peterhouse, Cambridge, 48, 50, 51, 61, 68,
    71–8, 88, 269
pets, 50–1, 52
Phillipps, Samuel, 271
Piedmont, 175, 176, 180, 183
Piers, John, archbp of York, 267

Piers Plowman, 11, 13, 14, 140
pigs, 104–5, 107, 164
Plompton Park, Lancs, 164
poaching, 158, 164–6, 167–8
Poland, 181
Pontigny, 68
poor, the, 49, 110, 127, 138–51, 227–8, 235–6, 242–54
Prague, 44
preaching, 51, 175, 177, 178, 182, 244–5, 248, 265, 272
Premonstratensians, 28–9
prosopography, 2
prostitutes, 99, 105, 106–7, 129
Pseudo-Dionysius, 192
Puiset, Hugh du, bp of Durham, 27
puritanism, 196, 242–54
Pysford, William, 101, 102, 104, 110

Queens' College, Cambridge, 76, 270
Queen's College, Oxford, 47, 49

Ramsey Abbey, 68
Redman, Richard, bp of Ely, 90
Reformation, 13, 54, 103, 175, 194–6, 199, 237, 264
Rewley Abbey, 72
Reyce, Robert, 250
Richard, duke of York, 88
Richard III, king of England, 166
Richardson, Richard, 266
Richmond, countess of, *see* Beaufort, Margaret
Rievaulx Abbey, 26
Ripon, Yorks, hospital, 266; town, 28, 115
Robin Hood, 4, 22, 60, 156–69
Robinson, William, 84, 90–1, 92
Rochester, bps of *see*: Brinton, Thomas; Fisher, John; Merton, Walter de
Rogers, John, 245, 247
Rome, 62–5, 66
Rotherham, Yorks, college, 52, 85; parish, 265
Rotherham, Thomas, archbp of York, 52
Rowley, Alice, 101, 104, 113
Rowley, William, 101, 102, 104, 109, 111
Ruysbroeck, John, 190

Sainsbury, John, 230, 238
St Alban's Abbey, 21
St Andrews, almshouse, 237; university, 271
St Bernard, 189–90, 190–1, 196
St Catharine's College, Cambridge, 263
St Cuthbert, 6, 68
St Etheldreda, 67, 78
St Ignatius Loyola, 193–4, 196–7

St John's College, Cambridge, 46, 84–94, 261, 262
St Margaret of Antioch, 213
St Mary's Abbey *see* York
St Pol, Marie de, 53
Salisbury, bps of, 261; city, 243; dean of, 232; earl of, *see* Montagu, Thomas
Sandys, Edwin, archbp of York, 267
Saunders, Laurence, 101
Savage, Thomas, archbp of York, 260
Savoy, Boniface of, archbp of Canterbury, 61–4
schools, 52, 85, 86–7, 130, 226, 263, 269–70
Scott, John, 88
Sempringham Priory, 28
Seneca, 118, 123, 124
serjeants at law, 139–40, 143
Shareshull, William, 146
Sharp, Richard, 262
Shere, Surrey, 205, 206–7, 210
Sherfield, Henry, 243
sheriffs, 22, 117, 150, 158, 159, 160–1
Sherwood Forest, 160
Shirley, John, 20
Shorton, Robert, 91, 93
Shrewsbury, earl of, *see* Talbot, George
Shute, Christopher, 265
simony, 64, 271
Smart, Peter, 196
Smyth, Richard, 101, 102, 108
Sodor and Man, bp of, *see* Stanley, Thomas
Southwell, Notts, 263
Staneley, William, 263
Stanford, Hugh de, 74
Stanhope Park, co. Durham, 160
Stanley, Edward, lord Mounteagle, 260
Stanley, Thomas, bp of Sodor and Man, 260–1
Staunton, Hervey, 146
Steward, John, 91–2
Story, Thomas, 266
Stow, John, 124, 253
Stratford, John, bp of Winchester and archbp of Canterbury, 50, 82, 207, 208
Suffolk, duchess of, *see* Chaucer, Alice; duke of, *see* de la Pole, William
Sutton, Roger, 102; Saer de, 34–5, 41
Swine Priory, 26–38
Swinfield, Richard, bp of Hereford, 207, 208
Syclyng, John, 88
Sykes, John, 266

Tadcaster, Yorks, 263
Talbot, George, earl of Shrewsbury, 265–6
Tarrant Crawford, Dorset, 213
Tate, William, 263
Tattershall, Lincs, 234

Thorney Abbey, 68
tithes, 35
Thurscross, Timothy, 271
tombs, 61, 78, 225, 238
Tomlyn, William, 90–2, 94
Trinitarians, 29
Trinity College, Cambridge, 269
Trinity College, Oxford, 269
Trinity Hall, Cambridge, 49, 50, 53
Tutbury, Staffs, 163
Tynedale, 163

universities, 43–54, 60, 237, 260–72; *see also individual entries*
Utopia, 117–30, 226, 259
Utye, Thomas, 265

Valence, 44
Vascy, Henry, 160–1
Vascy, Robert, 166
Venables, Piers, 163, 164
Verli, Robert de, 27–8
villeins, 68, 69, 145
violence, 158–61, 216
visitations, 11, 30–2, 53, 70

Waide, Peter, 263
Wainfleet, Lincs, 52
Wakefeld, Robert, 261–2
Wakefield, Yorks, 160, 264
Waldensians, 174–84
Waleran, John, 62
Walpole, Ralph de, 73
Warde, Joan, 104
Wars of the Roses, 157–8
Warwick, earl of, *see* Beauchamp, Richard
Watton Priory, 27, 28, 36, 38, 39, 263
Waynflete, William, bp of Winchester, 52
Weardale, 160, 164–5
weavers, 98–9, 249–52
Webster, Richard, 266
Wengham, Henry of, bp of London, 61, 63
Wensleydale, 167
Wesley, John, 242, 248

Westminster, abbey, 2, 72, 78, 90, 236–7; hall, 138
Whalley Abbey, 208
Whateley, William, 244, 246, 247
Whitacres, Edward, 265
Whitacres, Gamaliel, 265
White, John, 243
White, William, 262
Wigston, John, 101, 110
Wigston, William, 110
Wilkinson, Robert, 248
Willenhall, Staffs, 163
wills, 32, 210, 252, 253
Winchelsey, Robert, archbp of Canterbury, 149
Winchester, bps of, *see*: Beaufort, Henry; Fox, Richard; Stratford, John; Waynflete, William; college, 52; hospital, 230
Wincop, Thomas, 272
Windsor, Berks, 233, 263
Wisbech, Cambs, 68–9
Wolsey, Thomas, archbp of York, 48, 52, 85, 163, 260
Worcester, bp of, *see* Bell, John; city, 99
Wrotham, John of, 215
Wyclif, John, 44
Wykeham Priory, 40

yeomen, 157, 167, 253
York, archbps of, 63, 67; *see also*: Bainbridge, Christopher; Giffard, Walter; Greenfield, William; Grindal, Edmund; Heath, Nicholas; Holgate, Robert; Hutton, Matthew; Lee, Edward; Le Romeyn, John; Matthew, Toby; Melton, William; Murdac, Henry; Piers, John; Rotherham, Thomas; Sandys, Edwin; Savage, Thomas; Wolsey, Thomas; Young, Thomas; city, 105, 272; diocese, 259–73; duke of, *see* Richard, duke of York; minster, 5, 263; St Mary's abbey, 22, 162
Yorkshire, earl of, *see* Aumale, William of
Young, Thomas, archbp of York, 264

Zwicker, Peter, 178, 179, 180